Civilizing World Politics

Civilizing World Politics

Society and Community beyond the State

Edited by
Mathias Albert, Lothar Brock,
and Klaus Dieter Wolf

ROWMAN & LITTLEFIELD PUBLISHERS, INC.
Lanham • Boulder • New York • Oxford

ROWMAN & LITTLEFIELD PUBLISHERS, INC.

Published in the United States of America
by Rowman & Littlefield Publishers, Inc.
4720 Boston Way, Lanham, Maryland 20706
http://www.rowmanlittlefield.com

12 Hid's Copse Road
Cumnor Hill, Oxford OX2 9JJ, England

Copyright © 2000 by Rowman & Littlefield

All rights reserved. No part of this publication may be reproduced, stored in a retrieval system, or transmitted in any form or by any means, electronic, mechanical, photocopying, recording, or otherwise, without the prior permission of the publisher.

British Library Cataloguing in Publication Information Available

Library of Congress Cataloging-in-Publication Data

Civilizing world politics : society and community beyond the state / edited by Mathias Albert, Lothar Brock, and Klaus Dieter Wolf.
    p. cm.
    Includes bibliographical references and index.
    ISBN 0-8476-9802-5 (cloth : alk. paper) — ISBN 0-8476-9803-3 (pbk. : alk. paper)
    1. International relations—Social aspects. I. Albert, Mathias. II. Brock, Lothar. III. Wolf, Klaus Dieter.

JZ1251.C58 2000
327.1'7 21—dc21   99-044888

∞™ The paper used in this publication meets the minimum requirements of American National Standard for Information Sciences—Permanence of Paper for Printed Library Materials, ANSI/NISO Z39.48–1992.

Contents

Preface vii

1 Introduction: World Society 1
World Society Research Group

2 Debordering the World of States: New Spaces in International Relations 19
Mathias Albert and Lothar Brock

3 Collective Identities in World Society 45
Christoph Weller

4 'Community' in the Global Network: A Methodological Exploration 69
Emanuel Richter

5 The 'English School': International Theory and International Society 91
Chris Brown

6 States Are Not 'Like Units': Types of State and Forms of Anarchy in the Present International System 103
Georg Sørensen

7 The New Raison D'État: International Cooperation Against Societies? 119
Klaus Dieter Wolf

8 Time to Change: States as Problems or Problem-Solvers in World Society? 133
Hilmar Schmidt

9 Multilevel Governance: On the State and Democracy in Europe 149
Michael Zürn

10 Democratization without Representation 169
Hilmar Schmidt and Ingo Take

11 Neo-Medievalism, Local Actors, and Foreign Policy: An Agenda for Research 179
Jürgen Neyer

12 The Better Half of World Society 199
Ingo Take

Notes 215

References 237

Index 269

About the Contributors 275

Preface

Civilizing World Politics is the result of a research effort undertaken by the World Society Research Group. This group comprises project teams at Darmstadt University of Technology and the Johann Wolfgang Goethe University at Frankfurt/Main, Germany, and was first established early in 1994. The work condensed in this volume combines the ongoing conceptual work developed by the group collectively (chapter 1) with related work from within the group's individual projects as well as from scholars who are not part of the group in a technical sense, but very much so in that their ongoing engagement forms an indispensable part of the group's intellectual input.

The current volume takes a fresh look at the notion of *world society*. It thus reflects a more general tendency in current scholarship to explore the links between international relations research on the one hand and social theory on the other hand. The prominent role that the notion of 'civil society' has played in various discussions bears witness of this tendency. It is in this context that we feel that even the classical continental sociological tradition, based on such thinkers as Weber, Durkheim, Simmel, and Tönnies, remains notoriously underutilized in contemporary debates in International Relations (IR). Since a systematic remedy to this deficit exceeds the possibilities of one volume, we choose one specific entry point, the concept of *world society*, to explore how classical sociological thought can help to shape new research agendas in international relations. With this concept, we attempt to outline a research framework that is theoretically dense yet open enough to connect with a number of approaches within and beyond the discipline. We nonetheless trust that our proposal to read global change through the lens of the formation of *world society* allows a much more specific focus of research questions than is possible with the ever more fuzzy notion of 'globalization'.

The realization of this volume would not have been possible first and foremost without the intensive discussion of the draft chapters in their various stages during our regular research group working sessions in Darmstadt and Frankfurt as well as on the occasion of presenting the work-in-progress at a number of conferences and seminars. Invaluable advice for the final revision of the manuscript has been provided by Jennifer Knerr at Rowman & Littlefield as well as an anonymous reviewer. At an earlier stage, Margaret Clarke and Gerald Holden have translated some of the chapters that were written in German originally (if not otherwise noted, all translations of quotes from German originals are authors' own).

Funding for various parts of the group's research has been provided by the Ministry of Science of the State of Hesse, which in 1994–95 granted seed money to get the group's work off the ground, the German Research Community (DFG), as well as the Volkswagen Foundation, which awarded grants to various project teams in Darmstadt and Frankfurt since then.

We hope that with this volume we will be able to address not only an IR audience, but also to generate discussions that span disciplinary as well as geographic boundaries, and look forward to a continued engagement with what we feel is a fascinating and timely subject.

1

Introduction: World Society

World Society Research Group

The totality of transborder relations seems to be undergoing lasting changes, but we still lack coherent analytical categories that could reflect this process conceptually and identify its dynamic and implications. The concept of 'world society' is one attempt to supply such categories: a promising concept, but one that always has been and that remains ambiguous and disputed, since it is claimed by numerous parties to the debate and can be amplified in a variety of ways. This chapter sets out criteria for a conceptualization of world society with the help of which we want to analyze some of the core questions that political science addresses regarding the internationalization of politics. The research based on this concept and documented in the contributions to this volume opens up different dimensions of society formation beyond the state. It deals with the complex interplay between processes of transborder society formation *(Vergesellschaftung)* and community formation *(Vergemeinschaftung)*, a distinction we take up from Max Weber.[1] We are interested in the patterns of interaction between different collective actors on different levels and spheres of interaction against the background of new regulatory needs confronting the state and the simultaneous decline of its regulation competence. This implies looking at problems of government as well as governance. In what dimensions and at what levels can processes of change in the system of international relations be identified? What are their implications for effective governance and for legitimate government? How are actors responding to the new challenges?

Like world society, the concept of 'international community' has a well-established place in the standard vocabulary of political science. The idea of an international community is especially popular in the everyday language of diplomacy. Regular appeals are made to this community to deal with abuses and with problems that arise across borders. The difficulty with this usage, however, is that it can serve to disguise uncertainty about what exactly is being said. It insinuates that a fully anarchic state of nature no longer prevails in relations between states, but it also affirms the assumption of anarchy by appealing to the states to act together in the absence of rules that would prescribe to them to do so.

In what follows we will try to show how the terms 'international community', 'international system', 'international society', and 'world society' are related to each other. Our main goal is to advance the construction of ideal types, which will help us to prepare a foil against which a more precise reading of transborder relations can be developed. In doing so we include German literature in order to help to overcome language barriers that prevail and broaden even in International Relations (IR). We proceed by referring in the second section to earlier conceptualizations of world society, newer international political economy considerations pertaining to the concept, and the need to go beyond both. In the third section we take up Max Weber's distinction between *Vergesellschaftung* (society formation) and *Vergemeinschaftung* (community formation) and treat the international *community* as the concomitant of a *society* formation process. In the course of this discussion, the international system as a self-help system that is (at best) balanced in power-political terms, is distinguished from an interstate, rule-governed international society (Bull 1977) and, with the increase in the significance of societal actors, from world society (fourth section). Our concept of world society is designed to capture the growing complexity of world affairs in terms of the diffusion of actors as well as the differentiation of levels of interaction and of spheres of interaction. With the help of the distinction between society and community formation we also seek to identify integrative and disintegrative tendencies and to render them accessible to analysis (fifth section).

In our final section we deal briefly with the normative implications of the concept of world society. There is no doubt that positive expectations are frequently associated with the development of a world society. It must for the time being remain an unanswered question, whether the appearance of world society implies progress toward a more peaceful and just world order or whether it will simply lead to a transformation of collective violence.

COBWEBS, MARKETS, AND INSTITUTIONS

With the cobweb model presented in his book *World Society* (1972), John Burton aspired to overcome the state-centric view of the world expressed in the very name of the discipline Inter*national* Relations: "There are important religious, language, scientific, commercial and other relationships in addition to a variety of formal, non-governmental institutions that are world-wide" (Burton 1972: 19). Burton sees this distinction not as a play on words, but as an alternative approach to research. The state continues to be viewed as a prominent actor, but according to Burton an approach that remains focused on the state alone could not capture the genuinely new and important developments taking place in the international system: "The political and social life of people within states, which is always altering with changed thinking and new technologies, influences relations among states" (Burton 1972: 20).

Burton's cobweb model is an attempt to render visible these forms of interaction, which take place at the substate level and outside the state, and to make them accessible to analysis. Ernst-Otto Czempiel comments: "If we see the world as a world society, we must be interested in everything that happens, in every relationship. The model focuses on human behavior and on all human beings as its starting-point" (Czempiel 1981: 70). This, however, points directly to the weakness of the Burtonian concept. It offers no criteria according to which we could systematically select objects of investigation and specify research questions. The same holds true of Martin Shaw's recent definition of *global society* as "the entire complex of social relations between human beings on a world scale" or "a diverse social universe in which the unifying forces of modern production, markets, communications and cultural and political modernization interact with many global, regional, national and local segmentations and differentiations" (Shaw 1994: 17, 19).

Burton's critique of the realist school's model of the world of states rests on a liberal pluralist understanding of international politics. A contrasting treatment from the early 1970s is Klaus Jürgen Gantzel's globalist-emancipatory concept of world society (on these labels see Viotti and Kauppi 1993). Gantzel's main criticism relates to the neglect of historically rooted dependency structures. A lack of interest in domination and violence

> diminishes the political effectiveness of the scholarly effort to use critical elucidation to counteract a resigned acceptance of the apparently inevitable, and to empower human beings, above all the oppressed and suffering, to act effectively against violence and illegitimate systems of rule, in other words: to defend their own interests. (Gantzel 1975: 9)

World society is thus constituted through the social struggles to overcome dependency and domination.

Though the language has changed, recent years have seen a continuing interest in the political economy of international relations. As one of the most creative scholars in this field of study, Robert Cox has demonstrated the necessity to see interstate relations in the context of a complex interplay between the world economy and changing forms of political hegemony (Cox 1981: 126 ff, 1987, 1994: 45 ff). Cox studies social processes with transnational effects. According to this model the state has no role as an independent actor detached from its social base. Instead, state policy formulation is understood as a function of dominant social coalitions that use the state to further their own interests.

From this perspective, the creation of transnational interest groups that affect the political process at both state and interstate levels assumes a growing significance. Because of increasing transborder economic interdependence and the capacity of transnational companies to affect political structures, it is increasingly difficult to trace social processes back to causes within single states. Instead, social processes are seen as emerging from the transnational conditions dictated by an inter- and transstate coalition of political and economic elites functioning as a hegemonic 'historical bloc' (Gramsci). According to this interpretation, 'hegemony' means an international order that reflects the interests of dominant social groups and makes use of both national and international political institutions (like the International Monetary Fund, the World Bank, or the World Trade Organization).

The potential for conflict in world society arises, according to this view, out of the disparity between the political organization of individual states and that of their external environment. While the former, at least in the OECD (Organization for Economic Cooperation and Development) states, rests on the democratic principle, the latter is, as a result of the liberalization of the 1980s, characterized by market forces that are motivated neither by political loyalties nor by social considerations. Since the state has lost much of its competence as a regulator of interactions between intrastate society and the external environment, the consequence is a growing contradiction between the internal and international orders. Because of the qualitative increase in the interdependence of economic relations among states since the Second World War, the liberalized international order is gaining a greater influence on the structuring of intrastate social relations and becoming structurally contradictory to the social needs of communities constituted within state borders (among German scholars see also Altvater 1994: 517 ff ; Narr and Schubert 1994; Neyer 1995: 287 ff).

According to this view world society appears to be a world *market* society, in which the freedom of action of individual states to take decisions on political, social, and cultural questions is eroded by the increasingly transnational effects of processes determined by nonterritorial economic actors. Along this line, Jens Siegelberg, who is working on a critical theory of the causes of war, speaks of capital's inherent tendency to create a division of labor through which national class structures are being internationalized (Siegelberg 1994: 144; see also Wolf 1995). What emerges as the central attribute of world society then is not interdependence in the sense of balanced relations, which, in principle, give all participants a chance to realize their own goals, but, again, domination and dependency.

This concept of world society belongs to the critical tradition of theories of imperialism. However, it differs from the latter by freeing itself from a purely negative assessment of the world market and by taking up its civilizing functions. Nevertheless, the underlying assumption of a primacy of economics underestimates the dynamics of state policies in a states system (Shaw 1994: 15). As will be argued later in this volume (see Klaus Dieter Wolf's chapter), by entering into binding arrangements among each other, governments follow interests of their own and may not be conceptualized as mere handmaidens of dominant classes.

In our own conceptualization, we take up the challenges of both the cobweb and the world market approach. But in doing so, we look for the knots and tensions in the cobweb and its various layers, and we look at markets as only one element shaping public policies and the formation of polities. We want to address the interrelationship between integrating and disintegrating tendencies in present-day political, economic, and social developments in a world context, but we also want to allow for erratic movements that cannot be explained in a 'simple' dialectical fashion regarding the 'unity of contradictions' on the present world scene (see Albert and Lapid 1997). Our approach gives leeway to look at both, the chances for a more peaceful world and new constellations of conflict that could result in new forms of organized violence.[2]

Among the structural changes pertinent to our questions are the development of a routine in global sourcing and global strategic alliance building among the big firms, the inclusion of medium-sized firms in this process through 'deep' networks of production and marketing; furthermore the appearance of financial markets that are functionally off-shore though they remain formally within the reach of state control, and the relative dematerialization of the world economy, which is a corollary to the historical shift of major economic activities first from the primary to the secondary and now to the tertiary sector (service economies). The structural changes in the world economy do not entail that local, regional, and national locations lose their significance. On the contrary, they contribute to the political accentuation of local and regional differences by encouraging the pursuit of active policies by towns and cities, regions, and states to enhance their global competitiveness. Under the simultaneous influence of global sourcing and local differentiation, the role of territoriality is changing. Interstate transactions can no longer be adequately analyzed as simple crossings of borders; rather, the borders themselves are changing in the sense that they are now more porous, and transstate economic spaces and transnational communities are being formed. In this way economic, political, and societal spaces are becoming less and less congruent (see also the chapter by Mathias Albert and Lothar Brock).

These transnational communities serve as links among different societies, but also pose a challenge to the cohesion of national societies. New social conflicts arise which place in question the state's socially integrative functions. It is not convincing to analyze such developments as the 'abdication' of the nation-state. What we are seeing are the initial stages of new forms of statehood, 'transstatehood' and horizontal political integration, which go beyond the old forms of international cooperation and norm-building, and through which the mismatch between political territoriality and economic and societal developments is reduced. Michael Zürn (chapter 9) speaks of a decline in the functions of the nation-state as a result of globalization, which leads to an uneven denationalization. Albert and Brock develop the concept of debordering in order to grasp the dynamic and the direction of ongoing changes. Debordering may result in new forms of political integration. But it may also produce new inter- and transnational conflicts. The latter in our view are not incompatible with, but rather constitutive of, the development of world society.

DIMENSIONS OF WORLD SOCIETY

In our attempt to develop a more precise approach to the questions we have outlined, we start from Tönnies' and Weber's distinction between 'community' (*Gemeinschaft*) and 'society' (*Gesellschaft*). Ferdinand Tönnies' analysis builds on what he sees as a fundamental dualism in human purposes and experience. Every human being possesses a natural and unreflected 'inner will' (*Wesenswillen*) and an artificial and calculating 'will to choose' (*Kürwillen*). The former moves human beings to act out of an affective impulse, while the latter guides them to action in pursuit of external goals. According to Tönnies, the *Wesenswillen* therefore leads to a natural order in the community; differentiating it according to ties of blood, spirit, and location. Society, in Tönnies' view, has to be understood as a cultural or moral atrophy of community (Tönnies 1972: 208, 215). In society, human actions follow the calculating *Kürwillen*. However, if Tönnies' concept is applied to international relations, as Buzan (1993: 327 ff) has attempted to do, two major problems arise: a sense of community is dependent on a value context that does not exist on a global scale. In addition the specific conception of community results in a negative evaluation of the idea of society.

Max Weber turns the community-society distinction around. He sets out four different types of action:

- strategic (*zweckrational*) (means are adjusted to ends);
- value-rational (*wertrational*) (specific means are considered as ends in themselves);
- affectual or emotional;
- traditional (guided by custom).

According to Weber, social relations do not presuppose feelings of community, but manifest themselves as the behavior of a plurality of actors insofar as the action of each takes account of that of the others' (Weber 1968). According to Weber, social relations do not arise out of the higher functional requirements of a social system, but through subjective acts "which do not assume any 'whole'" (Bauer 1993: 25). For Weber, a social relationship is called 'communal' (*Vergemeinschaftung*) if and so far as the orientation of social action is based on a subjective feeling of the parties, whether affectual or traditional, that they belong together. A social relationship will, on the other hand, be called 'associative' (*Vergesellschaftung*) if and in so far as the orientation of social action within it rests on a rationally motivated adjustment of interests or a similarly motivated agreement, whether the basis of rational judgment be absolute values or reasons of expediency (see also Weber 1968).

In employing the ideal types of society formation (*Vergesellschaftung*) and community formation (*Vergemeinschaftung*), we are well aware of the fact that we may be facing some categorical problems. For Weber, *Vergesellschaftung* and

Vergemeinschaftung clearly were phenomena that referred to persons as actors. Thus, to extend the search for processes of *Vergesellschaftung* and *Vergemeinschaftung* to involve collective actors may mean that the clear Weberian definition of the ideal types as strictly actor-based is put in doubt, not least in relation to the question who or what can be the carrier of a collective identity.[3]

Emanuel Richter's methodological analysis of the notion of community (chapter 4) points in a similar direction. It may in the end very well turn out that in the light of global processes the very concepts of 'community' and 'society' will have to be redefined in a fundamental fashion. Richter reminds us, however, that this may be easier said than done, particularly regarding the idea of 'community'. While he shows and clearly dissects the immense conceptual baggage that this idea has accumulated over the centuries, he also points out that it is a concept normatively laden in a quite distinct fashion. Thus, while in communitarian thinking community has a decidedly positive connotation, it immediately arouses suspicions in any social science discourse in Germany. Instead of lamenting this state of affairs, however, Richter calls for research on the 'global network' to be supplemented by a research on such basic ideas as Gemeinschaft and Gesellschaft.

Since *Vergesellschaftung* and *Vergemeinschaftung* are ideal types, most forms of actually existing social relations are mixtures of communal and associative relations. Social relations described in this way create a coherent social context through the existence of binding rules and the expectation that these rules will be adhered to. This ideal-typical distinction can be applied to international relations in different ways. One way would be to follow Hedley Bull's perspective on international society (Bull 1977: 13–14, Bull and Watson 1984c: 430 ff). 'International society' refers to:

> A group of states (or more generally, a group of independent political communities) which not merely form a system, in the sense that the behavior of each is a necessary factor in the calculation of the others, but also have established by dialogue and consensus common rules and institutions, and recognize their common interest in maintaining these arrangements. (Bull and Watson 1984b: 1)

In Weberian terms we could speak here of international society as a rationalization of the order of an international system. Bull's concept serves to identify a central element of qualitative change in the system of international relations according to the criterion of its higher level of organization. However, Bull sees the 'common set of rules' and the 'common institutions' as pertaining only to states. They are the only actors involved in this society-formation. Buzan has subsequently attempted to incorporate different social actors in this concept by drawing a further distinction between 'international society' and 'world society' (Buzan 1993: 327 ff; the latter term is identical with 'world community' as used in Chris Brown 1995: 9 ff). While system and society are said to belong to the level of interstate relations, the transnational level (world society) is to be incorporated by means of the community dimension, which Bull ignores. Buzan conceptualizes the two terms as complementary and even symbiotic:

> International society provides the political framework without which world society would face all the dangers of primal anarchy. In return, world society provides the gemeinschaft foundation without which international society remains stuck at a fairly basic level. (Buzan 1993: 351)

Buzan's assignment of societal elements to the international level and of community elements to the transnational level is intriguing. But it is also problematic. The possibility that community formation could occur within the state system is ruled out in advance, and secondly (and this is the more serious weakness of Buzan's classification), this understanding of politics implies that only states can be political actors. It does not seem to us to be helpful to investigate the societal element exclusively at the interstate level, and the community element at the intersocietal level. In our view it is especially important to consider nonstate actors as agents of society formation, and state actors as being involved in community formation. We assume that it is in the field of societal actors and of transnational relations that structural elements of world society have been forming for some time now. Research that focuses either on interstate relations or on understanding intersocietal relations cannot live up to complexities of society and community formation at the inter- and transstate levels.

THE DIFFERENTIATION OF ACTORS AND LEVELS AND SPHERES OF INTERACTION

Regime analysis, too, with its focus on international *Vergesellschaftung*, namely international institutionalization, has remained basically state-centric. It is only very recently that research on international regimes, employing two-level games analysis, has corrected the neglect of interrelationships between political systems or parts of them, societal groups, nongovernmental organizations, and international institutions that resulted from a preoccupation with the 'state' as a black box. If one wanted to stick to a more state-centered approach, there would be the need to problematize the neorealist notion of states as like units. Systemwide processes like the development of a world society affect the structure of state units, and in turn, this affects the structure of the international system. In his contribution, Georg Sørensen (chapter 6) draws attention to the emergence of 'unlike units' as a result of the interplay between international and domestic factors. Sørensen identifies three different types of states in the present international system: the 'Westphalian state', the 'premodern state'—mainly in Sub-Sahara Africa—and the 'postmodern state' in the European Union. These different types of states point to the unevenness of world society formation.

Picking up on this issue, Zürn's analysis deals with the dilemma of uneven denationalization: Trying to maintain their political capacity to fulfill governance functions, the nation-states create international governance structures, which may be still inadequate in terms of effective problem-solving, but which certainly increase decision-makers' autonomy from societal control. This creates problems for democracy for instance in the form of the democratic deficit of the European Union (EU). Zürn suggests the democratization of the territorial representation of the EU by way of introducing elements of direct democracy in order to overcome the democratic deficit of international governance. Wolf approaches this problem from a different perspective. His treatment of the problem of the democratic deficit refers specifically to the differentiation of actors and levels of interaction and the growing institutionalization of international governance as the two basic elements of our concept of world society. It also underlines that this concept does not simply replace a state-centered point of view with a society-centered one. Rather, in trying to understand how different types of actors interact, strategic and concrete goals are attributed to governments and nongovernmental actors at the same time. In this context, the concept of world society serves to explain the democratic deficit not as a mere accident but as the result of the strategic behavior of governments striving for internal and external autonomy.

In the present debate on the formation of world society, on citizen participation at the international level, and the control of international decision-making processes, increasing attention is being paid to nongovernmental organizations (NGOs). In chapter 10, Hilmar Schmidt and Ingo Take consider the contributions of NGOs to the democratization of international politics. They ask under which conditions this democratization may be reconciled with the goal of increased efficiency in international problem-solving processes. Just as states' behavior is oriented toward strategic goals, so do nonstate actors pursue both substantial goals (in attempting to deal with specific problems) and strategic goals—understood here as goals serving the maintenance of these actors' general capacity to act.

With a view to the pursuit of active policies by towns and cities, regions, and states, it is important to realize, as Jürgen Neyer points out in chapter 11, that substate units that play a role beyond the confines of national borders (like global cities) have to be regarded not only as sites but also as actors. To a certain extent they are involved in global sourcing in their own right, though not independent from the states. By pursuing these activities, they not only make use of existing differences between economic sites around the world but also deepen the unevenness of world economic development, causing politically precarious social cleavages even in 'their own countries'. The state itself tends to react in a procyclical way by displaying a growing reluctance to supplying redistributive transfer-payments. Neyer also demonstrates that global cities, while being centers of economic command and control, are also sites of social poverty and inequality. This serves as a special incentive on the part of the global cities to combine strategic goals vis-à-vis the central state with substantial problem-solving. This is becoming more difficult because of the tendency on the part of the state to practice what may be called an 'internal externalization' of the costs of its own strategic goal attainment. In this respect, the principle of subsidiarity, which has been acknowledged within the European Union as a means for regulating competence in favor of the state level of action, has come to serve both the central governments in their endeavor to get rid of economic and social problems, and the globalized substate actors in their endeavor to widen their margins of action for the mobilization of international resources.

These aspects of world society formation need to be looked at in greater detail. Thus, the concept of world society we are proposing here is also designed to stimulate actor- and problem-specific case studies, which could address the questions that arise from the basic assumption that world society formation is actually taking place. One such actor- and problem-specific case study is undertaken by Ingo Take in chapter 12. He looks at the contribution of NGOs to international environmental cooperation. Like states, which form international alliances to deal with the new global challenges, NGOs build transnational networks and organizations to balance the institutionalization of interstate relations. By offering a systematic review of the mechanisms through which NGOs interact with domestic, national, transnational, and international actors, and through which they also influence international relations, Take shows how the differentiation in the levels of operation constitutes a dimension of change, which all actors, be they states or NGOs, have to take into account.

Another promising field of investigation is the development of world society via economic, political, and societal 'debordering' processes in the world of states (developed by Albert and Brock). The concept of 'debordering' seeks to understand substantial modifications in the interrelationship between territory and states as an increasing incongruence of political, economic, and social spaces. Debordering goes together with the emergence of new political spaces and new forms of politics that at least partly compensate for the functional weaknesses of the territorial state. Debordering is to be understood not as an abdication on the part of the state, but as a change in the nature of statehood. This change can be seen from the political ethical point of view as a positive development, as long as pluralistic community-building and effective and democratic control remain possible. However, debordering can also give rise to perceived needs for the drawing of new borders leading to new exclusions. This observation underlines the integrative functions of borders between territorial states, and the necessity of finding new functional equivalents to them.

It would also be worth asking what effect new world-societal regulation requirements have on state policies and on the actions of nonstate actors. Will state policies orient themselves toward the requirements of effective problem-solving, and so perhaps give societal actors more of a role in the policy process, in order to set free corporatist resources? Or will the states act strategically and try to win back freedom of action and autonomy from their societies by committing them to keep to binding international agreements? In chapter 8, Hilmar Schmidt shows that states, if understood as problem-solvers, must not only change their behavior toward the external world, but also adapt themselves internally to the new requirements of world society. States in world society face a rapidly growing agenda of problems and equally increasing demands of societal actors to participate in foreign policy decision making. Schmidt suggests that the specific design of domestic policy-networks has an impact on the problem-solving capacity of states and that therefore states should include their societal subsystems in the political process.

THE RELATIONSHIP BETWEEN SOCIETY AND COMMUNITY

Our concept of world society is summarized in figure 1.1, which depicts the growing complexity of social relations in world society.

At this point, changes in international relations may be understood as a process of global society formation (development of a world society), which goes beyond the mere intensification of interdependence and interaction. However, we still need to address the question of community formation and of the relationship between society and community formation. Weber himself stressed the reflexive dimension of community formation (*Vergemeinschaftung*). Collective identities are usually—if not always—created by the perception of difference and sameness. Members of the same community realize that they have one or more things in common, which distinguish the members of the emerging community from all those who differ from them in this (these) respect(s).

> All kinds of other visible differences can, in a given case, give rise to repulsion and contempt [...]. Seen from their positive aspect, however, these differences may give rise to consciousness of kind, which may become as easily the bearer of group relationships. (Weber 1968: Vol. 1, 365)

Figure 1.1   International System—International Society—World Society

International System	Interaction and interdependence.
International Society	In addition: institutionalized collective regulation of behavior between states, based rationally on shared interests. As relations between states intensify with the common aim of raising the level of organization of the international system, by means of the development of norms and institutions, 'international society' constitutes itself. In this sense, society formation going beyond the self-help system begins.
World Society	In addition: the diffusion of actors and differentiation of levels of action, in the sense of increased complexity and the continued existence of state actors; in this way the transnational dimension of world society as further transborder society formation between nonstate actors is opened up.

This does not presuppose that the members of a community know each other or actively pursue community formation (*Gemeinschaftshandeln*) (see also Weber 1968: Vol. 1, 365). The feeling of belonging together and of demarcation are sufficient: they form the social construction that is relevant to the members of a group.

The distinction between society and community formation is one between ideal types. In real life, social relationships consist of a mixture of these two types. Processes of community formation also play a role at the level of international relations. By 'community formation' we mean the coming into being of a feeling of solidarity that is not reliant on interests or calculations of benefit. Buzan sees nongovernmental organizations as the agents of such processes, and states (governments) as the agents of society-formation processes. As mentioned above, we regard this restrictive classification as problematic. It is true that transnational networks of action groups linked by affectual ties (for example, solidarity) are particularly noticeable in the areas of environmental protection, development policy, or the defense of human rights. But first, this by no means covers the whole spectrum of nonstate actors; it excludes those economic organizations that are for us especially important—multinational companies and economic interest groups. Second, a process of society formation is also taking place between the groups mentioned, to the extent that they set up permanent organizational structures whose own bureaucratic interests grow as their political weight increases. Third and most important, society formation at the international level is taking place in a complex interplay with processes of international community formation. There may be community formation at the interstate level—for instance in the form of the much acclaimed 'community of democratic states' or among heads of states in the course of international negotiations. For this reason, we consider the use of the term 'international community' to be more than just a figure of speech. It identifies an aspect of international cooperation and of the establishment of rules that we lose sight of if we exclude community formation at the outset from considerations of society formation in international relations. Figure 1.2 underlines this understanding of the different levels of society and community formation.

In his contribution to this volume, Christoph Weller (chapter 3) conceptualizes *Vergemeinschaftung* on the basis of Weber's understanding of the latter as the formation of collective identities. National identity as one specific type of collective identity has been and still is the most important form of *Vergemeinschaftung* in international relations (see also Anderson 1991). As long as the borders of *Vergesellschaftung* and *Vergemeinschaftung* were largely congruent, the interplay between the two processes was of minor relevance and rarely taken into consideration. As an intensive process of antagonistic community formation, the East-West conflict dominated collective identity building, because the demarcation against the respective adversary determined the perception of nearly all others. With globalization, more differences can be perceived. For example, in many places *regional* collective identities have emerged, which chal-

Figure 1.2   Positioning World Society

	Society Formation	*Community Formation*
(a) International Relations	*International society formation* among states (for example, international institutions)	*International community formation* among specific states or representatives of states (for example, heads of states in intergovernmental negotiations)
(b) Transnational Relations	*Transnational society formation* among nonstate actors (for example, pressure groups or private companies organized across borders)	*Transnational community formation* among nonstate actors (for example, sectoral or regional groups)
(a)/(b)	*World society* (includes processes of international and transnational society and community formation)	

lenge existing states. At the same time we can observe a growing significance of *transnational* collective identities through issue specific coalition building across borders. Weller offers some considerations in how to deal with these forms of community formation in the developing world society, which he views as Janus-faced pointing to both integrative and disintegrative effects. On the basis of social-psychological theories he addresses the new nationalism, understood as securing or as renewal of emotional demarcations that have been challenged through the increase of cross-border interactions.

If perceptions of differences between 'us' and 'them' converge in different issue areas, for example, security, welfare, and culture, confrontation becomes more likely (see Weller 1995), and global society formation could be accompanied by violence. This evaluation is also confirmed in Chris Brown's contribution to this volume (chapter 5), in which he points to the fact that within the advanced industrial world, a much higher level of *Vergesellschaftung* and *Vergemeinschaftung* exists than vis à vis and within the states and societies that make up the 'rest of the world'. This raises important questions about the universal applicability and viability of international and transnational society and community (see figure 1.2). A deepening sense of community in the advanced industrial world, Brown argues, would impede the formation of a universal international society (*Vergesellschaftung*) between states. We agree with Chris Brown that a universal world community remains an impossibility, since *Vergemeinschaftung* always rests on demarcations from others.[4]

International societies seem to perform particularly well when they are accompanied by well-defined elements of community formation. A good example would be the existence of a community among heads of states who have learned to trust each other as the result of regular interaction, including communicative action resulting in a better mutual understanding (Müller 1994).

The society of Western states during the East-West conflict could also be described in terms of a community of states in respect of its affirmation of certain shared values and conceptions of order. The European Union, too, is clearly based on something more than a strategically motivated coincidence of interests; there is also a shared perception of belonging together, a certain degree of solidarity that seems to be a prerequisite for including the needs of the other members of the community in the building of one's own preferences.

It is precisely the progress in society formation in international relations that has set in motion a reaction against universalism (see Axtmann 1995: 93). This can also be seen as community formation within a certain group of states. One example would be the question of the 'Western' character of human rights, which became a much-debated topic when the ASEAN (Association of South East Asian Nations) states, after the 1993 Vienna Human Rights Conference, spoke critically of what they saw as a particularist Western tradition of thought about human rights, and contrasted this with their own non-Western understanding of the term (Asian values). Our view is that the problem of interests in the human rights debate should be taken seriously. The fact that political elites can seek to instrumentalize particular concepts of human rights certainly does not mean that a discussion of the concrete validity of human rights is superfluous. Every right requires interpretation in respect of its validity or applicability in specific situations.

We take the view that every type of society formation in social relations develops in a positive interplay with at least a rudimentary process of community formation, and that society formation can also at the same time bring about or foster 'militant' community-formation processes. The boundaries of such communities need not be identical with those of the society. This is especially noticeable in cases where society formation leads to a loss of identity and/or an endangering of the positions of specific groups; these groups then try even harder to preserve or strengthen their own shared values and traditions. There is therefore both a positive and a negative interplay between community and society formation. Both forms of interplay can also be observed at the international level, in the form of nationalism, fundamentalism, or value-demarcation in the course of global society formation.

On the assumption that there is a close interplay between society formation and community formation we differ sharply from conventional views of a chronological sequence (from traditional to modern) or even of a zero-sum relationship according to which community will be sacrificed on the altar of society. Furthermore, we do not assign community formation to the transnational level and society formation to the international level (like Buzan 1993). Instead, our concept is designed to direct attention to community formation among states as well. This kind of *Vergemeinschaftung* may serve to advance and support global society formation (*Vergesellschaftung*), but may also provide a shield against the latter. Since the already existing relations of interdependence make self-exclusion possible only to a limited extent, we can expect a continuing tension between particularist community formation and universalist society formation. In the short term, at least, world society will not be able to provide a substitute for the identity-providing function of societies organized as nation-states.

THE MARCH OF HISTORY?

It should be clear from the argument so far that our concept of world society does not assume that the process thus described is irreversible, and does not imply any one-sided normative evaluation of this process. We take the view that it is inappropriate to commit oneself in advance to a positive or negative assessment of the global society-formation process and "to systematize the changing manifestations of a world entity in a normative way" (Richter 1990: 279). The concept we have developed here is open-ended. In contrast to other concepts (for example Lipschutz 1992: 389 ff, List 1992: 29 ff), it in no way assumes a linear process, but is intended to remain capable of incorporating contradictory tendencies, which may indeed be a reaction to globalization without being *determined* by it (Brock 1993: 163 ff). Nevertheless, the existing degree of inter- and transnational interdependence and institutionalized interaction renders the uncoupling of certain actors from these associative contexts unlikely.

Regarding the normative implications of global society formation, Ferdinand Tönnies, as mentioned above, treats the development from community to society within a general context of cultural pessimism. The latter is echoed in the views of some of the modern communitarians. In contrast, authors like Anthony Giddens or Ulrich Beck are quite optimistic. Beck, for example, sees world society as the only way of solving the global problems of 'risk societies' (Beck 1986: 63). Wolfgang Hein also associates global society with the concrete expectation that it could be the forum in which all kinds of global problems can be solved (Hein 1994: 108). The observation that problems of interdependence can only be dealt with collectively could indeed make people more aware of the need for cooperative action involving state actors and societal actors (Kohler-Koch 1993: 110). But it would be a mistake to conclude that, just because the necessity and certain opportunities are there for every one to see, the latter will automatically be translated into action. From an actor-oriented rather than a functionalist perspective, cooperative problem-solving capability by cooperation is only one among many other possible strategic options. Assuming that states have an interest in themselves they will be very selective gatekeepers when deciding on the admittance of non-state actors to international governance mechanisms (see Wolf in this volume).

For Norbert Elias (1976) humanity's capacity to control its emotions (*Affektkontrolle*) is not only constitutive of society, but also forms the core of the civilizing process. The diminishing of violence attributed to this process leads Elias, in contrast to Tönnies, to a positive assessment: violence is something outside civilization, it can only be understood as a relapse. Society formation is connected with control over the emotions with rationalization and an order of interpersonal and intercollective relations resting on cost-benefit calculations. However, Elias posits a close connection between the containment of violence and its monopolization. Such monopolization of power does not exist in world society.

If we follow Elias, the positive effects of world society formation would only appear when the system of states has been overcome. The realization of world society as a new stage in the evolution of human affairs would therefore depend on the formation of a world state. This conclusion points to a weakness in Elias' approach. It is a mistake to equate society formation in the sense of rationalization and control over the emotions with pacification and the diminution of violence. König has formulated this very precisely in his criticism of Senghaas' reception of Elias' theory of civilization: "The increased destructive capacity of the industrial age is the product of modern society, not the product of its regression" (König 1993: 458). It is, says König, the distancing of the individual from the consequences of his/her actions, the operative principle of modern society, which makes possible a moral indifference toward violent action.

A one-sidedly positive evaluation of the civilizing process not only overlooks the ways in which the use of force has been perfected, but also neglects the issue of domination in complex social relations. This criticism applies above all to Bull, who, by omitting any further discussion of the ethical or normative dimension, turns 'order' into a "value without an argument" (Harris 1993: 729). When Bull declares that the order provided by international society is a value that takes precedence over all others, "because it is the condition of the realization of other values" (Bull 1977: 96 ff), he is only describing the inherent potential of this order, which distinguishes it from international anarchy. The ambivalence of the structures of this international order is, as Brown (chapter 5) points out, excluded from consideration by definition as long as the institutions of international society are said to possess a universal attraction that can only be denied by those who do not want to live in peace. Contrary to this glorification, the normative impact of these institutions has to be regarded as much more ambivalent when judged from the perspective of legitimate governance (see the contributions of Zürn and Wolf).

If one were to accept the normative evaluation of societies and of world society that is central to the communitarianism debate (Fowler 1991; Avineri and de-Shalit 1992), the evolution of a world society would be positive if it were accompanied by spreading communal cohesion. A liberal society that relies exclusively on rational arrangements "is fragmentation in practice; and community is the exact opposite, the home of coherence, connection, and normative capacity" (Walzer 1990: 9). Stability, solidarity, and peace would be absent from a world society as long as communal factors are not present to underpin associative institutions. The community is therefore vital for communitarians in order to anchor norms in a society and to ensure that this society does not turn into something no better than a self-help agency (Taylor 1992: 42). Since it is harder to discern communal elements at the global level than in national societies, the emergence of a just or solidary world society would be unlikely (Purnell 1973: 8).

If we wanted to get beyond the ambivalent associative dimension of world society, we would in fact have to look for a possible normative-ethical foundation for world society. But if we did this, we would be jumping out of the frying pan of moral indifference seen in Bull's analysis ("agnosticism about values," according to Harris 1993: 733) into the fire of the impossible task of constructing a global feeling of community. That this would not lead us far is revealed empirically by the resistance that 'Western universalism' encounters in the rest of the world. The fundamental premises of social psychology rule out the development of a universal collective identity. Global society formation is therefore far from being a process without contradictions. Despite the development of shared interests and their manifestation in common institutions and agreed codes of conduct, and despite the fact that nonstate actors now have more opportunities to become involved, there is a substantial, if concealed, potential for violence in this process. We can at best speak of a rudimentary global feeling of community based on universally recognized ideas (such as the *idea* of human rights). And despite the deficits with regard to legitimacy, processes of policy-making in the emerging world society are also connected with civilizational achievements which open up new opportunities for hedging violence and tackling global problems in a cooperative way.

2

Debordering the World of States: New Spaces in International Relations

Mathias Albert and Lothar Brock

INTRODUCTION: STRUCTURAL CHANGE AND ADJUSTMENT

What has changed as a result of the collapse of real socialism and the ending of the East-West conflict, and whether these events signal epochal change still remain open questions (Holm and Sørensen 1995a). It is a dispute that extends far beyond the question of changing coalitions of interest and patterns of relations in the world of states,[1] but touches on the change of statehood per se. "What is required," wrote Ashley in the wake of the upheavals, "is the audacity to admit that...we really do not know who 'we' are" (Ashley 1989: 311). In view of the simultaneous globalization and fragmentation of public life that is currently under way, this conclusion would seem to be inescapable; and yet it is being resolutely resisted (see also Reich 1990; Lipschutz 1994) and accompanied by warnings not to throw away the concept of the state too soon (Krasner 1994a).

Respecting these warnings but more fascinated by the possibility and necessity of the new, this chapter seeks to conceptualize change in international relations by thematizing the relation between territory and state. The formation of sharply defined, mutually exclusive territories is one of the fundamental features of the modern, state-based world. More than anything else, a change in the territorial order would challenge the modern international political order. It is therefore all the more astonishing, as Ruggie observes, that the concept of territoriality has been accorded so little interest for so long in international relations (Ruggie 1993: 174). John Herz's thesis that in the age of nuclear threat the nation-state had lost its thick-skinnedness (Herz 1957, 1968, 1976) aroused considerable attention, but it did more to explicate problems of security policy than to set in motion a radical debate about the relationship between territory and politics.[2] To take up this question in a more comprehensive fashion, one can refer to valuable conceptual work in the field of political geography[3] as well as to numerous works dealing with the functions of interstate borders and changes herein.[4] Furthermore, even beyond political geography an increasing interest in the issue of the territorial references of politics (and polities) can be witnessed.[5]

Kratochwil (1986) and Ruggie (1993) see the increasing number of transborder phenomena as an 'unbundling' of the territorial state.[6] This points to the fact that states as spheres of power are coming under strain and that their ability to regulate economic and societal developments in the framework of fixed territorial boundaries is waning (O'Brien 1992). The diminishing regulatory competence is then translated into a loss of social competence (Narr and Schubert 1994). It is thus that one of the state's essential functions for ensuring the cohesion of society becomes threatened. The problem is aggravated by mounting problems to regulate the relationship between citizens and the state via the instrument of citizenship in face of a transnationalization of social relations.[7]

We propose to analyze these developments as an expression of *debordering processes in the world of states* that might lead to a *debordering of the world of states*. *Debordering processes within the world of states* is understood as an increasing permeability of borders together with a decreasing ability of states to counter this trend by attempts to shut themselves off. In contrast, a *debordering of the world of states* is a form of adaptation of statehood as a response to this increasing permeability of borders. By a debordering within the world of states we mean the often cited increase in transactions of all kinds across boundaries, which do not as such already question the world of states' constitutive principle of territoriality. By a debordering of the world of states, however, we mean changes resulting in the emergence of new political spaces that transcend territorially defined spaces, without necessarily leading to new territorial demarcations (in other words, not to a simple shift of boundaries). Elements of a debordering of the world of states may be found in the process of international organization and the self-restriction of states by means of a more intense regulation of international relations (Rittberger 1993), in the emergence of transnational 'issue coalitions' in the context of 'governance without government' (Rosenau and Czempiel 1992; Zürn 1995, 1998), in the transgovernmental interlocking of politics (*Politikverflechtung*) and the emergence of multilevel systems of governance in transstate contexts (see also Jachtenfuchs and Kohler-Koch 1996b). Our notion of a debordering of the world of states opens up the possibility to look for a common denominator of these diverse developments. Not only is this denominator to be sought in the emergence of new forms of governance in the international context, but also in changes in the form of statehood in the course of its adaptation to the increasing perforation of conceptions of sovereignty defined territorially.

It should be clear from the outset that the observed changes do not constitute one-dimensional nor, for that matter, one-way processes—that is to say, a disintegration of the territorial aspect of politics that progresses in a continuous and ubiquitous fashion (see also Newman 1999). On the contrary, our analytical approach remains open to the possibility of countervailing trends, of signs of the persistence and power of attraction of new border demarcations (see also Brown 1995). To be more precise, we regard the simultaneous occurrence of debordering and new demarcation, and the reciprocal effects between these, as the core issue (see also Brock 1994). However, we refuse to elevate a 'simultaneity of contradictory tendencies' to the rank of an almost universal-dialectical analytical concept (see also Albert and Lapid 1997). The factual debordering processes in the world of states nonetheless do proceed as a diffusion of patterns of collective orientation that rests on the imagined unity of state, economy, and society. In connection with worsening economic situations, this might very well result in political conflicts which, for example, could manifest themselves in the mobilization of nationalistic or subnational-particularistic orientations.

The question is to what extent a dominant trend can nevertheless be identified amongst the broad mass of seemingly contradictory developments. One of the issues that we encounter in this connection is the extent to which, given their mutual dependence, the processes of debordering and demarcation under discussion can be understood in the context of an *evolution of world society* (see chapter 1). We will return to this issue in the concluding section.

MEANING AND DIMENSIONS OF DEBORDERING

Territoriality and Space

Browsing through the catalogue of academic libraries, the items that come up first under 'territoriality' are texts about the significance of territoriality in strategies of self-assertion in the plant and animal kingdom. In the early days of political geography, this semantic association resulted in some dubious analogies where border areas were viewed as biological battlefields, in which societies vied with one another for *Lebensraum*, or 'living-space' (Ratzel 1896, 1903; Haushofer 1927; see Jones 1959). The ways in which such views of the territorial principle are open to political abuse are well known and much care needs to be taken in any interpretation of them. And yet, the historic omnipresence of territorial strategies of self-assertion, and thus also of the struggle over borders, is impossible to overlook as territoriality manifests itself in the demarcation, defense, and revision of borders.

The evolution of the modern system of states has taken the form of a comprehensive territorial division of the world into independent states. In this connection, colonialism constituted a transitional phase from the premodern to the modern age. Decolonization greatly accelerated the process of demarcation and circumscription of exclusive areas. That process continues today through a third round of state-formation triggered by the end of the East-West conflict. With the partial 'territorialization' of the high seas that has resulted from the Third Conference on the Law of the Sea, the process has attained unprecedented proportions (see also Kratochwil 1986: 49; Wolf 1991). Even in the domain of modern communication, states attempt to enforce territorially defined controls—in relation to the Internet, for example. The disputes about the international information-order that had been going on for a quarter of a century essentially concentrated on the question of the national-cum-territorial restriction of global communication flows. It is in this sense in which one might come to describe the process of civilization as a process of territorialization of the public sphere. Accordingly, it would be more appropriate to talk of territorial- rather than nation-states, because territorial delimitation antedated the policy of nation formation, and the latter, as a blanket principle, has as yet not been fully realized, whereas the principle of territorial statehood has established itself worldwide.

One historical perspective that views the formation of the modern system of states as the gradual enforcement of the principle of territoriality rests in part on the observation that territorial amalgamation and demarcation do not by any means fulfill the same function at all times, and have not always had the same significance as far as the organization of public life is concerned.[8] The multifariousness of border demarcations in history, and the diverseness of concepts of territoriality, can scarcely be overlooked. The borders of the Roman Empire and of ancient China marked the division between civilization and barbarity; despite their solid physical markers (*limes*, walls), they did not, in practice, constitute hard-and-fast demarcations but rather zones of transition between the empire and the surrounding world.[9] In contrast, the borders of modern states are divisions between political entities of equal legal status. The borders themselves are regarded as inviolable (Duchacek 1986).

As far as the significance of territoriality in the organization and representation of the public sphere is concerned: the feudal system of medieval Europe was founded not on a territorial but on a functional partition of political space (Strayer 1970: 152; Taylor 1994; Kristof 1959: 278). There emerged a complex division of labor between secular power and papacy, between feudal lord and peasant, and, in the transition to the modern era, between city and country. In the Middle Ages, kings, dukes, archbishops, and bishops could all render feudal service to one and the same person. A patchwork of interwoven, overlapping, redundant areas of power emerged, involving varying and sometimes conflicting relations of loyalty (Jones 1959: 247). In contrast, a central aspect of the formation of the modern system of states was the gradual establishment of the territorial contiguity and equal legal status of each of the respective spheres of power, with central control of internal territorial affairs and unambiguous requirements in terms of loyalty. The Peace of Westphalia marks the transition to this modern system of political rule—a system, which, at that time, already carried within itself the germ of its eventual spread across the whole world (Wallerstein 1991). The Holy Roman Empire of the German nation was nothing but a veil that wafted across from the previous age into the modern era. It could not mask Europe's new image for very long, even if, in Germany and Italy, territorial contiguity of political space was not achieved until the nineteenth century (see Spruyt 1994c).

If one considers the present system of territorial states as a product of specific historical developments, this implies that a radical revision of the relationship between politics and territory is possible (see also Anderson 1992; Ruggie 1993: 152). Such a revision does not take us back to the Middle Ages; the point of looking back into the past is rather to enable one to envisage alternatives to the present system. But where should the path out of the modern era and into the postmodern era take us? One possible vista opens up if a more precise definition is given of the relationship between 'territoriality' and 'space'. *Territoriality* is, as Sack observes, "the geographical expression of social power" (Sack 1986: 5; see also Ruggie 1993: 151). The aim is to control people and resources by demarcating a particular area—in other words, curtailing free access (Peter Taylor 1994: 151). Territoriality is also aimed at ensuring the security and well-being of those who live in the territory, to preserve communities, and to strengthen the ability of the latter to assert themselves in the international or global competition for scarce resources.

Space is a referential system for ordering our thoughts, our perceptions, our feelings (Sack 1980: 4; see also Harvey 1989: 201; Albert 1996; Lefebvre 1991). Territoriality is a particular way of arranging social relations. In the modern age, it is the dominant form of expression of a particular mode of representing these relations in abstract spatial arrangements. As an expression of a particular mode of representation, it regulates which of these arrangements do appear significant and which do not. It has thus a direct influence on the options that are available in a particular era for endowing meaning, for attaining self-assurance, for shaping identity, and also for being able to exist in the society (Foucault 1992: 276; Ruggie 1993: 157). The modern, territorial form of these kinds of spatialities means that demarcation vis-à-vis the other becomes an important element in the constitution of a 'particularity', a 'self', or, to put it generally, of a modern 'subjectivity' (Deleuze and Guattari 1987). In so doing it converts a striving for security into ownership-based thinking. Territoriality not only transforms power spaces into territorial states by means of abstract, spatial lines; through the necessary regulation of ownership claims in the form of abstract property rights, it reaches right into the structure of social spaces within these borders.

According to this perspective, what is new is that territorial determinants of social life and the political process are beginning to break down, and that the latter are being represented in other forms, which in their turn are beginning to allow new combinatory options. This could mean, for example, that the public tasks with which every society is faced will come to be viewed in state-transcendent and functional rather than in territorial terms (see also also Albert and Brock, forthcoming). Economic and political regions will take shape whose essence lies not in a national border (in the sense of a physical line persisting in space) but in the growth of communication, transport, and economic activity (as a purely abstract line tracing flows of information). Areas of joint responsibility will emerge, taking the place of territorial spheres of influence (Kratochwil 1986). Transnational coalitions, in which state and nonstate actors collaborate in varying constellations, will take shape around particular issues or public concerns. Not least, the internal spatial differentiation of states will also change, and this will take place not in the form of an intensified provincialism or local patriotism, but as a functional decentralization of 'public work' and as the restoration of new forms of hybrid public/private spaces.

In what follows, three aspects of debordering will be discussed as possible areas of theoretical development. These three dimensions also serve as indicators of the debordering of the world of states.

The Economic Dimension of Debordering

The emergence of the modern system of states went hand in hand with an intensification and globalization of interstate economic relations. To begin with, trade existed between Europe and the Far East, while looting and pillaging were used as ways of appropriating natural resources in Africa and America. Once the industrial revolution occurred, trade became a necessity for development, and despoliatory colonialism gave way to an international division of labor based on a territorial partitioning of the earth amongst the European powers. The United States was involved, at least indirectly, in this partitioning via the 'dollar imperialism' it exercised over Central and South America and via its pursuit of an 'open door' policy for China. At the same time, however, it anticipated the conversion of the various colonial empires into the building blocks of a worldwide system of territorial states. The perfection of that system was actively promoted by the United States after the Second World War.

Although the world economy and the world system of states evolved together, there is a tension between the two that becomes particularly marked (in the form of protectionism and trade wars) in periods of crisis (1930s, 1980s) and upheaval. That tension is growing even more acute in the context of increased globalization as a result of the rigidity of national borders. The function of these, in the context that concerns us here, is to mobilize and safeguard economic potential. At the same time, however, by virtue of what is, in economic terms, arbitrary territorial demarcation, the rigidity of national borders does block the full realization of economic potential, making access to the relevant economic territories more difficult and thus raising the transaction costs of international economic relations.[10]

One way of reacting to this is to internationalize production. Another is to institute globally agreed reductions in trade restrictions. A third is to conclude regional agreements instituting free-trade areas or—as in the case of the European Union—economic integration. With approaches such as these, borders are circumvented, obstacles resulting from the existence of borders are reduced, or borders are shifted from the internal relations between the states in a particular group to the external relations between these states and third countries (creation of the European internal market). In this latter case, an economic debordering takes place in the internal relations of the states concerned.

A *general* debordering of what have up to now been known as national economies is taking place as a result of the globalization of economic activities and the formation of new international economic centers at the local (subnational) and regional (transnational) level. 'Globalization' here means: the transition from the internationalization of production to 'global sourcing'; the incorporation of all economic activities into a global relationship of competition, with increased capital concentration and partial cooperation between major rivals associated in strategic alliances; the formation of a worldwide financial market combined with a revaluation of invisible trade; and a resultant pressure on all states to adjust their own economic structures to the worldwide economic situation. Multinational companies and financial institutions should not be regarded as entirely stateless bodies, given that they are still subject to the control of the states within which they operate, or of their home countries. In this sense, the world economy does not theoretically have any 'off-shore' zone lying entirely outside the borders of existing national economies (Kapstein 1993). However, the 'off-shore' activities of large 'global players' do effectively invalidate state controls. Even more importantly, the national provenance of multinationally operating firms ceases to have any bearing on their strategic planning and, above all, on taxation.

An additional factor is that globalization is not developing evenly all over the world as a result of the emergence of dynamic centers of international economic development at the sub- and transnational level. The territorially segmented world economy is being transformed into a functionally partitioned space with globalized locations (world cities) and transnationalized regions.[11]

As regards the underlying logic of this transnational subdivision of the world economy and the gradual attainment of relative independence by substate spaces as players and significant entities in the world economy, we can point, initially, to the theses about the spatial structure of capitalist economies that were elaborated during the 1960s and 1970s (Wallerstein 1974, 1980, 1989; see also Harvey 1982). The debate at that time made clear the significance of this kind of structure. However, the model on which it was based, the division of the world economy into center and periphery, was still geared entirely to *international* disparities in development, notably in the relationship between North and South. Keener insights, as far as more recent developments are concerned, are provided by the discourse that has been going on for the last few years about the significance that specific local combinations of locational factors have on the investment decisions taken by businesses in the context of globalization and the development of new technologies and new ways of organizing production ('lean production'/'just in time'). We agree with the proponents of the thesis of 'new localism' (Scott 1988) that local locational factors are gaining in importance precisely as a result of globalization (see also Johnston 1994): given the primacy of *relative location*— that is the possibility to disperse economic activity more and more—the challenges to local and regional actors to shape these locational factors to their own advantage are becoming more daunting. The reduction of transaction costs and an increase in flexibility on the part of the businesses concerned play a central role here. There may be good reason to counsel against overrating transaction costs but their fundamental importance is not really disputed in the debate about 'new industrial spaces' (Henry 1992; Amin and Thrift 1992). Irrespective of this, there are, of course, other factors, not subsumable under the argument about transaction costs, that have to be taken into account: economic traditions that lend themselves to innovation; favorable wage-costs, trading conditions (regional integration); local and meso conditions (Sharpe 1993; Henry 1992; Allen 1989). The latter factors are important in the formation of local 'issue coalitions'—drawn from the economic, political, scientific, and social domains—which can greatly improve the competitiveness of subnational, transnational, and also interterritorial spaces, regardless of their complement of natural resources.

Debordering, in terms of the new localism and regionalism, is thus here viewed as a reflection of the uneven distribution of locational factors combined with a revaluation of the locational issue in the wake of stiffer competition on the world market. It is true that one of the driving forces of globalization consists precisely of the efforts of businesses to reduce their dependence on factors that they cannot control—in other words, to ensure they can act globally. But global action always has a local dimension, and businesses cannot just choose as they please in this matter—in other words, play locations and their political representations off against each other as they themselves are interested in operating in *particular* regions. It is by no means the case that business gains in scope what the state loses through the material erosion of its sovereignty.

In this connection, one should also bear in mind that the centralization of economic decision-making processes does not necessarily increase at the same rate as international concentration of capital and alliance formation. It is true that too little attention has been paid—notably by the proponents of 'new localism'—to the aspect of centralization (Herrera 1992). Nevertheless, new forms of cooperation and communication at the global level are better described as networks and 'flattened hierarchies' (Amin and Thrift 1992: 575) than as a centralized command economy operated by a handful of strategic groups. Only from this standpoint can one explain the genuine scope that exists for local and regional politics.

It is clear that the regionalisms and localisms discussed here are not the same as the new regional arrangements on the interstate level. On the other hand, there is an unmistakable synchronicity between the globalization of economic activities and increased regionalism both within the OECD world and beyond it (continuation of European integration, Asian Pacific Economic Cooperation, North American Free Trade Agreement, etc.). Moreover, this regionalism is embedded in a global policy of liberalization. To this extent, the state-based regionalism also contains elements of the new transstate regionalism, and one might talk here of a convergent evolution of state regionalism and transstate or substate regionalism and localism.

One should not, of course, expect that debordering processes in this realm move ahead synchronically. Distinctions must be drawn, particularly in view of the significance of local and regional factors. Regions that have metropolises that are tightly bound up in the global financial system are hardly likely to view territorial borders as an obstacle. From their point of view, making use of the central state for their own purposes is more important than expanding transnational or interterritorial relations. In contrast, a region that has a modern secondary sector and is tightly linked into international production structures will have a relatively high degree of interest in maintaining its ability to adjust to changing international economic conditions. To the extent that territorial borders will prove to be an obstacle to the structural adjustments required here to satisfy functional demands, a region is more likely to pursue a policy of debordering. Therefore, a *Land* such as Baden-Württemberg, or indeed an American state such as California or Texas, which is characterized by a high proportion of capital and technology intensive industry geared to the world market, is likely to safeguard its ability to adjust by organizing economic spaces in a functional manner (Kline 1984; Goldsborough 1993; Berfield 1993).

A region characterized by structural weaknesses or by an economic setup geared toward local markets, and which regards the linkage to world markets via the national trading area as dangerous, will more seek to isolate itself from the competitive pressures of the surrounding regions in order to either preserve the peculiarities of its own economic structure, or to enable economic modernization to take place in the shelter of protectionist ramparts. Indeed, this issue was raised by weak regions in the United States, Mexico, and Canada during the NAFTA negotiations.

Multiple Statehood

In his well-known 1993 article, Kenichi Ohmae confronts readers with the assertion that, in a borderless world, "the nation-state has become an unnatural and dysfunctional unit for organizing human activity" (Ohmae 1993: 78; Delamaide 1994: 4). In Europe, North America, and East and Southeast Asia, he claims that intranational and transnational zones of economic growth and technological innovation are emerging, which break the bounds of the international territorial-state order. According to Ohmae, the task of states would be to create the legal, social, and infrastructural conditions that will ensure that these economic zones achieve their full potential, and to refrain from any other kind of intervention. Ohmae's vision is one of the transformation of the world of states into a world of marketplaces that is no longer steered by political ideas and interests but by the desire of customers to secure a maximum satisfaction of their needs and that this can only occur through the interactive communication of all market participants. The retreat of the state, not its transformation, is the message. The citizen remains no more than a consumer.

Arguing from the perspective of political geography, Taylor puts forward a thesis more akin to the idea of new political spaces. He claims that there are signs of a long-term transition from interstate to transstate relations. Such a transition would involve the convergence of two diverse trends: the formation of capital control centers that transcend state economies on the one hand, and the growth of new social movements operating on a global scale on the other. The activities of these groupings, according to Taylor, are examples of the increasing 'evasions of sovereignty' and the emergence of "global political agendas in which the states are not central players" (Taylor 1995b: 13, with reference to Friedman 1986 and Falk 1992). In his view, U.S. hegemony played a decisive role in fostering those forces, which he considers to now foster the transformation of the world of states (Rosenau 1995: 27).

What Taylor postulates is not the retreat of the state as envisaged in the liberal scenario presented by Ohmae, but a marginalization of interstate relations as a determinant of social life through the action of nonstate actors (social movements, major urban centers) who link up globally and determine the direction of interstate politics. The citizen in this case is an NGO member and inhabitant of a metropolis (see also Sassen 1991).

Responding to Ohmae's plea for a regionally based pursuit of deregulation, and to Taylor's vision of a gradual retreat of interstate relations in favor of transstate ones, Ralf Dahrendorf (1994) has expressed the fear that this new localism and regionalism will lead to nothing more than a fragmentation of the world of states, and thus also to a multiplication of conflicts with a simultaneous decrease in the willingness to seek compromise and assume social responsibility.

We offer a perspective that differs from these views. What is involved in these processes of change is not a further deregulation, nor the elimination of the world of states, or its reproduction in the form of a new particularism on a grand scale (that is, at the global level). Rather, it is the transformation of that world by means of a tempering of territoriality as an organizing principle. The decisive factor, in our view, is not how far intrastate competencies between territorially distinct entities are preserved or newly distributed, but how new forms of reciprocal action emerge between economics, politics, and society which are shaped more by functional needs and less by territorially determined notions of identity and difference. The point is that geographical classifications should not also be viewed as territorial demarcations. The economic regions identified by Ohmae (and here we go along with his view) are all geographically localizable, but they do not thereby constitute political territories with new claims to sovereignty. That is the challenging aspect of this view (see also Rosenau 1995: 25–27; Hettne and Inotai 1994). As Rosenau observes:

> [i]t seems clear [...] that cities and microregions are likely to be major control mechanisms in the global politics of the twenty-first century. Even if the various expectations that they replace states as centers of power prove to be exaggerated, they seem

destined to emerge as either partners or adversaries of states as their crucial role becomes more widely recognized and they thereby move from an objective to an intersubjective existence. (Rosenau 1995: 27)

Our argument is that the state should not simply be viewed as a fixed entity, and that it does indeed change in the wake of the developments mentioned by Rosenau, Taylor, and others. However, the nation-state performs normative-cum-integrative functions, one of which is the distribution of welfare. It will not be possible, for the foreseeable future, to reproduce these functions either at the supranational or transnational/regional level (Brown 1995; see also, however, Zürn 1998). As a consequence, debordering at first only seems to involve the creation of transnational structures that are reconcilable with the requirements of preserving national political systems. On the other hand, if the territorial principle were eroded, the basis on which states operate in relation to one another would be radically altered. It would then no longer be a case of sharply delimited entities set one against the other, but rather one of noncongruent, function-based spaces. Within these, it would not be *Britain*, *Germany*, or *France* that would conduct politics, but German, English, and French operators, interacting with 'social forces' in specific constellations of interests. Of course, that by itself would hardly constitute a new perspective for inquiry. What is new is that the "overlapping and interpenetration of regional functional spaces by national and supranational activities and functional spaces [may] obey an entirely different, and sometimes conflicting, economic, social, cultural, and political logic" (Grabher 1994: 64) without this having to be regarded as negative. On the contrary, the result, ideally, would not be wastefulness and confusion of competencies at the level of the system as a whole, but an increased ability, on the part of state and quasistate structures and procedures, to adapt to changes in framework (international economic) conditions. It is in this sense that one might talk of the emergence of multiple statehood. The new social movements and the 'global cities' will play an important role in this kind of development. They help alter the areas of reference for the conduct of politics (which continues to be a task performed — and performed primarily — by states).

This then leads on to the question of how multiple statehood can be democratically controlled. The creation of new functional spaces in politics at the local or regional level does no more to ensure the development of informed democratic opinion than does subsidiarity per se. A possible way of tackling this is indicated by the Euregio, set up in 1965 on the Dutch-German border near Enschede and Gronau (Scott 1996; Hrbek and Weyand 1994: 66 ff). The Euregio is an amalgam of one German and two Dutch local authority associations comprising over 100 parishes, towns, and districts. The purpose of the amalgamation is, on the one hand, to foster Dutch-German understanding in the European context, and, on the other, to rid the relevant border areas of their peripheral status and create a new economic center. The main executive body is the Euregio Council. It was set up in 1978 and consists of twenty-nine Dutch and thirty-one German representatives elected by the various local councils participating in the scheme. In accordance with the practice of the European Parliament, the representatives collaborate on a party rather than a country basis. The council oversees Dutch-German cooperation in the various fields of work (employment relations, social problems, environment, culture, economic issues, tourism, transport and traffic, agriculture, technology, education and training, routine problems). It also coordinates the activities of the regional authorities operating in these domains. In addition, it acts as a lobby for the region. The council also has advisory members drawn from representatives of the European Union, the Dutch and German governments, the governments of the participating *Länder* and provinces, and the *Regierungsbezirke*.[12] In this context, a public space has been created, which, though geographically localizable, is actually held together by functional cooperation and not by territorial borders, and in which public matters are dealt with in a procedure that is governed by internationally agreed provisions of private law, and whose operation is, at least to some extent, subject to democratic control. We do not intend here to discuss how far the Euregio might be used as a model for other European border areas — let alone for non-European border areas such as San Diego/Tijuana or El Paso/Cd. Juarez. The co-operation that is taking place in the Euregio region is of an entirely different kind, and an important feature of the emergence of innovative institutions in this area would precisely be a high degree of regional specificity (Scott 1989). What the Euregio demonstrates is that there are new paths not only of cooperation but also of political control, that could help bring about a peaceful transformation of the world of states starting from its periphery, which, given the significance of territoriality, means from the demarcations that constitute its very essence.

The Social Aspect: Transnational Communities and Coalitions

Economic globalization is founded on the steadily expanding mobility of capital, goods, and services. However, a proportion of the prospective workforce, increasingly together with a great retinue of dependants, is also on the move. One incentive for this movement is provided by globalization itself, which tends, in contrast to the 'classical' internationalization of production, to react to locational differences rather than disparities in development, but by so doing constantly produces new constellations of unequal development. As center and periphery shift in the wake of globalization, a proportion of the people in the affected areas shifts along with them. With the revolution in communications and transport, and with the continuing disparity in development, this kind of avant-garde nomadism will increase. Given this context of globalization, one could speak of a 'postmodern migration', as distinct from modern migration. The latter was set in motion during the last century, in the wake of the modern international division of labor, and came to a halt during the 1930s and 1940s. It was the *Gastarbeiter* ('guest-workers') who laid the ground for the present phase of migration. During the 'golden age' of economic growth founded on mass production and consumption, they began migrating, initially from the European and North American periphery to the respective centers, and then also between southern Asia and the Middle East, and finally within (and to) Southeast Asia. The guest-workers led the transition from classical to postmodern migration, though, as North American migration and the differing causes of migration in present-day Europe show, the distinction between the two should not be exaggerated.

The decisive difference is that present-day migration, as compared with the classical kind, is encountering a reduced ability and/or willingness in the recipient states to absorb migrants. It reflects a decline in living conditions in the areas of origin (push effect) and the expectation of the migrants that they will secure some share in the development of the dynamic centers of the world economy (pull effect). The barriers to absorption that it encounters in these centers are in part due to the critical state of economic development and the problems of structural adjustment in the target countries themselves. These discrepancies between the supply of immigration opportunities on the one hand and the demand on the other, as well as the conflicts that result from them, have made migration one of the chief vehicles for, and objects of, the new 'transitional societies" reflections about themselves.

Although, according to various estimates, more than 150 million people are living outside their native countries at the end of the 1990s, this is not a particularly impressive figure if compared to the overall size of world population. What makes it significant, however, is that migration, like globalization, does not take place evenly, but is concentrated in particular places/societies. Here, transnational communities are being formed, occupying spaces that are delimited not territorially but culturally or ethnically (Glick Schiller et al. 1992).

Transnational communities exist in, and at the same time beyond, the world of states. They thus transcend the classical categorizations of population and territory. The classical instrument by which that categorization is achieved is citizenship (see also Kratochwil 1994; Beiner 1995). As far as the world of states as a system of theoretically equal and sovereign political entities is concerned, granting citizenship is a constitutive element. It supplements external demarcation in ensuring the internal functionality of the state, that is, its ability to maintain a public order. This is why one of the essential features of citizenship is that its award is not arbitrary but selective. The question is to what extent the role and award of citizenship should be adapted to the emergence of transnational communities. The crucial importance of this question in relation to the possibility of epochal change is highlighted by the recent burgeoning of publications on this topic, with the reflections on citizenship being embedded in the current debates about nationalism, culture, identity, gender, and ethnicity.[13]

The reason for the attention devoted to the issue of citizenship is not only the spread of transnational communities per se, however, but also the changes that have occurred in the social context within which this spread is occurring. Globalization affects not only those who migrate, but also those who are left behind. The effect that globalization has on the individual societies prompts the latter to view themselves as multilayered communities of interests, values, and cultural habits distinct from outside communities. At the same time, intranational competition for foreign investments begins to develop, putting the states' internal social equilibrium in doubt.

In addition, the national community of interests, values, and cultural habits mentioned is being pervaded by a new universalism in consumption, involving globally standardized *world goods* and *world news* (CNN) and the propagation of a unitary *Weltlebensgefühl* or *worldwide sense of life* (music and dance as delivered by MTV). Besides this, there is the confrontation with new threats to individual prospects (environmental destruction, crime, new diseases, fundamentalism), and the experience of the emergence of a unified world order, which runs counter to the narrative constructions by means of which the nation-state, the national economy, and national society present themselves as the trinity on which life is founded.

States themselves have responded to these challenges by setting in motion processes of international organization and regime formation, which, in the view of liberal institutionalism, are capable of a relatively independent existence and are in the process of changing from a dependent to an independent variable of world politics (Rittberger 1993). Sections of national societies are reacting to globalization and the challenges that accompany it by organizing themselves to act as champions of global causes such as the safeguarding of human rights, democratization, equality, and the preservation of an environment that is conducive to life. In these domains, new forms of cooperation are emerging, sometimes through interaction with governmental associations, conferences, and negotiating processes. Thus, transnational coalitions that present a new challenge to politics in the world of states—if not to that world itself—are appearing alongside transnational communities.

Transnational communities derive their identity not so much from their national origins, but from the fact that they have left their native land. Their 'ethnicity' is not simply a throwback to premodern times; it can be interpreted as an attempt to gain a foothold in the new society as a member of it rather than as its adversary (De la Garza et al. 1996; Vila 1994). By their very action, however, such communities effect changes on the host societies. Similarly, the formation of transnational coalitions and networks is not generally aimed at eliminating the world of states, but at getting it to adjust to new problems and challenges. Transnational communities and transnational coalitions thus ideally converge in promoting both internal differentiation and a tempering of external demarcation, thus creating new spaces in which endowment of meaning, self-localization, and public commitment take shape.

In parallel to the idea of multiple statehood, one obvious argument here would seem to be to talk of *multiple identities* of the individual and of social groups, particularly given that, in psychoanalysis, there is said to be a close connection between territorial shaping or delimitation, and the idea of a unitary subject (Deleuze and Guattari 1987). The alternative to this line of argument would be to stick to the idea of unitary subjectivity. This would mean looking not for a spread of multiple identities but for the formation of a complex identity that enables the subject to withstand ambivalence and to transform contradictory experiences into an increasing willingness to learn. We shall not opt for one or the other view here; but we do wish at least to point out that there is no doubt that debordering as the dissolution of clear territorial demarcations during the period of radical change at the end of the modern era extends to configurations which, like the territorial state, can also be regarded as building blocks of the modern world order. One such configuration is the idea of a unitary, unfragmented subjectivity (Glass 1995; Miller 1993).

The construction of new public spaces that use up less energy on demarcation and thus open up more opportunities for organizing communal life is in a way a utopian project on which far-reaching, concrete expectations hang. Thus, Elisabeth Meehan, referring to the EU case, remarks:

> My thesis is...that a new kind of citizenship is emerging that is neither national nor cosmopolitan but that is multiple in the sense that the identities, rights and obligations, associated...with citizenship, are expressed through an increasingly complex configuration of common (European) Community institutions, states, national and transnational voluntary associations, regions and alliances of regions. (Meehan 1993: 1)

Of course, such expectations do not remain confined to the EU. The current discussion about citizenship extends far beyond the European framework.

DEBORDERING AND DEMARCATION: EMPIRICAL POINTERS

Changes in the Function of Borders, Political Innovation, and Transnational Communication

The above observations regarding economic, political, and social debordering point to a change in the function of borders. In the new scheme, they would cease to act as separators and would change from transit zones into spaces of economic cooperation, political-cum-institutional innovation, and transnational communication. It is in this respect that Lawrence Herzog, for example, perceives a sea change in the development of border regions. The time of the Maginot and Siegfried lines, he says, are over: "The most obvious change has been the shift from boundaries that are heavily protected and militarized to those that are more porous, permitting cross-border social and economic interaction" (Herzog 1992: 5–6). It is thus argued that border regions have changed from being peripheral areas to being the focus of new expectations in regard to growth:

> Where once boundaries were seen as marginal spaces in a world that was largely organized around centrist nation-states, the late twentieth century has seen the old system fade away; in the new global territorial order, boundary regions may become centers of production and urban life. Thus a new form of city has evolved: the international border—or transfrontier metropolis. (Herzog 1991: 520)

As far as the political side of these developments is concerned, the promotion of the regional level and consequently also the promotion of transborder cooperation between substate actors has been included in the policies of European integration since the late 1980s. At the same time, the number of transnational links at the regional level has increased significantly (Hrbek and Weyand 1994: 78).

The efforts, notably of the German *Länder*, to counter political centralization in the EU member-states in the wake of further integration, has resulted in a general tendency to decentralize national political systems (Scharpf 1994). With the aid of the *Committee of the Regions*, different subdivisions of states will be able to work together to extend their scope for action in relation to central governments, and to improve their access to the new central bodies in Brussels (Hrbek and Weyand 1994: 153). The heterogeneous nature of the Committee will not necessarily be a hindrance in this regard. We believe that in the long run it can be seen as an advantage, because the multilayered nature of the interests represented in the Committee, and the way in which they are represented, makes it more adaptable in its dealings with the Commission and Council. Thus, initiatives that fail when taken in relation to one category of Committee members can start afresh by linking up with the interests of other categories. There is thus a redundancy of options for action, allowing problems to be tackled in a variety of ways (even at the level of definition) (see also Grabher 1994).

In 1990, the *Linkage Assistance and Cooperation for the European Border Regions* (LACE) was created. It is administered by the Association of European Border Regions (1971), which has thereby won EU 'recognition' and acquired an enhanced status. LACE represents the kind of link-up and reciprocal interpenetration of public and nonpublic levels of action that is interpreted here as a debordering of the state, in the sense of a breaking down of existing rigidities. Local authority bodies, chambers of commerce, trade unions, and all other institutions and initiatives wishing to promote transborder cooperation, may take part in LACE. Also, the INTERREG program (now in its second phase), which provides funds for structural adjustment and development in border regions, was launched in 1990. These funds may be applied for by the various associations of border regions that currently exist across the whole integrated area and also in the areas adjoining some external borders (Hrbek and Weyand 1994: 76). In this development, Scott (1996) sees a change of paradigm in the European policy of integration toward border regions. What we, for our part, see in it is a variety of indications of the breakup of a territoriality that comes into increasing conflict with the material and nonmaterial (cultural) interconnections between states.

In North America, there too is a whole series of indications that the activities of substate actors in the domains of foreign policy and foreign trade are increasing, and that new institutions and new patterns of communication are being created that simultaneously bridge two dividing lines: that between states, and that between public and private institutions and groupings. This trend is more advanced on the American-Canadian than on the American-Mexican border, with the drifting apart of the peripheral regions of Canada lending particular weight to the North-South links of the East (Québec), the Center, and the West (British Columbia) (Duchacek et al. 1988). The most fascinating entity here is undoubtedly Cascadia, the West Coast region, which stretches from Alaska down to and including Oregon, and which also has affinities with Northern California, because here, the South, on account of its proximity to Mexico and Central America, is regarded as the source of all evils (Stanley Foundation 1994a). Up to now, Cascadia has taken the form of a number of mixed organizations and initiatives. These include the *Pacific Northwest Economic Region*, an association comprising the governments of the participating American states and Canadian provinces; the *Pacific Corridor Enterprise Council*, a private-sector regional organization; and the *Cascadia Transportation/Trade Task Force*, a strategic alliance of urban centers in the south of the region. The *International Center for Sustainable Cities* is also involved at the Cascadia level. It sees the task in hand being about strengthening Cascadia's position on the world market whilst respecting the precepts of ecological sustainability, the latter being seen as a means to international (market) standing.

Ecological issues also play an important role on the U.S.-Mexico border—but more in terms of disaster prevention than of creating an actual utopia. The Maquila program of industrialization, launched in 1965, not only boosted economic growth—chiefly on the Mexican side of the border; it also resulted in an enormous increase in environmental problems. This was one of the reasons for the creation of a *Border Environment Cooperation Commission* (BECC) in 1994, in accordance with an agreement concluded by the United States and Mexico within the framework of the NAFTA negotiations. The activities of the BECC, which is based in Ciudad Juarez (Mexico), are financed by the *North American Development Bank* (NADBank), which was also set up as part of NAFTA. The composition of BECC's executive committee once again conveys the now-familiar picture of the linking of the state with the nonstate, and of the national or international with the local levels of action. The board of directors includes representatives of the *Inter-*

national Boundary and Water Commission (a binational U.S.-Mexico organization set up in 1944), the border states, the border districts, and the inhabitants of the border areas. The directorate meets quarterly, and is required to hold public meetings at similar intervals, in order to ensure that the public is involved in BECC's work.

The fact that environmental issues (and issues concerning working conditions) were included in the NAFTA negotiations is, in turn, due to the formation of a transnational alliance of nongovernmental organizations, individual specialists, ad hoc local authority initiatives, and so on, which secured a voice in the NAFTA negotiations through trinational public relations work and the systematic lobbying of the relevant governments (Thorup 1991). This instance of influence on interstate negotiations is undoubtedly one of the most important examples of the significance that the formation of transnational alliances can have in shaping interstate politics.

As far as the activities of U.S. states in the domains of foreign politics and foreign trade are concerned, similar to Europe there are signs that these substate entities are gaining in self-confidence as international actors (see also Goldsborough 1993; Berfield 1993; Kincaid 1984). This trend was set in motion by, amongst others, the Kennedy administration, which was keen to involve the resources of the U.S. states and of its NATO partners in international development cooperation (Elazar 1988: xxi). As at the *Land* (state) level in Germany, what has resulted from this is a carefully targeted policy of safeguarding and promoting industrial locations in the context of harsher competition on the world market. As far as Texas and Southern California are concerned, an important role is played here not only by the Mexican economy as a whole, but also by—precisely—the border economy.

The border region between the United States and Mexico is characterized by a huge flow of immigrants from the south and center of Mexico toward the north. The greatest degree of immigration seems to have been experienced by Tijuana (Martinez 1994: 46). Most of those who cross the border, however, do not remain in the border area but migrate further to Los Angeles, where public and private life are dominated by transnational communities. As early as the beginning of the 1980s, the immigration from the south prompted Joel Garreau (1981) to describe 'Mexamerica' as one of the 'nine nations', which he regards as constituting the real communities in North America, based on shared lives and values, and in diametric opposition to existing political borders.

To summarize, one can say that although the process of transborder political innovation in North America does lag behind developments in Europe, one can, in general, agree with Elazar that,

> The transformation of the international system from one in which politically sovereign states under international law were the only legitimate actors to one in which other entities, particularly the constituent states of federal systems, are also involved is one of the major developments of the post-World War II period. (Elazar 1988: xix)

'Change, Change?' Counter-impressions

There is no dearth of counter-impressions to the observations made up to now. Krasner's impatience at glib evocations of change—cited at the start of this chapter—is quite understandable. By way of illustration, we shall mention here a few impressions that run counter to the arguments set out above.

If the developments described above are being considered in the light of possible radical change, they have to be viewed in the context of the entire historical process of international organization, integration, and regime formation. In order to do this, one needs to go a long way back into the era of modernization. The 'Rheinschiffahrtskommission' (the 'Shipping Commission for the River Rhine'), the first functional international organization, was created at the time of the breakup of the Holy Roman Empire. The Universal Postal Union, the International Telegraphic Union, and others followed, at a time when in Germany the territorial state was still being established. The process of political innovation which serves to dissipate the tension between political territoriality and material interdependence thus has a long history and certainly did not begin with the latest round of globalization. Set against this long and rich history of international organization, the present trend could be seen as a continuation, one that completes the process of modernization rather than ushering in a new era of postmodern politics. This being so, one is often ultimately overcome by doubt as to there actually being any change underway in the world of states.

Besides this, when it comes to the question of radical economic change in border regions, there is practically no information available on economic integration. It is easy to obtain figures on the foreign trade of Baden-Württemberg, Hesse, Texas, or California. In all of the statistics, however, only countries—that is, in this case nation-states—are cited as target regions. This is quite unsatisfactory if one wants to use these figures to say something about the debordering of national economies through the formation of transborder or interterritorial economic spaces. This blind spot demonstrates the undiminished authority of territorial references: the data continue to be geared toward a clearly demarcated, vertically-cum-hierarchically integrated territorial state.

As was demonstrated once again by some of the reactions in face of the Asian crisis, globalization is still accompanied by insulatory moves and deliberate attempts to protect 'national' economies by political means. New protectionisms and strategic trade policies also serve as cases in point: within the framework of cooperation and integration in a regional grouping of states, they are internationalized, but not eliminated. What is taking place is therefore only a specific, not a general, debordering of national economies. Thus, the 'local content' provisions through which Mexico sought to expand its industrial production before liberalization, reappeared in the framework of NAFTA. The formation of transborder economic spaces between Mexico, the United States, and Canada is promoted, but this happens behind joint external borders that are designed to attract foreign investors and at the same time impose a particular kind of behavior.

Nor is it true that globalization leads to straightforward political innovation. The political process follows its own specific dictates in relative autonomy vis-à-vis the development of the world economy. The avant-gardists of transborder cooperation can only dream of seeing the measures they consider necessary (and which they put down on paper—for example, as studies about joint regional planning) translated into reality—and sometimes that is precisely what they do (see also Ganster and Valenciano 1993; Schmidt and Lorey 1994). As in other domains, the actual course that things take depends on the people involved to a considerable extent. Thus, for example, the administrative provisions for intercity cooperation in San Diego was much more elaborate in the 1980s than it is today. Today, intercity cooperation with Tijuana is conducted by a single person who is responsible for the city's economic relations with the whole of Latin America. The visions to which the conclusion of the NAFTA agreement gave rise in this domain were followed by considerable disillusionment in the wake of the peso crisis. Things do look similar in El Paso/Cd. Juarez. Looking at a number of much-celebrated transborder initiatives, one often finds only lackluster support (and mostly but one part-time employee) following widely advertised initializing ceremonies.

Similarly, the personal factor was also of no little significance in the evolution of transborder cooperation in the Upper Rhine region. It was the visionary talents, organizational skills, and perseverance of Josef Briner that initiated the process now regarded as a pioneering paradigm for transborder cooperation (Scott 1989). The creation of the 'Four Motors' is sometimes regarded (by less internationally minded administrators) as a public relations ploy by enterprising industrial politicians of Lothar Späth's (Baden-Württemberg's longtime premier) ilk. And indeed, if one takes a closer look at many agreements on regional cooperation, one has the nagging feeling that they are more likely to arouse scholarly curiosity than prompt any relevant action.

And then, of course—to return to the U.S.-Mexican border, though it applies to other borders as well—there is the fence and the intensification of border controls that began in El Paso in September 1993 with the U.S. Border Patrol's 'Operation Blockade' (later renamed 'Operation Hold the Line'), and was likewise instituted in San Diego a year later by the Immigration and Naturalization Service (INS) as 'Operation Gatekeeper'. What this initiative, as well as similar ones conducted in other border town areas, achieved, was arguably not to curtail illegal immigration as such, but merely the illegal border crossings on a daily basis that upheld the informal economy *within* the border twin towns (see Bean et al. 1994). What came as a surprise to some, however, was that the majority even of Hispanic residents on the El Paso side were not only sympathetic to the initiative, but also receptive to the harsh rhetoric that came along with it. Empirical studies conducted in El Paso on the 'narrative identities' of the city's population match up with this observation, showing that the self-images, political attitudes, and behavioral patterns of the transnational communities mentioned above cannot simply be inferred from their ethnic origins. In fact, those who have 'made it' by migration tend to distance themselves from those who may follow, rather than show solidarity toward them (Vila 1994). Other research points in the same direction. It can be summarized in the thesis that the much-discussed phenomenon of ethnicity is a means not of essential but of instrumental demarcation from the country of immigration's society, the purpose of that demarcation being self-assertion as a means of integration into that society (De la Garza et al. 1996). Given these findings, there can be no talk of Mexamerica as a 'nation'.

As far as the Mexican side is concerned, the inhabitants of the northern border-regions—the *nortenos*—have never been held in very high regard by the Party of Institutionalized Revolution (PRI) in Mexico City. They were viewed (to put it mildly) as leaning too much toward the United States. However, when it came to 'selling' the idea of NAFTA to the Mexican public, Mexico City promulgated the thesis that closer economic cooperation with the United States, and the percolation of economic growth from the northern border-regions to the rest of Mexico, which, it was hoped, would ensue, would *enhance* Mexico's national profile vis-à-vis the United Sates. More recently, Mexico has instituted dual nationality (not citizenship!). One can, of course, view this as promoting the formation of transnational communities for its own sake. But another interpretation is possible: Mexican immigrants are to be encouraged to become American citizens by offering them the possibility of retaining all the rights due to a Mexican citizen, including the right to political participation. As citizens of the Untied States, the Mexicans will then be able to look after their interests better there and will therefore (it is hoped) be able to attain a better economic status. They will also have an incentive to pass part of their economic prosperity back to Mexico, without, from the PRI's standpoint, causing any political damage (as per the old *norteno* thesis). Viewed then, the formation of transnational communities becomes a tool in Mexico's promotion of its own interests (see also De la Garza and Velasco 1997)!

For the sake of clarity, it should be noted that these migration problems do not relate to the U.S.-Mexican border alone. They can also be found in the avant-garde area of radical change, namely the European Union. Examples here are the Schengen Agreement and the recently instituted entry restrictions introduced by the individual states (asylum regulations). The arguments about these regulations show that borders have not become obsolete as a result of globalization. Disputed divisions remain—and not only in places such as Kosovo or Eritrea/Ethiopia. They are also to be found at Frankfurt airport and other centers of the world economy, which are both levers and social flashpoints of postindustrial development. Whilst universalist-minded 'regionalists' present us with amazing post-state-age maps, national thinking, following the end of the East-West conflict, has once again become a subject of discussion in places where it was considered to have been largely resolved.

The observations set out above show that debordering clearly cannot be understood as a straightforward, linear process. It is accompanied by demarcatory, 'rebordering' processes about which one has to ask oneself whether these are regressive phenomena (in the sense of the aftereffects of a long history of influences of a territorial nature) or the consequences of debordering, in which case a further distinction then has to be drawn between countertendencies to debordering and functional adjustment to it. A few observations will be made on this by way of conclusion.

THE WORLD OF STATES AND WORLD SOCIETY

In the theoretical section of this chapter, we suggest that globalization be viewed as a process of debordering of the world of states, thus providing starting points from which to structure the question of continuity and change in (the continuity and transformation of) that world. Three dimensions of debordering were distinguished: the economic, the political, and the social. It emerged in the empirical section that developments are not proceeding in a straightforward manner, and that debordering processes are accompanied by new processes of demarcation. How can these countervailing trends be brought into symmetry with one another and be utilized in a way that helps tackle the question of how the world of states is changing? And how do the three dimensions of debordering relate to one another?

In approaching this question, we pick up on efforts that have been underway for quite a while now, centering on the question of how to develop a concept of international relations that moves beyond the realist school's 'hard core' billiard ball model but at the same time does not dispatch the state too precipitately. Following up on the arguments developed in chapter 1, we distinguish three structural elements of international relations, or of what has up to now been vaguely termed the world of states: the international system, the society of states, and world society. The international system is currently characterized by complex interdependence, and the society of states (the English School's 'international society') by anarchy kept in check by a process of regime formation. The 'world society' element, on the other hand, relates to the nature of international relations as a multilayered network. We here see the network as a metaphor for the reciprocal interpenetration of territorially and functionally defined spaces, and for a mixing of interstate and transstate patterns of interaction. The intention here is not only to highlight the fact that in any analysis of the external behavior of states, internal factors must also be accounted for. Our prime object, rather, is to make sure that the indistinct nature of the divisions between state and nonstate levels of activity, and between the political, economic, and social/sociocultural spheres (see also Albert 1999) is taken into consideration. We should make it clear immediately, however, that we do not regard the dissolution of borders, or their increasing indistinctness, as the end of politics, but rather as a change in the conditions under which politics is conducted. This also means that networks do not at all render the question of the control of economic and political power invalid, but they rather require to pose the question of the possibility of new forms of control anew. This must not be forgotten when it comes to *network design*. Our concept of world society is intended to draw attention to just these aspects of the new developments.

Within both the society of states and world society, processes of *community formation* occur—that is to say, the formation of state and nonstate entitities characterized by particular historical, cultural, ethnic, and/or ideological affinities. In this scheme of things, the much-sought-after international community should be viewed as a community based on law and solidarity, the functionality of which depends on the strength of its members' sense of belonging together. From a communitarian perspective, one has of course to remember that communities are always particularist, and that the formation of a global international community should therefore be viewed as at the very least unlikely, if not impossible. This is another reason why we talk of world society. The strengthening of the world society element may cause the demarcatory tendencies between different state or nonstate communities to increase—as seems to be the case when one looks at relations between the great cultures of the world (the Islamic world, the Christian world). The theses advanced by Huntington in this regard (Huntington 1993) cannot simply be dismissed by arguing that what is involved here is merely the enlistment of religion for political purposes. What is interesting is that this kind of enlistment is repeatedly successful. But demarcation can mean many different things. In its mildest variant, it would mean 'only' a more pronounced awareness of one's own cultural traits; in the worst case, it would mean attempts at mutual repression and annihilation.

Our structural scheme is also an evolutionary model to the extent that we assume that, as globalization proceeds, interdependence will grow deeper, regime-formation will continue, and the blurred area between state and transstate levels of activity, and at the junctures between state, economy, and society, will grow. Here, new areas of public (political) life will emerge in which the identity of the actors and their behavior will become in part interchangeable: states will behave like businesses, businesses like states, communities like societies (in Weber's sense that they will make use of the sense of belonging together for rationally calculated purposes), and societies like communities (that is, by satisfying particular interests they will produce a sense of belonging together).

With regard to the distinction between community and society, Buzan (1993), picking up on Tönnies and Weber, has attempted to identify community-forming tendencies (*Vergemeinschaftungstendenzen*) in international relations, and contrast them with society-forming tendencies (*Vergesellschaftungstendenzen*). He views nongovernmental organizations and social movements, which are increasingly operating across borders and on the basis of universal values (human rights, environmental protection, democratization), as the moving forces behind community formation, whereas cooperation and the setting of standards at the interstate level are what constitutes international society. Buzan thus extends the investigative horizon as compared with Bull (1977), but he conceals an important element of change: the transformation of the world of states *itself* through the process of debordering.

It is not at all our intention to neglect the various processes of transnational community formation. Indeed, we assume that the latter acts as an important stimulus in the emergence of tendencies toward the formation of world society. We do, however, counsel against idealizing everything transnational in terms of a positively weighted concept of community. A distinction has to be drawn in this connection between transnational communities that promote their interests through sociocultural demarcation, and transnational alliances that come together in order to defend or promote universalist values (peace, democracy, human rights, the environment). Transnational communities can be just as blinkered as national ones. And many universalist alliances also serve minority interests. Many government adversaries of transnational coalitions have, fortunately, come to realize that such coalitions are not merely internationally organized bands of malcontents, but groups with considerable expertise—sometimes greater expertise than that of government decision-makers (namely, the Nestlé campaign, the Anti-Fast-Track campaign relating to the NAFTA negotiations). That said, increases in the competence and political weight of international nongovernmental organizations also increase their value as instruments of minority interests. For this reason also, we do not regard it as sensible to ascribe the community element in the present developments to transnational organizations and to contrast it with the society-based nature of the world of states.

We see society-forming tendencies (*Vergesellschaftungstendenzen*) to emerge at those points where state freedom and the ability to subject international relations in their entirety to state control, that is, the large-scale application of the territorial principle, are declining. We work on the assumption that the increasing societization of the international system will reduce the likelihood of interstate wars (increasing indistinctness of borders, decreasing danger of international polarization of interests). However, this is not a foregone conclusion, because when the borders between inside and outside are indistinct, every part of society finds it difficult to orientate itself, and consequently new efforts to demarcate result (see above). The cry for 'more light!' (Goethe's dying words) indicates the intolerable nature of blurred contours and an existential yearning for sharp distinctions, for a clear view of a muddled situation.

Yet the simultaneous occurrence of debordering and demarcation does not in itself signal a zero-sum game. We view the processes of demarcation described above as social phenomena within the framework of an overall debordering of the world of states that is prompted by a global shaping of the economy, communications, transport, consumer expectations, and attitudes to life (namely, the worldwide change in family structures). One can go a step further and describe the demarcation phenomena as a specific reaction to the debordering processes that are actually taking their course within the framework of globalization. Viewed in this light, demarcation (rebordering) would be, first and foremost, a way of *regulating* the process of transformation, not of *arresting* it (by way of illustration: even the U.S. Border Patrol and the INS know that a tightening-up of border controls between the United States and Mexico cannot stem the migratory flow).

To put it in more general terms, borders are always the result of encounter, not of isolation. They are a way of regulating relations, even where they involve a complete cutoff. Borders are therefore not the product of a human weakness of character; they have a social function. When debordering happens, the question arises as to what new forms of social regulation come into being to replace the old ones. Developing these new forms, and getting them accepted, is not merely an exercise in optimization. A multiplicity of interests and power-related issues are at stake here.

This being the case, we do not believe it possible either for demarcation to be fully subsumed under debordering. Up to now, every attempt at regulating social relations has given rise to minority interests and created power constellations that gradually develop their own momentum in relation to the functional necessities of the social system and tend to interweave public function and aggregated minority interests. The course of social development simply does not lead in a straight line from segmentation, via hierarchization, to functional differentiation; rather, segmentation and hierarchization persist even when functional differentiation is taking place (Bauböck 1994). It would therefore be naïve to view the tendencies to demarcation that are currently observable only in terms of their functionality in global debordering, and thus to see nationalism merely as a phenomenon that makes internationalism possible. An even less tenable approach, however, would be to regard the debordering processes described above as mere epiphenomena. What should be done instead, as we see it, is to broaden the debate to include the question of how far particular demarcatory needs are not so much an expression of old attitudes (nationalism, racism, sexism), but more an expression of the need to find new ways of regulating social relations in the context of trends in world society.

3

Collective Identities in World Society

Christoph Weller

How should social scientists react to what appear to be increasingly contradictory developments in social relations at the end of the twentieth century? With a postmodern shrug of the shoulders? If familiar institutional structures are in an advanced state of decomposition, traditional scholarly methods of trying to get a grip on them are also likely to be of little avail. One often has the impression that 'anything goes': globalization proceeds alongside fragmentation (Zürn 1992c); supranational political entities develop at the same time as a renaissance of the nation-state (Langewiesche 1995); increasing international and transnational interdependence is apparently not inconsistent with strengthened nationalism and ethnicity (Elwert 1989; Leggewie 1994); integration and separatism are quite compatible with one another. In short, it looks as though reality is no longer paying any attention to traditional theories of society.

If we were to insist on hanging on to the idea of modernization as a process of ever-increasing rationalization, all these instances of a redrawing of borders would be no more than temporary anachronisms, momentary setbacks within a development that cannot ultimately be held back—from communal social relations to global society formation in the Weberian sense.[1] In this chapter, I put forward a different view, namely, that a significant portion of social action is "based on a subjective feeling of the parties [...] that they belong together" (Weber 1968: vol. I, 40), that is to say it is a matter of community formation (*Vergemeinschaftung*) rather than rationally motivated society formation. This means that society and community formation should be understood not only as ideal types existing side by side, but also as modes of social relations that exist in a constant interrelationship with one another, neither of which can replace the other because each of them performs a specific function within human society as a whole. Nationalism, ethnicity, separatism, and other forms of social fragmentation can thus be understood as specific expressions of community formation (see Connor 1994), which come into being under certain conditions and can serve either to advance or to hinder the society-formation process that is advancing at the same time.

Similarly, the extent and intensity of society formation influences in a number of ways the conditions in which community formation comes about and the effects it has. If, therefore, we understand community formation not as a leftover from premodern social relations but as a necessary form of those relations in the present, we have to ask how it occurs.

There is general agreement that globalization, increasing interdependence, integration, and the creation of supranational institutions as forms of international society formation can be interpreted in terms of rationally motivated adjustment of interests or similarly motivated agreement (Weber 1968: vol. I, 41).[2] However, some other kind of motivation may be at the root of the simultaneous trend toward social fragmentation. For Weber (1968: vol. I, 40–41), the ideal-typical distinction between society and community formation is based on a difference of attitude that lies at the root of these two forms of social relationship. Community formation is not motivated by interests, but comes about on the basis of a feeling of belonging. Assuming that nationalism, separatism, regionalism, and the formation of ethnic groups are forms of social relations in which community formation dominates over society formation, we must examine the motivations behind this community formation if we want to find out more about the conditions that encourage social fragmentation.

In this chapter, I seek to answer this question with the help of social-psychological theories. According to social identity theory, the desire and striving for a positive self-image is the driving force behind the evaluation of social categories and groups, because there is an individual advantage to be derived from a positive evaluation of categories and groups of which one is oneself a member.[3] 'Social identity' is understood to mean "those aspects of an individual's self-image that derive from the social categories to which he perceives himself as belonging" (Tajfel and Turner 1986: 16). This means that we can speak of 'collective identity' whenever a certain social identity is of overriding importance for the members of a collective, that is, when a number of individuals accept a social categorization that enables them to differentiate themselves as a group from the rest of the world, and in the process to value the group more highly—which in turn enables each individual to benefit in terms of his or her own self-esteem.[4]

The individual's need for a positive social identity can therefore be seen as the basic motivation for the construction of collective identities and thus for community formation in social relations.[5] But the individual's need for community is not enough to explain tendencies toward fragmentation that are extremely diverse in their scope and intensity. We therefore need to develop a model which can specify the factors that are significant in the creation of collective identities, in order to both answer the question of *which* collective identities emerge as world society develops, and to make it possible to make statements about the strengths of these identities. While society formation seems to involve a tendency toward debordering, community formation is always associated with the drawing of boundaries because identity formation requires a demarcation of one's own group from those who do not belong to it. It is this tension between society and community formation that makes it so important, in view of the increasing globalization of social relations, to ask precisely what effects those social relations in which community formation is dominant have on international relations; in other words, the question of central concern is that of the conditions under which collective identities are formed within world society.

In order to pursue this question, I begin by presenting a concept of 'world society' that provides a framework for the analysis of the various dimensions of transborder social relations already mentioned. The next step is an examination of the concept of identity, which, in contrast to other approaches to the term, stresses its reflexive dimension. Some concepts of 'identity' already employed in the IR literature are then examined in order to establish what contribution they are able to make to our understanding of collective identities and to the research question outlined above. A brief overview of the literature on national identity follows. In the fourth section I take up the social-psychological concept of identity, social identity theory and self-categorization theory, approaches that offer a good basis for an investigation of community-formation processes understood in terms of the formation of collective identities. The task here is to make plausible the claim that the categorizations involved in every perception of reality also fulfill the individual's need for social identity, and that this need provides the basic motivation for the construction of all collective identities. It becomes clear that these identities are constructed in accordance with Weber's ideal-typical category of community formation, not least because this social relation between individuals and larger collectives is based on a *subjective* feeling and not motivated by rational, objectively identifiable interests.[6] In conclusion, I offer some thoughts on the relationship between collective identity formation and the development of world society.

SOCIETY AND COMMUNITY FORMATION

Our concept of world society is an attempt to develop an analytical instrument whose primary purpose is to make possible a more differentiated investigation of globalization and its consequences than traditional concepts of International Relations allow (see chapter 1). By linking our concept to Weber's ideal-typical distinction between society and community formation, we are able to examine relations in world society in terms of the specific mixture of rationally motivated adjustment of interests and subjective feelings of belonging that are present in each case.

However, we should not forget that in each case we are dealing with ideal types, nor that society and community formation are, at both levels, *processes* that are interconnected with one another in various ways. An example will help to make this clear. Weber says that a national community is similar to an erotic relationship in being a typical expression of community formation, while a market exchange relationship or a purposive (*zweckrational*) agreement designed to ensure a constant balance of interests correspond to the ideal type of society formation (Weber 1968: vol. I, 41). In this sense globalization and the revival of nationalism do not contradict one another, but are distinct forms of social relationship whose interconnections can be investigated. This enables us to understand nationalism's stress on subjective feelings of belonging as a logical reaction to the advance of debordering processes brought about by globalization, which constantly place in question traditional feelings of community. As a consequence, existing borderlines are emphasized more strongly, which serves to put a brake on the debordering process. Globalizing society formation is able to satisfy certain interests, but not the need for positive social identity that lies at the heart of community formation. It is only the distinction between one's own group (for example, the nation) and the rest that can provide the individual with a feeling of social identity. However, it is also possible for society and community formation to have a positive interrelationship with one another, as Weber himself explains:

> Every social relationship which goes beyond the pursuit of immediate common ends, which hence lasts for long periods, involves relatively permanent social relationships between the same persons, and these cannot be exclusively confined to the technically necessary activities [...] there is always some tendency in this direction [to community formation], although the degree, to be sure, varies enormously. (Weber 1968: vol. I, 41)

For example, it may be that the existing transnational community in Western Europe, which exists in part on the basis of a shared cultural tradition, is partly responsible for the fact that society-formation processes at both the interstate and the transnational level continue to advance, and thereby have positive effects on transnational community formation in this region.[7] But it is only when the external borders of intensive society and community formation are congruent with one another that communal social relations can be considered a factor supporting, securing, and driving forward society formation.

This concept of an interrelationship between society and community formation seeks to distinguish itself from a model in which one stage succeeds the other, as is for example the case according to the frequently encountered thesis that society formation gradually replaces communal social relations. A much more satisfactory move is to integrate both forms of social action, together with the world-societal developments identified here as the institutionalization of transborder relations and the diffusion of actors, within one analytical concept that is not teleological, either in respect of any particular type of social actor or in respect of specific structures of social institutions. In view of the social fragmentation that can be observed everywhere, it is questionable whether it still makes sense to cling to a rationalism that insists on categorizing these developments as temporary obstacles encountered on the road to modernization. It is equally questionable whether states will remain the dominant actors in global social relations, and indeed they may already have lost this status in circumstances in which world-societal developments are passing them by in the shape of transborder institutionalization and transnational relations. An analytical concept put forward in this area should at least make it possible to assess how far states are being forced to share their dominant role in both society and community formation with other institutions and actors, and whether they are losing or regaining ground here. A state-centric constructivism (or to be more accurate, a constructivist realism) as proposed by Wendt (1992) cannot capture developments such as these.

Our concept of world society goes beyond this state-centrism, which can be explained by the fact that the American debate is still dominated by competition with realist theories, and examines states in their interactions with societal actors (see chapter 1). The more societal actors orient themselves toward transborder institutions and transnational relations become independent of events at the interstate level, the stronger is the tendency for other collective identities to be formed at the transnational, regional, or other levels. However, before developing a social-scientific approach to dealing with the conditions in which collective identities come into existence within world society, it is necessary to clarify what is meant here by the terms 'identity' and, still more important, 'collective identity'.

IDENTITY

The Latin root of the word 'identity' has as its main meaning 'unity of nature or being' (*Wesenseinheit*)—in other words something like total equality, congruence, or correspondence. Thus the initial connotation of identity is always complete correspondence with oneself, with one's own nature or being. This suggests that *individuals* should be seen as the bearers of identity, because one can hardly conceive of any way in which collectives could become conscious of correspondence with themselves.[8] Nevertheless, all these suggested definitions show that 'collective identity' certainly does entail the attribution of some kind of 'nature' to a group or society, which leads us to the conclusion that the identities of collectives are seen to reside in permanent features such as norms, values, and institutions.[9] If the identity of a collective could be determined on this basis, it may be possible to say whether collective behavior corresponds to or diverges from this collective identity. Collective identity could then be used as an explanatory variable whenever it is possible to generate statements specifying the conditions under which the established identity influences the behavior of collective actors. On the other hand, the idea that collective identities are also subject to change would require the expenditure of additional theoretical energy, because this would mean that their constitutive conditions would have to be specified independently of their effects; in other words, we would need a theory of how identities change. This would have to make it possible to specify how far an identity would have to change before we could speak of a new collective identity which, under certain conditions, influences the behavior of collective actors. However, one can also conceive of a concept of collective identity that treats the individual as the bearer of identity and uses the term 'collective identity' for the relation of correspondence between the individual identities of the members of this group. But first, some basic questions have to be asked: Who are the bearers of identity? What conditions the emergence of identity and changes in identities? How can we explain the effects of identity? Who is the subject of the identification process, that is, who attributes or ascribes identity?

The *bearer of identity* can be the individual within a social system; this identity reveals "a combination of characteristics and role expectations which render it recognizable and identifiable [...]. In this understanding of the term, identity is considered to be a complex of characteristics ascribed from the outside" (Frey and Haußer 1987: 3). In other words, identity is a matter of a specific combination of qualities belonging to an individual, which distinguish that individual from others. In much the same way, identities are often attributed to collectivities and social systems — groups, institutions, states, and so on — by the identification of features considered to be characteristic of that collectivity or social system. However, while an individual's identity can come into existence either via the attribution of characteristics from outside or, so to speak, from within as a performative self-reflection of the individual's consciousness, the identity of social systems or groups is only conceivable as a complex of features ascribed from outside, since "for any social system, the system cannot be identical with its members; each member is at most a part of the system" (Frey and Haußer 1987: 4). In the case of this kind of ascription of identity from without in which the subject of identification differs from its object, the most important questions will be related to the appropriateness and correspondence of the identification, questions of how identity comes into being and of its effects being of secondary significance only.

Things are quite different in the case of the *reflexive concept of identity*, where the subject and object of the identification process are the same person.

> In this case, identity is understood as a self-reflexive process initiated and carried through by an individual. A person constructs his or her own identity by processing his or her own experiences and knowledge of him/herself [...]. In every case, what happens is that a person identifies him or her self, or aspects of that self, from an internal perspective. (Frey and Haußer 1987: 4)

However, this kind of reflexive identity emerges not out of an internal monologue, but as part of a societal process. The social environment is a precondition of this form of identity (see Mead 1967: part III, especially ch. 29), which is why the term 'social identity' is so widely used. Most important of all, however, is the fact that this is a subjective concept of identity that results from reflection on one's own experience. On this basis, the individual constructs an image of him or herself. This identity then affects the behavior of the individual; in order to avoid identity conflicts, the individual will seek to act in conformity with his or her own self-image, and will orient his or her social relations toward the goals of developing and maintaining a *positive* social identity (see below, fourth section).

The foregoing discussion has offered a brief sketch of two different, and in many respects competing, concepts of identity, and has drawn attention to some of the most problematic issues that arise in any discussion of the term. The next step is to present the concepts of identity in current use within International Relations, and to examine critically how far they contribute to the investigation of collective identities.

Identity in International Relations

'Identity' has recently been discovered by IR scholars. "A swing of the pendulum toward culture and identity is [...] strikingly evident in post-Cold War IR theorizing,"[10] comments Lapid (1996: 3). The three traditional, classical schools of thought in IR—realism, pluralism, and globalism—are unable directly to integrate identity (however defined) into their explanatory models (on this point see Zalewski and Enloe 1995: 294–97; Jepperson et al. 1996: 68–72). This observation is perhaps unsurprising, but it means that a good deal of analytic work needs to be done before we can hope to apply fruitfully in IR the meanings that can be teased out of the term 'identity', and to develop the concept in such a way as to bring out its potential for this field of inquiry. The present treatment does not seek to explain what it is that makes 'identity' so attractive, and perhaps necessary, in explanations of international relations after the end of the East-West conflict.[11] Rather, the objective is to present briefly some significant recent contributions to IR that employ the term 'identity', and to specify more precisely the concepts of identity used. In this way I hope to be able to pursue the questions of how a fruitful concept of identity might be developed for use in IR, and whether this would help to advance the research project outlined at the beginning of this chapter— the investigation of the conditions in which collective identities are formed within world society.

Feminist scholars have singled out identity as an issue of particular importance (see Zalewski and Enloe 1995: 280), and have on this basis persistently posed questions about the identity of actors in international politics. "It is no exaggeration to say that feminist research as such revolves around the question of identity," observes Locher (1996: 385, fn. 7). Personal identity is central here, since gender is primarily a characteristic of individual persons. Zalewski and Enloe (1995: 280) ask: "Who do people think they are and how does this shape not just their local but their international actions?" although they are unable to offer a concept that might provide an answer to their own question.[12] They try to work with a very broad concept of identity, incorporating both the reflexive dimension and the attribution of identity from outside (Zalewski and Enloe 1995: 282). They fall back on a reflexive concept of identity in dealing with the significance of group membership for the identity of individuals, but also want to focus on the way in which identity is assigned from outside in 'identity politics'. This means that they are unable to take any clear position on how specific identities come into being, and their thoughts on the effects of identity are equally vague:

> The consequences of who we are, how we identify ourselves, how we are identified by others (parents, police, journalists) are enormous. Identity determines how you are treated, what is expected of you, what you expect of yourself, what jobs will be available to you, what jobs you will even apply for, what your health will be, whether you will be allocated as a primary carer for children, whether you will be seen as an enemy or a friend. (Zalewski and Enloe 1995: 282–83)

In Zalewski and Enloe's use of the term, therefore, both individuals and collectivities can be the bearers of identity, but there is no discernable mechanism connecting these two levels; rather, it looks as though collective identities are formed by some process analogous to that which produces individual ones.

There is a similar lack of clarity about the identity concept used by Ole Wæver, Barry Buzan, Morten Kelstrup, and Pierre Lemaitre (1993) in their definition of 'societal security'.[13] With one partial exception (Wæver 1993: 21), these authors see identity as an objective reality and so a quality of societies that is assigned to them from outside; there is no examination either of how it comes into existence, or of how it might change.[14] McSweeney's review points out how problematic this is:

> In their view, identity is a property of society, not to be confused with human beings. It 'emerges' (a frequently used term) from the peculiar interactions of people and institutions in each society, fixed and incorrigible like the computer output of a complex arithmetic. Identity describes the society, and society is constituted by identity. Since its computation or construction does not crucially depend on human decisions, it makes no sense to speak of correcting it. Societal identity just is. We are stuck with it. (McSweeney 1996: 87)

Wæver and his co-authors seem—and perhaps this is true of others as well—to have succumbed to the temptation to take up the concept of identity because it is currently fashionable; unfortunately, neither they nor anyone else seems to know where this trend is taking us: "Identity is a good thing, with a human face and ephemeral character which make it at once appealing and difficult to grasp" (McSweeney 1996: 82).

Another author who has taken up the concept, in the context of an ambitious project in the field of security policy, is Peter Katzenstein. Katzenstein sets out to investigate the significance of *Norms and Identity in World Politics*:[15] "This volume concentrates on two underattended determinants of national security policy:

the cultural-institutional context of policy on the one hand and the constructed identity of states, governments, and other political actors on the other" (Katzenstein 1996b: 4). Because it is increasingly difficult to explain the behavior of state actors on the basis of interests, which, as the theory requires, should be derivable from the structure of the system, additional explanatory factors that influence interest formation must be introduced. This brings us to the question of "'how people and organizations define self-interest.' The answer lies in the issue of identity, in variations to the degree of expansiveness and restrictiveness, with which people and organizations relate to one another. To what extent does the 'self' incorporate relevant aspects of the 'other' in its calculations of gains and losses?" (Katzenstein 1996b: 15).

The concept of identity being applied here is then explained in a densely argued theoretical chapter written by Ronald Jepperson, Alexander Wendt, and Peter Katzenstein. It is stated at the outset that 'identity' is treated simply as one of several influential cultural factors,[16] and that this concept is not to be understood "as a signal of commitment to some exotic (presumably Parisian) social theory" (Jepperson et al. 1996: 34). As a rule, the state is the bearer of identity, and "the concept of 'identity' thus functions as a crucial link between environmental structures and interests" (Jepperson et al. 1996: 59). 'Identity' indicates "the basic character of states" (Jepperson et al. 1996: 33), and Jepperson, Wendt, and Katzenstein see it as belonging, alongside 'capabilities', to the 'properties of actors' (Jepperson et al. 1996: 41). Various factors are involved in the formation of identity:

> Thus norms either define ('constitute') identities in the first place or prescribe or proscribe ('regulate') behaviors for already constituted identities [...]. Cultural and institutional structure may also constitute or shape the basic identities of states, that is, the features of state 'actorhood' or national identity. (Jepperson et al. 1996: 54, 58)

It will have become clear from the cited passages that this conception, like others already examined, does not employ a reflexive concept of identity—simply because the bearers of this identity are all collectivities.[17] This means that identity stands for characteristics attributed from the outside. The problem then arises of which identity is to be treated as primary when there is no agreement about these characteristics, or when there are contradictions between different characteristics attributed to an actor.[18] Moreover, the use of analogy cannot answer the question of which characteristics of a collectivity are used in the derivation of its identity. Without some way of answering this question it seems at the very least problematic to proceed, as Jepperson et al. (1996) do, to suggest explanatory models of political decisionmaking in terms of the causal effects of identities: "Variation in state identity, or changes in state identity, affect the national security interests or policies of states [...]. Configurations of state identity affect interstate normative structures, such as regimes or security communities" (Jepperson et al. 1996: 52).

Jepperson and his co-authors adopt more or less the conception of identity worked out by Wendt (1992, 1994, 1996) within his own specific, constructivist analysis. Wendt's critique of rationalism is developed on the basis of his contribution to the agent–structure debate (Wendt 1987) and the initial constructivist thesis developed there to the effect that, in Risse-Kappen's version, "social reality is a constructed reality in which agents and societal structures are mutually constitutive of one another" (Risse-Kappen 1995a: 175). Wendt's critique of rationalism is formulated as follows:

> Like all social theories, rational choice directs us to ask some questions and not others, treating the identities and interests of agents as exogeneously given and focusing on how the behavior of agents generates outcomes. As such, rationalism offers a fundamentally behavioral conception of both process and institutions: they change behavior but not identities and interests. (Wendt 1992: 391–92)

Identity is thus taken to mean those characteristics of actors that are largely generated out of the structures, which the actors constitute by means of their social action (Wendt 1994: 385). Thus societal structures constitute identities as characteristics of actors, and the actors form their own interests on this basis: "Identities are the basis of interests" (Wendt 1992: 398). But because of the assumption that social reality is constructed, this construction and perception of reality must itself be integrated into the analysis:

> A fundamental principle of constructivist social theory is that people act toward objects, including other actors, on the basis of the meaning that the objects have for them. [...] It is collective meanings that constitute the structures which organize our actions. Actors acquire identities—relatively stable, role-specific understandings and expectations about self—by participating in such collective meanings. Identities are inherently relational: "Identity, with its appropriate attachments of psychological reality, is always identity within a specific, socially constructed world," Peter Berger argues.[19]

Although there is a suggestion of a reflexive concept of identity here, Wendt's constructivism remains in the final analysis partly a prisoner of materialism because he always treats identity as a characteristic of states, and treats these states as actors rather than as social structures, which one has to do if social constructivism is to be applied consistently.[20] There may be good reasons why Wendt proceeds in this fashion, but theoretical problems and the associated failure to appreciate changes and transformations in the state system cannot be resolved in this way (chapters 1 and 2; see also Jaeger 1996).[21] The main challenge confronting this approach is that it will have to fill the gaps opened up by its concept of identity: "to focus more directly on identities and interests as the *dependent* variable and see whether, how, and why they change" (Wendt 1994: 331, my emphasis). Since the authors, whose views have been summarized here, agree that a whole bundle of independent variables are simply waiting for their chance to affect state identity, the greatest difficulty arising from this concept could in the final analysis be the problems it has in dealing adequately with state identity as a dependent variable.

Recent work by Thomas Risse-Kappen employs an equally underdetermined concept of identity, especially with regard to the fundamental question of who the *bearers of identity* are. In Risse-Kappen's work, these could be individuals involved in communication situations whose identities—in the sense of self-understanding (see Risse-Kappen 1995a: 176)—could be placed in question as the result of arguments (Risse-Kappen 1995a: 177, 178, 179); they could also be collectivities or states or their representatives whose identity is imposed upon them (see, for example, Risse-Kappen 1994: 175; 1995b: 205; 1995c: 505; 1996: 393). According to Risse-Kappen (1995b: 4; 1995c: 509), the values and norms shared by state representatives form the basis of collective identities; norms "shape the identity of political actors through processes of socialization, communication, and enactment" (Risse-Kappen 1996: 366).[22] But there remains a major problem with this nonreflexive concept of identity. Risse-Kappen provides no answer to the question of *which* of the many common features present are significant for the formation of a collective identity. If actors have a number of different identities (Risse-Kappen 1996: 370) and collective identity is to be an explanatory variable, this question cannot be left to be settled by empirical analysis alone (as Risse-Kappen 1996: 370 ff suggests). If different identities are in competititon with one another, it is not legitimate for the researcher to decide which identity is to be treated as the explanatory variable relevant to the resulting identity formation.

However, Risse-Kappen's writings on the conceptualization of identity in International Relations do make one important contribution: they examine the domestic preconditions of international relations and attempt to provide a systematic description of the connections between them: "A sociological interpretation of a liberal theory of international relations then claims that actors' domestic identities are crucial for their perceptions of one another in the international realm" (Risse-Kappen 1996: 367; see also Risse-Kappen 1995b: 7, 28). But the next step must be a theoretically oriented conceptualization of this connection, which implies that it would be most productive to treat individuals as the bearers of identity. Risse-Kappen himself has systematically elaborated concepts of norms, transnational relations and two-level games (see Risse-Kappen 1995b: 204–10), but no such concept for collective identities; hence, he can only make fairly vague statements about the effects of these identities (see, for example, Risse-Kappen 1995b: 32, 34, 184, 199–200, 205, 214, 218, and 223). It is also unclear how far his concept of identity is a reflexive one. On the one hand, Risse-Kappen refers to social constructivism and stresses that "state actions cannot be adequately understood without taking communications and *self-understandings* of actors seriously" (Risse-Kappen 1995b: 7, my emphasis), but at the same time a reflexive concept is inconsistent with the idea that collectives should be seen as the bearers of identity.[23]

We have seen that Wendt, by introducing 'identity' as an intermediate element situated between structures and interests, argues against the neorealist assumption that behavior is directly determined by structure, and that Risse-Kappen uses 'collective identities' as a tool designed to strengthen a liberal approach. An interesting additional argument has been put forward by Jonathan Mercer (1995). Mercer's response to Wendt is an attempt to use 'identity' in order to present the realist self-help system as an intergroup structure, which results from human nature itself, and from which there is therefore no escape (see Mercer 1995: 236, 252). He supports this argument by incorporating Social Identity Theory, which explains the relative preferences expressed by group members within the 'minimal group paradigm' (on this point see Diehl 1990; Weller 1993, 1995: 73; and Mercer 1995: 237) in terms of the individual's need for a positive social identity.

The central element of this social-psychological theory (see below for a more comprehensive account) is its exploration of the relationship between group membership and feelings of self-worth. In the individual's self-perception, membership in groups determines a person's position in society; this gives rise to the individual's social identity, which therefore contains those aspects of the individual's self-image that arise out of group memberships. Because the sense of individual self-worth is partially derived from the evaluation of those groups of which the individual feels him or herself to be a member, there is an ever-present tendency to intergroup comparison, and to contrast groups to which one belongs with others (see Rupert Brown 1988). And because this comparison is intended to produce a positive result—for it is only in this case that the individual sense of self-worth can benefit—the individual tries to find ways of making this possible. As a result, 'mistakes of judgment' are often made that are to the advantage of one's own group and the detriment of other groups (see Weller 1993: 213).

However, Mercer fails to appreciate two problems with this thesis: first, the incompatibility of Wendt's understanding of state identity with the individual-based and reflexive concept used in Social Identity Theory, and second the multiple social identities possessed by each single individual. Mercer's unthinking equation of intergroup with interstate relations (Mercer 1995: 243) prevents him from seeing the potential of the concept of social identity for the understanding of inter- and transnational relations.[24] Since Social Identity Theory only generates statements about the social identity of *individuals* it provides no "theoretical and empirical support for the neorealist assumption that states are a priori self-regarding" (Mercer 1995: 251). Indeed, Mercer himself refutes his own claim when he observes correctly that group boundaries are not fixed, and that in the case of the EU one could imagine an ingroup consisting of a number of states. The formation of social identity is not based on the state system, as Mercer would have us believe, but on the categorization that is performed in the course of the perception of the social world (see Tajfel and Turner 1986: 13–14; Oakes et al. 1994: ch. 4). These categorizations may in certain cases be congruent with state borders, as, for example, during the live broadcast of a football match between two national teams. But most of the time quite different categorizations determine our perceptions, and thereby the boundaries between ingroup and outgroup that go to create social identity—for instance, between men and women, rich and poor, 'First and Third World', Christian and Islamic worlds, and so on. In order to render the identity concept used in Social Identity Theory fruitful for IR, we need to know *which* categorizations determine the perceptions involved in inter- and transnational relations; only when we know this will we be able to say more about the borders along which the mechanism of attaching a positive value to the ingroup, and a negative value to the outgroup, functions, and only then will we be able to say when this can come to have major political consequences. After all, the political implications of international football matches for interstate relations are minimal.

National Identity

Perhaps the most frequently examined identity concept is 'national identity'. Discussions of the factors determining national identity frequently suffer from the normative weight carried by the term (see Westle 1994: 454–63). However, there are also cases in which a theoretical perspective dominates, and these are more productive. It is possible to find a number of points of contact with the concept of collective identity, which is taken up again in the following section.[25] National identity is most frequently taken up in connection with research on nationalism itself. Anthony Smith sees nations and nationalism as cultural phenomena based on national identity, which in turn is a specific expression of collective identity (Smith 1991: 3–8). Smith's concept of national identity is based on assumptions derived from his historical work on the origins of nations:

> The existence of these common assumptions allows us to list the fundamental features of national identity as follows: (1) a historic territory, or homeland; (2) common myths and historical memories; (3) a common, mass public culture; (4) common legal rights and duties for all members; (5) a common economy with territorial mobility for members. A nation can therefore be defined as a named human population sharing a historic territory, common myths and historical memories, a mass, public culture, a common economy and common legal rights and duties for all members. (Smith 1991: 14)

The bearer of national identity is a 'political community' (Smith 1991: 9), a collectivity that shares the common features listed. Smith's concept of national identity is a multilayered one, which not only comprises these material dimensions, but also incorporates the reflexive dimension in pursuing the question of the functions of national identity: "Finally, a sense of national identity provides a powerful means of defining and locating individual selves in the world" (Smith 1991: 17).[26] Like the authors considered earlier, Smith pays no particular attention to the connections between individual and collective identity, but concentrates on the substantive, historical-cultural common features that constitute collective identity.

For Smith, therefore, the question to be answered in connection with the possibility of a European collective identity is: "So what is common to all Europeans?" (Smith 1992: 70), although he does not entirely rule out the possibility that such common features could also be constructed (Smith 1992: 67–76).

The construction of national identity occupies a much more central place in Benedict Anderson's analysis (Anderson 1991). Anderson's view is that "nationality [...] as well as nationalism, are cultural artefacts of a particular kind" (Anderson 1991: 4). A nation is therefore 'an imagined political community', 'imagined' because "the members of even the smallest nation will never know most of their fellow-members, meet them, or even hear of them, yet in the minds of each lives the image of their communion" (Anderson 1991: 6). For Anderson, therefore, a nation is a societal construction of belonging and exclusion.[27] "The nation is imagined as *limited*" (Anderson 1991: 7, emphasis in original), and this 'nation' can be constituted in a number of different ways.[28]

> The nation is above all an imagined order, a culturally defined conception which designates a human collective as a single unit. The nature of this entity emerges out of the criteria laid down for the determination of national collectivity in the concept of order adopted by the nation. [...] Depending on these criteria and on the way in which they are mingled together, the results are various human collectives which are supposed to form an association characterized by national solidarity. The distinctive features which are acknowledged within the imagined order of the nation therefore form the basis of different sorts of nations. This means that the nation is by no means a natural and unambiguous form of social order; it can change over time and is capable of adapting itself to historical developments. (Lepsius 1990b: 232)

But even if this means that we can treat the nation and national identity as social constructions, we still have to explain the preeminent position occupied over a long period by national identity in relation to other collective identities, whether at the transstate level (for example, a European identity) or on a smaller scale (substate regional identity). All social institutions offer possibilities for identification, and can provide feelings of belonging (see Burke 1992: 305, and Axtmann 1995: 93). The particular prominence of national identity as a specific expression of collective identity formation is above all related to the societal norms governing legitimate violence. Before the nation-state took on its function in the formation of societal structures, individuals' primary emotional attachments were to other institutions—towns, villages or tribes "were the objects of common identification, the shared objects of individuals' emotional attachments" (Elias 1970: 151). From a functional point of view, these institutions serve the purpose of defense against external physical threats. The emotional attachment is therefore strongly rooted in the prohibition and the legitimate use of violence (see also Weber 1968: vol. I, 394; Assmann 1993: 245).

> When one examines what it is that unites the various figurations which at different levels attract this type of emotional attachment on the part of the individuals who

form them, the first thing one discovers is that they are all units which exercise a more or less strict control over the use of physical force in relations between their members, while at the same time preparing these members for the use of force in relations with non-members, and in many cases even encouraging this. (Elias 1970: 151)

The legitimation of this kind of destructive violence, which is forbidden within one's own society, both presupposes and strengthens the categorical distinction between ingroup and outgroup. If relations with members of another society differ from relations *within* societies in respect of such a fundamental issue as the use of force, this fact must regulate perceptions of the social world in a very special way, for a misperception could take on an existential significance. The distinction between 'natives' and foreigners is therefore extremely important for structuring perceptions of the social world. Moreover, this categorization involves an evaluation: the outgroup must be accorded a lower value than the ingroup, for this is the only way in which the use of force, forbidden in respect to members of the ingroup, can be justified in respect to the outgroup. The recognition of this normative basis of the state involves an identification with one's own state that will always be a positive one, because the ingroup is valued more highly than the outgroup.

In more recent history this understanding of the state has been decisively relativized, through the experience of transborder exchange and international interdependence, and also with the help of international agreements and norms, in particular the prohibition of the use of force in international relations, which is laid down in the U.N. Charter. In this way, intrastate norms have been carried over into inter- and transnational relations, and the significance of borders, and so the preeminence of social categorization on the basis of state citizenship has been reduced by the growing importance of societal actors in international relations. This means that developments toward a world society (see the introduction to this volume) are contributing to a decline in the significance of national identity, above all for those people whose social relations constitute this world society.

Identity as a Social-Scientific Concept

It seems that the decline in significance of national identity that can be observed in some areas is being more than offset by other forms of collective identity.[29] The mass media and political essayists are quick to assign a collective identity to any group as soon as it shows signs of understanding itself as such. Because collectivities now tend—especially since 1989—to stress subnational differentiations and exclusions more frequently, in addition to their common national elements, a number of new identity concepts have now joined 'national identity'. Common features such as culture, language, religion, descent, and region, which would be immediately noticeable if they had not already been used in the construction of nation-states, have been discovered as new fields of collective identity formation. Here a regional identity is said to be developing; there ethnic identity is playing a role; elsewhere religious identities are becoming more important; in certain places cultural identity formation has made a breakthrough; here and there national identity has managed to return with a vengeance.

Whenever groups stress one or more of their specific common features in order to differentiate themselves from the rest of the world and to emphasize their own exclusiveness, it is claimed that collective identity is involved. In this way, 'identity' can easily become a category that covers everything and therefore explains nothing, a reference to features common to collectivities on any scale whatsoever. The Bavarians, after all, have something in common. But why then have they not, up until now at least, developed a regional identity strong enough to make them want to secede from the Federal Republic of Germany? Europeans as a whole also have things in common, and one sometimes hears talk of a 'European identity'.[30] But why has this European identity begun to emerge in some places rather than in others? And would not the formation of a global identity provide the best hope for the end of war and the best opportunity for humanity to show that it is capable of rising to global ecological and economic challenges? After all, all of us living on the planet also have something in common. But it is clear that this alone is insufficient. A concept of identity that leaves out the reflexive dimension may make it possible to ascribe all sorts of identities from the outside, but it cannot help us to make generalizable statements about the formation and the changes of these identities.

Any attempt to assess the importance of 'identity' in social-scientific theories must make it clear what concept of identity is being used. The most promising starting point would be the roots of the social-psychological terminology of identity as used by authors like Mead and Erikson, rather than the philosophical usages to be found in Plato, Aristotle, Leibniz, and Kant (see Henrich 1979: 137–40). "In philosophical theory, identity is a predicate with a specific function: it serves to distinguish an individual thing or object as such from others of the same kind" (Henrich 1979: 135), whereas in social psychology 'identity' is a complex quality acquired by persons. Thus, although the differences of meaning in the different contexts are clear, it is equally apparent that there is something in the content that links them to one another (see Henrich 1979: 134–37; Elias 1987: 209–10; Luhmann 1990a: 21). However, a 'truly hopeless confusion' (Henrich 1979: 136) arises when the difference between these two concepts of identity is not taken into account. A social-scientific concept of identity will always emphasize the social dimension of the emergence and effects of identity (see Mead 1967: part III, especially ch. 19), so that "it makes most sense to understand 'identity' as the constant pattern of behavior, and of self-interpretation of this behavior, which is the definitive result of the development within a language community of beings capable of speech" (Henrich 1979: 134).

This specification of the term singles out human beings involved in social exchange as the bearers of identity. Identity comes into being and changes as a consequence of individuals' interpretations of their own behavior—which entails a reflexive concept of identity. This still does not go far enough to explain how identity has the effects it does, other than in the formation of patterns of behavior, but it is clear that the subject of identification is the individual. Therefore, identity involves attributing greater significance to the self-understanding of individuals in contexts of social action; their behavior cannot be adequately explained if their identity is not taken into account.

SOCIAL-PSYCHOLOGICAL THEORIES OF IDENTITY

Social Identity Theory

In the discussion so far I have on a number of occasions dealt briefly with Social Identity Theory and mentioned that the need for a positive self-image is the basic motivation in the evaluation of social categories. I have also, in the course of my criticism of Mercer (1995), emphasized the fact that social identity can only be formed by individuals in a reflexive process, and that the categories used to draw boundaries between groups and to attach a lower value to the outgroup are not given from the start, but are based on the respective perceptions of reality of those involved.[31] The decisive point that suggests that community-formation processes in a Weberian sense can be explained with the help of Social Identity Theory can be found in the basic human need for social identity. In order to orient ourselves within our social environment, we have to define who we are with the help of social categories. "We classify not only others as members of this or that group, but we also allot *ourselves* a place in relation to these very groups. In other words, our feeling of identity is closely connected with our membership in various groups" (Brown 1990: 420, emphasis in original).

As human beings create a social identity for themselves in this way, the categorizations made in the course of the perception of the social world acquire a special significance: they form the boundary between ingroup and outgroup. This means that a feeling of belonging arises among members of the ingroup when, in certain situations and in agreement with one another, they categorize the social world in such a way that each of them individually recognizes the others as members of this group.[32] In this way a certain social identity acquires a dominant significance for the members of a collectivity, and this can be termed 'collective identity'. However, it is important to stress that what happens here is not the attribution of an identity to collectivities or groups. Rather, the term 'collective identity' can be employed in the sense of an identity concept developed on a reflexive, individual basis, whenever each of the individual members of a collectivity perceives all the others primarily as members of precisely this collectivity. Only this conceptualization of collective identity makes it possible to keep a firm grip on a reflexive concept of identity that saves us from understanding identity as something that is arbitrarily attributed from the outside.[33]

The chief premise of Social Identity Theory is the categorization performed in the course of every act of human perception. On the basis of similarities and differences, the objects of perception are grouped in identical or distinctive categories. One of the main reasons why this happens is cognitive economy: without such a categorization we would be unable to deal with the enormous variety of stimulations reaching our consciousness. The order we create in this way, however, contributes not only to self-orientation but also to the structuring of the world in terms of categories and of the social world in terms of groups, and this enables each individual to find an answer to the question, 'Who am I?'

> Social categorization allows the perceiver to 'structure the causal understanding of the social environment' as a guide to action. Importantly, it also provides a system of orientation for *self-reference*, creating and defining the individual's place in society. (Oakes et al. 1994: 81, emphasis in original)

This is basically the same conceptualization of social identity as the one put forward by George H. Mead in his understanding of social theories of the self (Mead 1967: 222). Each individual can only create and perceive his or her identity through social contacts, which is why we speak of 'social identity'. This social identity then includes those aspects of an individual's self-image that emerge from the social categories to which the individual perceives him or herself as belonging (Tajfel and Turner 1986: 16). This perception is preceded by the structuring of the social world according to categories that are context dependent. The coming into being of a collective identity therefore requires that the members of a collectivity perceive the social world through the prism of a certain categorization, which is of great importance for the social identity of the individuals.

One can best illustrate this process of collective identity formation with the help of a conflict situation. If a demonstration leads to a confrontation with the police or other security forces, the perceptions of those involved will be structured by the distinction between police and demonstrators. This will undoubtedly be the dominant categorization, on the basis of which the members of both groups will form their social identities. For the police officers, the most important consideration in this situation is not the possibility that they might agree with the demands being made by the demonstrators, but their social identity as members of the forces of law and order. This self-perception results from the categorization that is dominant for all participants in the situation, and this leads to a subjective identification within the respective ingroups. Since the dominant identity on the police side is the awareness of being a police officer, a collective identity is formed, which without doubt decisively influences the actions of each individual officer. The maxim guiding action here is not so much individual advantage as the feeling of belonging to the collective of one's own ingroup. This is also the case for the demonstrators.

The example of this conflict situation is intended to make it easier to see how the perception of the social world is shaped by a particular categorization process. But collective identities can also come into existence without such a direct conflict, since categorizations must be carried out whenever the social world is perceived. However, it is necessary to offer a differentiated analysis of which specific categorizations are used to structure perceptions of the social world, and of the range of the collective identities that result—in other words, of the range of boundaries that separate ingroup from outgroup. These requirements can be met with the help of the meta-contrast principle developed within Self-Categorization Theory.

Self-Categorization Theory

Self-Categorization Theory is based on the findings of Social Identity Theory, but it is also in certain respects a further development of that theory (see Oakes et al. 1994). Its main goal is to illuminate the relationship between the cognitive categorization process and the reality of groups. The basic assumption is that the formation of social identity rests on a self-categorization. This means that the individual, in the course of his or her self-perception and the associated categorization of the social world, perceives him or herself as identical with others in a certain very specific dimension—in contrast to those individuals who are perceived in this dimension of the categorization as *other*. Thus, self-categorization can be carried out at very different levels of abstraction in different categories, and the category selected is context dependent. For example, in the context of the evaluation of university teaching, a professor will see him or herself as a teacher, a member of a group distinguished from the students. When it is a matter of a resolution protesting against cuts in the education budget, the same professor will perceive him or herself in the first instance as a member of the university along with the students. When a discussion about planned cuts in development aid takes place, people concerned about global justice and international solidarity will find their transnational identity activated as something that distinguishes them from those opposed to this form of aid. During the Olympic Games, on the other hand, national collective identity is likely to become dominant, because the differences that dominate perceptions revolve around nationality.

These examples also demonstrate that all social situations contain the potential for certain categorizations, according to which perceptions are structured and which are used as the bases of self-perceptions. The decisive contribution of Self-Categorization Theory consists in its capacity to explain theoretically which category is used for this categorization, and thus in the formation of social identity:

> This point is formalized in the principle of meta-contrast, which is so called because it involves a contrast between contrasts, a judgement of difference between differences. The meta-contrast principle predicts that a given set of items is more likely to be categorized as a single entity *to the degree that differences within that set of items are less than the differences between that set and others within the comparative context*. (Oakes et al. 1994: 95–96, emphases in original)

The decision about which categorization is to be made is therefore based on a comparison of the differences within potential categories with the differences between these categories. At the same time, however, it makes a difference which categories are, so to speak, made available through the social context and which of them are appropriate to this context. It is quite possible that in a personal, easily comprehensible context, one perceives oneself primarily as an individual rather than in social categories, so the social identity is less significant for the individual's self-perception. But "following the meta-contrast principle, *social* categorization of the self and others becomes more likely as intergroup differences increase and intragroup, interpersonal differences decrease" (Oakes et al. 1994: 99, emphasis in original).

The larger the perceived social space, the more each individual is forced to make categorizations that place more emphasis on differences *between* the groups and similiarities *within* them. In this way, the social identity becomes more significant. And the result of social categorization is the depersonalization of self-perception and behavior: "Most importantly, self-categorization theory proposes that it is this process of depersonalization that makes group behavior possible and produces its emergent, irreducible properties" (Oakes et al. 1994: 100). Collective identity comes into being when the members of a collectivity perceive themselves primarily as members of this collectivity, so that a depersonalization of both perception and behavior occurs.[34]

COLLECTIVE IDENTITIES IN IR THEORY

Collective Identities in International Politics

Collective identities are based on the categorizations carried out in the course of the perception of the social world, by means of which individuals allot themselves a particular place in that world. In cases where states and nationality dominate the perception of international politics, it will be national collective identities that guide actions undertaken in this sphere. But we should not forget that other collective identities besides national ones are also frequently formed and can acquire partial significance, which means that categorizations are made that do not coincide with national borders. This kind of shift in collective identities can be demonstrated by means of an example from the end of the Cold War.

During the Cold War, perceptions of international relations were dominated in a very special way by questions of security policy. Security policy laid down the categories used by each individual to find his or her own place in the context of international politics. Around 1980, in accordance with the meta-contrast principle, the difference between 'us' (the West) and 'them' (the East) was perceived to be greater than that between 'us' (Germans or Europeans) and the Americans. Therefore, the categorization of the social world, as far as international relations were concerned, was mainly drawn along the border between the systems. In this systemic conflict, we perceived ourselves as 'the West' and developed the corresponding collective identity. This provided us with a basis on which to develop military arsenals and strategies that seem so irrational in retrospective as to be hardly comprehensible. But when, at the beginning of the 1980s, the view that weapons and military strategies were more dangerous than the Soviet threat became widespread, the categorization involved in the perception of international politics also began to change. The most important difference was now seen by many to be the one between those favoring political detente and those who believed in the necessity of a military strategy based on nuclear deterrence and the balance of power, rather than between 'East' and 'West'. The resulting categorization drew boundaries that no longer coincided with the national borders: 'peace movements versus military strategists' replaced 'East versus West'. This also produced transnational collective identities, both on the peace movement side and within NATO (see Risse-Kappen 1995b), which led to deep divisions in many Western societies. From the mid-1980s onward, one of the determining factors in European security politics was the information being received about reforms underway in the USSR. From this moment on, a crucial influence on categorization was the division between those who were skeptical about and those who reacted more positively to Mikhail Gorbachev's reform policy, because many Europeans saw this as a more significant difference than the systemic conflict—even though this had not disappeared. For most Americans, however, the greatest perceived difference remained that between 'free West' and 'oppressed East'. The American understanding of the United States as the stronghold of liberty was only placed in question when the categories 'East' and 'West' lost their significance with the collapse of the Soviet bloc.

These changes in collective identities affected the West's decision-making on security policy. The loss of significance suffered by the collective identity 'the West' during the 1980s made it more difficult for NATO's member-states to pursue a confrontational policy toward the Warsaw Pact. As the new foreign policy pursued by the USSR after Gorbachev came to power provided impetus to the categorization 'supporters of detente versus opponents', especially in West European societies, well-defined collective identities developed along the line dividing those who thought there should be a positive response to Soviet disarmament and detente proposals from those who took a more skeptical view. During the period in which this question shaped the public debate, an important aspect of social identity for every individual was which school of thought one belonged to. Because there had been a change in the categories according to which international politics was perceived, and so also in collective identities, it was no longer possible for the West European NATO governments to stick to a security policy whose dominant collective identity was 'the West'. In the United States, on the other hand, no particular attention was paid to the opportunities that might be presented by the new Soviet foreign policy in the mid-1980s, and so no decisive shift in collective identities occurred—which meant that the U.S. administration remained attached to its old policy and oriented toward the East-West dichotomy much longer (see Risse-Kappen 1991 and Weller 1992, 1998).

The perception of international politics involves categorizations that are used by each individual as the basis of a social identity. Which collective identities emerge, in other words, which correspondences in the formation of social identity, depends on which categorization is used by the individual in his or her self-perception in the context of international politics. A decision on which of the available categorizations is to be used is taken with the help of the meta-contrast principle. Another factor that is at least as influential as the meta-contrast principle is the representation of international politics. It is the media's presentation of the world which more or less implicitly provides the categorizations that guide the individual's perceptions. Social Categorization Theory therefore provides us with a concept of social identity that starts from the individual perception of the social world and the categorizations involved here. The structuring of perceptions of the social world of international relations according to the categories of ingroup and outgroup provides the basis for the formation of collective identities, and so for forms of community formation that are not in all cases tied to state borders. By applying the meta-contrast principle to the presentation and perceptions of international politics, we can investigate the question of which dimension of collective identity formation acquires particular significance in specific contexts of action.

Collective Identities in World Society

Because of the individual's need for social identity, the life of social groups always leads to the formation of collective identities that can be understood as subjective feelings of belonging, or, in Weber's terminology, as community formation. If we therefore accept that community formation needs to be treated as a form of social relations that is just as significant as society formation, we should expect that as global society formation proceeds and leads to the development of a world society, we shall observe not the disappearance of communal structures, as is frequently predicted, but simply a change within the collective identities underlying these communal structures. On the basis of the interrelationship between society and community formation, we can expect shifts in the formation of collective identities whenever there are changes in society formation (in its intensity, its boundaries, in the actors involved). In a world dominated by states, national identities will be the dominant form of collective identity formation, and in a world characterized by power blocs and/or global conflict formations (for example, Cold War or North-South conflict), collective identities first of all form along the boundaries set by these categorizations.

With the end of the Cold War, one categorization that characterized international politics has disappeared, so that today—in accordance with the meta-contrast principle—other categorizations are affecting the formation of social identity and so the emergence of collective identities. As this happens, states remain the prototypical institutions producing community formation, because they are still the guardians of the prohibition of violence internally and responsible for the instruments of force in external relations, and so national identities are still a dominant expression of collective identity formation. But as world society develops, states are losing their significance for collective identity formation. The first reason why this is happening is that the distinction between legitimate outwardly directed violence and the prohibition of violence in domestic affairs, a feature of states that is decisive for national identity, is declining in significance as norms and institutions are established between states. Secondly, perceptions of international relations are increasingly affected by other institutions that offer alternative categorizations and thus alternative ways of forming collective identities: communities of states, trading blocs, regional economic communities, substate regions and transnational organizations.[35] The changes in international politics brought about by the development of a world society may give rise to new collective identities.[36] These new identities will always mean some kind of social fragmentation, since the categorization underlying them always involves a differentiation between ingroup and outgroup, on the basis of which individuals assign themselves a place in the social context of international politics.[37]

The perception of international relations as consisting of a world of states characterized by the Cold War clearly provided the dominant categorization for the creation of collective identities during the whole period from 1945 to the end of the 1980s. National identities and the feeling of belonging that arose from the overkill capacities of both sides characterized the emotional involvement of each individual in international politics. The end of the Cold War and increasing globalization not only means that we currently lack clear categorizations for the perception of international politics; regional and transnational connections are also increasingly coming into being in a way that makes available alternative forms of collective identity. Since the development of world society reduces the significance of the nationality of actors on the world stage, other collective feelings of belonging come into play. Today we can observe more intensive community-formation processes at various levels: substate (secessionist movements) regional (for example, border regions), transnational (for example, the environmental movement), state (nationalism) and transstate (for example, the 'Clash of Civilizations'). This means an increasing fragmentation of international politics, even though it is not possible to say what effects this has on globalization and on interstate relations. Community formation can either strengthen or slow down the development of inter- and transnational society formation; it all depends on whether the external borders of society formation are the same as or different from those of community formation (see Weller 1995).

Samuel Huntington's 'The West versus the Rest' thesis (Huntington 1993) is a weak one (for a critical response see Senghaas 1995). However, it is not inconceivable that as globalization, which we can see primarily as an 'OECD-ization' of the world, proceeds, a clearer dividing line between North and South, between the rich and the poor world, will come into being. This dividing line would not only be the place at which the majority of societized interactions come up against their limits, it would also serve to identify the boundary between ingroup and outgroup for the purposes of community formation.[38] If perceptions of international politics come to be more strongly influenced by the idea of a North-South conflict, there is a danger that a 'Northern' collective identity will emerge on the basis of this categorization.[39] If the external borders of intensive society- and community-formation processes coincide with one another and there are only a few collective identities that cross these boundaries — for example, transnational collective identities based on international solidarity — the result will be a much stronger tendency toward escalation and violence in the event of conflict (see Weller 1995). This makes it especially important for the analysis of world-societal developments not only to direct its attention to the increasing intensity and scale of social relationships, but also to ask what changes can be observed in communal relationships. Where collective action is concerned, we must above all be interested in the external borders of subjectively experienced feelings of belonging, that is, of intensive communal relationships, which may perhaps undergo radical transformation as a result of changes in international structures and institutions. Community formation can be understood as a form of collective identity formation, the conditions of whose emergence can be investigated with the help of social-psychological theories. The empirical analysis of collective identities in world society should therefore begin by investigating the ways in which the categorizations governing perceptions of international politics are determined.

4

'Community' in the Global Network: A Methodological Exploration

Emanuel Richter

The social-scientific literature on 'globalization' continues to grow rapidly. As a result of the intensification of global interdependence via flows of goods and capital, migration, technological communication and the media, and also through global threat constellations in the military and environmental fields, no work published in the area of International Relations neglects the question of the global network.

But there has been a change in the way this subject is dealt with. More and more frequently, analyses of globalization are going beyond pure description. Because globalization is by no means synonymous with social, political, and economic integration or with the harmonic unity of 'one world', but also gives rise to tensions in the form of fragmentation, disintegration, and regionalization, social scientists are unsure how to proceed. There seems to be a need for a classification that is more sensitive to the normative aspects of the problem, and there is an increasing preparedness and need to draw up a systematic account of globalization processes that clarifies their potential for both integration and disintegration. 'Community' is one of the concepts most frequently employed in attempts to provide this sort of evaluation. The most straightforward usage of this term serves to identify groups characterized by a strong, stabilizing, and coherent identity. While the distinction between exclusive group egoisms and an integrative preparedness to cooperate leads to considerable analytical problems, a world of communities or even the unity of the 'world community' remains a conceptual symbol standing for successful global integration and peaceful global coexistence. It is more difficult to evaluate 'community' as a general moral orientation to action. How is community to be distinguished from global actors' strategic or instrumental orientations, and what normative impulses is it able to provide to the global network? These difficulties confront us in the end with epistemological questions. What normative criteria should we use to evaluate the formation of communities or the realization of community-based action orientations? Can the discipline of International Relations associate itself unhesitatingly with pleas for the further diffusion of communities in world politics, for the strengthening of these community-based orientations, or even for the conceptualization of a 'world community'? Is the term 'community' adequate for the task of getting an analytic and normative grip on the extraordinary diversity of worldwide communication at the end of this millennium, a phenomenon for which I use the neutral term 'global network'?

There are therefore a number of questions that we need to ask of the category 'community'; on closer examination it turns out to be far from self-evident that we can use the term as a way of classifying global interdependence. The term itself is enigmatic, contested, and in need of further clarification before we can judge how meaningful it is. Moreover, the field to which it is applied is so complex, and so difficult to evaluate in normative terms, that a single concept, however crucial, is unlikely to be adequate as an instrument of classification. For these reasons, some justified skepticism has been expressed about the use of the term 'community' in connection with the analysis of globalization processes. Booth suspects that talk of an 'international community' is merely "a platitude, trotted out by the powerful when they want to legitimize a particular action" (Booth 1995: 121). As a way of distancing the analysis from such ideological diversions and making it easier to draw clear distinctions, a number of authors distinguish world society from world community. They seek to use this distinction to determine more precisely the degree of cohesiveness, the intensity, the persistence, and the institutional stability of the global network (see chapter 1). Another move that has been made is to paint a broad picture of the global situation, and then to attempt with the help of additional concepts and categories such as 'world system', 'international society', and 'transnationalism' to describe in a systematic way integration and disintegration potentials (see chapter 2; also Buzan 1993). The conceptual debate is being stimulated further by the growing number of authors who are introducing 'ideas' as an analytical category in International Relations. This brings into clearer focus aspects traditionally considered to belong to the sphere of shared life-contexts—worldviews, moral concepts, and individual identities (Jachtenfuchs 1995; Weller 1995). Attempts have also been made to describe the cohesiveness of community by using the very term usually regarded as its antithesis—'society'. One example is the use of the term *Gesellschaftswelt* (societal world), which, within the global network and as something that goes beyond conventional political internationalism, is seen to be extending its reach as the basis of integrative models of action and as a contribution to global democratization:

> The increase in the interdependence of the societal world as a result of the activities of societal actors is clear for all to see; in the world-view of the societal world, the societal environment is no longer seen merely as an object, but rather as a subject enjoying equal rights because it bears equal responsibility. (Czempiel 1991: 106)

This chapter is an attempt to provide some clarification of this tangle of concepts and categories. It is intended to assist in the search for the distinguishing features of 'community', to help answer the question of the normative characteristics of the cohesiveness of community, and to provide some guidance on how community relates analytically and normatively to the global network. The task is to classify the attributes of 'community', and also to assess the analytic and systematic power of the normative category 'community' in International Relations. Attention is focused both on the conceptual substance of 'community', that is to say, on the diverse understandings of the content of the term and the problems of applying it at the global level, and on its potential efficacy as a category to be used in political science research. These methodological considerations serve to make it easier to assess the explanatory value of the category 'community' in attempts to understand the integrative and disintegrative potentials of globalization.

My exploration of these fields proceeds in two stages. In the next section I begin with some remarks on the history of the concept itself, which lead to a sketch of its place in the history of political theory. I show briefly how theorists from Immanuel Kant to Michael Walzer have used the term community, in order to illustrate the different understandings various authors have had of the term and the diversity of the areas to which it has been applied. I then go on to use the findings of my theoretical-historical sketch to develop the project of using 'community' as an instrument in the analysis and normative classification of international relations. The main objective here is to shed light on the explanatory value of community in respect of the integrative and disintegrative potential of global interdependence. In my concluding remarks I offer a brief assessment of the methodological force of the category 'community'.

'COMMUNITY' IN POLITICAL THEORY

As far as its etymological origins are concerned, 'community' is by no means a precise concept that would be well-suited to the task of classification in the social sciences. The meanings attached to the term vary, and are to some extent divergent in the most important modern languages (for further details on these etymological questions, see Richter 1992).

Although usages of 'community' and 'communal' can be traced in almost all periods in the history of political theory, the concept has still not acquired any kind of central terminological or conceptual position within the Western philosophical tradition. If anything, the history of political theory reveals a predominance of cautious and sometimes even openly negative positions on the question of according 'community' a central role. In this section I use the work of selected political theorists to illustrate the breadth of interpretations and the different understandings of the term that can be found within this tradition.

Immanuel Kant assigns 'community' to a variety of dimensions of human knowledge and experience. Kant sees community as forming, alongside substance and causality, one of the bases of experience. The term refers to an interaction between objects—or, to be more precise, a relationship under conditions of simultaneity—without which human perceptions and the establishing of connections between different perceptions would be impossible (Kant 1902–1955, *Kritik der reinen Vernunft*, vol. III: 27). Subjective experience is inseparable from the ability to relate perceptions to one another and to grasp their interactions (see Richter 1991: 191). In the *Kritik der Urteilskraft*, 'community' refers to the capacity to communicate to other's judgments on questions of taste. But Kant fails to make his position entirely clear: does this communicability presuppose an imaginary community of all subjects able to make aesthetic judgments, thereby already entailing the idea of human universality, or is it no more than the solitary subject's solipsistic projection onto the possible aesthetic judgments of other subjects? In the latter case it would serve to construct a human community rather than presupposing such a community (Kant 1902–1955, *Kritik der Urteilskraft*, vol. V: 214).

Kant goes further in his philosophy of religion and enriches his understanding of community by adding normative content. Here he argues that 'nature' is the basis for the development of the good in man. Human freedom is directed toward furthering this development in an autonomous way; this is the active human employment of reason, described as the 'common purpose' of humankind (Kant 1902–1955, *Die Religion innerhalb der Grenzen der bloßen Vernunft*, vol. VI: 97). However, the force that drives this unfolding of community is not the human capacity to acquire knowledge or any reasonable moral behavior, but simply a moral impulse nourished by the obligation to do one's duty, according to which the individual subject functions, unconsciously, as an organ responsible for fulfilling certain predisposed, rational goals of existence. Kant does not go into detail about the foundations or content of this community—they remain no more than the expression of a human duty that has been carried out. It is this tracing back of the communal unfolding of reason to a self-constitutive but nevertheless empty human 'duty' that has earned Kant harsh criticism from some of those who have engaged with his thought. Hegel was the first scornful critic; he sardonically dismissed Kant's theory of duty as 'empty formalism' (Hegel 1975: 120).

Hegel keeps his distance from Kant's implied conception of a social a priori that establishes some kind of human community as a starting point for the unfolding of reason, for experience or for aesthetic judgment. Consequently, the term 'community' is not accorded any particular conceptual significance in Hegel's thought. For Hegel, '*das Gemeinsame*' ['the common'] is no more than a coincidental agreement and arbitrary attachment that emerges out of an intended coincidence of interests. This *Gemeinsame* emerges, in Hegel's view, in bodies like corporations and associations as societal interest groups pursuing their own goals (Hegel 1975: 78–80). 'Community' is nothing more than the sum of congruent interests and goals.

But Hegel, like Kant, pursues the idea of an unfolding of reason that rests on the foundations of human existence. In the place of Kant's duty-driven community of interests, Hegel proposes *das Allgemeine* ['the universal'], which has a concrete point of reference in the 'reasonable' state. This universality is not the 'communal' sum of congruent interests but rather a higher stage of attachment that individuals reach through reasonable coherence. "Unification pure and simple is the true content and aim of the individual, and the individual's destiny is the living of a universal life [...]. Rationality, taken generally and in the abstract, consists in the thoroughgoing unity of the universal and the single" (Hegel 1975: 80). In concrete terms, the unity of the universal and the individual comes about in the form of the state.

Hegel moves semantically onto a quite different path from that taken by Kant. It is not an original form of social behavior—Kant's shadowy social a priori— that provides the foundation for the unfolding of reason, but the not-yet-achieved fusion of the 'individual' existence with a form of life that is binding for 'all'. An artificial attachment takes the place of an organic social attachment. In this way, paradoxically, Hegel's 'common' comes close in terms of content to an important aspect of contemporary understandings of community: the problem of universalizability. Under conditions of globalization, it is not only the social coherence of a community that becomes a central characteristic, but also the possibility of projecting that community's characteristics and normative orientations onto all conceivable life-contexts. This brings us to the problem of universalizability, an area in which fierce controversies have arisen within the ongoing debate about tensions between culturally specific communal orientations and universal normative orientations. Hegel's understanding of 'the universal' is close to the general test of universalizability: he considers a form of life reasonable only if it can elevate itself above its own accidental development and find a constitutive base that it can share with 'all' others. Hegel provides some fruitful indications of how we might approach the analysis of concepts of community in the global network, precisely because of this continuous tension between the concrete forms of human life and the abstract justification of reason. One must, however, stress that 'community' as such has only a subordinate, systematically and normatively insignificant status in Hegel's thought. Between Kant's implicit and Ferdinand Tönnies' explicit references to community, Hegel occupies the position of a methodologically refreshing skeptic.

Tönnies developed his understanding of community seventy years after Hegel, an interval that arguably saved him from overestimating the state as the embodiment of reason. What Tönnies does instead is to focus his critical attention on the contradictions of modernization in industrial societies and to locate these analytically in the tension between *'Gemeinschaft'* and *'Gesellschaft'* ['community' and 'society']. Tönnies understands community as the expression of a *Wesenswillen*, which is methodologically derived from an inevitable human physiological disposition and represents human beings' fundamental mode of living together, prior to any particular goals or strategic projects. In other words, it is closer to Hegel's *das Allgemeine* than to his understanding of community. 'Society' symbolizes for Tönnies a system of anonymous, functional relationships, which is nevertheless a necessity in the history of human evolution. However, on the basis of the Western orientation toward progress in the form of the modern capitalist, industrial society, 'society' takes on the pathological features of a collective human arrangement dominated by functionalist action orientations (Tönnies 1972). Taking up an idea of Kant's, Tönnies tries, with the help of the concept of community, to elaborate the ontological foundations of experience that remain unclear in Kant's own writings. He argues that experience is derived from the 'organic life' represented by 'community' (Tönnies 1972: xvi). Although Tönnies himself does not put it quite as bluntly as this, he is saying that human beings can accept their social, 'communal' existence, but they cannot understand it cognitively as a part of their individual experience. In this way community, understood as organic determinism, acquires, in contrast to society, a self-evident 'empirical-historical' dynamic (Zander 1982: 26) that can be captured in a general statement about human evolution: the functionalism of industrial society eclipses the social community.

In this way Tönnies leaves unanswered the instructive question of how human beings should deal with the communal disposition at the various stages of historical development. Does reflection on organic determinism suffice to activate the defenses of community against societal functionalization? How can the human subject identify the value of social community in the life-context of an industrial society? How can community be recultivated in a way that avoids reproducing the social deficencies of society? Tönnies treats community as something that determines directly the existence of empirical subjects, but he fails to provide any guidance on how we could make epistemologically critical use of the concept of community and thus develop it as a practical and critical political instrument. To the contrary, because Tönnies himself has no understanding of community that is applicable to the contemporary world or could be used in a critique of modernization, he makes use of a dubious explanation of the term that refers to ties of blood, spirit, and location (Tönnies 1955: 465). This is why Tönnies repeatedly found himself confronted with a specific misuse of his concept of community and why he was forced to criticize those aspects of community that later provoked general reservations about the concept. Community came to be instrumentalized as a way of legitimizing an arbitrary group ideology or a blood-and-soil way of thinking geared to exclusion and social ostracism.

Max Weber's understanding of community tries to escape the possible misuse of the concept of community by embedding 'community' in the description of a large number of stages of social attachment and organization. This sober but very precise categorization seems most helpful as a way of getting to grips with the problems of using 'community' in the contemporary context. Weber's accounts of 'community' and 'community formation' succeed in capturing the terms' characteristics at three levels: the composition of the attachment, its degree of cohesiveness, and the normative bases of community.

Weber characterizes community as the expression of a "subjective feeling of the parties, whether affectual or traditional, that they belong together" (Weber 1947). Community symbolizes the irrational attachment, any addition of rationally created attachment places the relationship in the category of *'Vergesellschaftung'* ['society formation']. It is instructive to note that Weber attributes this affective type of bonding not only to small groups like the family, but also in principle to collectives such as large religious groups or national communities.

Weber classifies the cohesiveness of a community with reference to experienced feelings of belonging together. This sentiment produces, by means of a kind of subjective adaptation to communal features, a lasting social relationship that gives the community the cohesiveness of a social group. Common features that arise accidentally, such as similar biological characteristics, are, in accordance with this argument, excluded by Weber from being considered as a form of community.

Weber also turns his attention to the difficult question of the normative foundations of community formation. Like every social relationship, the community has a meaning, a constitutive order that can come into being either traditionally and affectually, or rationally in relation to goals or values. It is the group's way of dealing with its own internal meaning that decides whether this group is open and prepared to accept new members, or whether, either through strict exclusionary criteria or through specific conditions imposed on new members, it fences itself off sharply from the outside world. By means of these characteristics, Weber comprehends controversial aspects of the constitutive conditions of community formation that are extremely important in the analysis of global problems: the relationship between inclusion and exclusion.

Weber constructs a borderline case in his exposition of 'political community', which he identifies via the characteristics of territorial sovereignty and the preparedness to defend this sovereignty. In this way, and surprisingly, the modern nation-state can be understood as a community. Strangely enough, the definitional criterion for a political community is not community of culture, language, or common descent, but the preparedness of those living in a certain territory to risk their lives in order to preserve or even expand it. At this point, Weber abandons the careful distinctions he makes in his exposition of community formation. He does not examine the political community in respect either of its characteristics or of its meaning, but contents himself with describing indicators of cohesiveness that appear outdated even in the light of the stage of development reached by the industrialized European nation-states during Weber's lifetime, and which can best be explained by his susceptibility to German nationalism.

One must of course not forget that for all its plausibility, Weber's drawing up of clear categories rests on the construction of ideal types, which, as he himself recognizes, hardly correspond to reality. It is more realistic to start from an assumption of mixed types, which lead to an opaque interpenetration of community and society formation. The three groups of features serving to distinguish community formation will not be found in the pure form portrayed by Weber anywhere in reality, although this does not detract from the value of his systematization and the heuristic productiveness of his contrast between community and society formation.

The sociologist and philosopher Helmuth Plessner made a strongly critical intervention in the debate about community in 1924. Prompted by his concern about the growth of a sentimental youth movement appealing to the spirit of community and over the nihilistic contrast being drawn at that time between culture and civilization, and also by a lively debate about the relationship between politics and morality, Plessner considered that it was necessary to demonstrate as clearly as possible the limitations of the concept of community. Plessner takes the view that the recourse to community is an overreaction against the functionalism of societal relationships.

> The idol of community exercises its fascination on the weak: it is to be understood as the ideology of the excluded, the disappointed and the stalling of the proletariat, of the impoverished and of youth, a generation that has only just become aware of the chains that bind it; it is justified as the protest of those suffering under the modern metropolis, the machine age and social uprootedness. (Plessner 1981: 28)

This orientation to community is therefore born out of weakness, and it gives rise to a dangerous preparedness on the part of the weak to offer themselves as affectual sacrificial lambs to the plans of the unscrupulous and powerful, to dependence on authority and a susceptibility to doctrinal extremism that in the long run opens the door to a racial ideology with dangerous consequences. Plessner sees community as inescapably connected with the shaping of a male master race, the leadership principle and the preparedness to follow leaders unquestioningly (Plessner 1981: 43). In cases where no ties of blood exist, symbolic or spiritual rites and ties take their place. Affectual ties are raised to the level of 'love' for a community or within that community. Plessner unmasks this affectual bond as a sentimental attitude, which raises fragile identifications with individuals, groups, associations, or nations to the level of stable social relationships: "We have always been too generous in our use of the words brother, sister, comrade, people's community, human community; this generosity flatters our belief in our own capacity to love our fellow men, and exaggerates the ingenuity of our emotions" (Plessner 1981: 46). Those who think in this way fail to see that in fact, linking 'community' with 'love' serves to draw attention to a clear boundary beyond which community formation cannot go: "The prospects of a community being formed worsen as the probability of love declines, that is to say as the distance from individual reality increases" (Plessner 1981: 47). There are therefore good reasons why we should be extremely skeptical about heady talk of popular or national communities.

Plessner distances himself both from any understanding of community that characterizes a social a priori and from any sober description of social cohesion. His disapproval of 'community' is a radical one: the use of the term is for him nothing more than an irrational flight from social and political maturity toward the seductions of populistic authoritarianism and messianic ideology. Communities such as these abandon precisely those qualities, which, in Plessner's view, distinguish 'society' and prevent the reduction of social relations to the affectual: the structuring of social reality in a way that is rational, oriented toward the long term, rooted in tradition and concerned to ensure peaceful social relationships. The affective community orientation is nothing more than a social and political radicalism that descends into fundamentalist extremism (Plessner 1981: 14).

Plessner's critique is the harshest that has been formulated of the appeal to community, and it rejects both the social and political implications of community and the analytical use of the term in the social sciences. Plessner's severe verdict has affected the German-speaking world up to the present day, contributing to fundamental reservations about 'community' and a very hesitant analytical use of the term. Plessner clearly anticipated fatal political instrumentalizations that retrospectively justify his skepticism. The talk of 'people's community' during the National Socialist period and the appeal to the 'socialist people's community' in the official jargon of the German Democratic Republic were attempts to activate those affective attachments that Plessner clearly and reasonably rejected.

The affective attachment, which Weber had accepted as one neutral possibility for a stable structuring of social bonds, is turned by Plessner into an emotionally overloaded, irrational offensive against the operation, calculability, and peaceful structuring of social reality. Community might cause disastrous political developments. Plessner points to the highly problematic ideological roots of communal patterns that are played down in the sober categorization of their manifestations drawn up by Weber. This also entails a skeptical assessment of Tönnies' polarization between communal solidarity and cold social functionalism, which has to be considered in the application of 'community' in the analysis of global political problems.

A further important aspect of the discussion of community is revealed by the American social-scientific debate between 'liberals' and 'communitarians'. This debate directs our attention away from abstract normative discussion toward concrete social manifestations and their political implications. Although this discussion turns out to be a theoretical discourse, it refers concretely to the social and political characteristics of American society. This is particularly instructive because in American society, liberalism and community represent two traditional social principles that have over a long period existed in a relationship of tension with one another. The contribution of the American philosopher and social scientist Michael Walzer to that debate demonstrates how useful it can be for the critical discussion of community.

The U.S. debate differs from its German counterpart in that an uninhibited, mostly benevolent use of the key concept of community dominates in the United

States, both in analytical debates and political contexts. In the American tradition, 'community' has preserved the semantic vagueness that was lost in Germany because of the misuses identified by Plessner. The category can be used to refer neutrally to family structures, neighborhood relations, and local or regional attachments, as well as to affective bonds within particularistic groups or even the patriotic sentiment of a whole nation (see Joas 1993: 50). In the United States, the debate on community has always been closely related to the theory and practice of political liberalism; this also holds true for communitarianism. This tension can be traced back to the first European settlers who approved Christian ideals of fraternity through the affective appeal to community, but who also characterized local and regional authorities as rational and formalized contract 'communities'. The polarization between community and society has never been enforced and has been replaced by the pragmatic idea of the integration of affective and rational elements. At the beginning of the twentieth century, John Dewey shaped a catchy formula by interpreting the rational principles of democracy as the emanation of those traditional values that result from the communal life of individuals. Dewey focused this concept in the idea of the 'great community'. However, this concept was intended neither to introduce emotion into politics, nor to emphasize the local patriotism of independent communities. It simply reveals the desire to integrate the intended and non-intended results of collective action and autonomous spheres into a whole that seems to be reasonable from the perspective of the affected persons (Joas 1993: 61). The continuous activation of communal resources has to supplement the complex liberal construction of American society and its political institutions.

For contemporary American society, the diagnosis of a drying up of communal orientations in favor of an economic understanding of liberalism that is purely directed toward competition seems to be correct. This, at least, is the basic analytical insight of the communitarians. Walzer's position within the American debate on community is that of a liberal thinker who is sensitive to communitarian arguments. Walzer takes the view that contemporary American society is characterized by a loss of community in four major spheres of orientation that can be summarized under the notion of 'mobility'. What he means by this is a disintegrative mobility, caused by social structures, in the fields of geography, social organization, family life, and political attitudes (Walzer 1990: 11–12). Walzer takes up the communitarian concept in order to express regret, following Dewey's tradition, for the loss of communal orientations through enforced mobility. "The liberal state is not a home for its citizens; it lacks warmth and intimacy" (Walzer 1974: 606). American society is increasingly dominated by an egoistic individualism in which elements of solidarity are minimal.

However, the principle of community can be reactivated, and Walzer sees a possibility of introducing communal orientations into contemporary American society in spite of the dominance of mobility. In Walzer's perception, liberal society notoriously tends to restrict the development of community, but this only reflects traditional tensions between liberal principles and communal orientations. "It is a matter of principle that communities must always be at risk" (Walzer 1990: 20). Walzer emphasizes that communal orientation and communal faith are much more stable than laments about the decline of community would suggest. He considers ties of place, class or status, family, and even politics to be remarkably resistant to the disintegrative tendencies of mobility. This does not necessarily mean abandoning liberal principles and values, but rather correcting social and political individualism by a stronger supplementary consideration of communal bonds. Walzer defends a 'critical associationalism' (Walzer 1995: 25).

This does not tell us much about the composition or coherence of the community involved. At no point is Walzer as precise as Weber or Plessner. However, Walzer makes some clear and concrete remarks about the problem of the development of community in the macropolitical sphere. The larger the political unit, the more difficult seems to be the development of community, which is principally bound to small units, into a macropolitical principle (Walzer 1995: 17). Demands for macropolitical communal orientations frequently express totalitarian tendencies. Even patriotism, especially in connection with populism, might develop a dubious dynamic that threatens liberal principles and values (Walzer 1974: 607).

Through communitarian theory and Walzer's expositions of community, the concept acquires a greater degree of precision than in Weber's and Tönnies' analyses. Community cannot be developed apart from society, only within it. Within this framework, community is much more pragmatic than in the European analytical context, and it represents a social principle that—under the prevailing conditions of American society—must be balanced with the predominance of liberal principles and values. The recourse to the social capacity of affective attachment represents an indispensable element of the durability of large social groups. For Walzer, communitarianism and liberalism belong together. This concept appears to be realistic and plausible from the viewpoint of cultural theory (see also Brunkhorst 1996). However, it is very difficult to apply Walzer's concept to global political problems: here, the structural differentiation between 'community' and 'society' represents an initial attempt to remove precisely those analytical confusions, which, in the end, are confirmed by Walzer's integrative viewpoint.

PROBLEMS IN THE APPLICATION OF THE CONCEPT OF COMMUNITY

The perspective of the history of political ideas has revealed many controversial aspects of community, and the concept of community has provided considerable methodological stimulus to the analysis of the global network. But an analysis of contemporary global problems clearly requires more than a chronologically reappraised fund of political theory. A systematization of the different community concepts seems to be necessary, an examination of the possible fields of global political application and the analytical capacity of these concepts. The methodological variety of community concepts uncovered by my discussion of political theory must be focused, and explained with clear reference to possible fields of application. This systematization will make it easier to evaluate the methodological productivity of the concept of community.

Due to the overlapping circles and ambiguous processes of group formation in global politics, it remains *analytically* difficult to identify 'communities' and to evaluate their coherence. These difficulties will be plainly revealed in the following review of the fields of application. *Normatively* the problem arises of finding criteria for judging communities. When is community formation to be considered helpful for the solution of global political problems, and when should it be rejected?

These questions force us to examine more precisely the general goals of global political developments, because the hope that global politics will develop more 'communally' represents one element in the discussion of these goals. The difficult methodological problem here is that, conventionally, the goals of global politics are mostly described in terms of a positive concept of community even before the concept has been approved as normatively appropriate for such a characterization. The analytical difficulties revealed by my examination of political theory show that this positive evaluation is unjustified. Therefore, a brief review of the normative goals of global politics seems to be necessary.

Discussion of the purposes of global politics is often linked to the concept of 'order'. Order is required to diminish the dominance of unpredictability, contingency, arbitrariness, aggression, and competitive claims in international relations. Order strengthens community orientations (Bull 1977). Order is to be preferred to chaos; thus it is in the interests of all relevant global actors, and of social scientists and their scholarly ethos, to direct their efforts toward the possible identification and affirmation of order and community formation. Another analytical concept of value in the clarification of global political purposes is 'integration'. However, integration revolves around the relationship between dependent and independent variables. Karl W. Deutsch and Amitai Etzioni used the concept as long ago as the 1960s in order to evaluate flows of communication and interaction in global politics (see also Deutsch 1968; Etzioni 1962; as a survey and critique Fisher 1969; Zimmerling 1991). The concept of integration describes continuous developments and characterizes the increasing density of communication and interaction at all levels of globalization as a process of community formation. Integration leads to a kind of 'transnational assimilation' which is called 'community'. This community represents a very general normative orientation that can be projected onto all social, economic, and political aspects of globalization. All possible flows of communication and interaction have the potential to shape integration and community; the characterization of community by placing emphasis on its fixed specificity no longer seems to be possible, and even integrative elements of world *society* might become constituent elements of a world *community*.

This positive relationship between global politics and community fails to take account of all the normative reservations about community reviewed above. If community means nothing more than affective susceptibility to the requirements of group behavior, it cannot take on a positive role with regard to order, stabilization, and integration at the level of global politics. Community should not simply be incorporated into the positive normative purposes of global politics. We should first of all examine critically the conditions under which the term can be accepted as a plausible normative element of global politics. A more general classification system is required so that we can distinguish between the integrative and disintegrative effects of community building. For this task, the concept of *democracy* seems to be appropriate.

It is no accident that numerous studies of political globalization call for the development and institutionalization of democracy. The key concept of 'democracy' focuses a whole set of normatively fruitful, reasonable values aimed objectively toward the peaceful, integrative stability of a global network and subjectively toward broad public consent and the preparedness to identify with those values. 'Democracy' means the acknowledgment of popular sovereignty with regard to the constitutional political unit, equality and freedom, submission of all political power and institution building to the people's will, and a guarantee of participation in and control over all political decision-making. Although some traditional elements of democracy might not occur or cannot be identified at the level of global politics, the concept nevertheless helps us to classify plausibly the purposes of political community formation in the global network. Practical political community formation can be subordinated to a normative evaluation with regard to democracy, and can thus be assessed in respect of its global political capabilities (see also Archibugi and Held 1995).

The understandable misgivings about democracy as a reference point, which stem largely from the dubious forms it has taken in European modernity, have to be considered here (see also Greven 1993). This should prevent us from jumping to the hasty conclusion that each social or political group that appeals to democracy must necessarily be characterized as a community; it should also prevent us from rejecting normatively, from the point of view of global politics, any community that cannot be traced back to democratic ideals.

We must also take into consideration the fact that democracy does not necessarily refer to an existing or conceptional uniform 'collectivity' of global politics. It might equally well be conceptualized as a combination of particular democratic institutions and procedures, which seems to be much more appropriate considering the 'denationalization' of global politics (Zürn 1998). The autonomy of small communities does not represent a threat to the congruence of global politics with democracy if the global network of those particular autonomous communities on the whole strengthens democracy. To the contrary, it might reasonably be argued that democracy is better served by the subsidiarity concept of the greatest autonomy of small units than by the concept of a homogeneous global unity. To some authors, such a principle of global political democracy seems to be the only appropriate concept of contemporary democracy:

> The problem of democracy in our times is to specify how the principle of autonomy can be enshrined and secured in a series of interconnected power and authority centres. For if one chooses democracy today, one must choose not only to operationalize a radical system of rights but also to do this in a complex, intergovernmental and transnational power structure. (Held 1991b: 165)

With the help of this concept of democracy, a plausible global political classification system for the characterization of community formation in the global network can be established: does a specific case of community formation further the concept of democracy generally or in particular areas, is it indifferent to democracy, or does it even aim at the violation or destruction of democracy? The methodological challenge of the combination of 'global politics' with 'community' lies in the exploration of specific conditions in which community formation can have positive effects on global politics.

With the help of the key term 'democracy', many of the concepts of community examined above can be set aside as meaningless in the global political context: namely, those concepts of community that exclusively characterize an abstract social principle. A community concept that only describes the insurmountable embedding of man in social perception and social reality is not close enough to reality to be applicable in the global context. Neither Kant's account of the foundations of experience and the origins of aesthetic judgments nor Tönnies' organic determinism, with its derivation of community from the physical disposition of each individual, can be regarded as an element of community that is decisive for global politics.

The attempt to adapt the concept to reality could only go as far as to elevate the abstract social principle to a normative reason for the development of 'global solidarity'. However, this would do no more than begin to raise questions linked to global politics, questions that would relate to the composition of this solidarity rather than to the plausibility of social determinism. Even if we assume that democracy is bound to a fundamental human social disposition, this provides no criteria according to which we could measure the conformity to democracy of actual social and political groups, because numerous other elements determine the effectiveness of democracy. Thus, a 'communal' attitude that accepts an abstract social principle could be characterized by social disrespect, aggression, and disintegration—because other concrete political attitudes obscure the abstract social determinism. Islamic fundamentalism seems to confirm this argument: it acknowledges the social determinism of human existence and appeals to 'homo politicus', but at the same time it challenges the justification of Western culture by means of an aggressive claim to exclusive global recognition (Tibi 1995: 29, 41). As we have seen, Plessner was well aware of how easily community can be used for purposes of concrete political instrumentalization.

In close affinity to the sociological version of the abstract social principle, there exists another basic philosophical concept that is also extremely relevant for communities in global politics: the principle of universalism. Justifying universalism means testing to see whether specific norms are valid for all human beings in any context regardless of space and time—'quod semper, quod ubique, quod omnibus' (see also Tönnies 1995: 15). The abstract social principle is adopted to the extent that both principles have to reflect in the same way on the reasonable combination of individual existence with the undifferentiated totality of all human beings; however, the test of universalizability is implemented as a formal justification of individual norms, not as an anthropological reflection on social determinism. Although the test of universalizability seems at first to be even more general than the abstract social principle, it nevertheless becomes more important politically because it aims at the constitution of man with individual rights and thus is promoted as a critical standard for real political power. The strengthening of the global network gives the test of universalizability even greater relevance: its omnipresence is simply equated with globalism, which thereby erroneously loses its contextuality. The test of universalizability is raised to the status of a sufficient principle for the justification of global political norms: correspondingly, the particularistic orientation of a community that is in accordance with the test of universalizability and can thus be extended to all human collectivities could be applied to each sector of the human collectivity that is represented by contemporary global society.

This projection of universalism onto global politics is reductive and not as harmless as it appears. In Western societies there is a growing suspicion—set off by doubts in non-European societies—that, although universalism seems to be a formal principle of generalization, it is nevertheless characterized by specific concepts of generalization that vary according to their social origins. The concept of an abstract social principle is, to some extent, applied to the test of universalizability itself, and this reduces its credibility. If all human experiences and ideas have a specific social origin, then the principle of universalism must have its specific roots as well.

It is unsurprising, therefore, that the test of universalizability as a classification system for particularistic values is being viewed with increasing skepticism. It turns out to be a typical 'Western' belief in the possibility of treating values formally, and one that stands squarely in the tradition of the European Enlightenment. Even 'classical' universal concepts like the idea of human rights are falling into disrepute because of their general claim to legal force. Such concepts seem to reveal the dominance of traditional European ideas about a balanced relationship between individual and public power, which can by no means be treated as common to all cultural areas, and to suggest the untenable idea of a general ethical consensus on human rights that embraces the whole earth (Nuscheler 1995: 200). The concept of the test of universalizability is based on a moral subject that only formally decides about ethical problems, an attitude that has been correctly classified as a reduction of man to a purely rational nature (Kondylis 1992: 110 ff). In Western societies, universalism has turned into a rational substitute for the intuitive justification of norms and affective social relations; it is thus opposed to the constitutional characteristics of communities. Even Tönnies regarded the legal and political rationality of universalism as a 'social' advantage in comparison to purely communal social bonds (Tönnies 1972: 212). A particularistic community based on universal norms would represent a successful combination of affective attachment and rational legal relations without exclusive validity. However, the contemporary models of a 'discourse ethics' argue against any affective cohesion and proclaim the model of a necessarily 'universal understanding' among all individuals, which is rational and 'common' at the same time: the normative ideal of a 'community of communication' (*Kommunikationsgemeinschaft*, see also Apel 1988, Habermas 1981, 1983). In any way, the reality of global politics raises the tension between universalism and community to an analytical challenge. This point will be taken up again later in connection with the notion of 'particularity'.

The legitimate critique of the test of universalizability by no means compels us to relinquish it as a normative classification system for the concept of community in global politics. Rather, Hegel's reservations about 'community' can be developed as a critical tool for the clarification of the unreflected premises of the test. Following Hegel's argument that 'community' only represents the accidental, not the general, the test of universalizability should accept the skeptical suspicion that a formalistically disguised cultural relativism is involved rather than an abstract generalization independent of all practical considerations. In accordance with this skeptical position, particularistic norms of communities can be evaluated in terms of their global political potential. Can the normative characteristics of a specific community coexist with other norms? Can they be made valid for everybody in every context? Which alternative norms are excluded by those of that particular community? Is it reasonable to extend the particularistic norms beyond limited contexts of realization toward an abstract principle of validity? Finally, the inclusion of the question of democracy can provide some guidance on whether particularistic norms can be generalized in political contexts. Is this particular communal orientation helpful for the realization of democracy outside the limited scope of its own constitution? Can democratic norms be identified in this community that might attain global political relevance? The example of the reappearance of small scale nationalism in different parts of the world underlines the relevance of these questions. The application of the test of universalizability and the question of whether national communal orientations can be extended toward a democratic principle of nationalism that can be globally applied facilitates the critical assessment of the claim made by these orientations to general validity beyond particularistic contexts.

The fundamental tensions between universalism and community suggest that it may be productive to reverse our analytical perspective and raise the question of the legitimacy of *particularism*. Walzer emphasizes that the formation of communities is restricted to small units, and so he does not consider the possibility of a world community based on universal values. Can community only be developed in functionally comprehensive and geographically small contexts? What about coexistence between these particularistic communities? Can a particularistic communal orientation be helpful for the development of general democratic ideas?

If the claims to validity made on behalf of particularistic communal values and global political democratic concepts were mutually exclusive, the normative implications of these questions could be disregarded: either a world community would exist, or the particularism of strategic interests and instrumentalized actions would have to be accepted. Because such a polarization cannot be perceived at first sight, the overlaps and borderline cases deserve more detailed consideration. The relevance of the question of particularism can be deduced from the fact that, in spite of the intensification of globalization, cultural divergences between the different areas of the world are growing and it is difficult to assess whether this reflects peaceful coexistence between communities or latent hostility. This situation is analytically difficult to deal with and potentially explosive in social and political terms. Samuel Huntington has focused this anxiety about latent aggression in his scenario of a 'clash of civilizations'. He sees a danger of territorial conflicts between small ethnic groups, and also of nation-states in different cultural areas developing aggressive foreign policies toward one another (Huntington 1996; see also Senghaas 1995: 207). Cultural relativism and its political implications correspond to the historical findings of cultural theory: it seems to be extremely difficult to develop values and norms that transcend the limitations of a specific cultural areas and that match those of other areas. The preeminent position of diverging religious beliefs as a characterization of specific cultural areas demonstrates the political difficulties of regarding a general religious belief, in the sense of an ecumenical 'global ethos', as a generally accepted normative consensus between particularistic communities (see also Küng 1990).

Particularism therefore raises the question of the possibility of democratic coexistence between particularistic communities belonging to different cultural areas. In view of the serious ethnic conflicts that can be observed in all parts of the world, the claim to communal orientation would seem to have a good deal to answer for. But regardless of these political difficulties, the attempt should be made to distill a classification system for 'community' from this problematic global political situation.

The problems of particularism that I have outlined lead us to the question of how communities handle their genuine characteristics of inclusion and exclusion. Weber connects this question with the 'reason' of a community and emphasizes the necessity for that community to differentiate itself from other external communities as well as the need to be prepared for peaceful coexistence with other communities—which he regards as a reasonable characteristic of community itself. Global political problems demonstrate the relevance of two aspects of the assessment of communities: the degrees of inclusion and exclusion, and the relationship between inclusion and exclusion.

Degrees of inclusion and exclusion should be discussed in terms of how intense they need to be in order to identify communities in the context of global politics. Weber addresses this problem by distinguishing between different stages of coherence, which he interprets as specific levels of 'emotional attachment'. A community can sometimes be reduced to a latent traditional element, scarcely coherent and unstable, so that it has no relevance for global politics. However, such a low level of emotional attachment can be succeeded by a reactivation of coherence and thus can at once confer global political importance on the community. Communities based on religious beliefs, ethnic homogeneity, or ideological concepts often exist at a low level of coherence that can, if necessary, be transformed into close affective coherence. The shifting political relevance of religious beliefs and their associated political images demonstrate how quickly and with what far-reaching consequences the coherence of a community can be transformed.

The characteristics of the self-understanding and the clarity of aims of a community are another, closely related element in the analysis and assessment of these degrees of coherence. 'Contingency' and 'teleology' mark the spectrum of possible characteristics. A community can arise from such a high level of affective spontaneity that its continuity comes to depend on random conditions. Such a community will be judged as having a low level of coherence. On the other hand, a community might be based on such an intense degree of strategic rationality that it acquires a teleological validity, which deliberately brings a high level of coherence into play. The common interests of the victims of spillage from an oil tanker might turn into communal coherence among those affected; this, however, has arisen accidentally and will only exist as long as the damage remains perceptible. Such coherence will hardly reach such a degree of intensity that its 'reason' acquires global political relevance, although this is conceivable, for instance in the form of a legitimate demand for a worldwide coordinated system for supervising the sea lanes, preventing accidents, or restricting the damage caused by such accidents. In quite a different way, an institution like Amnesty International rests on a communal attachment that draws on intense personal engagement opposed to political injustice and can attain the affective strength of a community. Its political project is based on a rational definition of instruments and aims, and uses rational strategies in an attempt to reach a global political goal: the ostracism and prevention of politically generated injustice by means of personal engagement and public pressure.

The problems of how the members of a community perceive their membership have also to be subsumed under the aspects of contingency and teleology. The affective attachment can be so dominated by tradition or ideology that the individual members are no longer conscious of the constitutional reason of a community. In this case, reservations arise with regard to the group's tendency to be seduced by communal orientations, which is what led Plessner to reject on principle the concept of community. However, even rational reflection about membership does not provide any guarantee against ideological misuse. Certainly, a higher degree of rationality facilitates the analytical classification of the community in question. But the mere fact of belonging to Western culture, with its dominant position in the global economy, does not represent a sufficient indication that any particular individual shares a communal orientation, which makes a dubious claim to global power.

The 'reason' of a community in relation to global political problems is closely related to the intensity of attachment of that community. On a spectrum from 'contextuality' to 'abstraction', many grades of concreteness of this basic reason are possible. An ideological movement, which campaigns for the strengthening of parliamentary principles in all parts of the world is from the start closely concerned with global political problems. A small ethnic group, on the other hand, is far removed from global political issues—as long as its coherence does not develop into an international problem touching on the defence of minority rights. It is also conceivable that the global contextuality only results from a sort of summation of different basic 'reasons' that do not individually pertain to global politics. Such a contextuality would produce a communal orientation through global uniformity. In the field of global environmental problems and through the strong political engagement of numerous interest groups, a new communal orientation arises, which results from the accumulation of individual actions and from the identification of individuals with the group ideology and the global relevance that arises. Only this 'deliberate' affiliation produces the 'reason' of a community. Thus, the genesis of 'epistemic communities' in the sphere of environmental protection can be explained: a 'transnational network of specialists' produces scientific knowledge and access to specialists' 'know how' that is open to all environmental movements. "Epistemic communities are likely to be found in substantive issues where scientific disciplines have been applied to policy-oriented work [...]" (Haas 1993a: 187). The 'ecological epistemic community' shapes global political contextuality and provides the engaged participants with the coherence of a global political communal orientation—the transnationality of the movement for the protection of the global environment.

At each level of coherence, we have to ask how the specific community handles the necessary elements of inclusion and exclusion. In the global network, the problem arises of the relationship between cutting oneself off and opening up, between being prepared to coexist and an exclusive claim to validity. In social groups, 'strong' and 'soft' states of inclusion and exclusion can be identified. In a 'strong' state, the characteristics of inclusion can be clearly distinguished from the characteristics of exclusion. In this case, inclusion incorporates strict selection procedures for membership and demanding criteria for its maintenance. The characteristics of exclusion are shaped accordingly: open or hidden hostility to nonmembers, strict and enduring barriers designed to keep these out, and controls and selection with regard to communication with the outside world. Democratic values cannot be integrated into such a polarization between inclusion and exclusion. The normative deficits of such a community are clear, but this does seem to be a realistic description of a projected future 'clash of civilizations' scenario. In conditions of such segregatory particularism, the appeal to 'community' turns into an explosive charge threatening peaceful global coexistence.

'Soft' states of inclusion are characterized by less formalization and low thresholds for membership, and variable requirements for the maintenance of the communal orientation. Correspondingly, the general awareness of the modes of exclusion is weak. This sort of relationship expresses a kind of coherence of individual communities that is politically adaptable rather than aggressively restrictive. In view of global cultural divergences, such a differentiation is often regarded as an appropriate foundation for contemporary concepts of democracy; democratic values cannot be implemented through a striving for global identity of interests, but only through the democratic resolution of normative and political conflicts between groups with 'communal' orientations (Dubiel 1994: 113 ff). Communities blur the strict distinction between inclusion and exclusion if they do not turn the inner need for homogeneity into an outward demarcation, and so permit 'differences'. This kind of community is therefore much more appropriate to the characteristics and problems of the global network than a segregational particularism.

The relationship between inclusion and exclusion raises specific problems at the level of global politics, because the communal orientation of large groups necessitates sharp demarcations, which are themselves opposed to the demand for democracy as the normative classification system for global political community. In general terms, greater coherence at the macropolitical level will impede basic democratic structures, because it is generated through appeals and is accompanied by pressure for conformity. The price of inclusion, as an enduring principle that can be clearly assessed, is an evident and usually codified exclusion. Taking into consideration all these problems of inclusion and exclusion, the normative demands of a community can be characterized as the need to level the exclusive homogeneity of a particularistic community with the inclusive strive to recognize other communities' orientations. This task consists of an "un-levelling and un-impounding inclusion of the other in his or her distinction" (Habermas 1996: 58).

CONCLUSION

This chapter has demonstrated that the concept of community has many facets, both in its general use and in its concrete applications. All in all it seems to be necessary to connect the assessment of community to a systematic analysis drawn up on the basis of a consideration of political theory. Has 'community' as a characteristic of groups any global political significance? Is 'community', due to its variety and contested nature, meaningless as a normatively demanding action principle in the global network?

'Community', despite the numerous different understandings of the term that can be identified within political theory from Kant to Walzer, clearly provides a focus for analysis of different degrees of social coherence. As a contrast to 'society' as a term describing rational, anonymous coherence in large social groups, community aims at affective attachment that develops in a comprehensive, reasonable setting. The difficult implementation problems that arise require a clear analysis for the purpose of identifying and systematizing 'communities'.

The question then arises of how communities can be evaluated, especially in the complex field of global politics. An investigation of political theory reveals that the assessment of communal coherence is extremely variable and dependent on historical context. In terms of normative democratic ideas, community sometimes seems to represent a unilateral claim to validity and influence and a basic attack on the political development of freedom and equality—and, consequently, of *democracy*. Sometimes it seems to represent the necessary social foundation of all forms of political bargaining and thus an indispensable element of the realization of democratic ideals. Its classification in the field of global politics is extremely difficult. Although globalization is advancing rapidly in all spheres of social life, there is no comparable homogenization of or adaption to democratic ideals like freedom and equality. World society is turning out to be not a symbol of Kant's peaceful cosmopolitanism, but a disparate, fragmented, and hierarchical interdependence between individuals, social groups, and states—a "stratified world society" (Habermas 1995: 306). Instead of homogeneity, we are seeing the advance of segmentation, segregation, and domination. In view of the dominant role of economic actors in the process of globalization, a description in terms of the 'world market' would seem to be much more precise than one employing the concept of community. Although the term is a rather awkward one, we could speak of a 'dissociative social attachment'—the production of inequality lies at the the social core of the processes of transnationalization (Narr and Schubert 1994: 43, 162). Against this background, talk of a—normatively demanding—*global community* seems to be rather far from the mark. Even the contribution of fragmented communities to global democracy has to be skeptically analyzed and needs to be examined in each individual case. However, processes of fragmentation bring up the necessity to critically assess the inclusive and exclusive characteristics of globalization and thus stimulate new insights into the democratic potential of globalization (Beck 1997: 188; Richter 1997). A variegated and largely unexplored field for research is opening up here.

The concept of community is gaining in influence in the social sciences, but this is happening hesitantly and unsystematically. The need for further work is clear, but it is difficult to say what path this work will take. I have shown in this chapter that there are certainly possibilities for systematic classification that encourage us to deal analytically and normatively with 'community' and 'communal orientations'. Classification systems can be developed along the axes of universalism and particularism, inclusion and exclusion, contingency and teleology, contextuality and abstraction, all of which open up possibilities for the systematic analysis of these terms. With the help of these classifications, even such an enigmatic concept as 'world community' can be critically analyzed.

Dubious though the concept of community may seem as a classification system and a normative element of global politics, it has nevertheless been introduced here as a key concept for the characterization and assessment of degrees of political coherence in the global network. This represents a challenge for further research. The concept of community has the potential to be able to help in the classification of coherence in global politics; community can also, if related to democratic ideals, be of value in the normative assessment of coherence in the global network. The methodological remarks made in this chapter seek to make clearer the analytical usefulness of community and to contribute to a more systematic application of the term.

5

The 'English School': International Theory and International Society

Chris Brown

From the perspective of a particular kind of international theorizing, foundational questions about the nature of international society are a central concern. "Does the collectivity of sovereign states constitute a political society or system, or does it not?" is, according to Hedley Bull, the first of a series of questions that, taken together, constitute 'Classical' international relations theory and distinguish it from the 'Scientific' approach to the subject (Bull 1969). Similar sentiments could be drawn readily from the work of the other authors whose writings collectively make up the International Theory, or International Society, or 'English School' approach to international relations theory. I have argued elsewhere that there are reasons why this emphasis on international society is mistaken (Brown 1992b, 1993). To cut a long story short, the burden of the argument is that an approach that places primary emphasis on the nature of *international* society is likely to isolate itself from the wider discourses of political and social philosophy in ways that cannot be defended in terms of any alleged *sui generis* features of international relations. Rather, international relations theory is best understood as an aspect of political theory and not as a discourse with its own rules and subject matter. The purpose of this article is to sketch the outlines of an examination of international society that would be less tied to traditional categories and in closer contact with broader movements in social thought.[1]

The primary concern of this chapter is with characterizations of international order, and, to this end a number of connected arguments and propositions are set out. First, international *society* is identified as occupying the middle position of a triptych, the other two elements of which are *system* and *community*. Next, it is examined whether international society as a 'middle way' between system and community is to be understood as a 'happy medium' to be defended in its own terms, or as a 'second best', defensible only because no better international order is on offer. Cases can be made for both these characterizations—the argument forks and there are, in effect, two quite different justifications for the notion of international society. However, and finally, it seems that whichever fork of the road is taken, the route to an international society is far less straightforward than the international theory tradition suggests; the viability of the middle way is open to serious question, and it may be that 'international society' is a conception of international order that is only available under very limited circumstances.

SYSTEM, SOCIETY, COMMUNITY

International relations theory is bedevilled by neologisms, and—worse—by the use of terms in ways that are subtly, or, in some cases, radically, different from the usages employed by other branches of social philosophy; hence an article of this nature always has to begin by stipulating meanings, rather than by adopting a currently dominant vocabulary. Thus, first, *international order* is taken to be a neutral term that encompasses any characterization of the total complex of relationships that are, provisionally, to be understood as 'international'—the only baggage to be carried by the term order is the assumption that these relationships are not random; they may be anarchic in the sense of 'nongoverned' but the use of the term 'order' conveys the idea that they are not anarchic in the sense of chaotic. There are regularities and these rest on some kind of rules; the different conceptions of international order outlined below rest on different conceptions of these rules.

One conception of order suggests that whatever rules and regularities exist in the world are the product solely of an interplay of forces and devoid of any kind of normative content. This account of international order is here characterised as a *system*. One version of this kind of order, associated with neo-Marxist, 'dependency theorists' such as Immanuel Wallerstein, works in terms of a 'world system' in which the forces are socio-politico-economic, and the components states and classes (Wallerstein 1974). However, in mainstream international relations the most influential account of an international system is that of neorealism or 'structural realism'. Order here is understood as the product of a balance of power, in turn understood as systemic in origin, rather than as the product of the intentions and wishes of diplomats.[2] This fits the stipulated definition by attempting to exclude any kind of normative component of world order—except possibly the sort of norms that might emerge after order is established by the balancing process.[3]

The polar opposite of an international system is a world *community*. The nature of 'community' is heavily contested, but at the center of the concept is the idea that whatever order exists in a community is normatively grounded, based on relationships that constitute a network of mutual claims, rights, duties, and obligations that pull people together in ways that are qualitatively different from the impersonal forces that create a system (Brown 1995). Community implies the idea of common interests and, at least an emerging, common identity. The notion of community on a world scale implies a cosmopolitan belief in the oneness of humanity, a belief that might find expression in the structures of a world government, or might be incorporated in an account of obligations compatible with a range of institutional schemes short of world government.[4] What is central is the idea of unity based on notions of fellow feeling, a resistance to social forces — and ideas — which divide loyalties and weaken the sense of a common humanity, and a refusal to see order as something that emerges simply from the interplay of countervailing forces.

Society emerges in contrast to both community and system. Social philosophy since Tönnies and Maine (if not before) makes a clear contrast between *Gesellschaft* [society] and *Gemeinschaft* [community] where the former is an association that lacks the affective unity of the latter. Society is a norm-governed form of association, but the norms in question emerge out of the requirements for social cooperation and do not necessarily require commitment to any common projects, common interests, or common identity beyond what is required for social coexistence. On the other hand, societies are norm governed, and as such differ from systems as that term is defined above. The norms that underlie cooperation in society may be limited, but they do exist, and whatever cooperation could exist in the absence of such norms would not justify the qualifier 'social'.

Out of these two contrasts a picture of international society can be made to emerge. An international *society* differs from an international *system* because it is a form of order that is normatively based, and not simply the outcome of an interplay of forces. On the other hand, in common with neorealist theorists of international systems, and in opposition to the idea of a world community, theorists of international society assume that states are the primary members of this form of association. Both system and society in their international usages are 'state-centric' in their terms of reference.[5] The point is that the latter envisages a world of states that is partly normatively governed, the former does not. Further, the norms that constitute international *society* are different from those that would constitute a world *community*. They are essentially the norms that are required for the successful pursuit of peaceful coexistence by states, whereas the norms involved in world community are neither limited to those of coexistence, nor restricted in their application to inter*state* relations.

Two preliminaries remain; how is international society distinguished from Burtonian *World Society*, and what is the relationship between the theory of international society and *neoliberal institutionalism (neoliberalism)*? The first of these questions is relatively straightforward. When John Burton uses the term world society, he has in mind an essentially empirical account of interlocking systems of social action, overlaid maps of interaction in which the state ('administrative system' in his terminology) disappears and which together create the famous 'cobweb model' of world society.[6] This world picture is much more compatible with ideas of world community than with international society; however, Burtonian thought lacks the normative dimension common to both these latter approaches. Indeed, Burton's positivism has, in recent years, pushed him in the direction of sociobiology and the more scientific end of 'needs' theory precisely in order to expel normative questions.[7]

More interesting, and certainly more significant, is the relationship between the theory of international society and neoliberalism—which of course is, along with neorealism, one of the two major branches of orthodox U.S. International Relations theory. Unlike Burtonians, neoliberals actually stress norms, and indeed, on occasion, refer to a 'Grotian' tradition of regime analysis, thereby touching base with some international society theorists.[8] However, the correspondence is, I feel, limited. Neoliberals share with neorealists the assumptions of anarchy and rational egoism; they focus on the 'tragedy of the commons' and their point is that the tendency of states toward self-destructive behaviour can be tempered by norms of reciprocity that emerge out of cooperation in institutions. The problem is that they generate only a very thin notion of norms—much thinner than is to be found in the international society tradition—because only a thin notion of norms is compatible with the assumption of rational egoism.[9] In effect, neoliberals are trying to solve problems of cooperation set up on Hobbesian lines but without resort to a Hobbesian sovereign—which as neorealists are fond of pointing out, correctly in this case, will not do. Rational egoists will only behave in accordance with norms of reciprocity if it is in their interests to do so; however, it is precisely at the point at which self-interest cannot be relied on to prevent cheating to achieve short-run advantage that norms become important. In effect, neoliberals are optimistic—and rather less rigorous—neorealists, and, in the terms of this chapter, theorists of the international *system*.

THE DESIRABILITY OF INTERNATIONAL SOCIETY

Although international society has been described as the middle term in the triptych 'system, society, community', it is not intended to suggest that there is here necessarily a progression—clearly this is not how all theorists of international society have seen the matter. Two generalizations are common to such theorists: first, it is generally agreed that an international system—that is, to reiterate, a form of order effectively devoid of norms—is not a desirable version of international order nor, probably, is it sustainable for more than short periods of time.[10] Second, it is generally agreed that a world community is an unattainable version of international order given current circumstances and, for that matter, any plausible variation on current circumstances. However, what is not agreed is whether this latter point should be seen as a matter of regret. One approach suggests that world community is not simply unattainable but would also be undesirable; on this count international society is to be valued in its own terms. But a second, minority, approach disagrees and holds that international society is a 'second-best' form of international order, an incomplete realisation of our common humanity that is defensible solely on pragmatic grounds, as the only available alternative to the moral wasteland of a purely systemic approach.[11] Later the international society approach will be considered as a whole, but it may be helpful in the meantime to outline some of the arguments deployed in support of these two different conceptions of the moral significance of international society.[12]

Those who see international society as a desirable endstate are probably the majority amongst international theorists. The bare bones of their argument were articulated in the eighteenth century when the (international) world was young. An international society preserves the independence of its members, the 'liberties of Europe', in a way that a single community would not, but it allows for such 'difference' to exist within a common civilization, whereas a purely power-generated order would destroy that civilization (Vincent 1984; Welsh 1995).[13] Amongst moderns, Bull in *The Anarchical Society* adopts a similar position, but the most convincing defence of international society as a desirable state of affairs in its own terms is that of Terry Nardin in *Law, Morality, and the Relations of Nations* (1983).

Nardin's approach is based on a distinction elaborated by Michael Oakeshott in *On Human Conduct* (1975). Oakeshott distinguishes between 'enterprise' association and 'civil' association. The former brings individuals together in the pursuit of common interests, is essentially voluntary, and, according to Oakeshott, nonpolitical; the latter is concerned with laying down the terms for the general arrangements of a society, is not voluntary, and is the only true form of political association. Nardin takes from this the idea that civil association is the only form of association compatible with freedom of the individual, and translates this into an account of an international society that guarantees the individuality of the states of which it is composed. Enterprise association becomes 'purposive' association, and civil association becomes 'practical' association, where practices are standards of conduct "considerations to be taken into account in deciding and acting, and in evaluating decisions and actions" (Nardin 1983: 6) and a practical association is built solely around such common standards of conduct, and not around the pursuit of substantive goals.

The value of practical association is that it both reflects and promotes the pluralism characteristic of the modern world. The practical association of international society is "an association of independent and diverse political communities, each devoted to its own ends and its own conception of the good" (Nardin 1983: 19). There is no reason why these diverse communities should be expected to agree on any kind of substantive common purpose, but it can be expected that they will agree on certain common practices that will allow them to co-exist, and relate to each other peacefully, securely, and with justice.[14] These practices are those embedded in the institutions of diplomacy and customary international law—respect for sovereign equality, non-intervention, *pacta sunt servanda*, diplomatic immunity, and so on. It is not within the competence of individual states to reject these practices; in effect they define what a state is—and in any event, there is, Nardin suggests, no reason why any state would want to reject them. Obviously it would be possible to say much more about this approach (Chris Brown 1988); for the time being it suffices to summarize that for Nardin international society as a practical association is an attainable form of international order that is desirable in its own terms, and in no sense a 'second best' option. This is the central position of the international society approach to international relations theory, and Nardin is one of its best modern representatives.

There is, however, an approach to international society that does see this form of international order as a second best. This approach is certainly less prominent than the alternative and less easy to associate with particular, significant, writers, but it does exist. Indeed, arguably, it can be found in the work of at least two very famous names—Immanuel Kant and Martin Wight. This characterization of Kant is doubly problematic; some would say that he is not a theorist of international society,[15] while those who do see him in this way might well resist the idea that he saw international society as a second best. However, both propositions are defensible. As to the first, neither in the Provisional nor in the Definitive Articles of a *Perpetual Peace* does Kant envisage the formation of a world government (Kant 1970). In the world envisaged by the Definitive Articles, members of the 'Pacific Union' are states, and the restrictions placed on them—essentially to avoid going to war with one another—are compatible with the pluralism of an international society. Although this pluralism is somewhat undermined by the First Definitive Article, which requires a Republican constitution, this provision does not of itself signal the establishment of a world community. Equally, Kant's requirements vis-à-vis Cosmopolitan Right in the Third Article are not very demanding, constituting no more than a right of refuge.

More to the point, there are quite good reasons to think that Kant did not regard even the Definitive Articles as more than a second-best approach to international order. His thinking is partially driven by the desire to abolish war, and since it would seem that the obvious solution to this problem would be to create a world republic, it is interesting to examine why in *Perpetual Peace* Kant does not go down this route. The main, albeit rather tangled, reference here is to his discussion of the Second Definitive Article establishing a 'Federation of Free States'—actually a treaty rather than a federation in the modern meaning of the term (Kant 1970: 103 ff). In this text he examines all the reasons why the present order is intolerable and why states should renounce their independence, but then concludes: "But since this is not the will of the nations, according to their present conception of international right (so that they deny *in hypothesi* what is true *in thesi*), the positive idea of a *world republic* cannot be realized" (Kant 1970: 105).[16] It seems clear that Kant here is acknowledging that his so-called Federation is only a second-best solution to the problem of international order.[17]

The identification of Martin Wight as a theorist of international society as a 'second best' is rather more tentative. It is grounded in the first place on what is known of Wight's religious convictions—the Christian pacifism that led him to be a conscientious objector in the Second World War. It seems plausible to assert an a priori case for saying that someone with such views would be likely to be supportive of some notion of a world community and to regard the limited normative base of an international society with suspicion—although, of course, as a believer in Original Sin, Wight would have denied that a fully functioning Christian World Community would be a possibility in this sphere of existence.[18] It is difficult to be sure that this a priori position is confirmed in his writings because he is an author whose convictions are notoriously elusive in his texts, but there do seem to be one or two points at which a sense of the 'second-bestness' of international society come through. The ending of *Power Politics* is articulately relevant here; citing Julien Benda to the effect that "mankind has always betrayed its obligations, but so long as it continues to acknowledge and believe in them, the crack is kept open through which civilisation can creep," he continues. "Powers will continue to seek security without reference to justice, and to pursue their vital interests irrespective of common interests, but in the fraction that they may be deflected lies the difference between the jungle and the traditions of Europe" (Wight 1978: 293).[19] This looks very much like a resigned acceptance that some kind of international society is the best we can hope for in the current circumstances, given our inability to achieve any deeper commitment between and among the 'powers'.

The aim in this section has been to show that a generally agreed upon notion of what international society might entail is compatible with two quite different *evaluations* of the concept. On the one hand, international society could be seen as a desirable form of international order, more in keeping with the essentially pluralist nature of the modern world than a world community would be, even if the latter could be achieved, which is not possible. On the other hand, the same international society, with the same institutions, could be seen as a very shabby, incomplete and unsatisfactory form of international order, tolerable only because no better form is attainable. These positions clearly share the view that community is not attainable—but they also share the view that society is, that it is actually possible to see international order as normatively based whether at satisfactory level or not, that some move beyond the moral wasteland of an international system is a possibility. It is this common view that will be examined in the next section of this chapter.

THE VIABILITY OF INTERNATIONAL SOCIETY

Both versions of the case for international society believe that it is an attainable, not-utopian goal, but there is an interesting difference in the way in which adherents of the two approaches—for the sake of convenience let them be called the 'pluralists' and the 'second-besters'—set up the argument. Pluralists see the institutions of international society as possessing an appeal that is universal; according to Nardin, only those who do not want to live in peace-with-justice could rationally reject the terms of practical association, and his assumption is that virtually no state will fall into this category for more than the briefest of revolutionary moments (Nardin 1983: chap. 12). Second-besters seem to be less sure of this. Kant's version of the second-best, the treaty between free states abolishing war, is only available to 'republican' political systems. Wight is more direct. It is the traditions of *Europe* that distinguish international relations from the law of the jungle.

It is clear that this difference between pluralists and second-besters is of very great significance for any account of the viability of international society under contemporary conditions. We no longer live in a world in which the 'traditions of Europe' have any kind of automatic appeal—if they ever did. International society as a general account of international order will have to have a wider appeal than that if it is to survive into the next century; it will have to be shown— perhaps through an argument such as that presented by Nardin—that the European origins of international society are not of great significance. As for Kant's argument, while it is just about possible to see the states of 'really-existing liberalism' as the descendants of Kant's 'republics', nonetheless an international society that requires all its significant members to be republican is, again, likely to lack universal appeal (Brown 1992b). On these terms, international society will be an option for some, not for all. If this is right, the implication is that in terms of its future prospects, as opposed to past history, all of international society's eggs are in one basket—the 'pluralist' basket that is constructed out of the belief that the institutions of international society, properly understood, can have an appeal divorced from their political and geographical point of origin. In other words, if the argument is to succeed it needs to be shown that institutions such as diplomacy and customary international law can be defended as practices that all members of international society must obey, where the strength of 'must' is divorced from considerations of power, culture, or history; some pluralists claim to be able to make this demonstration.

Some, but not all. Clearly Nardin believes that this is possible, but it is doubtful whether more conventional international theorists such as Bull would make such a claim; certainly Burke would not have. Both the latter writers are clear that they are thinking of a specific society rather than some generic international society.[20] Nardin does cast his argument more widely, but in order to do so it is necessary for him to conceive of coexistence as possessing a positive value in itself, independent of the values tied up in the forms of life it protects. This is a position analogous to Rawls's formula of 'justice, political not metaphysical'—and open to the same objections.[21] The basic problem is that it requires a level of broad-gauge, across-the-board tolerance that is unavailable. Virtually no one actually believes in toleration at the level that would be required for a worldwide scheme of coexistence to be ethically grounded. It has become customary at this point in the argument to make some reference to the difficulties that Islamic societies have in accepting some of the practices of international society such as diplomatic immunity and domestic jurisdiction, but, in reality, this is far too restrictive a frame for the point being made.[22] Those who, within the West, overtly promote the virtues of toleration almost always have limits in mind which, in practice, restrict the range of social practices that should be tolerated quite markedly and in this respect are no less intolerant than apologists for non-Western cultures sometimes seem to be.

Anyone who doubts this should contemplate the history of international human rights protection.[23] Declamatory statements such as the 1948 Universal Declaration are sometimes taken to establish universally agreed minimum standards, which have become part of the list of 'settled norms' of international society (Frost 1986). This is hardly the case. The Declaration expresses an explicitly 'Western' viewpoint. At the time of the 1948 Declaration, Saudi Arabia, one of the few U.N. members whose social system was based on a non-Western world view, abstained, ostensibly on the grounds that the right to change religion (Article 18) contravened Islamic law, but, presumably, also on the wider grounds that, if taken seriously, the Universal Declaration amounts to a root and branch condemnation of Saudi society.[24] It might be argued, rather cynically, that later non-Western, nondemocratic adherents to the Declaration were able to sign, because they realized that it was not meant to be taken seriously—or because having fewer financial resources than the Saudis they were more concerned at the economic implications of Western disapproval. Nothing in the recent history of human rights protection gives reason for believing that a meaningful consensus on human rights—as opposed to a willingness to subscribe to unspecific norms, which do not, in practice, affect state behavior—actually exists.

The wider point here is that there is no universally accepted standard for judging the internal arrangements of states that could provide some kind of objective yardstick for determining which forms of life ought to be allowed to coexist in an international society based on practical association. The doctrine of human rights, which is so important in the Western conception of politics, is essentially an *intolerant* doctrine, one that stands against the pluralism that characterizes international society understood as a practical association. Human rights have been stressed here as a key issue in relation to coexistence, because Nardin in *Law, Morality, and the Relations of States* seems, at times, to regard the protection of human rights as something that could be equated to a 'practice' of international society authoritatively binding on all states irrespective of their wishes.[25] If this is, indeed, his argument, it is unconvincing. His essential defense of the notion that the practices of international society are authoritatively binding is that of reciprocity; these practices are equivalent to rights that cannot logically be claimed for one's own state without extending them to other states. There are problems with this formula—what of those 'states' who do not think of themselves as states? in any event, when has logic ever governed these matters?—but even if it is plausible with respect to a practice such as diplomatic immunity, it seems highly unconvincing if applied to anything connected with human rights.[26]

The best defense of 'international society as practical association' would escape from this difficulty by relying on a very strictly defined notion of which practices are to be regarded as authoritatively binding. The normative base of such an international society would have to be very thin and matters of 'domestic jurisdiction' such as the treatment of one's own nationals would not be covered, except, perhaps, in very extreme circumstances—genocide and the like. International lawmakers would have to be careful not to breach this basic position by attempting to establish authoritative rules in 'inappropriate' areas. Even if it could be established, this kind of international society would, at best, produce peaceful relations and basic procedural justice—not, perhaps, so bad a fate—but, in any event, it is very difficult to imagine that the sort of self-denying ordinance that even so limited a form of association would require could ever be established in practice.

There is an analogy here with the fate of the source of Nardin's thinking, Oakeshottian thought in general. It seems unlikely that Oakeshott's distinction between—nonpolitical—enterprise association, and—political—civil association could 'work' in any actual, functioning, political system. Irritatingly, ordinary citizens, being unfamiliar with the finer points of liberal political philosophy, insist on trying to use the power of the state to improve their position in life, and so cross the line between Oakeshott's categories. Individuals have projects that they pursue in the political sphere, and it is highly unlikely that they can be persuaded that they are making some kind of category error by so doing. In much the same way, states have interests and projects that they attempt to pursue internationally by establishing authoritative rules, and they are unlikely to be deflected from this pursuit by the thought that they are straying beyond what 'practical association' allows. In his account of international institutions, Nardin makes the interesting point that the United Nations is less firmly based in practical association than was the League—and this, he suggests, accounts for many of the difficulties that the former body has experienced (Hardin 1983: chap. 5). This is both plausible and insightful, but, of course, as Nardin recognizes, the United Nations is as it is not because of some drafting mistake in 1944, but because that is the way in which states want it to be—even if they are not always happy with the consequences of their wishes.

This section began with the proposition that 'second-best' accounts of international society presumed that the members of this putative society have something substantial in common—being 'republican' or European—and that the only account of international society with genuinely global implications is the pluralist account best articulated recently by Terry Nardin. An examination of the latter has, however, suggested that the universalist quality of this approach is achieved only by an implausibly rigorous exclusion from the terms of international coexistence of many features of international life that most states would consider suitable for normative regulation. Combining these points, it would seem that there are real difficulties in finding any sense of international society with universal applicability. However, the possibility remains that an international society with a more limited membership is viable—in other words, a Kantian union, or a Wightian 'European' society may work, albeit for Republican or European states only.

In these two cases the pluralism required for an international society to work is bounded; the tolerance required is not open ended. For a Kantian international society, the pluralism of different kinds of republican states is acceptable, but no other kind of political order needs to be, or can be, tolerated. Wight's 'traditions of Europe' can also be translated into a proposition about the acceptable range of variation in domestic structure and, perhaps especially, culture amongst the members of an international society. In practice, the two approaches probably merge nowadays; that is to say, the current meaning of both 'European' and 'Republican' is much the same—such societies as are liberal-democratic and essentially capitalist in economic structure fit the bill. Nowadays the 'Europe' of the mind stretches from Vladivostok to Vancouver (perhaps in both directions to include Japan), while some of the most successful 'republics' are constitutional monarchies. Another way of making the point is to say that the only functioning international society today is that which exists between and among the advanced industrial countries. However, if pluralist accounts of international society fail, while within a restricted terrain a 'second-best' international society is possible, is the pessimism with which theorists of the second best treat the possibility of moving beyond society to community still justified? Perhaps community is now available—albeit only for some of the states and peoples that make up the modern world.

CONCLUSION: THROUGH SOCIETY TO COMMUNITY—FOR SOME ONLY?

Within the world composed of advanced industrial, liberal-democratic states, something like an international society does exist. These states do seem to accept that their mutual relations are, to a considerable degree, norm governed. On the whole, they conduct their relations with one another in a lawful manner. This international society is no longer a 'war-system', and, potentially, this has profound consequences for the way in which states regard each other. However, what is most interesting about this international society is that relations among its members seem to be much closer than is implied by the term 'society'. As suggested above, perhaps the proposition that 'community' is unattainable needs to be modified—at least for this 'world'.

The case for the unattainability of world community has always rested on the ultimate unwillingness of states to surrender sovereignty. Clearly this unwillingness undermines 'institutional' cosmopolitanism, but it is equally subversive of any attempt to cash out 'moral' cosmopolitanism in practical terms—that is, that recognition of moral obligation is undermined if states reserve to themselves the right to determine when and if these obligations will come into operation, and to make this determination on the basis of self-interest. Since the states that make up the international society of the advanced industrial world show no general inclination to surrender their sovereignty it might be thought that any move to community is doomed. However, this may be too premature a judgment. In the first place, many states have given up elements of their sovereignty in the European Union, which, Murray Forsyth has convincingly argued, is already a Federal state of a kind (Forsyth 1994).[27] Second, it could well be argued that if physical violence is no longer a serious option, then in practice, sovereignty has been seriously weakened, whatever the legal position. But third, and most of all, it can be argued that the *feel* of politics in the advanced industrial world goes beyond what is usually thought of as implied by an international society. Complex interdependence is a confusing theoretical term, but a lived reality, part of the life experience of modern industrial societies—and, as against this reality, the formalities of sovereignty seem relatively unimportant. The states of the advanced world may not yet form a community in the full sense of the term—common identity is not yet fully present—but they seem to be heading in that direction.

If this is right, then, perhaps paradoxically, there are reasons why we should be deeply concerned about this situation—why we should regard the future of international order with great foreboding. This is so because a deepening sense of community in the advanced industrial world seems to be accompanied by an increasingly 'system' oriented set of relationships between this emerging community and the rest of the world—and in relations amongst and between the states that make up the rest of the world. The picture that seems to be emerging is close to that portrayed in an American study, which touched a number of nerves—*The Real World Order: Zones of Peace/Zones of Turmoil* by Max Singer and Aaron Wildavsky.[28] The 'zone of peace' (an international society tending toward community) pursues its own concerns, no longer required to take seriously the interests of the rest of the world because the rest of the world is no longer capable of doing it serious damage. Meanwhile, the 'zone of turmoil' sinks into ever greater distress. Singer and Wildavsky helpfully point out that there are reasons 'Why We Will Be Better Off'—but they also indicate, with an appropriate air of resignation, that in the zone of turmoil, "We must expect violence and poverty to take millions of lives" (Singer and Wildavsky 1993: 12).

As things stand, this chilling dystopia is a serious prospect. The only steps that might be taken to prevent it from materializing would involve citizens and governments in the zone of peace making a conscious effort not to allow their own moves toward community to involve the imposition of 'outsider' status on the rest of the world—in other words, to preserve the norms of international *society* in their dealings with the rest of the world even while transcending these norms in their dealings with each other. Such a position is unlikely to stand unless the countries of the zone of turmoil adopt a similar normative stance in their dealings with the zone of peace and, as suggested above, there are reasons for pessimism on this count. However, it is in the context of the response of states, elites, and peoples in both zones to this emerging situation that the viability of the middle way of international society must be, and will be, judged.

6

States Are Not 'Like Units': Types of State and Forms of Anarchy in the Present International System

Georg Sørensen

(Neo-) Realist International Relations (IR) theory insists that sovereign states are 'like units'.[1] In this article, I argue that some states in the present international system are highly unlike units, not only in terms of their relative power capabilities[2] but in other important respects as well. I will demonstrate how the existence of unlike units is tied to how systemwide (international) forces affect the structure of units. And I contend that the existence of unlike units has consequences for the international system. Different types of state units exist in different forms of anarchy.

Over time, systemwide processes of a political, economic, cultural, and social nature change unit structures. Changed units, in turn, affect the structure of the international system. In more concrete terms: systemwide political and economic processes have changed the units that made up the international system in 1945. If we consider the modern states emerging from the Westphalian revolution as the prototypical state unit,[3] there are at least two groups of unlike units in the present international system: the 'premodern' states in Sub-Saharan Africa and the 'postmodern' states in the European Union (EU). To appreciate current developments in the international system, the existence of these different types of units has to be acknowledged.

I thus use a 'second image reversed' approach first and a 'second image' approach next. But whereas most previous employments of these approaches have focused on specific aspects of the international-domestic and the domestic-international connection, the scope here is more comprehensive[4] in that it seeks to characterize some main types of units in the present international system and to draw implications about how they influence systemic structure and forms of anarchy. Moreover, I 'play it again': the 'second image reversed' analysis does not stand alone; it is followed by a 'second image' inquiry.

The following section discusses political and economic processes in the international system between 1945 and 1990 and traces their effects on units. These changed units, in turn, are the source of structural changes leading to different forms of anarchy, each of which significantly deviates from the traditional neorealist picture of states in an anarchic self-help system. The present chapter intends to clarify the meaning of anarchy as a context in which world society formation takes place. It pursues this goal by emphasizing the differentiation of types of states as a feature of global structural change that conditions the functional differentiation of the international system as world society.

SYSTEMWIDE PROCESSES CHANGE UNITS: POWER AND INTERDEPENDENCE IN POST-1945 DEVELOPMENTS

Several types of systemwide processes are relevant candidates for investigation; a comprehensive analysis would have to include economic, political, social, and cultural factors. Some theoretical grip is needed in order to make sense of the multitude of ways in which international forces affect the structure of state units. Two main theoretical perspectives on IR suggest themselves. The first is realism; the second is liberal interdependence theory.

According to realism, distribution of power is the crucial determinant of processes in the international system. In the case of a highly asymmetrical distribution of power, powerful states not only constrain the weak; they may also undertake direct intervention in weaker states, that is, strong states may intervene and change the structure of weak states (see, for example, Krasner 1994b and 1995). For example, the United States and its allies intervened heavily in West Germany and Japan after the war. And the United States was also 'interventionist in other states which seemed in danger of slipping out of its orbit.'[5] In the East, the Soviet Union intervened as massively, or even more so, in its sphere of interest in Eastern Europe. The pattern repeated itself in the context of cold war and bipolar confrontation. Nearly all of the post-1945 interventions were related to this conflict: Hungary, Vietnam, Laos, Czechoslovakia, the Dominican Republic, Afghanistan.[6]

Direct intervention was only one of the ways in which the powerful affected the structures of state units in the international system. They also affected such structures by way of decolonization. Decolonization was more than a mere process of accepting sovereign independence for former colonies. Decolonization effectively meant a change of the constitutive rules of the institution of sovereignty in that a new, weak player was allowed entry into the exclusive group of sovereign states.

The moral basis for the demand of colonial independence was the notion of the right of colonial peoples to self-determination. Colonialism, in contrast, "became an absolute wrong: an injury to the dignity and autonomy of those peoples and of course a vehicle for their economic exploitation and political oppression."[7] In the course of relatively few years, the right to self-determination became the accepted international norm leading to independence for the colonies. The right to self-determination stands in stark contrast to the view that dominated before the war, reflecting the position of the colonial motherlands. In that outlook, there was no room for swift independence; the majority of colonies were not ready for that. Only a prolonged effort of institution building, creation of national unity and a proper economic basis would be able to establish the necessary prerequisites for independence.

According to the official British view in 1946, there were four obstacles to 'early and effective self-government': (a) the colonial populations were 'too unaware' of the operations of modern government to be capable of citizenship; (b) there was no national unity; (c) there was no economic basis that could support a modern state; (d) a number of colonies were simply too insubstantial to allow for "anything more than a limited internal self-government" (Perham 1946: 295, 336–37). What the British suggested as an alternative to independence was a diverse range of forms of semi-autonomy that were seen as appropriate for the different levels of development of the colonies. There was nothing new in this; the League of Nations had employed a distinction between 'A', 'B', and 'C' Mandates indicating different degrees of 'readiness for independence' for territories that were perceived incapable of sovereignty.

But in the post-Second World War world, it quickly proved difficult to defend the 'degree of readiness' argument other than on paternalistic grounds reasoning in terms of higher and lower levels of civilization. The leading postwar states rejected this whole way of thinking. Both the United States and the Soviet Union pressed for rapid decolonization. They were supported by Latin American countries and by the U.N. General Assembly. In other words, the leading powers of the postwar world had the support of the majority of states in the international system in demanding swift decolonization from the European colonial powers.

In 1960, the United Nations passed a Declaration on the Granting of Independence to Colonial Countries and Peoples which emphasized that "all peoples have the right to self-determination," and "inadequacy of political, economic, social or educational preparedness should never serve as a pretext for delaying independence" (Jackson 1990: 77). The road to independence for the colonies was now open. This happened in a way that changed the preconditions for qualifying for statehood and thus paved the way for a type of sovereign state that was qualitatively different from previous types. The powerful had achieved the decolonization they wanted; but the outcome was also the admittance of a new kind of weak player with very little substantial statehood to the society of sovereign states. The weakest of these new, sovereign entities were situated in Sub-Saharan Africa.

In summary, two ways in which powerful states influence the structure of sovereign units were identified: direct intervention on the one hand and redefining the criteria for sovereign statehood on the other. Direct intervention has most often been used to create like units—after World War II, for example, defeated states were restructured in the image of the winners—but the new criteria for sovereign statehood created in the context of decolonization helped establish a new category of sovereign states that were unlike units compared with previous members of the system of states; they were premodern states possessing formal, but very little substantial statehood.

Let me turn to the other main theoretical perspective, liberal interdependence. This view emphasizes the effects of increasing interdependence on unit structure (Keohane and Nye 1989; Rosecrance 1986; Cooper 1968). In economic terms, the period since 1945 has been one of intensification of economic relations across borders, that is, of economic globalization. The process is uneven in both intensity and geographical scope. A distinction between two principal dimensions of globalization is helpful; one is 'intensified economic interdependence'; the other is an 'emerging global economy.' The former is increase in trade, investment, and other economic transactions between national economies. The latter involves a qualitative shift toward a global economic system that is no longer primarily based on national economies, but on a consolidated global marketplace for production, finance, distribution, and consumption. In this case the "global economy dominates the national economies existing within it."[8]

It is the aspect of an 'emerging global economy' which is of interest in the present context. When Charles Kindleberger declared, in 1969, that "the state is just about through as an economic unit," Waltz conceded that if he were right, "then the structure of international politics would have to be redefined" (Waltz 1979: 94). The position taken here is that Kindleberger is about half right when his statement is applied to the highly industrialized countries in the present international system. The current process of economic globalization includes both the 'interdependence' and the 'global economy' aspect.[9] The former aspect came first, as part of the Second Industrial Revolution. The centerpiece of the Second Industrial Revolution was 'Fordism', that is, scientifically supported mass production in the context of primarily national economies. The railroad system tied the national economic spaces together; the heavy industries of steel, chemicals, and other producer goods developed in conjunction with consumer goods industries. The automobile industry became a role model for both sectors. The national political systems helped create a framework conducive to rapid economic development. Indeed, "the development of the nation-state in the late 19th and early 20th centuries was inextricably intertwined with the so-called 'Second Industrial Revolution'" (Cerny 1994: 15; see also Reich 1983).

It is the Third Industrial Revolution, currently taking place, that contains the strongest tendencies toward creating a global economy. First, an increasingly globalized financial sector is of growing importance:

> Instead of a series of national financial systems linked by a few operations buying and selling credit across the exchanges, we now have a global system, in which national markets, physically separate, function as if they were all in the same place. The

balance has shifted from a financial structure which was predominantly state based [...] to a predominantly global system in which some residual local differences in markets, institutions and regulations persist as vestiges of a bygone age. (Stopford et al. 1991: 40–41)

Second, and facilitated by the globalization of the financial system, 'Fordism' has given way to flexible manufacturing involving the differentiation of production processes on a worldwide scale (see also chapter 2 in this volume). Flexible manufacturing involves both highly skilled labor and the latest production technologies as well as unskilled labor, sweat shop producers in subcontracting networks. Third, technological change is faster while product lifetimes are shorter. This creates a growing need for investment in research and development, which forces firms "to seek additional markets abroad to gain the profits necessary to amortize their investments in time to stay up with the competition" (Strange 1994a: 104; see also Cerny 1994: 26–33).

The result is an increasingly globalized economic system that is no longer reproduced in the form of territorially based, national economic units.[10] Yet states have not been passive victims of economic globalization. States are active players and their policies are probably the single most important determinant of the scope and direction of globalization.[11] States get involved in economic globalization in order to promote economic growth and welfare. Under present conditions, growth and welfare require participation in economic globalization; "opting out of the world market economy is no longer an option" (Strange 1994b: 215).

In sum, economic globalization has changed state units in a way that calls for differentiation. It is premature to talk about the state being 'through as an economic unit'; but it is also misleading to continue as if nothing has happened and assume that the traditional way of dividing the international economy into distinct national units remains as valid as before.[12] Intensified globalization not only narrows policy choice in the sense that protectionism is no longer a viable option in times of crisis (see Milner 1983). As emphasized by Philip Cerny,[13] globalization affects all of the main areas for state activity in economic affairs: (1) the provision of a 'market framework', such as property rights, a stable currency system, and a legal framework for economic activity; (2) industrial policies, including subsidies and infrastructural support for private firms; and (3) welfare procurements or economic redistribution.

Counterfeiting, copyright violations, transnational capital flows, tax havens, and intrafirm trade undermine property rights; the globalization of finance has created a volatile market where currency and interest rates are increasingly difficult to put under political control; legal rules as well as demands for welfare provision and high social standards are undercut by the improved exit opportunities of firms. Industrial policies can no longer discriminate between national and foreign firms; the option is one of providing an environment basically conducive to private companies, whether they are of foreign or domestic origin.

The argument is not that states have necessarily become less important or weaker overall; the progress in areas of communication, organization, and information that has accompanied the process of economic globalization has also led to increased state capacities for regulation and surveillance.[14] But economic globalization radically changes the 'traditional' national economic context for state activity. Decisions made by other states as well as by firms operating on a global basis have significant consequences for developments within one's own borders.[15] In this sense, economic globalization changes "the character of the state and of the state system" (Strange 1994b: 212). States heavily involved in economic globalization depend on the world market context for their economic growth and welfare. They are involved in an economic welfare community based on the world market economy. By contrast, the conventional neorealist view is that while states may be economically interdependent, they continue to basically take care of themselves economically and they strive to keep it that way: "Nations pull apart as each of them tries to take care of itself and to avoid becoming dependent on others" (Waltz 1979: 143).

One important consequence of this structural change is increased demand for international cooperation, for example in the form of regimes or other forms of governance at the supranational level.[16] In that way, states attempt to compensate the decreased ability to autonomously control activity within their own borders with an increased capability of regulation at a supranational level, through cooperation with other states. It will be contended below that this leads to changes in the institution of sovereignty for some states and thus to functional differentiation of state units.

In summary, I have looked at two aspects of systemwide processes. One is economic globalization where I argue that in some states globalization has progressed to a point where it is misleading to talk about purely 'national' economies. The other aspect of policies relevant for my purpose here concerns the way in which powerful states define the criteria for sovereign statehood. Through the process of decolonization, colonial territories that a few years earlier had been seen as completely unfit for independence suddenly became sovereign states. It will be argued in the following section that the impact of economic globalization and decolonization makes both structural and functional differentiation of units necessary.

IMPACT ON UNITS: FUNCTIONAL AND STRUCTURAL DIFFERENTIATION

The economic and political processes described in the previous section have had significant consequences for the units affected by them. They have led to functional as well as structural differentiation of the state units comprising the international system. This differentiation cannot be comprehended within a purely neorealist framework that takes the existence of states as like units for granted. For neorealism, sovereignty means autonomy (states are independent, free to choose their policies), as well as identity of purpose and function (all states have to fulfill the same tasks, all states are rational utility maximizers). "Like the Hobbesian model of the autonomous individual, states are assumed to 'spring out of the earth' and suddenly, like mushrooms, come to full maturity, without any kind of engagement to each other" (Cronin 1994: 11, quoting Thomas Hobbes). But on the one hand, states do not spring out of the earth. Newcomers are admitted to the system according to the rules defined by the powerful. Change in these rules in the context of decolonization gave sovereign statehood to a new type of weak player that is functionally and structurally different from modern states. On the other hand, economic globalization has also led to structural and functional differentiation for a group of states.

Identification of the unlike state units in the present international system requires some simplification. The purpose is not an exhaustive characterization of units, but an identification of significant dissimilarity between main types of units. A suitable instrument for this purpose is Weberian ideal types.[17] I shall identify a 'premodern' ideal type, which emerged in the context of decolonization, and a 'postmodern' ideal type, which has emerged in Europe in the context of economic globalization. Each of these types differs in distinct ways from the modern state, which is normally considered the prototypical 'Westphalian' state unit.[18]

Let me begin with the 'premodern' ideal type. In the neorealist account, states become like units through competition and socialization. Applying this reasoning to much of the Third World around the time of decolonization would mean that the new states-to-be had learned their lesson and acquired the necessary prerequisites for substantial statehood. The whole neorealist idea of domestic realms as hierarchic orders presupposes state institutions that embody authority, administration, and law.[19] The neorealist account fits reasonably well with the situation before World War II, where sovereignty was only bestowed on countries that were able to demonstrate a capacity for self-government (Jackson 1990: 34, 38). Previously then, positive sovereignty (demonstrated capacity for self-government) preceded and was indeed a precondition for negative sovereignty (that is, formal-legal recognition by other states and freedom from outside interference). But in a large number of cases, this is not what happened in the context of decolonization. The territories that had previously been regarded unfit for self-government did not all of a sudden acquire the attributes of substantial statehood. Their institutions were as weak, their lack of nationhood as evident, their economic resource base as insubstantial as before World War II. Compared with the established states they were not like, but highly unlike units. Conferring juridical sovereignty upon them did not change this state of affairs. What changed, then, was not the territories, but the international legal framework deciding which type of units could become sovereign.

Substantial statehood is thus no longer a prerequisite for juridical statehood. The new sovereign states were given the latter without having the former. Premodern[20] states are functionally different from the typical modern state that emerged from the transformation of the absolutist state in Europe. The premodern state has statehood only in the formal sense of juridical sovereignty. In the modern state, the juridical shell of sovereignty is filled with substantial political, economic, and military capacities. In the premodern state, domestic order in the form of hierarchy is not well established; premodern states have not solved 'the Hobbesian Problem' of creating domestic order (see Gaubatz 1994). It would be misleading to consider this difference only in terms of a difference in capabilities between otherwise like units. I shall argue below that the anarchy pertaining to premodern states is different from the anarchy characteristic of 'Westphalian' states.

Structural differentiation concerns variation in the internal organization of states in political, economic, social, and other relevant areas. The notion of a premodern state implies contrasts between modern and premodern states in a number of respects. In political terms, premodern states are characterized by weak and underdeveloped state institutions with state power concentrated in individual political leaders, the system called personal rule. There is no monopoly of violence vested in the state, but an armed force personally loyal to the strongman. The military and the police are not primarily concerned with the creation of domestic order or the protection of the population in general. The coercive apparatus is an instrument in the hands of the ruler, used against political opponents or for making profits in the protection market (see e.g., Apter and Rosberg 1994; Jackson and Rosberg 1982).

It is misleading to speak of a coherent national economy in premodern states. There is a highly heterogeneous domestic economic space, consisting of sectors on very different levels of development with low levels of intersectoral exchange. The economy is highly dependent on the world market for critical inputs. Finally, there is no developed nationhood in premodern states, neither in the sense of a shared common ethnic and cultural background, nor in the sense of a national political community where different groups support the national political space delimited by the state's boundaries. Ethnic and communal divisions were exacerbated in the context of personal rule and against the background of post-colonial borders arbitrarily splitting some groups with a common ethnic-cultural background and putting together other groups without it.[21]

The states in Sub-Saharan Africa are the real world states closest to the premodern ideal type. Premodern traits also characterize the Central Asian states emerging from the former Soviet Union, the least developed Central American states, a group of the least developed Asian states including Afghanistan and Bangladesh, and even some of the East European states such as the three Baltic republics, Romania, and Albania. These latter countries are not premodern in all the dimensions described above; yet they may as soon deteriorate to fully fledged, premodern states as they may become modern national states. The direction of development is not given beforehand.

Let me turn to the 'postmodern' state emerging in the context of economic globalization. The countries most intensely involved in economic globalization are the industrialized countries in Western Europe, North America, and, to a lesser extent, Japan. As indicated above, this has led to structural differentiation in the economic realm. Economic globalization involves more than intensified economic interdependence; the Third Industrial Revolution has established a world market economy with a measure of specialization. This economic system is no longer reproduced in the form of territorially based, national economic units. There is an economic welfare community based on the world market economy. In that sense, heavily globalized economies are structurally different from the national economies characterizing the traditional 'Westphalian' state.

What about functional differentiation? Can we speak of a postmodern state with a distinctive kind of sovereignty? It was mentioned earlier that economic globalization does create more demand for cooperation, but whether such demand is translated into ad hoc agreements or into regimes of differing types depends on a number of intervening variables.[22] That is, there is no deterministic link between economic globalization and specific forms of cooperation between states. Certain trends are clear, however. There is currently a tendency to promote regional cooperation in various forms (headed by the United States in America, by Japan in East Asia, and by the European Union in Europe) as new political-economic frameworks of capital accumulation.[23] There is also a trend toward states increasingly choosing to limit their substantial, operational sovereignty through international agreements. That is, states allow other states a measure of influence on activities within their own borders in return for a measure of such influence on other states. According to Robert Keohane, sovereignty is becoming "less a territorially defined barrier than a bargaining resource for a politics characterized by complex transnational networks" (Keohane 1995: 252).

The members of the European Union (EU) have taken this process to a point where they have developed a political space organized on a nonstate territorial basis. The EU has autonomous power, which has consequences for the sovereignty of the participating states. In some areas, especially those related to realization of the single market, the EU is able to make binding rules for its members (see Nørgaard 1994: 245–87; see also Sørensen 1994: 33–36). States involved in that form of cooperation can be called 'postmodern' states. They are functionally different from modern states in that sovereignty is no longer exclusively vested in the state.[24]

There is a big debate about what the EU cooperation really is.[25] It appears easier to determine what it is not;[26] on the one hand, it is not state-state cooperation in the conventional form of intergovernmental organization (IGO).

In contrast to IGOs, the EU can make binding rules for member countries in certain areas. On the other hand, it is not a federal state either, although there are some federal traits (Pedersen 1992). In other words, the EU does not fit well into conventional schemes of cooperation between states. It is a hybrid, qualitatively changing some aspects of sovereign statehood, while retaining the single member state as the key player, albeit within an increasingly strong transnational policy network.

The power and influence that have been transferred to EU institutions encourages political and interest group organization on an EU-regional basis. When the single member state is deprived of the veto weapon, the incentive for transnational lobbying increases, both in the private and the public sector. Transnational policy networks are strengthened and the role of the state as a coordinator of policies is made more difficult.[27] Philip Cerny emphasizes that globalized societies such as EU members are characterized by "diffusion and decentralisation of power," resulting in "an enmeshing of traditional power structures, such as the state, in a web of overlapping affiliations and fractionalised, cross-cutting conflicts" (Cerny 1993: 28, 31). The new 'structure' is thus a patchwork of many different types of actors involved in many types of conflict at various levels: multilateral, regional, state, and substate. Cerny calls it a "quasi-anarchy in which the differentiated units are not merely states but a wide range of differentiated and unevenly developed sub-structures."[28]

The notion of cooperation between postmodern states also indicates a change in identity and loyalty of citizens, away from the 'we-ness' singularly based on nationhood toward a more mixed palette of identities; identities are simultaneously local, regional, national, supranational, and universal. The populations of EU member states are not switching their loyalties to the supranational level. But there is change in this area, away from the uniform national identity tied in with the 'Westphalian' state. James Rosenau's concept of 'sovereignty-free' individuals and Lothar Brock's notion of 'identity-surfing' individuals both try to capture this change (Rosenau 1992b: 272–94; Brock 1993: 163–73). Seyom Brown points to the emergence of "a *polyarchy* in which nation-states, subnational groups, and transnational special interests are all vying for the support and loyalty of individuals" (Brown 1988: 245).

In sum, systemwide processes change the structure of units in the international system. It is relevant to perceive the state units of the present international system as functionally as well as structurally differentiated. I have identified a premodern and a postmodern ideal type. The former is the prevalent state form in Sub-Saharan Africa, while EU-members are the best current example of the latter. Their respective main characteristics are condensed in the following table, where they are contrasted with the 'Westphalian' state ideal type, as perceived by neorealists.

Table 6.1 State Units in the Present International System: Three Ideal Types

	'Premodern'	'Westphalian'	'Postmodern'
Sovereignty	Juridical, negative, formal	Substantial, internal and external state autonomy	Operational, shared with supranational institutions
Economy	Dependent, structural heterogeneity	Self-sustained, no specialization, a coherent national economy	Globalized, some specialization, part of larger welfare community
Polity	Personal rule, weak institutions	Polyarchy, strong institutions	Plurilateral emerging transnational policy network
Nationhood	No	Yes	Yes, but challenged by competing identities

The following section discusses how these different types of units affect the international system. I turn, in other words, from a 'second image reversed' to a 'second image' inquiry.

UNIT IMPACT ON SYSTEM: DIFFERENT FORMS OF ANARCHY

We saw earlier that Waltz conceived of an unbreakable link between like units on the one hand and anarchy and self-help on the other. In neorealism, sovereignty leads to anarchy, and anarchy and self-help are two sides of the same coin. There is a false and a true element in that understanding. It is true that all sovereign states are constitutionally independent,[29] and therefore the international system is anarchic in the sense of absence of systemwide government. It is not true that such anarchy necessarily must lead to self-help. Premodern and postmodern states are each characterized by distinct types of relationships that are different from self-help. These relationships each entail different, specific patterns of conflict and cooperation.

The international system is not one of self-help for premodern states; they would be completely unable to survive in such a system. Premodern states need special, preferential treatment from the developed world; that is, the background for the development of assistance regimes where economic aid flows from rich, developed countries to poor, underdeveloped countries. In other words, decolonization created a number of premodern states that lack substantial statehood. In order to achieve substantial statehood, they need development; hence the development assistance regime that includes the large number of international organizations with the U.N.-system at its center. U.N. organizations devote most of their resources to the promotion of economic development in premodern states.[30]

At the same time, premodern states want to have their cake and eat it too: to enjoy sovereignty in the form of formal equality, and freedom from outside intervention (that is, to be recognized as equals in the international society of states); and to enjoy development assistance and other preferential treatment (that is, to be recognized as unequal in the international society of states and thus qualify for aid). In Robert Jackson's words:

> The new ethics of international development are obviously difficult to reconcile with historical liberties of sovereign statehood. If developed states have obligations to come to the assistance of underdeveloped states—as is often claimed—they certainly have no corresponding rights to ensure that their assistance is properly and efficiently used by governments of the latter. [...] There is a fundamental incompatibility, therefore, between classical liberal rules of reciprocity and commutative justice and contemporary doctrines of nonreciprocity and distributive justice. [...] southern governments have only rights and northern only duties. The former have no obligations to use foreign aid properly or productively. The latter have no right to demand it. (Jackson 1990: 44)

Given this situation, the principle of nonintervention, which is normally a corollary of juridical sovereignty, is difficult to uphold. Economic and other aid gives the donors an amount of influence over the domestic affairs of recipients. Economic conditionalities and, of late, political conditionalities have been tied to development assistance (see, for example, Sørensen 1993). Yet in a large number of cases, such measures have not radically improved domestic conditions in premodern states. With the Cold War overlay gone, the early moves toward more democracy have fuelled conflict in many premodern states. Hence the current debate about 'saving failed states'.[31] The last two U.N. Secretary Generals have argued for a further move away from the principle of nonintervention. In 1991, Javier Perez de Cuellar stated that all nations had a responsibility to live up to the U.N. Charter requirements concerning human rights and democracy. Failure to do so, he indicated, could provoke U.N. intervention. In 1992, Boutros Boutros-Ghali claimed that "the time of absolute and exclusive sovereignty [...] has passed. Its theory was never matched by reality" (Helman and Ratner 1992–93: 10).

In summary, anarchy in the international system involves a situation of non-self-help for premodern states; they would not be able to survive without economic support and security guarantees from the international community. In the domestic sphere, by contrast, order and security are lacking due to the very nature of premodern states. Over long periods of time, there has been more anarchy than order in several premodern states (for example, Mozambique, Angola, Somalia, Sudan, Ethiopia, Uganda, Zaire). Violent conflict is thus chiefly domestically generated in premodern states. The security dilemma in premodern states is domestic, not international.[32] This, then, is the basis for the substantial levels of domestic, violent conflict in areas such as Sub-Saharan Africa. These conflicts are responsible for by far the largest number of casualties in recent years.[33]

The relationship between postmodern states in the EU is not characterized by self-help either; it is based on cooperation and non-self-help. First, a framework has been created that allows for legitimate outside intervention by member-states in national affairs. The Single Market Treaty permits a majority of member-states to define rules applicable to all members. The Council can do this by way of qualified majority. The use of qualified majority is intended for several other policy areas, even though it is presently restricted to measures related to the single market. Rule-making powers are complemented by the EU administrative apparatus and the European Court. There is, in other words, an element of authority, administration, and law in the relationship between EU members, precisely the words used by neorealists to describe the hierarchic orders of domestic realms.

Second, economic cooperation involves a measure of redistribution that is not solely based on redistribution between member countries, but also on regions within countries. At the same time, it is recognized that some states are better off than others, that is, there is a 'North-South' division within the EU. Poorer members' support for the Single European Act creating the single market was thus compensated in the form of economic support for development projects in those member-countries.[34] Instead of national economies, there is an increasingly integrated economic space with a measure of redistribution.

Cooperation and non-self-help in the context of the EU should not be taken to mean that harmony has descended on EU members. Close collaboration has increased rather than decreased the areas of controversy and potential conflict between member-states. Diverging national interests remain in place in many areas. But there is no longer the prospect of disputes leading to violent conflict between states, as is a likely outcome in the neorealist conception of anarchy as self-help. Robert Gilpin recently speculated what it would take to make war between states impossible: "Humankind [...] would need to reject the anarchy of international relations and submit itself to the Leviathan of Thomas Hobbes" (Gilpin 1989: 35), a development Gilpin deems inconceivable. The EU is no Leviathan, but it does embody an element of authority, administration, and law, as emphasized earlier. Anarchy in the context of the EU has been modified to an extent where the use of military force is no longer considered a viable polity alternative; the EU constitutes a security community.[35]

Republican liberalism has developed the argument about a liberal zone of peace between democracies. Commercial liberalism argues that economic exchange leads to interdependence, which increases the incentives for cooperation.[36] Cooperation between EU members has gone a step further, both politically and economically. There is not merely liberal democracies with common moral values; there is an integrated polity with consequences for sovereignty. There is not merely economic interdependence; there is an integrated economic space, which is no longer based on purely national economies, that is, a welfare community. The entire group of OECD states are characterized by similar traits as those identified for the EU: involved in economic globalization, cooperating in international regimes, and so on. Accordingly, they may be part of a larger security community encompassing the OECD area. Yet the scope and intensity of cooperation and thus the modification of anarchy is strongest within the EU.[37]

CONCLUSION

States in the present international system are not like units. In addition to the traditional 'Westphalian' state, there are two main types of state units in the present system: premodern and postmodern states. Unlike units emerge as a result of the interplay between international and domestic forces. It is thus necessary to pay more attention to this interplay, not merely in the form of decision-makers playing two-level games, but in the theoretically prior format of the consequences of systemwide processes for unit structures and, in turn, the effects of such change in unit structure on the international system.

Unlike units exist in different forms of anarchy. The neorealist claim that anarchy invariably leads to self-help must be abandoned. For premodern states, anarchy in the international system involves a situation of non-self-help; economic support and security guarantees from the international community is a condition for their existence. In the domestic sphere, by contrast, there has been more anarchy than order in many premodern states.

The relationship among postmodern states in the EU is not characterized by self-help either; it is based on cooperation and non-self-help. The EU is both a welfare community and a security community. There can be intense conflict between member-states, but solving conflict by means of force is out the question.

In sum, the interplay between international and domestic forces leads to unlike units, which exist in different forms of anarchy that may or may not be based on self-help. The examination of these unlike units is a precondition for understanding why the post-Cold War world is simultaneously characterized by increasingly violent conflict and more intense peaceful cooperation. Analyses of world politics after the Cold War have focused exclusively on relationships between states. Those have led to the currently dominant consensus about a 'liberal' Zone of Peace among developed countries in the core, based on "a shared set of liberal beliefs, institutions, and practices" (Goldgeier and McFaul 1992: 478), and a 'realist' Zone of Conflict in the less developed periphery, where "power and wealth are still linked in ways recognizable to the realists, and the security dilemma is paramount" (Goldgeier and McFaul 1992: 479). This understanding is not wrong, but it is highly abstract and imprecise. Further scrutiny of unlike state units and various forms of anarchy is needed in order to arrive at a more precise analysis, especially as regards domestic conflict in premodern states and as regards the 'liberal' peace among postmodern states.

Neorealists may object that the unlike units identified here merely represent limited, regional phenomena in Western Europe and Sub-Saharan Africa. That is, relationships between the great powers still correspond to the neorealist picture of anarchy as self-help and that is what is really important.[38] But on the one hand, the notion of premodern states as an ideal type helps us understand the nature of conflict in Sub-Saharan Africa and elsewhere in a more complete and thorough way than the blunt neorealist analytical instruments. On the other hand, even the great powers are affected by the processes of economic globalization which change the national economies characterizing the traditional 'Westphalian' state. In other words, the neorealist picture of the 'Westphalian' state unit may be outdated in several respects. This leads to the question of whether such a 'like unit' as the standard 'Westphalian' state was ever, at any historical point, an adequate description of the sovereign states in the international system. It probably was not.[39] That means that we need to identify the unlike state units for each relevant historical period, not just the post-world war period that I have focused on here. Only in that way will we be able to understand the nature of conflict and cooperation characterizing different periods in the history of the international system.

7

The New Raison d'État: International Cooperation Against Societies?[1]

Klaus Dieter Wolf

Within the analytical framework of the international society, cooperation among nations attracted the attention of International Relations primarily as a means of civilizing conflict regulation and of enhancing problem-solving capabilities. The limits of this state-centered approach to the project of world order became evident when the issue of the legitimacy of intergovernmental cooperation was first identified in regard to the European Union. This previously neglected new focus of research initiated a lively debate about the democratic deficit of governance in Europe. However, in this regard the European Union is not a special case. As I will try to show in this chapter, de-democratization by internationalization is a characteristic feature of governance beyond the state in general.[2]

It is no accident that the notion of a democratic deficit first entered circulation in connection with the European Union. Its multilevel *sui generis* character has attracted the attention of several subdisciplines of political science, including normative political theory, much more than ordinary international institutions. Elmar Rieger expresses a view shared by many commentators when he says: "The complex machinery responsible for the preparation of decisions taken by the Council of Ministers, and the Council itself as the central decision-making body, have, in association with the principle that this body's negotiations and deliberations should remain confidential, become the ideal type of an *arcanum imperii*" (Rieger 1995: 363). I will attempt to locate this phenomenon in the broader theoretical and conceptual landscape as an instance of a new form of raison d'état that has emerged as a feature of international society formation.

Reflecting on the legitimacy of governance beyond the state obviously requires a departure from the state-centered analytical framework of the international society. It involves the complex interplay between political systems or parts of them, societal groups, nongovernmental organizations, transnational economic corporations, and international institutions. The concept of world society as developed in the introductory chapter of this volume can provide us with an appropriate analytical model for an overdue enlargement of the research agenda. It directs our attention to patterns of interaction between different groups of actors in different spheres and on different levels. The interplay among the three spheres of interaction which may be distinguished as the system of states, the international civil society, and the world market, defines exactly the context in which the problem of legitimate governance beyond the state has emerged and must be addressed. Intergovernmental governance may originally have been developed by nation-states in order to cope with problems of interdependence more effectively. But along the way it has also contributed to distributing and diffusing responsibilities in such a way that nongovernmental actors' opportunities to participate are reduced and general limitations are imposed on the domestic political process.

The state-centric answer to the problem of the democratic deficit, to the effect that democratic structures of international governance are already adequately realized in the form of decision-making practices such as the principle of one-state-one-vote, is an inadequate response. Structural realism, a prominent representative of this view in International Relations theory, conceives of intergovernmental cooperation as a matter of self-organization within the system of states. Its subjects and addressees are nation-states. The world society perspective can address the democracy question more broadly, not only by drawing attention to the complex relationship between different levels of interaction, but also by treating societies and/or individuals as the actual subjects of democracy. However, in order to make the societal dimension meaningful for the analytical purpose of this chapter, a basic assumption of the traditionally society-centered perspective offered by political liberalism has to be dismissed as well, namely its notion of international governance as a form of collective self-organization with the sole objective of satisfying societal demands. This assumption may help to explain the degree of mutual self-commitment that puzzles political realists, and it may also account for much of what is going on in multilevel governance arrangements, but it can give no explanation of the numerous cases in which government representatives instrumentalize intergovernmental patterns of interaction in order to manipulate their respective domestic context. Put shortly, the perspective of political liberalism on the relationship between state and society fails to give a convincing account of the de-democratization process, which goes along with the internationalization of governance.

Although the literature contains no shortage of references to the problem that politics becomes less democratic as it is internationalized, none of the suggested approaches enables us to get to grips with this in a systematic way. The democratic deficit of governance beyond the state is thus portrayed as an unintended product of state policies. Michael Zürn's concept of 'uneven denationalization' (Zürn 1992c) captures very well the complexity of a situation in which the pressure of economic globalization leads to an internationalization of political attempts to solve problems. This process, however, is portrayed as proceeding too slowly to permit the reconstitution of the individual states' weakened regulation capacities, but too fast to enable the existing localized structures of democratic participation, particularly at the individual state level, to adapt to the unfolding of governance and regulation in increasingly complex multilevel systems. As a consequence of these assumptions, Zürn's answer to the puzzle of the democratic deficit goes no further than a shrug of the shoulders: democratization is lagging behind the internationalization of regulation mechanisms, and these in turn are lagging behind globalization. Other authors, for example, Robert Dahl (1994: 34), do not see the problem in terms of a delay in the democratization of international politics but view the democratic dilemma as a reflection of the impossibility of any attempt to achieve 'system effectiveness and citizen effectiveness' simultaneously in conditions where the fields of reference are expanding. According to Dahl, the constant pressure to internationalize politics should therefore lead to efforts to strengthen national and substate democratic structures. Such views raise the question of whether blame for the democratic deficit can really be laid at the door of overstretched problem-solvers.

Intergovernmental cooperation seems, in most of the relevant literature, to be reduced to an orientation toward the most efficient way of going about problem-solving. But politics does not only have this dimension of *governance*, in the sense of coping with problems by regulating behavior; it also has to do with *government*, in the sense of striving for power. The different ways in which the representatives of nation-states make use of international insitutions cannot be sufficiently described by only addressing the first (that is, governance) dimension. We also have to look at the government dimension, that is, at those patterns of intergovernmental interaction that aim at self-assertion, at staying in power, at getting reelected, or at favoring specific interest groups the support of which is important to them. If we assume that national governments have these objectives, we must also concede that their preferences may not always be in complete accordance with those of the societies the demands of which they are supposed to represent. This leads to a further assumption: in order to be able to follow such preferences of their own, governments can be expected to have an interest in governance arrangements that provide them with the autonomy to do so. The intergovernmental arena offers this opportunity exactly because of its potential as an *arcanum imperii*.

This aspect of institutional arrangements for governance beyond the state is forced into the background and cannot be examined as a motive for intergovernmental cooperation on the premises of the existing approaches to international governance. Confronted with the complementary shortcomings of both political realism and liberalism, in regard to accounting for both sides of the puzzle, that is, self-binding and de-democratization, an integrated approach seems to be more promising. Such an approach is suggested in this chapter. It conceives of international governance as a multifunctional institution created by national governments under the pressure of their respective domestic environment. Its subjects are national governments, but its addressee is civil society. In order to elaborate this approach, which can provide a more satisfactory account of the simultaneous occurrence of mutual self-commitments among governments on the one hand, and a creeping de-democratization of governance on the other, I apply the classical maxim of raison d'état to the multilevel policy context of world society, and use the striving for domestic autonomy as a way of accounting for the undemocratic structures of binding intergovernmental agreements.

Political autonomy is understood here in Georg Simonis' or Eric Nordlinger's sense (Simonis 1972: 293; Nordlinger 1981: 19), to mean the capacity of an actor to form its own preferences, to convert these into collective action, and to shape its environment in accordance with these preferences. Striving for autonomy in this sense can be treated as a synonym for terms like self-assertion or the maintenance of freedom of action; it is understood here as an *instrumental* meta-strategy pursued by an individual rational actor, something to be distinguished from concrete, *substantial* preferences based on policy content. This meta-strategy is of prior character because it provides the very preconditions for the realization of substantive goals pursued in specific constellations. Such concrete goals can consist of attempts to keep certain political programs out of the public sphere, but can also involve attempts to improve sectoral regulation capacities by granting access to nongovernmental actors, as long as this helps to foster legitimation and the overarching instrumental interest is not adversely affected. Autonomy or self-assertion therefore identify the lowest common denominator in the goals of each acting unit: the preservation of that actor's general freedom to specify its own goals as independently as possible and to shape the environment accordingly. Using a term by Claus Offe, I will attribute to states an 'interest in themselves' (Offe 1975: 13), which can clearly be distinguished from societal interests and which Nordlinger characterized by the striving after "autonomy-enhancing capabilities and opportunities to somehow forestall, neutralize, transform, resist, or overcome the societal constraints imposed upon them" (Nordlinger 1981: 30).[3] If we assume that states remain interested in their own self-preservation even when they are cooperating, the unavoidable conclusion is that they cannot be interested in overcoming the democratic deficit that characterizes governance beyond the state.

DOMESTIC DIMENSION OF RAISON D'ÉTAT

In the following I will use the term 'the new raison d'état' to situate conceptually and theoretically the mutual self-commitments of national governments as just another variant of a traditional kind of state behavior, which serves the purpose of self-assertion in the face of domestic and transnational societal challenges. Intergovernmental cooperation offers a new strategic option for the self-assertion of governmental actors. The formation of the international society of states has made possible the practices of this new raison d'état by making available the instruments, that is, the institutional setting, by which states can enter into self-binding commitments among each other. Even though the focus of attention here is exclusively on the adoption of intergovernmental self-commitments, the basic world society concept's picture of diffusion of actors and multilevel politics suggests that self-binding as a way of preserving autonomy in such multilevel policy contexts need not remain a strategy employed by the state alone, but can also be used by different actors at various levels of this mechanism.

Since the first use of the term 'raison d'état' toward the end of the sixteenth century, the state's relationship with both its societal and its international environment has changed significantly, and so have the strategies pursued by the state. But the logic of raison d'état has remained in essence unchanged, even though this logic has become far more complex as a result of the demands of the world society that is developing. From the very beginning, the concept was oriented toward both the external preservation of state independence and the internal monopoly on the use of force. When a civil society demanding a political space free from the state began to emerge, the nation for some time served as an integrating concept for the conservation of the unity of (national) state and society. In this context, raison d'état has been used for purposes of *Realpolitik*, to provide the foundation of a supposed harmony between state rule and society, and so as a way of resisting citizens' demands to be allowed to participate. It is therefore clear that the concept of raison d'état never could, and cannot now, be used meaningfully within a purely state-centric worldview, despite political realism's attempts to restrict the term to this usage. The appeal to raison d'état has always been also, and much of the time even principally, a technique of rule applied to relations within the state. Among the goals pursued in this way are the elimination of competitors, and so the autonomy of those already occupying positions of power, and the political-administrative system's strategic interest in maximum autonomy in relation to its societal environment. The precise nature of this doctrine's domestic functions has changed appreciably in the era of transnational society formation and intrasocietal democratization. Today, an appeal to raison d'état, that is to say, the attempt to justify decisions by means of reference to a real or putative state interest, which is supposed to overcome all opposition (see Quaritsch 1975: 53), is less likely to perform a societally integrative function than to be an attempt to secure political-administrative autonomy against challenges from the societal world.

CHALLENGES OF THE SOCIETAL WORLD TO THE AUTONOMY OF THE STATE

Considerable attention has already been paid to the challenges presented to the territorial state and to the state system itself by the societal world. In order to support the thesis that the state has been losing its problem-solving capacity, reference is made to technology-driven economic globalization, in the course of which transborder problems arise that cannot be adequately dealt with by territorially segmented political decision-making units. The political-administrative systems can only retain their problem-solving capacity if they utilize the resources of other actors. One way of regaining this capacity is by drawing societal actors into corporatist structures. There is, however, a price to be paid in the currency of state autonomy. Fritz Scharpf (1991: 622) has described this price aptly as "the de-hierarchization of the relationship between state and society."

This de-hierarchization is highly ambivalent if examined from the perspective of a government's interest in itself. On the one hand, it serves this interest because it makes the state more effective as a problem-solver and thus substantially adds to its legitimacy. On the other hand, however, the de-hierarchization, which results from the substitution of the vertical interaction modes of subordination and control by the horizontal interaction modes of arguing and bargaining, which are typical of the policy networks that have emerged, also cuts down governmental freedom of action considerably. This process of change would cause no problem for governments if we conceptualize them in the terms of political liberalism, that is, as 'honest brokers' with no interests other than those they pursue on behalf of society. It becomes, however, highly problematic if the national government is understood as a societal subsystem charged with carrying out certain functions but also retaining its own interests. While globalization challenges the states primarily in respect of their regulation capacity as problem-solvers (that is, their *governance* function), domestic pressure and the growth in the importance of transnational actors place in question their autonomy of action itself, especially in relation to the actors of the societal world (that is, their *government* function). These developments lead to a situation in which the individual political-administrative systems are less and less capable of structuring societal contexts in accordance with their own preferences. But which options do governments have if they want to escape from the dual challenge by which they are confronted?

MANIPULATING THE DOMESTIC CONTEXT BY INTERGOVERNMENTAL SELF-COMMITMENTS IN THE EUROPEAN UNION

If we assume a basic and general inclination to self-assertion as an actor's preference that is of prior character and that is ranking higher than substantive goals determined by specific situations, and if we furthermore attribute this striving to the political-administrative system, we can interpret a wide range of types of behavior as strategies designed to maintain or recover state autonomy threatened by globalization and the rise of civil society. Intergovernmental self-binding is one of these behavioral options. At first glance it may seem as though this characterization stands in sharp contradiction to the prevailing view, which sees international institutions as a kind of self-government by the states with the goal of pooling and consolidating their problem-solving capacities. I am by no means seeking to deny that the internationalization of governance still does, and was perhaps even originally designed to, serve the purpose of recovering problem-solving capacities that have been lost at the nation-state level by means of a refocusing of state competences at the intergovernmental level. But just like the raison d'état, mutual self-commitments have from their very beginning always had a power dimension as well that cannot be captured by a problem-oriented understanding alone. Robert Keohane argues that considerations of domestic policy already played a part in the original agreement on mutual recognition of sovereignty and the renunciation of intervention: "Intervention [...] reduced the power of monarchs vis-à-vis civil society. Hence, agreement on principles of nonintervention represented a cartel-type solution to a problem of collective action" (Keohane 1995: 172). The rise of civil society that has gone along with the emergence of world society has revitalized this cartel. Increasing global and intrasocietal pressures have reinforced the search for external support in order to gain strength domestically (see Hudson et al. 1993: 79, 90). The strategy of this new raison d'état makes use of a reorganization of statehood by means of international governance with the goal of reaching agreements and making commitments, which can be removed as far as possible from the sphere of domestic political debate and thus rendered immune to revision.

In his comprehensive analysis of the development of the world of states and of future state survival strategies in the face of societal emancipation, Hendrik Spruyt too singles out international institutions as strategic instruments "deliberately designed [...] as protection to individual governments from irate domestic constituents" (Spruyt 1994c: 190). A development that looks at first like a loss of autonomy in relation to the other members of the world of states gains in plausibility once we see it as a successful isolation of the government from societal control.

The importance of society for state action is no longer a consequence of its capacity to produce tensions threatening stability (which make it an object of authoritarian integration), but rather a reflection of the fact that it has become a competitor, presenting the state with a choice between dominance and submission. Theda Skocpol identifies the state's internal interest as the political-administrative system's pursuit of ways in which it can strengthen its autonomy in relation to societal groups. State action, previously accorded the highest priority as the instrument of preservation of the public good, is thus demystified and classified as the reflection of only one of a number of rival interests emerging out of different societal subsystems. We can expect the state to carry out both its function as a synthesizing force in bringing together societal forces directed outward and its mediating function in relation to the adaptation pressures exerted by the international environment, not only actively but also in an *interested* way, in the sense of its own self-assertion. The consequence for the analysis of foreign policy is the suspicion that the state apparatus may also use international interactions for its own benefit as it pursues this interest: "Indeed, a state's involvement in an international network of states is a basis for potential autonomy of action over and against groups and economic arrangements within its jurisdiction" (Skocpol 1979: 31).[4] This return to the original idea of raison d'état as an internally directed technique of rule establishes a connection with the origins of the concept itself: "The traditional theoretical location of the concept of raison d'état has been the very point at which an assumption is made that there is an actual or potential conflict of interest between the governing and the governed, between state and private affairs" (Maluschke 1975: 573). Just such a context is provided by the emergence from the societal world of demands to be allowed to participate.

In this way, interstate cooperation is acquiring a new function. It can no longer restrict itself to the task of setting the margins of maneuver enjoyed by states in their relations with one another, but has now become a suitable forum for strategic interaction designed to maintain an internal autonomy that is increasingly under threat. There are good grounds for suspecting that the motivation "to maintain or regain control over the domestic exchange process" (Hudson et al. 1993: 53–54) is playing a role whenever we observe agreements being reached in the framework of intergovernmental self-commitments, which seek to remove certain controversial questions from further societal discussion or participation. The more irreversible this separation from the public sphere, the clearer it will be that this is what is happening.

Intergovernmental agreements can obviously serve a number of purposes simultaneously: by means of a mutual restriction of external autonomy in the relations between states, it is possible both to reestablish shared problem-solving capacities and to regain domestic freedom of action. The European Union is, in terms of its implications for external autonomy, the most radical project ever undertaken by a group of states. It provides a particularly graphic illustration of the ways in which governments can adopt binding mutual self-commitments but at the same time cast off certain shackles and in the end acquire increased autonomy and discretion to act. The EU case demonstrates both a high level of interstate self-binding and a marked democratic deficit. In the far-reaching commitments entered into by its member-states, the EU comes closer to the ideal type of a supranational organization than any other international institution. In the course of the creation of this complex decision-making system there has been a shift in favor of governmental and executive actors at the interstate and supranational levels, which has reduced nongovernmental actors' opportunities to exert control.

It does not even run counter to the basic argument presented in this chapter to acknowledge that the process of European integration has developed a dynamic of its own, and that the European polity has become much too complex to be reduced to the role of a mere tool in the hands of the national governments. This is neither how Euro-skeptical governments would perceive the European Union, nor could this view account for the influence of supranational institutions such as the European Court of Justice. On the contrary, I would argue that European integration has set in motion several, intended and unintended, dynamics, among them the emancipation of norms and institutions from their creators *and* the opportunity for national—and also supranational—executives to evade the control of civil society.

No one would seriously call into question that Europeanization has weakened the exercise of parliamentary control at the national level without reestablishing comparable procedural possibilities at the Community level. As long as the key to legislation is in the hands of the European Council supported by the Commission (which has the right to take initiatives), a major portion of political power is removed from the hands of those who are in theory sovereign. The executive functions of statehood have become autonomous in the European polity (see Neyer and Wolf 1996: 414). An especially important aspect of the loss or assertion of internal autonomy is the strengthening of national governments' positions in relation to societal interest groups, which is connected with Europeanization. The confusion occasioned by decision-making structures distributed at multiple levels and the fragmentation of competences have also reduced the prospects of successful lobbying, if we compare these relationships with the clientilistic relations between bureaucracies and large firms within individual states. Since national governments are no longer the decisive addressees of societal interest groups' demands, they can respond to the pressure exerted by these groups by referring to the fact of European political integration. Edgar Grande has used the striking formulation 'the paradox of weakness' to describe this "gain in autonomy achieved by state actors in relation to societal interests that has come about as a consequence of the former's loss of autonomy within integrated decisionmaking structures" (Grande 1996: 392). The suspicion that the ostensible maze as which the European polity may appear did not entirely come about by chance, but is at least to a substantial part also the result of interstate coordination efforts designed to maintain the national governments' own freedom of action in the domestic context, is reflected in Andrew Moravcsik's comment that "the unique institutional structure of the EC is acceptable to national governments only insofar as it strengthens, rather than weakens, their control over domestic affairs" (Moravcsik 1993a: 507).

The convergence criteria laid down in the Maastricht Treaty for the introduction and membership of a European Monetary Union provide some grounds for interpreting the self-commitment of the EU member states as an instance of the new raison d'état. This case demonstrates how, within the framework of a multilevel decision-making system by the establishment of which the initial instrumental goal of setting up a polity that provides broader and adequately isolated governmental action potential has been realized, a substantial program can also be made binding on subsequent governments if, at a given moment in time, this program is supported by the governments involved. It shows how a monetarist stabilization policy that has been secured at the interstate level can be put into practice domestically with the help of references to international obligations.

The momentum toward closer integration in the shape of the Single European Act and the Maastricht Treaty, which is at first glance difficult to explain theoretically, is in fact "sustained and driven forward by the shared interest of the member-states' governments in bringing about strategic changes in domestic structures and institutional orders by means of a policy of supranational integration" (Rieger 1995: 365). Two requirements must be met in order for there to be any prospect of achieving substantive domestic policy goals such as regaining international competitiveness, attracting investors, or flexibilizing the labor market at the expense of existing welfare provisions. First, the goal of restructuring the welfare state on the basis of a specific political program, and in the face of predictable societal resistance, must be a shared one. This condition of a self-commitment to a substantive political program is fulfilled only temporarily and in certain circumstances. It requires a specific political constellation characterized by agreement on concrete political goals (in this case monetary stabilization on the basis of a shared neoliberal economic philosophy) and on strategies for achieving these goals—in other words, policy and politics. Second, a polity framework must also be available, which makes it possible at any time to make use of specific possibilities for action and policy justification. This is available in the shape of the EU's multilevel system, which is largely isolated from nongovernmental political influences and is permanently supervised by the member-states' governments. This system, as the consequence of a general agreement to ensure the widest possible freedom of maneuver, is available at all times and can be activated whenever there is consensus on policy and politics. In order to remove certain political goals from societal interference, degrees of self-commitment can be increased or extended in specific sectors, as has been done under the provisions of the Maastricht Treaty. It is vital that these agreements be negotiated in fora to which the public has no access or in which government representatives can act as gatekeepers.

EXPLOITING TWO-LEVEL GAMES: THE NEW RAISON D'ÉTAT AS A GENERAL FEATURE OF INTERNATIONAL GOVERNANCE

How can the pattern be conceptualized that characterizes the interplay between domestic and intergovernmental interaction? Furthermore, is this pattern just typical of the special case of European governance and not applicable beyond the European polity? The full complexity of the self-assertion problematic identified by the term 'new raison d'état' becomes visible as the international political environment differentiates itself so as to become a multilevel system. Treating intergovernmental cooperation as a reaction by governments to challenges from the societal world means analyzing the political-administrative systems as actors in a multilevel game. They have to play at a number of different tables simultaneously, and in doing so they can try to achieve certain goals in internal and external interactions that are all related to one another. In this process, both the governments' relations with each other and their relations with their respective societal environments are characterized by both congruence and differences of interest. The concept of world society provides us with the model with which to analyze the *content* of this new raison d'état, and the two-level game model furnishes the appropriate *formal* framework that marks out the field within which we can analyze the various strategic options. If we add to this picture the theoretical assumption that the interacting governments are themselves interested in self-assertion both internally and externally, it follows that the mechanisms of international governance they create cannot be democratic, because the governments wish to preserve for themselves the broadest possible freedom of action both within and with the assistance of this two-level game. This does not entail the assumption that the governments must always form alliances against their societal environments, but they do want to have this option available at all times—just as they want to be able to play the two-level game in order to achieve their preferences in areas where they compete with each other. The new raison d'état aims at self-assertion by self-commitment at both levels. In fact, two-level games provide the participating governments with numerous opportunities "to manipulate domestic and international politics simultaneously" (Moravcsik 1993b: 15).

Identified as a general strategic option offered by contexts of two-level bargaining this way, it would be surprising if autonomy-seeking self-commitments on the intergovernmental level were limited to the European Union alone. But are there issue areas or segments of world society that are more conducive to practices of the new raison d'état than others? As far as types of issues are concerned, the classical literature on two-level bargaining (see, for example, Putnam 1988; Evans, Jacobson, and Putnam 1993) suggests that the strategy of intergovernmental self-binding is especially attractive for the realization of political programs that would otherwise be hard to push through domestically. The example of the European Monetary Union chimes perfectly with the empirical case referred to by Robert Putnam when he first introduced the metaphor of the two-level game: governments that enter into a program with the International Monetary Fund without necessarily needing a loan. Agreements on fiscal adjustment programs "that are (misleadingly) said to be 'imposed' by the IMF" (Putnam 1988: 457) are often sought by governments not because they want an IMF loan but because they are actually interested in a scapegoat for being able to push through unpopular measures internally. The IMF conditions are instrumental in order "to achieve internal reform in situations where constituency pressures would otherwise prevent action without the pressure [...] that an external partner could provide" (Putnam 1988: 447–48). Here, the same pattern is at work as in the EMU case: governments instrumentalize two-level games in order to tie their preferred policies to an international commitment.[5]

The numerous cases of IMF-scapegoating, which include developing countries from very different regions, also serve as evidence against the possible assumption that we can expect to observe practices of the new raison d'état most likely in regions where transnational society formation or intrasocietal democratization are already farthest advanced. Practices of the new raison d'état can be attributed to governments of very different types of states; they are neither restricted to Western Europe nor to the OECD world. The contributions to the volume on *Double-Edged Diplomacy* edited by Evans, Jacobson, and Putnam (1993) hint at further cases in which governments have used the leverage provided by two-level negotiations "to undermine the bases of their domestic opponents' power" (Evans 1993: 400). Their findings underline the assumption that it is by no means exclusively in liberal democracies that governments perceive domestic pressures or domestic opponents as incentives to enter into intergovernmental self-commitments. Examples such as Egypt and the USSR show that states that are 'weak' in the traditional sense can also attempt to overcome suspected domestic resistance to a policy course pursued by the government with the help of a self-binding strategy whose goal is internal autonomy.

If we take a look at different issue areas that are regulated by intergovernmental self-commitments, such as international security or the international protection of human rights, a whole variety of manifestations of the practices of the new raison d'état can be discerned. In regard to the international security system the expectations to be derived from our assumptions correspond with our observations: the principles of non-intervention and sovereign equality on which the international law of coexistence is based protect the autonomy of nation-state governments externally and internally. The Charter of the United Nations, which is still the world's most comprehensive framework for peace and security, lends external authority to the governments of the member-states. Michael Barnett speaks of "(t)he UN's stamp of approval" (Barnett 1997: 544) in regard to the authority claims of member-state governments. The price that governments have to pay for this is comparatively low because the horizontal mode of coordination is favored over the vertical mode of subordination in the U.N. context. Mutual recognition can therefore be obtained without sacrificing too much external autonomy. The societal world is hardly present at all in this intergovernmental arena. As Erskine Childers and Brian Urquart (1994: 171) put it: "The peoples of the United Nations introduce the Charter and then completely disappear from that document."[6] Even the welfare components that found their way into international law with the introduction of redistributional issues in the seventies have not very much increased the weight of societal demands vis-à-vis their governments: the still significantly soft international law of cooperation remains within the realm of solidarity among states, not among peoples.

Demands and concerns of civil society have, however, not completely been excluded from this arena. In fact, representatives of numerous nongovernmental organizations were present at the founding conference of the United Nations in 1945. Until today, even more of them have participated in a number of U.N. conferences. But nation-states still try to protect their leverage on them eagerly by acting as gatekeepers. If at least a modest degree of recognition and access has been achieved, this is less the result of friendly invitations from national governments to NGOs to offer their resources and expertise, but mostly the result of a struggle against the heavy, but not always successful resistance of nation-states (see Clark, Friedman, and Hochstetler 1998).

There is no more significant instance of the ongoing competition between the recognition of fundamental concerns of civil society and nation-states' interest in maintaining internal and external autonomy than the scope and the monitoring mechanisms of the existing international agreements that deal with the protection of human rights. Although national governments proved unable to prevent the establishment of international human rights regimes altogether, they were hesitant vis-à-vis respective civilian initiatives and took a defensive line in regard to supplying human rights regimes with effective compliance mechanisms. Responding to the overwhelming impetus that was given to human rights norms repeatedly by humanitarian disasters and so on, governments did what they could in order to prevent human rights initiatives by mostly civilian protagonists from violating their interest in themselves too much. As the result of competing interests in, on the one hand, the effective protection of human rights by strong compliance mechanisms, or on the effective protection of the principle of non-intervention, on the other, international human rights regimes share certain significant features. These features exhibit governments' interest in themselves in regard to (a) what kind of human rights are protected, (b) how these rights are protected, and (c) which countries have accepted what kind of protection of what kind of human rights.

Without much exaggeration one may say that the answers to these questions do not contradict but support the assumption that governments pursue interests of their own when they enter into international agreements, including the resistance against any attempts initiated by civil society to impose restrictions on their domestic autonomy. The general impression of the weakness of international human rights regimes, despite all the merits they do of course have, reflects the success of national governments in trying to avoid autonomy-consuming monitoring mechanisms. The standard procedure to which more or less all governments have committed themselves consists in the presentation of reports about the efforts they have undertaken in order to guarantee certain human rights the protection of which they have explicitly recognized. The applicability of any stronger mechanisms is again contingent on a government's explicit acceptance. If compliance procedures are accepted that could be regarded as substantially interfering with a state's internal autonomy, the parties to such an agreement usually consist of states that would have to comply anyway because of national human rights provisions. In sum, the high level of formal acceptance of human rights agreements corresponds with the weakness of the latter's monitoring mechanisms. So even international agreements on the protection of human rights carry the trademark of national governments defending their internal autonomy.

CONCLUSION

Intergovernmental agreements and self-commitments that respond to the changes in background conditions described here promise to become more effective methods than the traditional practice of mutual threat as ways for the governments to support each other in their efforts to maintain internal autonomy, or, as Janice Thomson puts it: "The international system lends domestic autonomy to the state through institutions such as international law and diplomacy, which empower the state to overcome societal resistance to its policing practices" (Thomson 1995: 226). However, this new raison d'état is far more complex than the old, one-dimensional version, because it has to deal with challenges to state autonomy from two directions simultaneously and every possible strategy can have consequences along both of these axes; internal autonomy can be pursued and gained at the expense of external autonomy, and vice versa. But this securing of internal and external autonomy is not a zero-sum game, and it is quite possible for a skillfully conducted policy to follow the logic of the new raison d'état and to increase overall autonomy.

In their efforts to pursue a successful policy of the new raison d'état by following Thomas Schelling's classical maxim that "the power to constrain an adversary may depend on the power to bind oneself" (Schelling 1960: 22), the political-administrative systems have to perform a difficult balancing act. Self-binding measures designed to increase autonomy must be so irreversible that it is not possible for them simply to be abandoned as a consequence of a change in societal demands; this concerns the political-administrative system's internal freedom of action. But they must also be reversible enough for governments to be able to retreat if necessary from commitments entered into in the interstate context; this concerns the external freedom of action.

The full ambivalence of the new raison d'état policy becomes visible if we consider a further dilemma in which, in particular, those (democratic) governments are caught whose self-assertion also depends on their ability to present themselves as effective problem-solvers. As has been mentioned above, this dilemma has already resulted in the de-hierarchization of the relationship between state and society in the domestic context. It may well soon spread to the level of governance beyond the state as well and devour what appeared to be the last resort of maintaining (inter-)governmental leverage vis-à-vis civil society. If they tried to escape this dilemma by excluding civil society from what at present is still predominantly *international* governance, the national governments would in the long run damage their own interests. Isolation from societal actors who were seen primarily as rivals would inevitably lead to a loss of or failure to use the problem-solving capacities that these actors might be able to make available as a contribution to effective governance.

8

Time to Change: States as Problems or Problem-Solvers in World Society?

Hilmar Schmidt

"Why study world society?" John W. Burton's classic study of the subject-matter and research program of international relations begins with this question (Burton 1972: 3). Burton proceeds immediately to offer a large part of the answer. One of the main reasons for undertaking the scholarly analysis of world society, he says, is its influence as a 'new whole' on the behavior and actions of actors both in their interactions with each other and in their inner lives: "There are many domestic problems that are more readily understood by examining the same kind of problem on the larger scale of relationships in world society" (Burton 1972: 5). Although this concept of world society has been developed further (see chapter 1), it can still be seen as following in Burton's footsteps. The basic approach is to investigate the behavior, options, and new responsibilities of particular actors in the new space of world society (Banks 1984). For Burton, however, the nation-state is an actor that declines in significance as world society develops. My own approach focuses on the problem-solving capacity of nation-states. The central thesis is that if the nation-state wishes to maintain its capacity to solve problems (and it must attempt to do this, if it is not to end up in the dustbin of history), it must not only change its behavior toward the external world, but also adapt itself internally to the new requirements of world society. This chapter ignores the strategic capacities and goals of states, understood as those goals serving the maintenance of states' general capacity to act (Wolf 1999). It focuses instead on states' concrete goals, which always exist in addition to the strategic goals. In order to pursue concrete goals, state decision-makers must enter into long-term, norm-bound, and institutionalized forms of cooperation not only with international, but also with their own societal actors. Only states with a high problem-solving capacity are able to sustain the costs of seeking international solutions to globalized problems. These states are particularly well suited to taking the lead in promoting international cooperation. This chapter tries to sketch the influence of intrastate capacities on the performance of states in international problem-solving processes in the field of ecology.

NATION-STATE AND WORLD SOCIETY

John Herz's article *The Rise and Fall of the Territorial State*, first published in 1957, represented one end of the spectrum in the debate on the future of the nation-state. Since the nation-state that had emerged out of the territorial state was in the nuclear age no longer able to defend its own territory adequately, it should be replaced by a new system of collective security (Herz 1976). Among the models proposed as ways of overcoming statehood and dealing with problems collectively were a world state and world society (Burton 1972). Although the world state idea became less attractive as a goal in the light of criticism of its democratic credentials (Czempiel 1981), the idea of world society remained, in two forms: (1) as a normative goal at the end of a process of development, and (2) as a model for the analysis of international relations (Burton 1972). The continued existence of the nation-state was used as a convincing argument against the normative perspective. Czempiel argued that this perspective's flirtation with the idea of overcoming the nation-state placed it in the realm of the idealist and even of the spiritual (Czempiel 1981: 71; more recent criticisms of the concept can be found in Czempiel 1991: 168).

The (Darmstadt/Frankfurt) World Society Research Group has proposed an alternative approach in the shape of a concept of world society, which focuses not on denationalization, but on interaction, institutionalization, and diffusion of actors as the constitutive features of a world society (see chapter 1). This approach makes it possible to investigate the 'state of the state' (Litfin 1993) without leaving one open to the charge that one is hanging on to an outmoded model of the nation-state. The decisive characteristics of the development of international relations from international system, via international society to world society are threefold: the institutionalization of international relations, the differentiation of levels of action, and the diffusion of actors. Even the international society stage could be distinguished from the international system by virtue of the institutionalization of collective rules of behavior between states. However, not only the international society model but also the analytic treatment of the establishment of international systems of regulation remains captive to a perception of the world through lenses that only permit the viewer to see interstate relations. The concept of world society seeks to remove these lenses by taking into consideration new forms of transnational integration and politics whose agents are no longer just transnational concerns. In this sense societal actors are becoming increasingly significant in the way international politics is made. The work of these actors is not just concentrated on their 'own' state or society, but is increasingly being directed toward other states and societies.[1] It is no longer just economic or state actors who join together in international alliances; societal actors too are forming international networks, organizations, and alliances. In addition, these actors are seeking new ways of participating in and controlling state policies (for instance, by means of monitoring). But this development cannot be captured adequately by describing it as the abdication of the state, but as "the initial stages of new forms of statehood, 'trans-statehood' and horizontal political interdependence, which go beyond the old forms of international cooperation and norm-building, and through which the mismatch between political territoriality and economic and societal developments is reduced" (quoted from chapter 1).

The driving force behind the development of a world society as described here is globalization. The world society concept provides a background for the investigation of changes in interstate relations set off by globalization. This means that the development of interstate social relations is not just an indicator of globalization, as in Beck's account (1996). Beck nevertheless draws attention once again to a decisive point: in addition to globalization from above (interdependence, international institutions), we also have globalization from below. Among the distinguishing features of globalization from below are "new transnational actors operating outside the parliamentary-political system and challenging conventional politics and interest organizations" (*Das Parlament,* no. 30–31, 19 July 1996: 12). Beck helps us to add a further element with considerable explanatory power to the concept of world society: the existence of risks caused by global dangers against which no insurance is possible. Beck's view is that the global adoption of capitalist technical processes and production methods, and their further development during modernity, leads to a situation in which the societal production of wealth is systematically inseparable from the societal production of risks (Beck 1986: 25). This applies to societies organized in the form of states and also at the level of international relations. The risks described by Beck are above all the effects of the advancing destruction of the natural environment. On top of these come the manufacture and proliferation of weapons of mass destruction and the poverty of a large part of humanity. While it is possible to identify local sources of the creation of these problems, especially the environmental ones, virtually all parts of the earth are affected by the consequences of such environmental problems as the destruction of the ozone layer and the greenhouse effect. World society therefore contains elements of risk society, and is also itself a risk society.

Our concept therefore identifies the most important conditions in which state governance must seek to solve problems arising within world society: (1) economic, political, and societal integration; (2) demands made by societal actors at the systemic and intrastate levels in the framework of societized foreign policy; (3) an ever-growing agenda of problems caused by modernization risks on a global scale (Beck 1986; Prittwitz 1993a).

The world society concept by no means denies that world politics lacks a central authority that could regulate the distribution of goods and take on control functions. Nevertheless, the classical security dilemma no longer exists in this world society. As a result of the proliferation of weapons of mass destruction, international terrorism, and the numerous forms of connection between the nation-states (see below), the security logic of this world society is no longer "trust no-one," but "trust no-one, not even yourself"—"anarchy [...] is withering away" (Lipschutz 1992: 418). Even 'security' itself is a collective problem in world society. Attempting to assert one's own interests to the exclusion of all others' is an inadequate strategy in this international system. In addition there are new dangers, which are characterized by Beck (1986) as 'modernization risks' (*Modernisierungsrisiken*), in connection with which the term 'ecological security' has been used. Although these issues do not follow the logic of the classical security problematique, in some cases (for example, climatic changes) they pose security problems in the sense of the survival of entire populations. Because of the problem of collective goods (Hardin 1968), it is usually the case that global environmental problems can only be solved when all the important actors cooperate. Power as an instrument for dealing effectively with such problems becomes relatively unimportant (Benedick 1991).

CONCEPT OF WORLD SOCIETY CAPACITY

What, then, are the tasks confronting the nation-states under the new world-societal conditions? Burkhard Wehner sees state communities as having four distinguishing features and four main categories of tasks they have to carry out. Nation-states must provide problem-solving capacities (efficiency in security and administration), tradition, identification, and solidarity (Wehner 1992: 2–4). During this century, however, the nation-state has developed increasingly as a community whose priority is efficiency in the sense of problem-solving, so that only efficient nation-states have maintained their organizational forms and been able to determine the course of history. According to the prevailing view, nation-states must accumulate goods in the three classical areas of policy—rule, welfare, and security (Czempiel 1981). The nation-states' provisions in these areas include foreign policy strategies involving some combination of confrontation and cooperation, and inwardly directed adaptation strategies (for example, democratization, liberalization, the establishment of the rule of law). The following sections present the strategies that can be derived for actors in world society, and develop criteria for what I call world society capacity, that is, the capacity to pursue policies appropriate to world society.

I now come to the main thesis of this chapter: if the nation-states wish to find solutions to the global problems that have developed and are still developing, they will need not only to change their external behavior but also to reorganize themselves internally in a very specific way. They must pursue an internal inclusion policy, that is, adapt their relationship to societal subsystems with the goal of finding the most effective ways of dealing with these global problems. The existence of these problems and the state's regulation difficulties are linked by a number of authors with the decline in significance or, as Ralf Dahrendorf puts it, the helplessness of the state: "The nation-state is no longer a very useful instrument for creating welfare; the days of the 'national economy' (Volkswirtschaft) are over" (Dahrendorf 1994: 756). The development of world society seems to emphasize more than ever the failure of the state in the sense of its weak capacity for political intervention, its functional ineffectiveness, and economic inefficiency in settling domestic political problems (Smith 1992; Jänicke 1993b). On the other hand, the nation-states have proved to be extremely stubborn (Weißmann 1993), and are still seen as the only institutions capable of guaranteeing societal security and freedom (Dahrendorf 1994: 760). What is more, only the nation-states seem to have the capacity to furnish the resources needed to solve global problems in world society, or at least to call for the provision of these resources. Smith draws the conclusion: "Equally, it can be argued almost in the same breath both that the state is being or has been weakened by the changes relating to globalization, and that it has been strengthened by precisely those changes" (Smith 1992: 256). This is true in virtually all fields of policy, but can be seen particularly clearly in international environmental politics:

> Only the state has the human and financial resources to mount the large-scale scientific and technical projects for detecting, monitoring and preserving the global environment. Only the state, standing at the intersection of domestic and international politics, has sufficient authority, political legitimacy, and territorial control to influence the myriad causal agents of environmental deterioration. Thus, global ecological problems can be expected to bolster the power and legitimacy of the state in new ways. (Litfin 1993: 95)

The debate over 'global governance' has provided an initial answer to the question of what forms of rule might be appropriate in conditions where the problems confronting humanity are globalized and world-societal:

> If state policy still has any capacity at all to contribute to effective solutions for intrasocietal and global problems, this will not come about through sovereign decisions but above all through involvement in pluralist, corporate and intergovernmental negotiation systems, in transnational regimes and in international organizations. This is the plain fact of the matter: hardly anyone denies it and there is no need to make any further effort here to offer supporting arguments. (Scharpf 1993b: 165)

It is no longer the case that any one state can solve its citizens' problems alone; if this can be done, it will usually only be possible in cooperation with other actors from the area around that state's borders. The international coordination of policy is becoming more and more important. This kind of international policymaking, which is for the most part more strongly oriented toward the search for consensus, is quite different both from the realist image of governance and from the usual picture of politics as conducted between the members of an international society. For one thing, it is not just the large and powerful but also the smaller states that have an opportunity to participate in managing international affairs, and indeed to act as driving forces. Even more important is the fact that the state-centric analysis of international relations is now being corrected and even transcended via the incorporation of the interrelations between political systems (and their component parts), societal groups, NGOs, and international institutions. This correction also needs to be made to the picture of policy-making painted by Scharpf, because intergovernmental negotiation systems are bound to exclude other actors, including other corporate actors, from the initial stages of policy formation and problem-solving. As long as this procedure is followed, the capacities of scientific communities or NGOs to contribute to problem-solving can only be called on when it is too late.

The capacity to solve problems in this way is attributed not to all nation-states, but only to the democratic, industrialized nations (Dahrendorf 1994; Liftin 1993). Even so, one cannot say that adaptation to world society is only a matter of democracy and the market economy; it would be more accurate to say that in a sense this is where it begins, since world society is constantly developing and there are constant changes in the demands it makes of the nation-state. Solving globalized problems in world society is therefore a matter of addressing a wider array of problems at the same time as allowing for a higher level of societal participation in the foreign policy-making process. There are two possible ways of going about this: by means of democratic corporatism, or by means of political modernization.

STATE AND SOCIETY: DOES POLITICS MATTER?

It should be clear by this point that the search for solutions that are appropriate to the demands of world society takes place in the political space between a significant growth in the agenda of problems to be addressed and the increasing participation of societal actors in the foreign policy-making process. Problem-solving with such aspirations must attempt to integrate both of these developments. It should be noted that a further, hitherto undiscussed assumption lies behind this statement, an assumption that underpins my whole argument. I am assuming that internal circumstances have an influence on states' problem-solving capacities, that is, that these are determined by more than just external factors such as a given state's general position in its international environment. I have also argued, following Scharpf, that the search for adequate solutions to globalized problems must take place at a level above that of the individual state. According to this argument, single states do not possess the capacity to solve these problems on their own. But why do different states participate to very different degrees in international problem-solving processes? Why do the economic and societal costs of international cooperation take on different dimensions in different states? My argument in this chapter concentrates on the constellations that exist within states and the effects of these on the states' performance in world society. Preparatory studies (Schmidt 1996) and an entire school of research within International Relations have dealt with the influence of intrastate factors on foreign policy,[2] and other studies with states' capacities to manage the effects that the international system has on them (Katzenstein 1984, 1985). Especially in the field of environmental policy, intrastate influences on environmental foreign policy have been repeatedly analyzed, but this has hardly ever been done in a systematic way.[3] One particular finding appears in almost all of these studies: the decisive factors determining policy outcomes were the influence of interest groups (economic associations, but also nongovernmental organizations) and the prevailing political style in the individual states (Jänicke and Weidner 1995: 19–23; Breitmeier 1996: 236). If we combine this finding with the new world-societal conditions for state policy, we can draw up the following working hypothesis: the way in which the societal interest groups are incorporated has a decisive influence on the policy outcome. Smith has formulated a similar hypothesis in the following terms:

> [This] suggests that more consideration needs to be paid to the broad context within which groups operate. The important variables in understanding decisions are the nature of the relationships that exist between groups and the state—the types of policy networks—and the interests and activities of state actors—the degree of state autonomy. (Smith 1993: 1)

Volker von Prittwitz's research on international environmental policy led him to a puzzling finding: environmental policy does not emerge as a reaction to a catastrophically high level of damage to the environment; rather, it develops in phases in which environmental damage is either declining or is already at a relatively low level (Prittwitz 1990: 27). This means that in the sphere of international environmental policy, no support can be found for a general statement that the worst affected countries pursue a particularly active environmental foreign policy while less seriously affected countries tend to be more passive (Prittwitz 1990: 236). The explanation for this paradoxical situation ('the catastrophe paradox') is to be found in variations between different capacities for action (economic, scientific, and political-institutional) and the development of the interests of those affected and those attempting to help, which clash with the interests of those who cause the environmental damage. The decisive factor in determining whether or not a particular state develops an environmental foreign policy is the constellation of interest profiles within a policy field, in other words, the relationship between these interests and the strength of each in relation to the strengths and/or weaknesses of the others. These interest relations are in turn influenced by the state's own capacities. Independent associations' chances of obtaining access to the political process are among these political-institutional action capacities (Prittwitz 1990: 176). The question that remains to be answered is that of the type of democratic system that makes this kind of access to the political process, legitimized participation and influence more likely, that is, the question of whether the organization of the political process has any influence on the policy outcome. This, at any rate, is the claim made—on the basis of a substantial amount of empirical corroboration—by political-institutional theorists. A decisive role in the emergence of policy outcomes is played by the "institutional conditions of the formation of opinions and decisionmaking" (Schmidt 1993: 397) between economic, political, and societal actors. This analysis differs from the classical field of institutional research in that it also examines, within the framework of a state-society model, the informal rules and norms, the institutions and independent elements within decisionmaking structures considered both as barriers and as features, which make certain policy outcomes possible. In the study presented here, I attempt to use network analysis to track down these state-society connections and to establish the effects they have on specific policy outcomes.

Network Analysis as a Method

Network analysis came into being as a reaction to criticism of 'traditional' policy research. It serves to correct an overly schematic view of politics by "concentrating on the interaction between private and state (organizational) actors" (Héritier 1993b: 16). It also rejects the idea that state actors automatically enjoy a dominant position in relation to societal actors:

> The question of who occupies such a dominant position is an empirical question which can be answered with the help of theoretical considerations; however, the public actors are the only ones with the privilege of making rules, which means they can redistribute institutional action resources—for example, by changing formal decisions or introducing the right to take an issue to court. (Héritier 1993b: 16)

Social networks are systems of social units, linked by social relations. The decisive element in the proposed analysis of these networks is that not only the units, but also the relations between them, are described. The analysis proceeds by examining these networks in terms of their structure, the kinds of communication occurring within them, and the symmetrical or asymmetrical nature of the relations between their component parts (Pappi 1993: 85). Network analysis has the advantage of being able to shed light on social structures in which relations are interrupted, since these interruptions are sometimes deliberately employed as a tactic by certain actors (Pappi 1993: 87).

Policy Networks as a Phenomenon

Political networks are becoming more and more important, and are increasingly recognized as such (Scharpf 1991). Societal actors increasingly seek recognition as participants in the political process, and at the same time cooperation with these actors gives the state an opportunity to acquire information (Mayntz 1993: 41).

> Policy networks with the potential for voluntary and conscious collective action only come into being in societies in which there are corporate actors who are in a position to take strategic decisions, to negotiate with other corporate actors, and to reach compromises. The existence of policy networks is therefore not only an indication that the state's role is restricted to the specific dimension of rule, but also an indication of societal modernization. (Mayntz 1993: 43)

Policy networks are treated here as a particular feature of politics that only manifests itself in modern political systems. These networks seem to be a more or less natural concomitant of structural change in modern societies, "and one can even see them as a central expression of societal modernization" (Mayntz 1993: 41). In my own work, the primary function of the network approach is an analytic one. Networks' influence on policy outcomes depends on their composition, that is to say, the actors making them up and the relations between those actors. It has become customary to contrast traditional pluralistic models with two organizational types of networks; corporatist networks and networks that come into being in the course of political modernization.

Pluralism

Pluralist theories have for many years exerted a dominant influence on research on the state and on the role of associations. Most pluralists see associations as the decisive factor in the analysis of political behavior. The original version of pluralism took the view "that power is distributed equally, that the state is neutral and that the access to the state is relatively open" (Smith 1993: 15). Elite associations are seen as bridges between members of society and the political system, and they transmit society's claims to the system. Political decisions are negotiated by the interest groups, and the state functions as a neutral judge or referee. If interest groups make no demands of the political system, no political decisions will be taken. This means that the state cannot pursue any policy independently of these groups, and new subjects are placed on the agenda by these interest groups. An interest group's influence is decided by the level of societal support on which it is able to draw (Easton 1965: 37).

Corporatism

The start of the corporatism debate was heavily influenced by a fierce, sometimes polemical controversy between corporatists and liberal theorists (Streeck 1994b: 8). The advantages of the concept of corporatism became clear when it was applied in comparative empirical studies. Liberalism, argued the neocorporatists, was empirically neither universal nor the inevitable outcome of a long-term trend:

> To the contrary, empirical research seemed to show that societies whose real conditions came reasonably close to the liberal model were often politically and economically inferior to others, especially to those 'associative democracies' or 'bargained economies' which conceded a legitimate place to the corporatistically organized collective actions of social interest groups. (Streeck 1994b: 9)

Peter Katzenstein reached the same conclusion after posing the question of why different democratically constituted industrialized nations have enjoyed varying degrees of success in their attempts to balance the costs and benefits of their involvement in the world economy. Katzenstein starts from the assumption that almost all states were affected by the changes in world markets and economic crises that characterized the 1970s and 1980s. He goes on to identify a group of nation-states that were more successful than most others both economically and politically (in the sense of maintaining stability). These findings illustrate "a traditional paradox in international relations concerning the strength of the weak" (Katzenstein 1985: 21). This more successful group of 'small European states' consists of Switzerland, Austria, Norway, the Netherlands, and Denmark. They were more successful in containing unemployment, in keeping the inflation rate down and in maintaining the internal legitimacy of the political system (a high level of acceptance of the political parties and infrequent changes of government). The explanation offered by Katzenstein is that the smaller European nation-states had no choice but to adapt themselves to the world economy, since they were dependent on it and had no way of influencing the rules of the game. As a result, democratic-corporate structures have developed in these states; Katzenstein describes these as follows:

> Democratic corporatism is distinguished by three traits: an ideology of social partnership expressed at the national level; a relatively centralized and concentrated system of interest groups; a voluntary and informal coordination of conflicting objectives through continuous political bargaining between interest groups, state bureaucracies and political parties. (Katzenstein 1985: 32; see also Katzenstein 1976)

Political networks with corporate structures seem not to be dominated by particular interests, as in the USA, but rather to function as ways of carrying out specific political tasks: 'The dominant function of the network [...] is policy formation and implementation, with centers of decisionmaking being difficult to locate' (van Waarden 1992: 139). Corporatist structures therefore seem to be better equipped than straightforwardly pluralist structures to respond to world-societal requirements (above all those derived from interdependence and modernization risks), and so able to keep the societal and economic costs of this response as low as possible by means of a deliberate attempt to involve the society as a whole. In my opinion, corporatist structures are not completely incompatible with a growing post-industrial society, although some authors take the view that the two things are incompatible (Crepaz 1994: 47). In environmental policy and also in other fields, social partnership and corporate actors are visible and have an impact on the formulation of effective results, and these structures are compatible with the development of policy networks in postindustrial societies (Czada 1994: 57). The discussion of the decline of corporatism is not ignored in my analysis of world society capacity, but it is not helpful to talk about the decline of the corporatist state, as this entity cannot be found in anything like a pure form at any time in European history.[4]

Exclusive and Nonexclusive Corporatism

A comparative study of policy networks in the United States and the Netherlands has shown that in these countries both citizens' movements and small parties have been able to engage with corporatist structures and have thus been able to exert a lasting effect on the political process (van Waarden 1992). It is difficult to explain this within the framework provided by classical corporatist theory, since centralized (exclusive) negotiations are part of the definition here. It is therefore useful to draw a distinction between 'exclusive' and 'nonexclusive' corporatism. The main characteristic of exclusive corporatism is the fact that the 'classical' actors, workers' organizations, and capital, make sure that new societal actors such as environmental groups are not allowed to participate in corporatists arrangements (Therborn 1992: 42). The consequence of this is either the reduction of the environmental factor to something that is used and instrumentalized, or a situation in which the classical corporatist actors seek to meet the challenge of environmental management by concluding agreements with the government (Hukkinen 1995: 69). All the new societal groups can hope to do in these circumstances is to monitor governmental actions from the outside and to alert public opinion to the problems. The nonexclusive form of corporatism, on the other hand, attempts to involve all relevant interest groups in the negotiations. Alliance formation can sometimes lead to a reduction in the number of interest groups. Attempts are made in the course of negotiations to find solutions that reflect the widest possible societal consensus. However, consensual negotiations require both that the point at issue be generally recognized as important and that the new societal actors be prepared to modify their positions. In addition, there must be a guarantee that the negotiating parties enjoy legitimate authority to make decisions that will then be translated into action by their organizations. One of the interesting questions that remains unanswered is how far the societal actors are prepared to accept this role.[5]

Political Modernization

Like neo-corporatists, modernization theorists are concerned with states' capacities to act. In this context, modernization means "the further development of the modern welfare state as it has emerged in western societies in the course of the 19th and 20th centuries" (Hesse and Benz 1990: 14). A requirement for further modernization has arisen toward the end of the twentieth century not simply because of complex and subtly differentiated problems of economic development, but also because of simultaneous changes in ecological and social conditions. Traditional methods of regulation seem outmoded, and the functioning of centralized regulation can no longer be guaranteed (Hesse and Benz 1990: 50).

In his theory of state failure, Martin Jänicke has attempted to explain the nation-state's reduced regulation capacity. Jänicke identifies three weaknesses of the disenchanted state, of which so much is demanded, but which can in reality do so little:

- The state's weak capacity to intervene politically; in other words, its structural incapacity to counteract trends that are widely seen as negative;
- Its lack of functional effectiveness, as manifested in a preference for tackling symptoms rather than trying to deal with the root causes of problems;
- Economic inefficiency in the form of a systematic mismatch between the quality and the price of public goods, a consequence of an economization of attempts to deal with problems, which is the industrial system's way of using the state apparatus for its own purposes (Jänicke 1993b: 64).

Two circumstances made it possible for these tendencies to develop: changes were ignored, and interests "for which the persistence of the problems was not inconvenient" (Jänicke 1993b: 65) were able to institutionalize themselves. Jänicke identifies these as above all bureaucratic and industrial interests; Prittwitz (1990) calls them the interests of those who are at the root of the problem. But since not only the population as a whole, but also some parts of industry and of the administration are affected by state failure, new, decentralized, and cooperative structures have formed below the state level and in cooperation with the political systems. Jänicke's term for this development, which is still in its early stages, is 'political modernization'. It leads to the following changes:

- from the bureaucratic regulation of details to stronger regulation of framework conditions and contexts of action;
- from the bureaucratization of ways of dealing with problems to a socialization of this process with the state continuing to play a role;
- from centralized to decentralized problem-solving;
- from an exclusive to a more inclusive and participatory decision structure (a partial opening-up of established policy networks);
- from an imperative political style to the search for solutions through negotiation;
- from a reactive to a more anticipatory pattern of politics;
- from the regulation of public expenditure to a strengthened regulation of public income (taxation, duties and other forms of revenue) (Jänicke 1993b: 70–71).

Political modernization is to be understood as an ideal type of politics, as "a change in and significant extension of industrialized societies' capacity to solve problems, in the sense of a tendency towards debureaucratization, decentralization and problem-solving at the societal level" (Jänicke 1993b: 72). Modernization understood in this way includes above all a redefinition of the relationship between the political system and the other societal subsystems, which is becoming necessary in the conditions of world society. The inclusive and participatory decision-making structure that lies at the root of the concept of political modernization also makes it impossible to exclude the policy networks from the political process. The debate over environmental policy has itself demonstrated that an open political process within a policy network can be a decisive resource in the search for solutions to ecological dilemmas (see Prittwitz 1993a). In Beck's concept of reflexive modernization, which is offered as a way of beginning to get a grip on the harmful consequences of 'simple' modernization, the central idea is that of the decentralization of politics. Beck (1991) sees an emerging category of 'sub-politics' as offering a possible way of countering risk society. According to this conception, state politics are becoming less and less significant, and societally coordinated politics more and more decisive: the first indications of this development can be observed in the putting into practice at the local level of Agenda 21, the central document of the Rio Conference. However, it would make more sense to see this 'subpolitics' as a complement rather than an alternative to traditional politics, as it would be preferable to resist the further disintegration of societies into new sub-units rather than to encourage this process (Prittwitz 1993b: 37). The process of modernization also includes elements of intentional political regulation.

INITIAL FINDINGS AND PROSPECTS

Before approaching political decision-makers with well-meaning advice, scholars working in this area should try to identify a causal relationship between the desired and in part already formed structure of the decision-making process and a more effective political output. The first task, therefore, is to show to what extent already-existing modernization capacities or corporatist features have an effect on a given state's competence in problem-solving. The author is presently conducting research in the field of global climate protection, seeking to establish whether and in what respect the behavior of states already possessing these capacities differs from the behavior of those in which these capacities have not yet been developed.

The central issue here is the content of democratic structures in western industrialized systems, in other words, the "'intensity problem' of democracy" (Lewin 1994: 59). The question of societies' participation in the political process is posed in a wider sense once we have the context of 'societized foreign policy' (Czempiel 1994); it is not just a matter of the implications for the theory of democracy, but also a question of the connection with the state's competence in problem-solving. A political modernization process or elements of a corporatist structural development could bind societal actors into the political process in an effective manner that is well-adapted to the development of world society. In this type of political process, there are better prospects for consensus-guided problem-solving and for using capacities from nongovernmental actors and a kind of pooling of know-how. Whenever a cooperative policy-style brings together actors from different parts of society, the prospects of an integrated and consensus-based form of policy implementation improve. The earlier the social and economic actors are involved in dialogue and cooperation, the easier it is for these actors to provide inputs and to see how important they are in the search for effective solutions. Another point worth stressing is the capacity of innovative firms in this process (Business Council for a Sustainable Future 1994); these firms are able to introduce new discussions to the industrial sector and to mobilize resources in this part of society. The main role of nongovernmental organizations is generating public awareness and solidarity. Both concepts improve the prospects of problem-solving competence by employing a horizontal style of politics, which permits the participation of societal actors and which is partly guided by the political system itself.

The author's research project attempts to detect corporatist and/or modernization tendencies within political networks, which can be considered as indicators of a state's capacity to adapt to world society. The case studies will seek to establish whether these states are better equipped to deal with transborder ecological problems. Initial findings from the work of the author (Schmidt 1996) and other scholars (Breitmeier 1996; Jänicke and Weidner 1995) lead to the conclusion that a cooperative policy style, an open information system, and the involvement of societal actors allow the state to cope with environmental problems faster and more easily. States with these features often play major roles in international negotiations in the field of environmental politics. Japan, nowadays a pacesetter in air pollution control policy, has, as Weidner has shown, a high effectiveness in 'meta-instruments' and policy instruments as a result of "certain unique developments and events in Japanese society in the 1960s and 1970s as well as of certain characteristics of its political, cultural, and social system" (Weidner 1995: 169). The result of this development is the creation of new basic conditions in the environmental conflict area, a governmentally guided cooperative policy style and the very early participation of the most important economic and societal forces. These developments are even visible in the German policy-making process related to global warming. In 1987 the German Bundestag established the Enquete-Kommission 'Schutz der Erdatmosphäre' [Protection of Earth's Atmosphere]. This commission made it possible to bring together all political parties, scientists, industry, and NGOs. Like the NGOs, different parts of industry even joined together in concentrated bargaining groups. While the commission was to some extent critical of government policy, it also played the role of a partner. In this political climate, an early consensus developed on the need for a reduction in German carbon dioxide emissions, and like Japan, Germany played a leading role in negotiating the framework convention on climate change.

A major finding of the research done so far is that in none of the cases examined has there been a withering away of the state. State decision-makers concerned with Japanese pollution control or German climate policy had a major impact on the political process as well as the policy result. These findings suggest that: first, analyzing states in world society will remain a necessary research topic in the future, because states are still playing the dominant role in international politics, even (or may be even more so) in world society; second, it is important to analyze states' behavior in relation to their own societies, even in an international context.

9

Multilevel Governance: On the State and Democracy in Europe

Michael Zürn

Has the West European integration process seriously weakened the nation-state, or has it effectively strengthened it and thereby damaged the fundamentals of the democratic constitutional state? How should a European political system be shaped in order to avoid such damage and ensure that politics remain democratically legitimate? More generally, how can democracy be established in a world society?

With regard to the first question, I argue that the recent thrust toward integration in Europe, which was initiated by the Single European Act, can be seen as the result of a globalization thrust that began in the mid-1970s. This globalization thrust decisively weakened the capacity of the modern nation-state to effectively fulfill some of its governance functions, in particular the provision of social welfare and security. In reaction to this development, governments established international and supranational institutions in order to regain policy effectiveness. Although they have in part succeeded, on balance political control over markets has been weakened. Moreover, insofar as the real significance of international institutions has increased, this has also led to an increased independence of political decision-makers from their national constituencies.

Against the background of this predicament, I would like to join in the discussion on a democratic design for the European multilevel system of governance. I shall introduce four criteria that are imperative for a democracy to function and that are all affected by the aforementioned transformation processes. Against these criteria the two currently most prominent points of view in the debate on European democracy will be evaluated. Both perspectives, the one demanding a strengthening of the European Parliament (EP) and the one demanding a form of coordination that is compatible with national autonomy, reveal shortcomings when measured against these criteria. In the light of this discussion I would finally like to put up two new institutional proposals for discussion. One proposal advocates a democratization of territorial representation in the EU system and the other recommends the strengthening of elements of direct democracy at the European level with a view to promoting cross-border public discourse in Europe. In principle, the analysis of the democratic problems for governance beyond the nation-state and partially also my own institutional suggestions are both applicable to fields and areas outside the European Union as well. In this sense, this chapter is a general contribution to the issue of democratic governance beyond the nation-state.

MAASTRICHT: THE ZENITH OR THE BEGINNING OF THE END OF THE NATION-STATE?

Up until well into the 1970s, the analysis of Europe in political science was very straitlaced, assigning the process of West European unification almost completely to the subdiscipline of International Relations and discussing it in the context of integration theories. A little later, independent research on the EC developed, but this soon turned out to be an academic form of commentating stagnation. It was only with the Single European Act that political science research on Europe was endowed with theoretical issues. Today, the analysis of West European integration has taken on board concepts such as 'state', 'nation', and 'democracy'[1] that are constitutive for the discipline. The European Union is now the empirical focus of debates about postnational politics. One of the central questions in this debate is whether the European territorial state, which during the seventeenth and eighteenth centuries was able to prevail over a series of institutional rivals, is now in a process of dissolution. The debate thus centers on the immodest question whether politics is at the threshold of a new epoch.

A considerable number of experts claim that, in the words of the British political scientist Barry Buzan (1994: 97), "states are steadily dissolving, leaving their societies increasingly exposed to the cultural, economic, and human dynamics of the whole continent." The Frenchman Jean-Marie Guéhenne (1994: 13) prophesies that an 'imperial age' will follow the era of the nation-state "just as the Roman Empire succeeded the republic." The German Tilmann Evers (1994: 125) already perceives within the present 'European architecture' more similarities with the constitution of the Holy Roman Empire than with the concept of competing and cooperating nation-states. In the United States, too, analysts of West European integration discern a diffusion of power centers and consequently a 'hollowing out' of the nation-state, "[pulling] some previously centralized functions of the state up to the supranational level and some down to the local/regional level" (Marks 1993: 392; Hughes 1993).[2]

Andrew Moravcsik (1994: 52) seems, however, to come to a contrary conclusion: "EC policies tend, on balance, to reinforce the domestic power of national executives."[3] Along the same lines, Milward, Brennan, and Romero (1992: 5) introduce their monumental book on the *Rescue of the European Nation-State* with the following words: "It is the argument of this book that [...] the evolution of the European Community since 1945 has been an integral part of the reassertion of the nation-state as an organizational concept." And, with a view to the European state system in general, Robert Jackson (1994: 367) rhetorically asks, "Why should anyone expect such a system to be abandoned at the very moment of its greatest success?"[4]

Who is right? Which of the two opposing sides can present the more convincing arguments? In my opinion both sides present good arguments, but both sides also draw biased conclusions, the reason being that they fail to draw an important distinction between the different dimensions of statehood. On the one hand, the state is seen as a political and administrative system that achieves its autonomy from society on the basis of specific resources such as the monopoly on the legitimate use of force, the right to impose taxes, and the authority to assign decision-making competencies. From this resource-oriented, or realist, point of view, the state mainly means *government* with superior means of power.[5] On the other hand, the state is defined by its capacity to fulfill specific functions for the society such as ensuring peace within and beyond its borders (protective function), the protection of property rights and the provision of common goods (efficiency function), and the (re-) allocation of material and immaterial goods (distributive function). From this functionally oriented or liberal point of view, the state means *governance*, that is, the fulfillment of economic and societal functions.[6] Both dimensions of the modern nation-state belonged together for a long time. It was regarded to be a general rule that sufficient resources and an autonomous political and administrative system result in highly effective policies. These two dimensions in the customary definition of the state, however, are not irreversibly connected (see Ronge as early as 1979; Mayntz and Scharpf 1995).[7]

In the remainder of this section, I want to evolve the thesis that the formerly close connection between the autonomy of the political and administrative system and the state capacity to fulfill governance functions will be further loosened in the course of European integration. According to the functional definition (as governance), nation-states will be hollowed out, while political decision-makers become more independent of societal control than they have ever been under the welfare state. While one side observes the increasing erosion of the effectiveness of national policies, the other side perceives a growing autonomy of the political and administrative system. The reason for the divergence of both these dimensions of traditional statehood is uneven denationalization.

States have never been able to achieve political goals without taking the activities of other states into account. The activities of others were always a decisive factor for the effectiveness of policies, especially with regard to security. In this sense, the interdependence of states is a constitutive characteristic of the modern state system. With the spread of industrialization in the nineteenth century this interdependence extended into the economic, and thus the societal sphere. Only since the end of the Second World War, however, has the western world been able to cooperate on a long-term basis to overcome the inevitable friction resulting from the interdependence of societies. This success can be attributed to the international institutions established after World War II under the leadership of the United States, of which the economic institutions were of foremost importance.[8] The international trade regime (GATT) and the regimes for regulating currency and financial affairs created an institutional framework that made the postwar worldwide economic boom possible. The principle behind these international institutions has been summed up in the term 'embedded liberalism' (Ruggie 1983, 1994). Embedded liberalism made relatively unrestrained economic trade between all industrial countries possible while at the same time leaving room for different national political and societal structures. In this way, corporatist welfare states of Scandinavian origin were able to coexist successfully with liberal Anglo-Saxon systems and Eastern Asian state-oriented societies and economies. International institutions were a form of international governance, which enabled national governance to continue, and led to a hitherto unknown expansion of state activities. As trade barriers fell, the states intervened with measures to offset the domestic political consequences of free trade by embedding free trade within the interventionist welfare state. It therefore comes as no surprise that the majority of national economies that are integrated in the international market are governed by states with proportionately high social expenditures.

The European Economic Community was an important component of this institutional arrangement, which cogoverned the western world. Regional tariff unions, that is, regions in which tariff restrictions on trade were completely lifted, were perfectly legitimate within GATT, even if they partially contravened the most-favored-nation clause. Accordingly, the EEC was also based on the principle of 'embedded liberalism'. Within the EEC, goods were exchanged duty-free without preventing national governments from independently determining the institutional framework of their domestic markets. As with the GATT, problematic sectors such as agriculture and the steel industry were excluded from the principle of free trade.

The international economic institutions of 'embedded liberalism' were successful: they nurtured stable growth in the western industrial societies for almost thirty years; they fostered the integration of the world economy and consequently strengthened the role of export-oriented industries within the national political systems; and they have up until now helped to prevent a spiraling of protectionism and devaluation as occurred during the world economic recessions after the Second World War. Furthermore, these institutions allowed the development of welfare states, through which almost half of the gross national product is channeled in some West European countries.

Yet the international economic institutions have been too successful in some respects, as the recent globalization—or better: denationalization—thrust has increasingly undermined the national impetus in the postwar system. The process of societal denationalization, seen as a process in which the boundaries of social transactions increasingly transcend national borders,[9] violates the traditional notion of a nation-state that regulates transactions within its own national territory. While up until today the implications of interdependence were that social and state activities abroad had considerable effects on an individual country's policies and society, in many ways the distinction between domestic and foreign affairs are now neutralized. Since the mid-1970s, hidden but significant changes have been taking place, all of which have been an expression of a 'devaluation of borders' (Lothar Brock). The trend of these changes has been to transform the international economy into a global economy, national welfare states into risk societies and international relations into a world society.[10]

A major result of these developments is that national policies have become less effective in bringing about desired social outcomes. Evidence shows that the effectiveness of state policies is reduced in those issue areas where the jurisdiction of national regulations does encompass the borders of social spaces (defined by a decline in the intensity of transactions), that is, in those areas where political and social spaces become increasingly incongruent. The paradox of postwar liberalism is that it has ruined its own shock absorbers by undermining the congruence of social and political spaces. Ruggie (1994: 8) himself writes:

> By lowering and eliminating point-of-entry barriers to the flow of economic transactions and by encouraging cross-border corporate ties and market forces, governments have also inadvertently undermined the efficacy of some of their standard policy tools of managing the consequences of liberalization.

Therefore, the ability of an individual nation-state to intervene in world market processes in order to absorb undesired effects has weakened: both protectionism and generous welfare benefits are increasingly perceived to be self-defeating.

Against this background, we are currently witnessing a process that can be labeled 'uneven denationalization' (Zürn 1992c, 1995). This process comprises three phases. In the first phase, as a result of societal denationalization the effectiveness of national policies is reduced in those issue areas where social spaces are larger than political spaces. In the second phase, in an endeavor to restore the effectiveness of their policies, nation-states strive to establish international regimes and institutions, thus adapting the scope of political regulations to the boundaries of social transactions (political denationalization). However, international institution building takes one or two decades to be accomplished[11] so that international institutions cannot completely compensate for the growing ineffectiveness of national policies so far. The effectiveness of international regulation has by no means improved to the same degree as it has deteriorated under nation-states. Moreover, international institutions that have facilitated the extension of social transactions possible (negative integration) have to be distinguished from those built to mitigate the effects of globalization by regulative measures (positive integration). On balance there has been more deregulation, which has above all aggravated social inequalities within national societies. The third phase comprises a rapid growth in the number and importance of internationally negotiated regulations, while at the same time the democratic control of international organization lags behind. We are currently in a situation in which the *bourgeois*, who have thought and acted in transnational categories for some time, can pursue their economic interests at will, despite the lacking democratic legitimacy of denationalized economic networks, because they are liberated from the norms and rules of collective political rationale, which still imprison the *citoyens* within national confines.[12]

The particularly rapid rate of uneven denationalization in the context of the European Community is due to two distinctive features of European integration: First, the traditionally, particularly dense cross-border transactions within Europe and second, the existence of supranational European institutions that have manifestly accelerated the processes described above. Although the high degree of integration of West European societies makes them in any case highly susceptible to processes outside their national borders, the creation of a Common Market certainly fostered this. Nevertheless, the national deregulation necessary to create a common market would not have been accomplished so fast and so forcibly without the European Court of Justice (see Burley and Mattli 1993; Joerges 1995). At the same time, reregulation efforts at the European level are also largely attributable to one supranational institution, the Commission (see Majone 1993). Reregulation thus regularly raises issues of democratic legitimation.

The recent move toward European unification can thus also be understood within the context of the above-mentioned processes of uneven denationalization. Concern about a drop in competitiveness between European industries and Japanese or American enterprises initially led to the formation of the Common Market to improve the economies of scale and eliminate national regulations that hampered growth (see Sandholtz and Zysman 1989). Soon after this, an attempt was made to complement the "market without state" (Joerges 1991) with European regulations that were functionally equivalent to state regulations (see Tsoukalis 1993). The outcome of this combined process was on the one hand a reduced effectiveness of national policies, but on the other growing evidence of a democratic deficit within the European Union. Due to the difficulties involved in reregulation there has been an overall decline in the political effectiveness of state policies[13] and, from a material point of view, reregulation is taking place too slowly. However, from a procedural point of view, reregulation is progressing well ahead of the process, which renders it democratically legitimate. As a result, national governments are now in a much better position to evade societal influence and are gaining more autonomy from their constituencies.

With the help of the European decision-making level, governments can at the national level

- better regulate the domestic political agenda,
- restrict the options in domestic politics,

- gain privileged access to information on internationally relevant facts and situations, and
- gain privileged access to exclusive information on international decision-making processes, which makes credit claiming and scapegoating easier (see Moravcsik 1994).[14]

In other words, the sources from which social groups have been able to gain influence are gradually coming under government control. Moreover, social groups are only just beginning to resist this development by setting up European interest and pressure groups. This reorganization of interest groups initially takes place asymmetrically to the benefit of the employers,[15] which increases the difficulties in implementing positive regulations. Even for the relatively well-organized industrial interest groups it is, however, difficult to exert influence in the conventional way. At the European level, the degree of autonomy of political decision-makers is very high, because:

- They have more leverage in relation to social and economic interest groups.
- The decision-making process in the Council of Ministers takes place in camera, thus reducing the influence of interest groups.
- Due to the complexity of decision networks, economic interest groups experience great difficulties in finding the right access point for exerting influence.[16]

To sum up: although there has been a drop in the effectiveness of positive policies or regulative power, executive decision-makers have otherwise been able to sidestep societal control and thus gain more autonomy. This has two implications for the controversy between those who see the nation-state as having reached a new zenith of institutional dominance, and those who see Maastricht symbolic of the downfall of the nation-state. Worldwide economic and social change, which formed the basis for the recent thrust toward European integration, was facilitated by international postwar institutions. The result of this has been a considerable reduction in the effectiveness of national policies. In this respect, those who discern a decline in the significance of the state with regard to its traditional functions are right. However, states are reacting to these unintentional effects of social change by drawing up, in cooperation with supranational institutions, Europe-wide regulations, which, to a large extent, appear to be outside societal control and influence and at the same time forestall national decision-making processes. In this respect, those who point to the greater independence of the political class from society are also right. On balance, both sides lose out: the societies, which are cut off from the resources needed to participate effectively and voice their opinions, and the states, which have lost some of their regulative power due to the rapidly improved exit options of a few privileged economic actors. In this respect, Maastricht neither represents the zenith nor the end of the nation-state. It rather signals

DEMOCRATIC PROCESS IN A MULTILEVEL GOVERNANCE SYSTEM

Turning to the second question—that is, "how can democratic legitimacy be achieved in the European multilevel governance system, which developed out of uneven denationalization?"—one can take two conclusions drawn from the first question as a starting point. The first conclusion is that there is little point in discussing the problem of a 'democratic deficit' without taking both the effectiveness and control of policies into consideration. It is not enough to endorse the democratic principle by simply emphasizing 'the people'; the people must also be able to 'govern', that is, they must be in a position to use political measures to achieve what they desire. The right to choose freely must be complemented by the factual freedom of choice. Even if the national decisions are perfectly democratic, a democratic deficit can also arise if, due to structural restrictions at the international level, a political community is not able to pursue the objectives desired by the majority.[17] This 'democratic deficit in the broader sense' is very similar to the 'non-decisions' that were debated in the 1960s and 1970s (see Bachrach and Baratz 1970). The second conclusion is that the much deplored 'democratic deficit in the narrower sense' actually lies in the advantage political decision-makers or the executive have over society. The problem is not that the decisions of one or the other EU institution are lacking in legitimacy. The EU is a multilevel governance system that is constituted both by nation-states and European institutions, each of them being defined only in relation to the other. It is governance in Europe as a whole that is the problem.[18] Decision-making processes in complex multilevel governance systems generally give decision-makers, and particularly national governments, more power to prevail. Consequently, the question is not so much how individual EU institutions can be democratized but rather how a complex multilevel governance system as a whole can be democratically legitimized.

For a long time it was claimed that the democratic process (Dahl 1989) is only possible by means of representative majority decisions within a constitutional system. Although parliamentary democracy is an institutionalization of the democratic process that was quite appropriate as long as nation-states were the dominant form of political organization, it should not be confused with the democratic process itself. When nation-states came into existence, the Athenian form of city-state democracy no longer seemed adequate. Representational systems were better able to cope with the size of nation-states. In a similar way, parliamentary democracy may well become outmoded in the age of uneven denationalization. Hence, we need to identify the features of the democratic process itself and then seek institutional forms that best fulfill them in given circumstances. In order to do so, I distinguish among three questions:

1. What are the preconditions for a democracy in terms of community scale? In other words: what association of people should constitute the demos?
2. What are the characteristics inherent in a democratic process itself?
3. What institutions are most appropriate for opening up a democratic process within the current structures?[19]

Each of these questions necessitates the discussion of a large number of prerequisites, characteristics, institutions, and conditions. In this chapter I wish to pinpoint only those aspects that seem to be of particular significance in connection with uneven denationalization (see Held 1991b; Scharpf 1993b). Turning to the first question, I argue that in the context of denationalization the issue of membership of a *demos* raises new problems (criteria 1 and 2). With regard to the second question, two characteristics of the democratic process will be elaborated, which are neglected by the European multilevel governance system (criteria 3 and 4). These criteria are considered here as the four criteria for a democratic process that are most severely affected by uneven denationalization. They are considered in their ideal-type form, in the knowledge that although, historically, they never actually existed as such, deviations from them were and still are generally perceived as 'deficient'. Turning to the third question, the institutional strategies for overcoming the democratic deficit within the EU have to be evaluated, in the context of these four criteria. In current discussions there are two salient points of view. One calls for a strengthening of the European Parliament in the institutional system so as to improve the legitimacy of decisions made at the European level; the other advocates an 'autonomy-sensitive form of coordination', which aims at circumscribing the policies of nation-states as little as possible. It will become apparent that neither of these two strategies are convincing in the light of the four criteria affected by uneven denationalization.

Limits of Democracy

Time and again the purpose of theoretical discourse on democracy has been to find out which associations and communities should be organized in a democratic form. Do only states have to be democratic, or all social institutions that make binding decisions for their members? Which areas of life are supposed to be private and thus elude public decision-making processes? Now a new issue has been taken up in discussions on the limits of democracy: what is the appropriate size or scope of a political institution?[20] In the light of the current denationalization thrust, the question of the right size of a democratic community is of prime importance. There are two aspects of a democratic community that are affected by the extension of the boundaries of social transactions.

1. Congruence: The objects of governance and the subjects of governance must be identical, that is, there must be a "strict convergence of those involved in making collective decisions and those affected by these decisions" (Scharpf 1993b: 167). In other words, the spatial scope of political regulations must not be smaller than the boundaries of social transactions. If this congruence is not given, the self-determination of the people is overridden. The modern infringement of the principle of self-determination is brought about by a lack of congruence between the scope of democratically legitimate political regulations and the space of relevant social transactions. In a globalizing world governed by a system of formally independent nation-states, the identity of the subjects and objects of governance — a fundamental requirement for political self-determination in a democratic collective — is challenged. There are two reasons for this: First, within an integrated social space the decision of one political unit necessarily affects people who are not members of this unit and who thus have no say in such a decision. The non-avoidance of cross-border pollutants is an example. Second, if political communities are not able to reach a desired objective because structural conditions outside of their influence render it impossible, then there is a 'nondecision' situation, which is a democratic deficit in a broader sense. The realization of these problems, however, should not result in ignoring the congruence criterion or calling it unrealistic. The question to be asked is to what extent do the different institutional arrangements allow a reconciliation with the congruence criterion so that the number of 'nondecisions' and those affected by, but with no voice in, a decision is reduced.

2. Identity: Democratic decision-making processes are based on the assumption that those involved in the decision-making process have a collective identity. A demos does not, of course, have to be an ethnos, but the members of a demos have to recognize each other as members. It must be noted that the boundaries of national identity are by no means automatically the same as the boundaries of social transactions that are initially defined by a high density of transactions within the realm of economics, culture, ecology, or information. Such interconnectedness gives rise to an interdependence of the effects of social decisions and indicates an 'objective interconnectedness'.

The formation of a community is a much more complicated process. According to nationalism theory, the essential prerequisites for this process, besides the increasing density of transactions (see Deutsch 1953), are the functional requirements accruing from the latter (Gellner 1991), the existence of an administration (Breuilly 1994), and sufficient means of communication (Anderson 1991). This set of conditions raises the hope that all components of a community may eventually develop within the EU. At present, however, this is clearly not the case. Although the transaction component is without a doubt given, the general view is that a strong sense of European identity does not yet exist. Peter Graf Kielmansegg puts it this way:

> A stable, traditional, collective identity develops out of communities of communication, experience and memory. Europe, even the smaller Western Europe, is no community of communication, hardly a community of memory and a community of experience only in a very limited sense. (Kielmansegg 1994: 27)

This is alarming enough. Even worse, though, considering the requirements of a democratic community in terms of size, we appear to be facing a genuine structural dilemma. While the congruence criterion recommends an extension of the scope of political regulation, the identity criterion points in exactly the opposite direction. In other words, the origin of our current democratic problems lies in the divergence of the criteria of congruence and identity. Therefore, the alternative institutional arrangements discussed here must be evaluated on their capacity to resolve this dilemma.

Democratic Process

Once the boundaries of a community have been defined, the decision-making and will-formation process must fulfill a couple of additional requirements before a community is worthy of being called democratic. In the current European multilevel governance system, two of these prerequisites are particularly problematic.

1. Reversibility: Democratic majority decisions are based on the conviction that political measures are not an expression of an enduring and universally valid truth, but arise out of the interplay between interests and convictions that can change over time. This prior conviction requires that once decisions are made they can be revised. Claus Offe (1984) has pointed out that in society with high-risk technologies some material decisions are irreversible and therefore defy the principle of majority voting. In multilevel governance systems like the EU an additional problem arises: The 'joint decision trap', identified by Fritz Scharpf with respect to the EC in the early 1980s, renders decisions almost irreversible.

> In long-term decision-making systems without exit options or with high exit costs, the reversibility clause is changed. With an increasing density of regulations, the failure to reach an agreement means that earlier decisions are upheld, and there is no return to a state in which there is no collective regulation. (Scharpf 1985: 337)

Any institutional design for the EU must therefore be examined as to whether and to what extent it fulfills the requirement of reversibility.

2. Accountability: Representative democratic systems must be able to reverse not only material decisions, but also personnel decisions. Constituents should regularly be able to reelect representatives and the executive or to vote

them out of office. At the same time, legislators should be in a position to control the executive by ballots and elections, which require a minimum of information on the achievements and activities of the representatives. The problem of multilevel governance systems is, however, that this information is not sufficiently provided:

- The democratic legitimacy of the Council of Ministers through national elections is undisputed. However, it is only indirectly guaranteed, and as a 'collective organ' the Council is not subject to any form of democratic scrutiny. This makes accountability problematic insofar as "democratic chains of legitimacy can only fulfill their function if they are not arbitrarily long" (Claasen 1994: 252). There are no constituents who can by election 'punish' the Council as a whole. The Council is constituted by means of elections, which are generally held on the basis of national, but not European issues.
- A further characteristic of the Council of Ministers is that internal discussions are highly nontransparent. This is exacerbated when the Council of Ministers arrives at decisions in close but equally obscure cooperation with the Commission. For the constituents and representatives this leads to a high degree of uncertainty as to what international institutions stipulate and what is nationally permitted, what could have been enforced at the European level and what could not. As a result of this opaqueness, the accountability of decision-makers declines while at the same time politicians increasingly seize this opportunity for credit claiming and scapegoating (see Moravcsik 1994).

The fourth criterion for assessing alternative proposals for the institutional design of the EC is thus accountability and transparency. Can the proposed institutional structure provide the legislators as well as the electorate with sufficient information for them to determine who is responsible for which policies and not to lose complete control of the voting agenda?

STRENGTHS AND WEAKNESSES OF ALTERNATIVE FORMS OF THE EUROPEAN MULTITIERED SYSTEM

The rejection of the Maastricht Treaty by the Danes at their first referendum highlighted how the democratic deficit has become a real problem of West European governance. Since this referendum, the suspicion has grown that the democratic deficit is not only a normative defect, which theorists of democracy are attempting to reveal or to conceal. The democratic deficit has meanwhile become a major contributive factor to the diminishing acceptance of West European integration. In the light of the growing impact of the questions discussed here, it can also come as no surprise that in academic discourse, a whole series of proposals has been made as to the institutional restructuring of the EU in order to fulfill the requirements for a democratic community. In simplified terms, there are now at least two institutional options favored in academic discussion: 'strengthening the European Parliament' and 'autonomy-sensitive coordination'.

Strengthening the EP

Since the early 1990s the EC has introduced more regulations into French legislation than the national bodies themselves (see Majone 1996: 159). The binding force of EC legislation increasingly permeates the legislation of its member states, although—as it is argued—this 'European state power' does not derive its authority from the people and, above all, its powers are not controlled by special legislative authorities. The Council of Ministers' decision-making power makes the German federal government both legislator and executor of EC law in Germany at the same time. Following this argumentation, then, it is not merely a question of strengthening the European Parliament, but above all a question of protecting the principle of the separation of powers and consequently protecting parliamentarianism in general. The former president of the EP, Klaus Hänsch (1986: 191), put it in a nutshell when he stated:

> Those who do not want a parliamentarization of the Community, must, for the sake of parliamentary democracy in their own countries, reject integration. Those who want integration to continue must, again for the sake of parliamentary democracy in their own countries, promote the parliamentarization of the EC. (see also Möller and Limpert 1993; Schmuck and Wessels 1989; Williams 1991)

In a number of ways a strong parliament contributes to the safeguarding of the democratic process. It fulfills the principle of the separation of powers, which protects the system against encroachment by individual state institutions, and gives the system scope for innovation due to the plurality of the state institutions. A parliament is made up of representatives who are usually elected in territorial constituencies. In effect, a strong European Parliament that is empowered to elect its commissioners from its own ranks and with a mandate for EU directives and rules, could reduce information deficits and mitigate the problem of accountability.

The problem with strengthening the European Parliament lies in the ambivalent effects of such an institutional reform on the three other criteria outlined above. The demand to bring the integration process to a halt for the sake of parliamentary democracy if the Community is not parliamentarized sounds rather unrealistic in the light of the problem of congruence. The national parliaments' loss of decision-making power is actually caused by the growing incongruence brought about by rapidly increasing transnational interdependencies. This has increased the volume of 'nondecisions'. The recent thrust toward European integration is a reaction to this development in an attempt to win back political powers. If the reaction process is halted, the Parliament will not be strengthened, but all the political agencies will be weakened, including the national parliaments.

Reinforcing the 'principle of the separation of powers' in the EU is also rather ambivalent. Given the strength of the European Court, a not-insignificant European Parliament and a far from homogeneous Council of Ministers, the problem of the EU appears to lie not in an unsatisfactory separation of powers but in too many checks and balances. Too many checks and balances can result in a 'conservative democracy'—as the U.S. system is sometimes termed—because it calls the condition of reversibility into question. Strengthening the European Parliament in order to solve the problem of accountability could adversely affect the condition of reversibility.

The third objection to a strengthening of the European Parliament is sufficiently expounded in the relevant literature. It concerns the condition of identity and is based on the argument that in the absence of European media, European parties, and a European public opinion, a strengthening of the European Parliament is an inappropriate means of closing the democratic deficit.[21] As long as there is no political community with which all Europeans can identify, a stronger parliament would not be characterized by public debates concerning public welfare, but instead the professional confrontation of national interests would only be transferred into Parliament. In an extreme sense the consequence of this objection is that "as far as social legitimacy is concerned there is no difference between decisions made in the Council of Ministers and those made in the European Parliament" (Weiler 1989: 85). There is certainly some truth in that argument, which rightly warns against naïve ideas about a European state. I would like to add, though, that it appears a little bit static. When territorial states were established in Western Europe, the formation of national political institutions also preceded the development of a national identity.[22] Institutions are not just the instruments of ready-made social entities, they usually also have a generative function for a community. In terms of institutional modernization policies,[23] a strong European Parliament would, due to the very weak identification of European voters with it, not directly solve the problem of accountability, but it could over the medium term help to alleviate the problem of a missing European identity.

On balance then, strengthening the European Parliament would hardly solve the problem of accountability because the precondition of identity is not fulfilled. Furthermore, there is the danger that a stronger European Parliament would even exacerbate the problem concerning reversibility and possibly even that of congruence. At the same time, it must not be overlooked that the strengthening of the European Parliament is not just a conditional instrument and therefore does not merely rest on the criteria stated above, but may also help generate new identities itself. In this respect, the proposal to strengthen the European Parliament is a step in the right direction: the process of West European integration must not necessarily culminate in a European superstate, but it has already led to a political system *sui generis*, which as such must be legitimized and democratized.

Autonomy-Sensitive Coordination

The second proposal described here is based on the assumption that democratic legitimacy can only be achieved within the framework of a community with which people can identify. The starting point of this proposal is thus the identity criterion. From this perspective, the connection between nation and democracy is not regarded as an historical accident, but as logical and inseparable. As long as there is no European nation, the national components of the multilevel governance system should not be weakened more than necessary. Cooperative solutions to problems are needed, but they must be compatible with national autonomy so that they do not unnecessarily restrict the power of the national units. Thus, it is accepted that wherever "democratic and federalist principles are linked, [...] the result is modifications of the principle of democracy" (Kielmansegg 1994: 25). In order to restrict these 'modifications' to an acceptable level, those two elements must be separated as clearly as possible. Instead of an integrated multilevel governance system, an institutional framework with nation-states as distinct entities that are interlinked in clearly defined areas is advocated. There are two concrete recommendations in this direction:

- The procedural recommendation is closely connected with the name of Joseph Weiler (1987, 1989). According to his analysis, the democratic principle of majority decisions should only be applied in communities with which people can identify. If seemingly democratizing majority procedures are introduced at the European level, the veto position of the individual member states is weakened. It is this weakening of democratic nation-states that leads to a legitimacy deficit.
- The substantial recommendation focuses on the content of European policies. European policies should be formulated in such a way that they are compatible with the autonomy of the individual nation-states. This recommendation, which is expounded by Scharpf in particular (1993a, 1993b), suggests restricting decisions made at the European level to general mandatory regulations and prohibitions, and waiving integrated community planning. For this coordination, interstate financial adjustments may be necessary, but European funding programs should otherwise be dispensed with.

The strength of this recommendation lies in its pragmatism. It is neither committed to obsolete hopes for a European superstate, nor is it unrealistic in its expectations of a European identity. Nevertheless, the necessity of coordinated policies is acknowledged. If the different levels are distinctly separated and the national level is given enough room to maneuver, then this proposal would reduce the restrictions on democracy to an acceptable limit.

There are other difficulties with this approach when it is viewed in the light of the four criteria outlined above. As far as congruence is concerned, the need for the identity of objects and subjects of governance is certainly recognized by the advocates of the proposal. Scharpf (1993b: 167) writes: "Thus, if the prevalence of external effects is not to thwart all hope of the deliberate shaping of a community's fate as interdependence increases, the attempt at a coordinated solution, negotiated among the entities involved, is the only solution." Nation-states would therefore have to act in agreement with the community. The question is, however, whether this statement conceals the desire to return to the age of 'embedded liberalism', when it was the express purpose of international institutions to make national governance possible. This would by no means be reprehensible, but it is questionable whether this option is still open after the thrust toward societal denationalization in the mid-1970s. The institutional arrangement of 'embedded liberalism' did not begin to falter because of exaggerated desires for political integration, but because of an unintended thrust toward social integration, which transcended the boundaries between domestic and foreign affairs and dramatically curtailed the effectiveness of national policies. The recent thrust toward integration in Europe was nothing but a reaction to this. Democracy oriented toward the nation-state is in danger of losing the means to fulfill popular will. Democracy not only requires control over the means of governance, but also requires that these means have the potential to achieve desired ends. In this respect, the option of autonomy-sensitive coordination seems to fall short of an essential criterion for the democratic process.

My second point of criticism of the concept of autonomy-sensitive coordination concerns the criterion of accountability. A non-integrated multitiered system with distinct boundaries between the levels is extremely harmful to this criterion. Autonomy-sensitive coordination aims at extending the real power of national decision-makers again. The ability of constituents to reverse decisions via their representatives and to be self-determined depends, however, not only on the existence of real power at the national level, but also on the existence of sufficient information about the activities of political representatives. Similar requirements apply to the representatives when controlling and instructing the executive. But it is precisely those decision-making systems with strictly separate decision-making levels and which adhere to the international diplomatic rules of top-level secrecy, which do not deliver the information constituents need. The opportunity of strategic manipulation of information is wide open to decision-makers.[24]

A final criticism is that autonomy-sensitive coordination in the EU—at least if it followed the procedural recommendations of Weiler—would fall straight into the joint-decision trap. This would adversely affect reversibility as an integral part of the democratic process. A political multitiered system, which is structurally not in a position to eliminate policies that are generally considered as irrational, is bound to lose social acceptance sooner or later.

WHAT CAN BE DONE?

Both major positions in the discussion on the institutional formation of the EU have proved to be problematic for different reasons. The recommendations of both positions, when examined against an extended set of criteria for and characteristics of the democratic process, reveal remarkable weaknesses. Against this background, I would like to finish by offering for discussion two proposals for the establishment of democratic legitimacy in the European multilevel governance system. These proposals intentionally neglect the constitutional difficulties and questions as to their chances of success. The initial objective is to find the appropriate institutional structures to facilitate a democratic process in a complex multilevel governance system. The discussion of these questions should not be hampered right from the start by thoughts on whether or not it will succeed.

To start with, the postulate of autonomy-sensitive coordination is absolutely right for the regulation of all social transactions, which do not transcend national borders and do not have any externalities. *Ceteris paribus*, the democratic process is easier to organize in smaller communities than in big ones. There is no reason for Europeanizing housing policies, for example. However, with regard to all those policy areas concerning social transactions that cross national borders, a strategy aimed at restricting the undemocratic part of the European system in its significance for the democratic part is bound to fail.

Since the extension of real social and economic relations cannot easily be thwarted, institutional mechanisms need to be identified, which allow the scope of political regulation to be extended without creating problems in terms of identity, reversability, and accountability. The following proposals thus follow a Pareto-criteria: they qualify by improving at least one of four counts of the democratic process without deteriorating any of the others.

Europe-wide Referenda

Political institutions are not only based on certain premises of identity, they can also generate and broaden identity (see also below). The aim must therefore be to establish institutional procedures that are able to function without a fully developed European identity, and at the same time work on broadening it. Europe-wide referenda on matters of some importance could be such an instrument. Although the national referenda on Maastricht made the problems of legitimacy of the EU quite clear, they also showed that momentous political events like these can spark off a public debate.[25] Referenda are more than just ballots. They are distinguished from a 'teledemocracy' by a phase of discourse, which is at least as important as the voting itself. If the outcomes of such referenda were determined at the European level, then attempts to instrumentalize them for national issues not relating to Europe would be ineffective. In this respect, European referenda seem to be an appropriate procedure for political decision-making for an extended political space, which would at the same time foster elements of a European community spirit. Furthermore, this procedure could be specifically used, for instance, to increase the potential for the reversibility of policies. Referenda are particularly appropriate for breaking down real or perceived cartels of the political class.[26] As referenda are an element of direct democracy, the problem of accountability of policies to representatives by definition does not arise — on the contrary, they return control to the voters.

Nevertheless, the question of which decisions should be taken by Europe-wide referenda remains open. Clearly, there are some issues for which referenda are unsuitable for such a form of decision-making, at least initially. First, the issue to be voted on needs to be substantial enough to have the hoped-for generative effects on the public. A new milk quota regulation should certainly not qualify for a Europe-wide referendum. Second, the issue to be voted on should not primarily be a matter of distribution, as this involves the risk of conflict between member states, which in turn could jeopardize the existence of the community. Redistributive policies are in general only acceptable if a sense of identity has already developed, and are not suited for generating a European sense of identity. The European agricultural policy therefore does not appear to be a valid issue for such referenda either. Third, constitutional matters[27] should only be put to the vote under the application of strong restraints and with a guaranteed qualified ratio of representation. So Maastricht II as a whole should also not be voted on in an Europe-wide referendum. This finally leaves those policies resulting from non-constitutional majoritarian politics (Wilson and Dilulio 1995). These are decisions in which both costs and benefits are widely spread and whose significance exceeds that of individual or particular interests. Defense measures are good examples of majoritarian policies. They would be suitable for Europe-wide referenda if the common foreign and security policy were extended. The same applies to environmental policies, the costs of which would primarily give rise to higher prices for consumers and which would be valid throughout Europe.

Democratization of Territorial Representation

In the discussion on the democratic deficit in the EU, the problem of accountability has not been taken sufficiently into consideration. The activities of one and the same politician at different levels give him or her a chance to obtain an informational advantage, which can be put to strategic use and, of course, abuse. The growth of credit claiming and scapegoating and the loss of agenda-determining competence outside of the executive is an expression of this problem. It therefore seems advisable to appoint separate — democratically elected — delegates to the relevant national and European political institutions. In other words, the national representatives of the Council of Ministers should be elected directly by their national constituents in a separate election from the national government election. In this way, the chain of legitimacy leading to the Council of Ministers would be drastically shortened, and at the same time the Council would be legitimized as a collective organ. Both the national governments and the national delegates in the Council of Ministers would then be forced to justify their policies individually to the national public. This would certainly lead to frequent conflicts, but could also promote more transparency and make it clear to the public what role they have in a multilevel governance system. It would then be much easier for the national public to decide who bears the responsibility for which policy. The modern U.S.-American political system, in which governors are elected separately from senators, demonstrates the potential feasibility of such an arrangement.[28] Democratizing territorial representation in the European decision-making system could also foster the growth of a European identity, given that national representatives would have to emphasize the European dimension of their policies in order to maintain the support of the electorate. Finally, with regard to the requirements of reversibility and congruence, I fail to see how such a measure could further impede the reversibility of European policies (condition of reversibility) or systematically increase difficulties in obtaining European policies (condition of congruence), provided that national and European areas of competence are clearly separated.

Transparent Decision Networks

Particularly in the realm of international environmental politics, the admission of nongovernmental organizations (NGOs) has given interstate negotiations a momentum that differs widely from negotiation processes on more conventional matters. Thanks to these NGOs, so-called 'epistemic communities' (Adler and Haas 1992) are in a better position to convey their knowledge to the public. In turn, epistemic communities have contributed to the fact that in international environmental negotiations arguing lags far less behind bargaining than it does in many other issue areas (see Gehring 1995). As a result, 'sectoral publics' have evolved, thus strengthening the representation of diffuse interests in European politics. A similar development at the European level could better redress the imbalance of interest groups and strengthen the criterion of congruence. To the extent that these sectoral publics are able to capture wide attention—as with the prevention of the sinking of *Brent Spar*—they could even contribute to the generation of a European identity. Conversely, I see no reason why more transparent political networks should adversely affect reversibility and accountability. If NGOs either codetermine or coimplement collective binding decisions, however, they themselves must be organized democratically. The same applies to those NGOs in which the exit option for their supporters (that is, their source of influence) is not cost-free.

In conclusion, then, it must be kept in mind that all three suggestions are formulated against the background of those criteria for the democratic process, which I see are most affected by the process of uneven denationalization. There may easily be further requirements that would be negatively influenced by the proposed procedures. And even with respect to the four analyzed conditions a closer inspection of the suggestions is certainly necessary. The thrust of this chapter is therefore mainly critical: measured against the four discussed criteria for democratic processes, both the strategy of strengthening the EP and the strategy of autonomy-sensitive coordination reveal significant weaknesses. A simple parliamentarization of European politics would certainly fail due to a lacking sense of European identity. The strategy of autonomy-sensitive coordination seems to underestimate the transformation of statehood. On the one hand it underestimates the dwindling effectiveness of national policies, a process that is emphasized by those who note a long-term weakening of the nation-state. On the other hand, it also underestimates the broadening of the national governments' scope for manipulation, which accompanies international institution building and which is emphasized by those who believe that the nation-state is reasserted through European integration.

10

Democratization without Representation

Hilmar Schmidt and Ingo Take

As globalized links develop in daily life and politics, and as global problems like the man-made greenhouse effect and the destruction of the ozone layer emerge, political models for solving these problems seem inevitably to gravitate upward to the international level. Political action to solve international and intrasocietal problems occurs, if it does so at all, through a number of governmental collaborations, that is, in various systems of negotiations, in inter- or transnational, and in international organizations (see also Scharpf 1993b). In addition to this internationalization of politics, there is also, as Beck recently described it, globalization 'from below'. This is being driven by new transnational actors who are seeking to influence and challenge established political processes by means that go beyond the political system (Breitmeier and Wolf 1993: 355; Beck 1996). It is in this area of tension that the problem of the realization of democracy, in both the international and transnational context, poses itself. This present chapter considers the contribution,which social actors, notably nongovernmental organizations (hereinafter 'NGOs'[1]), make to the democratization of international politics, and it asks under what conditions this democratization may be reconciled with the goal of increased efficiency in international problem-solving processes. In our view, the main way in which NGOs help democratize international politics and foreign-policy decision-making is by creating transparency. In the following section, we attempt, within the framework of the concept of world society (see chapter 1), to clarify the importance of transnational actors in regard to processes of globalization and socialization. In the next section, we describe the ways in which NGOs can influence international politics, and evaluate these from the point of view of democratization and problem-solving. In the final section, we pose the question of how NGOs might be linked into not only national, but also—and most importantly—international problem-solving processes. Against the background of a normative notion of democracy, and taking into account the problems that result from this as regards increasing the efficiency of globalized problem-solving, we arrive at the position of rejecting the call for NGOs to be given a participative status.

CONCEPT OF WORLD SOCIETY

The defining characteristics of the formation of world society have been identified as: the institutionalization of international relations; the differentiation of spheres of interaction; and the diffusion of the actors concerned. The concept thus clearly allows for an increase in the importance of social actors in the international formulation of policy.

These three components of the formation of world society also influence the behavior of the social actors. Thus, not only do governmental and economic actors come together in international alliances; social actors also form transnational networks and organizations.[2] The differentiation in the levels of operation is discernible in the fact that the work of social actors is no longer focused on these actors' 'own' states or 'own' societies, but is increasingly directed at other states, other societies, and international organizations[3] (Colás 1996: 12). The degree of dispersal of the actors is also easily demonstrable—over 1,500 NGOs of the most varied kinds are now accredited with ECOSOC (Willetts 1996c: 38).

The trends toward a world society have undoubtedly weakened the ability of modern nation-states to direct affairs[4] (see chapter 9; Schmidt 1996); but they in no way signal those states' demise. Rather, there are early signs that new forms of statehood ('trans-statehood', horizontal political links) are beginning to develop via the old forms of international cooperation and regulation (see chapter 1). This development is driven by globalization.[5] The formation of transnational economic areas and transnational communities is leading to a curtailment in the power of states to direct affairs. In addition to the problem of change and of the permeability of borders, there is the problem that economic, political, and social spheres are becoming less and less congruent (see chapters 1 and 2). The differing styles of government—'government' and 'governance' (see chapter 9)—no longer have any equivalents in the sphere of political control. Both effects of globalization—namely, the diminished power of states to direct affairs when it comes to solving global problems, and the process of 'de-democratization' that is a concomitant of international governance—harbor the danger of a loss of confidence in state institutions, leading ultimately to a loss of legitimacy for representative democracy. The next section will endeavor to show what contribution NGOs can make to the democratization and increased efficiency of processes for solving global problems at the international and national level.

NGOS AND INTERNATIONAL POLITICS

Helping Democratize Global Governance

The proper functioning of democracy as a complex form of political coexistence depends on many variables (Lenk 1993: 986). According to Lenk, the factors that determine whether or not a vital democracy emerges are, in addition to general rules of behavior: the political culture, the needs of the citizens, and the general public. Transparency in political decision-making processes is therefore a crucial factor in tying political power into the social fabric: "Political power must be open, so that it can be controlled by the public; and the public itself, in the form of public opinion, plays a considerable part in determining how policy is to be shaped for the common good" (Göhler 1995: 7). So that the public can exercise its functions of control and the issuing of demands, information must be made available to it, and processes by which political decisions are made and the procedures whereby specific political outcomes are opted for, must be made transparent. But precisely in the case of foreign-policy decision-making processes and international politics, the role of the public is regarded as of minor significance. This perception is based on the supposition, first, that the public sees decision-making processes at this level as too complex, and, second, that it does not feel itself sufficiently affected by the problems in that sphere—a fact that is explained in terms of the distant nature of international political concerns (Zürn and Take 1996: 8). But the influence of the public depends crucially on "whether public opinion figures at all in the particular area concerned" (Müller and Risse-Kappen 1990: 384). NGOs therefore also seek to acquire competence in foreign-policy and international issues (at least in relation to their own particular concern) and thus to put themselves in a position where they are able to comprehend international decision-making processes. In this connection, we see the role of NGOs in the democratization or redemocratization of international politics/foreign-policy decision-making processes as being that of creating transparency by informing and enlightening the public about these processes. Transparency through information is, in our view, the basic precondition for public control, and thus constitutes an important contribution to democratization. In what follows, we attempt to show, by means of concrete examples, what contribution NGOs make to the creation of transparency in political decision-making processes.

In the debate about the formation of world society, about citizen participation at the international level, and about the control of international decision-making processes, increasing attention is being paid to NGOs (see also Agenda 21, Chapter 7,[6] Kößler and Melber 1993: 256). As transnational actors of world society, NGOs are organizations which, though seeking to secure particular political objectives and working in concert with local communities, regions, states, and international organizations, nonetheless also endeavor to preserve their status as independent players. Publicly effective campaigns are used to highlight practices that are dangerous or illegal, or are felt to be immoral, and activists take personal action to oppose them. Such activities at the same time also point the finger at governments for having failed in their duty of care toward their citizens. The large NGOs in particular usually seek out symbolic issues for their campaigns, of a kind they know will touch a chord with people. The methods they use provide them with a special way of strategically realizing their goals. The way those goals are chosen is therefore not arbitrary. Besides the link with social movements, there are various other factors that indicate that NGOs, though not enjoying democratically constituted legitimation, do not act in ways entirely disconnected from major social concerns. Their choice of action is initially made in an internal decision-making process and is generally geared to the presumed acceptability of the action to the public.[7] This function of representing public interests is acknowledged both by the public and by officialdom. The reasons for the public acceptance lie in the way in which the stuff of political decision-making has become differentiated and interests have become particularized, such that political parties, with their generalized programmatic claims, and interest groups aggregated into national entities are no longer doing justice to these new challenges (Kitschelt 1996: 26). As a result, the public is increasingly trusting to 'issue-oriented' NGOs to provide an appropriate response to the new problems.[8] The case of Greenpeace's successful campaign against the deepwater disposal of the oil rig *Brent Spar* showed that, when taking far-reaching decisions, neither multinational concerns nor ministers can afford to ignore responding NGOs whose campaigns have won backing from the public. Public acceptance of NGOs is also mirrored in the media coverage. Quite often, media reporting on conferences is based on information that NGOs provide there for all interested parties. NGOs are enjoying increased acceptance and recognition from official quarters as well. This is reflected in their involvement as participants or *rapporteurs* in international meetings, and in the inclusion of their representatives in national delegations. In connection with the Rio conference, Princen and Finger talk of 150 delegations in which NGO representatives were included (Princen and Finger 1994: 4). The importance of the NGOs as representatives of the public interest was also highlighted by former U.N. Secretary-General Boutros-Boutros Ghali when he described them as a basic form of representation, which in some sense guaranteed the political legitimacy of the United Nations (Das Parlament, 42, 13 Oct. 1995: 13). The way in which the NGOs' consultative status is constantly being enhanced endorses this idea. Again, because of the increasing personal burden that environmental damage is imposing on individuals, ever more urgent calls are being made for social actors to take part in the shaping of international environmental policy.[9] This is the basis from which the NGOs derive their demand for participative status. In addition, they point to the democratizing effect that such a status would bring with it.

The collaboration with the media ensures that internal NGO structures are rendered transparent[10] and that the NGOs themselves, as new actors in international politics, at least partially satisfy the transparency criterion. To this extent, their incorporation into international politics at least does not lead to any additional loss of transparency.

The additional democratization of international decision-making processes, which NGOs bring about, can be convincingly demonstrated by reference to the various activities by which they seek to promote transparency. These include both their repeated provision of information to, and enlightenment of, the public about political decision-making processes,[11] and also the independent specialist information and recommendations for action, which they make available, thus obviating a situation where political decision-makers are reliant solely on their own advisers. Examples of such material are regular magazines for members, documentation to accompany conferences, and annual reports such as that published by Amnesty International. In addition, the NGOs help monitor the implementation of internationally agreed measures. Thus, by providing additional information, making decision-making processes transparent, and monitoring the implementation of particular policies, the NGOs create an additional degree of transparency, which in its turn gives citizens greater scope in forming their opinions.[12] This thesis is supported by amongst others, Karin Stahl, who, having analyzed the UNCED process, concluded that the NGO presence had "undoubtedly resulted in greater transparency and openness in the negotiations, and [had] facilitated access to important information" (Stahl 1995: 251). Furthermore, within the NGOs, activities that promote transparency are not hampered by a restrictive administrative apparatus.[13] The NGOs can therefore carry out their prime functions—which consist in monitoring, criticizing, challenging, and condemning political processes and their agents—unhindered. However, it also has to be noted that the larger NGOs at least find themselves in the quandary of, on the one hand, having to demarcate themselves from governmental policy and economic activities, and, on the other, having to rely on issues being formulated in a connectable way if they are to be promoted at all.

NGOs' Contribution to International Problem-Solving

The process of informing the public should not be seen only as an aid to the democratization of international politics; it is also one of the important functions that NGOs exercise within the framework of a multistage 'global governance' aimed at finding solutions to global problems (Take 1996: 64). Through such public information, pressure is exerted on political decision-makers to put certain problems on the political agenda or to get on and deal with them.[14] The environmental movements, as is clear from Ulrich Beck (Beck 1995: 15), have often emerged from this 'exposure-centered conflict' as the victors (Basle convention on toxic waste, ban on disposal of sulphuric acid in the sea, moratorium on underground nuclear tests, and so on). In the debate, which then follows about the most effective strategy for countering a particular trend, the 'accountability-centered conflict' comes to the fore (Beck 1995: 15). This involves the responsible parties being identified and made answerable for their actions. Here too, NGOs manage time and again to chalk up successes (see Shell or McDonalds).

Another important contribution to the solution of global problems is the monitoring and, where appropriate, imposition of sanctions on 'free riders'. Thus, at international conferences, NGOs check to see whether participants' resolutions do not fall short of regulations that have already been agreed. They also monitor implementation at the national level, generating the pressure needed to persuade legislators to translate internationally agreed measures into national laws. This pressure results from the creation of openness and the dissemination of counter-ideas amongst 'leader states' at international conferences. Practical implementation at the individual level (for example, inside businesses) is also promoted by means of these strategies. In most cases, local authorities do not have enough capacity to check whether environmental laws and regulations are actually being adhered to by industrial concerns.

NGOs aid problem-solving at the international and national levels by putting forward alternative proposals and ideas and by calling on their own expert resources (Morphet 1996: 141). In this connection, NGO information-input sometimes shows a greater degree of competence than equivalent studies commissioned by governments.[15] By acting as mediators between state actors, and by supporting leader states, NGOs time and again manage to help carry agreements on a stage further (Potter 1996: 38–41). As an example, one might cite the mediating activities of the Pugwash Club, which played a crucial part in bringing about a ban on the testing of overground nuclear weapons. The involvement of the NGOs in the decision-making process also means that the laws ultimately passed by a government have greater legitimacy in the eyes of the public. The same is true for the agreements concluded at the international level (Leatherman et al. 1993: 27; Willetts 1982: 194).

NGOs in International Politics: More Democratic and Better?

We have tried to discuss the influence of nongovernmental organizations on international politics from two standpoints: (a) the democratization of foreign policy and international politics, and (b) improving the problem-solving capacity of foreign policy and international politics. As we have shown, NGOs not only help increase the transparency of political decision-making processes, provide extra controls on national and international decision-making and implementation processes, and extend the public's competence; they also help identify solutions to global problems. In this last section, we shall first highlight the potential for problem-solving and democratization that can be created by deliberately integrating NGOs at the national level. Following on from this, we shall set out, according to our guiding categories (democratization/problem-solving) to discuss the problems associated with the call for NGOs to be given participative status at the international level.

Integration at the National Level

As the debate about corporatism has already shown, it can, as far as states are concerned, definitely make sense to give space to social interest groups and their corporatist approaches, thus making productive public use of organized private interests (Streeck 1994b: 9. See also: Katzenstein 1984, 1985; Schmitter 1981; Lehmbruch 1982). These corporatist structures can have a marked effect on the nature of political networks. In the context of the dispersal of actors and the emergence of new levels of operation associated with the trend toward world society (Czempiel's societized foreign policy, 1994),[16] policy networks can have an integrating effect, "because on the one hand, social actors are seeking a part in the political process, and, conversely, co-operation with the state offers such actors an opportunity of obtaining information" (Mayntz 1993: 41). It is true that, by this route, the NGOs would not be conceded any direct participation (for example, voting or veto rights);[17] but because of their close proximity to the decision-making process, their views would have a more direct influence on the learning process of other actors (Stewart 1992: 254; Waarden 1992: 139) and would bring additional transparency into the foreign-policy process. At a further stage, they could, within the framework of the devolution of governmental power—or, as in Jänicke, within the framework of political modernization—be tied into national governmental activity, and thus help to ensure the governability of developed industrial societies when it came to solving global problems (Schmidt 1995: 12; Streeck 1994b: 16; Jänicke 1993a).

Integration at the International Level

If problems of a global nature are to be solved, "international regulation of them," so Zürn concludes (1992c: 491), "must stop being reactive; it must acquire a capacity for active direction by virtue of non-state actors also having a direct role in the development and transformation of international institutions." In this connection, not only NGOs and researchers,[18] but also representatives of the UN are calling for social actors to have participative status in international organizations. One example of this is provided by Agenda 21: "With a view to strengthening the role of nongovernmental organizations as social partners, the United Nations system and governments should initiate a process, in consultation with nongovernmental organizations, to review formal procedures and mechanisms for the involvement of these organizations at all levels from policy-making and decision-making to implementation" (U.N. Doc. A/Conf.151/4 (Part III), para. 276).

What is being called for is actual incorporation into the political decision-making process—that is to say, granting of the right to vote. This is intended to bring political internationalization into congruence with social internationalization and thus to regain a minimum of democratically controlled steering power. In what follows here, we should like to discuss the positive and negative implications of this kind of participative status.

Advantages

As mentioned above, participation by social actors in the legislative process would give national laws and international regulations additional legitimacy. Direct involvement by the NGOs could, furthermore, reduce political reaction times—in the sense that new issues would get onto the political agenda more quickly (Cohen 1995: 150). The information and evidence collected by the NGOs would enter the political decision-making process directly, and this could help bring about policies that were more 'in touch with' the citizen. Up to now, it has cost the NGOs considerable time and money to secure access to the political decision-making levels. If the NGOs were formally tied into decision-making processes, they could use these resources for other purposes—such as gathering additional information. If, in addition, one considers the fact that citizens no longer rely on governmental bodies alone to take effective action against life-threatening dangers, and believe instead that the NGOs are the ones with the power to do this, the direct involvement of NGOs in the political decision-making process seems a legitimate objective.

Problems

The Problem of Legitimation

Yet this kind of involvement—which is often called for—harbors major problems. One can, for example, justly criticize the fact that NGO representatives have not been legitimated by universal public suffrage. Indeed, they represent only particular interests, and it is ultimately not known what degree of public approval they have behind them. The idea of national or international NGO assemblies, from which delegates for a specific international forum would be selected, was conceived as a way of overcoming this deficiency. But this kind of procedure harbours the danger that the very different points of view that exist even within the NGO community would be neutralized and would thus become politically largely irrelevant at the international level.

The Problem of Internal Structure

One recurrent criticism is that the NGOs themselves do not satisfy democratic requirements as regards their structure (see also chapter 9). Greenpeace is not the only one to have hierarchical structures. For reasons of efficiency, almost all the organizations of any size have confined the power to make decisions to a limited number of members. Behind this lies the assumption "that democratic organizational forms such as majority decisions within specialist forums and the unrestricted admission of members of the association would critically curtail effectiveness" (Bode 1995: 122). And, in the view of Greenpeace International's head, Thilo Bode, effectiveness is precisely what determines NGOs' success (degree of influence) or nonsuccess: "In my view, it is essential that an association such as Greenpeace, which works confrontationally and has to deal with powerful interest-groups, should be able to react quickly and flexibly" (Bode 1995: 122).

The Problem of Delegation

The rapid growth in the number of NGOs, and their increasing need to win attention at the international level, will, in the medium term (for purely organizational reasons), lead to a situation where a selection has to be made from amongst the host of U.N.-accredited NGOs, and only those chosen will ultimately be allowed to take part in meetings and express their views orally. But this kind of selection process is open to the danger of being guided by the political calculations of the government representatives.

The Problem of North–South Relations

A further problem results from the unequal distribution of resources between the NGOs from the North and those from the South. The rich NGOs in the North subsidize the poor ones in the South and thus ultimately decide which Southern NGOs may attend which conferences. The structural defects of the international system of states is thus reflected at the NGO level. At the UN Conference on Environment and Development, for example, there was a clear preponderance of Northern—notably North American—NGOs (Stahl 1995: 246). Since then, however, there have been a number of indications of a change in relations between Northern and Southern NGOs. Such a change was detected by Skriver in regard to the 1993 human rights conference in Vienna (Skriver 1993: 525). Additional structural inequality results from the practice—established within the framework of ECOSOC—of dividing the NGOs into three categories with graduated rights of participation. This leads to preference being given to the established international NGOs—such as the international umbrella-organizations of employers' associations, the trade unions, and women's and youth organizations—rather than the specialized and partially political NGOs from the environmental, development, peace, and human rights spheres. The most that national NGOs can do is to get registered on the 'roster', but this does not entail any actual rights of participation for them (Martens 1992: 160).

The Problem of Integration

Participative status entails a responsibility to ensure that political decisions actually come about, and this would force the NGOs into compromises, which in each case would only embody the lowest common denominator (Willetts 1996b: 6). This kind of imperative for consensus would not only curtail their ability to engage in criticism; it would also restrict the systematic and independent representation of public interests. Furthermore, the call for increased public participation can also embody "the articulation of purely egoistic, particularist interests" (Schmalz-Bruns 1996: 41).

The Problem of Instrumentalization

One last objection points in quite another direction and emanates from the NGOs themselves. They fear that, against the background of worldwide economic deregulation and privatization, governments, acting under the cloak of participation and democratization, will evade their social responsibilities by passing on to the NGOs even such quintessentially governmental tasks as emergency services. But this point reflects a general problem of the NGOs—one that they are already experiencing, without being directly integrated into the decision-making structures. A further problem results from the need to allocate resources, which means that the NGOs have largely to adapt to the operational logic of governmental organizations and allocating bodies. In addition to the danger that NGOs will be exploited or co-opted for extraneous purposes, there is also a risk that they will use up all their energies in obtaining and administering resources. Exploitation of a somewhat different kind occurs when NGO representatives are admitted to national delegations merely in order to increase the legitimacy of the agreements concluded at the international level.

In the light of the opportunities and problems, which participative status for NGOs would thus entail? Our conclusion is as follows: If the NGOs are to obtain the right to share in decision-making, the shortcomings in their internal structures must first be overcome and a more systematic distribution of resources must be achieved—between Northern and Southern NGOs, for example. Even if the NGOs were able and willing to enter upon this democratizing path, the question of whether, in any case, participative status is advisable, remains open. Besides the reduction in effectiveness which the democratization of internal NGO structures would bring, the disadvantages would also include a curtailment of the ability to criticize (the consensus imperative) and a restriction of independence (system-determined bias). Given these problems, each NGO must ultimately decide for itself whether it is prepared to pay this kind of price. If it accepts these restrictions, there is, in our view, no longer any guarantee that NGOs will still be able to make the kind of contribution to democratization and to the solution of global problems, which they have been able to make up to now. They would, furthermore, run the risk of losing the moral charisma with which they are credited as the 'avant-garde of world citizenry'. We therefore do not believe the call for participative status is wise, either from the point of view of democratization or from that of problem-solving.

11

Neo-Medievalism, Local Actors, and Foreign Policy: An Agenda for Research

Jürgen Neyer

FROM INTERNATIONAL SYSTEM TO NEO-MEDIEVALISM?

One of the main topics in international relations theory over the last decade has been the investigation of changes in the international system. The number of contributions that argue either for a decline in importance of the principle of territoriality (Ruggie 1993), the demise of the state (Mann 1990), the end of sovereignty (Camilleri and Falk 1992), or even a general trend of debordering of political structures (chapter 2) is substantial. James Rosenau, for example, has portrayed international relations as 'postinternational politics' (Rosenau 1990) and Mark Zacher has traced the "decaying pillars of the Westphalian Temple" (Zacher 1992). As a consequence, the concept of sovereignty has come under severe attack by political science scholars who state that the growing interdependencies of states and the rise of international organization have led to an effective erosion of state autonomy. Mark Zacher, for example, argues that "it is no longer accurate to conceptualize states as having their traditional degree of autonomy because of the network of formal and informal regimes in which they are becoming increasingly involved" (Zacher 1992: 60). Others argue that states are becoming obsolete and even dysfunctional since they can neither guarantee peace and security at the global level, nor fulfil the goals of economic and social justice and are unable to resolve global ecological crises that transcend political borders. Consequently, Ruggie has argued for the need to conceptualize "post-modern forms of configuring political space" (Ruggie 1993: 144).

In international political economy, a number of contributions have similarly highlighted that the concept of an international economy composed of nation-states is challenged by the emergence of a global market for goods, capital, and services (Dunning 1994), the rise of the region-state (Ohmae 1993), and a transnationalization of social processes (see chapter 1). The most basic concepts of an international order, such as territoriality and international law, are treated as categories whose descriptive value is rapidly being eroded by the activities of transnational nongovernmental actors. The common feature of these approaches is to argue that world politics are undergoing profound change because of the emerging importance of a growing heterogeneity of actors. It is no longer only nation-states that influence global politics but also nongovernmental actors such as multinational corporations, nonprofit nongovernmental organizations (NGOs), subnational territorial units, and even individuals. And indeed, there can be little doubt that in the modern international system, nongovernmental organizations are no longer bound to their national territory by the restrictions of international anarchy and legal insecurity but have high incentives to exploit the opportunities of global markets and an internationalized political system. The growth in cross-border trade, traffic, and communication in the postwar era can be understood as a function of the growing density of international institutions and the improving relationship between the costs and benefits of cross-border interaction. Increasing transnational interaction by nongovernmental organizations, however, is not only a result of the "civilization of international relations" (Rittberger and Zürn 1990), but is at the same time its independent variable: the more interdependent the relationship between two countries, the higher the costs for one of the countries to break this relationship and the lower the probability that this will indeed happen. International institutionalization therefore leads to intensified transnational cross-border interaction and vice versa. Conceptualizing cross-border interaction, as some argue, therefore may no longer mean focusing solely on the interaction of states but requires the integration of a variety of nongovernmental and nonterritorial actors such as multinational corporations, those with individual cross-border interests (for example, cross-border refugees or couples living in two different countries), or nonprofit humanitarian organizations like the Red Cross, Amnesty International, or Greenpeace. Recent estimates account for about 18,000 transnational nonprofit organizations (Smith et al. 1994) and about 30,000 multinational corporations (UNCTC 1992) that engage in cross-border interaction. Some observers interpret their rise as the emergence of a "nonterritorial 'region' in the world economy—a decentered yet integrated space-of-flows, operating in real time, which exists alongside the space-of-places that we call national economies" (Ruggie 1993: 172). It is argued that in this nonterritorial global economic region, the distinctions between external and internal to a state are losing their territorial meaning and are rather becoming social categories of a debordered world society.

Not surprisingly, some argue that the explanatory value of the concept of an international system composed of unitary nation-states is restricted to a specific historical context. Furthermore, some even argue that the states system is undergoing profound change by the transformation of its dominant units, namely the states themselves: it is argued that states are not only subject to an intensifying assertiveness of nongovernmental actors but are actively deterritorializing by strengthening transgovernmental and interregional links, and thereby contributing to an order that is characterized by debordered governance structures and multiple administrative interfaces linking departments of states across borders (chapter 2). Indeed, there can be little doubt that modern governance[1] today bears only little resemblance to the classical Weberian model of a centralized bureaucracy with decision-making at the top and implementation at the bottom. Today, transgovernmental policy formulation, deliberative interaction among a multiplicity of actors (Joerges and Neyer 1997), and the delegation of governance functions to private bodies are well-known phenomena (Majone 1996), particularly in highly interdependent international contexts like in the European Union. The important question is: to what extent can we derive from these phenomena a reduced relevance of the states system in monopolizing cross-border politics? If we seriously accept the challenge that the concept of world society poses to international relations theory, it is once more necessary to examine the question asked by Hedley Bull twenty years ago: "The crucial question is whether the inroads being made [...] on the sovereignty or supremacy of the state over its territory and citizens is such as to make that supremacy unreal, and to deprive the concept of sovereignty of its utility and viability" (Bull 1977: 264).[2]

In addressing Bull's question, this chapter aims to contribute to the recent debate on the role and functioning of states in world society. It is conceived as a conceptual chapter that investigates the heuristic value of the world society concept by questioning the notion of a 'neo-medievalism' in global governance. Hedley Bull envisaged it as an option for the future of the international system that denotes a structure in which the sovereign state shares the stage of world politics with other actors and associations, at subnational, international, and supranational levels. This includes the overlapping of authorities, loyalties, and identities at all three levels, with a resulting order based on a variety of actors and authorities— territorial and nonterritorial—and a multiplicity of loyalties, identities, and rivalries (Bull 1977: 264–70).[3] In assessing the heuristic value of the concept for understanding governance among the highly developed countries, this chapter concentrates on analysing to what extent sovereignty is challenged by nonstate actors. This will be done in four steps: after arguing that neither multinational corporations nor nonprofit nongovernmental organizations seriously challenge the authority of the state, the chapter assesses the potential of subnational territorial units for doing so. This is followed by an analysis of the incentives that subnational territorial units have to 'go abroad'. In the next section, a brief overview is given on some of the main characteristics of the cross-border activities of subnational territorial units in the European Union and the United States. It will be assessed why and under what conditions those activities are furthered by the state or perceived as a threat. Finally, this chapter concludes by arguing that subnational territorial actors do indeed play a far more significant role in cross-border affairs than international concepts of global governance imply. It is also argued, however, that their importance should not be overemphasized but contrasted with the still dominant role of state actors in global politics. This chapter does not promise to realize an overall assessment of the importance of nonstate actors in global politics. Its aim is insofar more limited as it only aims at sketching some possible lines for further research and providing evidence in two policy areas for the relevance of such an undertaking.

SOVEREIGNTY, AUTONOMY, AND NEW ACTORS IN WORLD POLITICS

Although the empirical evidence of a growing transnationalization of cross-border affairs cannot be challenged, the independent impact of nongovernmental organizations on the behavior of state governments is difficult to qualify. For example, there is strong evidence that the emerging importance of the multinational corporation correlated with the decision of almost all governments to liberalize investment regimes and has provided strong incentives for further deregulation (Biersteker 1992);[4] but it is not at all clear whether the rise of the multinational corporation has been the cause of deregulation or its effect. Liberalization, as some observers argue, may be much better understood as a deliberate effort by Western countries to cope with competitiveness than as a function of the multinationals' threat to use the exit option (Helleiner 1994). Even if it may be a truism, it is necessary to mention that markets do not exist under conditions of anarchy and apart from political authority; without a legal framework guaranteeing property rights backed by public authority, no market could exist. The argument, put forward by authors like Ohmae (1993), that the importance of the nation-state in a globalizing economy is rapidly diminishing and that its competencies may be restricted to locally providing the public services that the global economy requires of them, needs to be viewed skeptically too. The underlying assumption of this argument, firms becoming truly global players and loosening ties to their former home economies, is contradicted by more balanced accounts. Kapstein (1991; see also Tyson 1991), for example, points out that U.S. firms derive very real benefits from remaining distinctly American firms, benefits that stem directly from the power and functions of the nation-state: among these benefits are the ability to have access to regulatory and standard-setting bodies like the Federal Aviation Administration (FAA) and Food and Drug Administration (FDA), to subsidies provided by the American government for research and development (R&D) and, last but not least, having protection when it comes to conflict with foreign governments.

As to nonprofit nongovernmental organizations (NGOs), skepticism about their independent impact on the state system is supported by even stronger arguments. It may be true that organizations such as Greenpeace under certain conditions do indeed command sufficient resources to change the behavior of individual governments. The *Brent Spar* issue (where Shell gas stations all over Europe were boycotted by consumers because of the intended sinking of an oil platform in the North Sea) or the debate on the introduction of genetically engineered foodstuffs to the European market are cases in point. There can be little doubt, however, that these conditions are of a rather restricted nature. The power resources of NGOs are limited to those areas that have the potential to mobilize high public awareness and are rather insignificant when it comes to technical issues. Nongovernmental organizations can therefore very often do little more than direct already existing public awareness to political issues that are already high on the political agenda. If this awareness does not exist, however, mobilization is difficult if not impossible, and the power to influence decision-making is severely restricted.

The most serious weakness of multinational corporations as well as NGOs is their lack of procedural legitimacy: none of them represent a democratic political constituency, and all are exclusive expressions of particular subnational or transnational interests. The goods they are aiming to provide are not public as such but are, by definition, club goods that serve the ends of a certain group. To be sure, even democratic nation-states do not in general act with regard to the collective good of the global community but are constitutionally bound to maximise the individual utility of a certain (territorially defined) social group. But the important difference to nongovernmental actors is the fact that their preferences result from political processes that have a high degree of procedural legitimacy and that encompass territorial units. By aggregating their preferences, international institutions can therefore claim an indirect legitimacy that is based not on some autonomous deliberation by special interest groups, but on the preferences of highly legitimized nation-states.[5] An important caveat has to be inserted at this point: obviously, the whole argument of an indirect legitimacy of international institutions depends crucially on the question to what extent the preferences of governments themselves result from domestic democratic processes.[6] If and when governance by international institutions is merely the aggregation of the preferences of totalitarian regimes—or is at least heavily influenced by them—little remains that can be perceived as normatively acceptable. The applicability of the normative argument is therefore restricted to international institutions covering democratic countries like the EU or the OECD and applies to the U.N. system in general only to a limited degree. As the analytical focus of this chapter is restricted to assessing the relevance of state sovereignty for governance structures among the highly industrialized societies of Europe and the United States, however, the caveat does not contradict the argument in general.

Taking into account the factual as well as the normative shortcomings of nongovernmental actors, sovereignty still seems to be not only one of the most contested, but also one of the most important categories of modern international relations theory.[7] In order to clarify the concept, this chapter argues that *sovereignty* needs to be sharply distinguished from *autonomy*, for analytical as well as for important practical reasons. Whereas sovereignty denotes the central legal ordering principle of the international system,[8] autonomy refers to the ability to determine policy outcomes independent of the preferences of other actors. Keohane (see also 1989a) conceives of national sovereignty as a relatively precise legal concept. It denotes a legal status that is characterized by: (1) the denial of any political authority above the state, so that the state claims supreme decision-making authority both within its territory and over its citizens, and (2) the acknowledgement by other states that it is legitimized to do so.[9] Sovereignty therefore refers to a legal relationship between states as well as between domestic societies and governments by granting the latter the legal monopoly to represent the political cross-border interests of the former. Autonomy, on the other hand, rather refers to the degree to which state actions are *in fact* independent from actions taken by other states as well as nonstate actors. States are only autonomous if none of these actions have a significant impact on them (which is purely fictional under conditions of interdependence). Both concepts may be closely related in practice: the fact that it is the People's Republic of China and not Taiwan that is recognized by most states as being the sovereign of the Chinese people is difficult to explain without taking into account the different power resources that the two Chinese states command. It also highlights, however, that acknowledgment by the international system as the legitimate representation of societal interests is an important power resource in itself: it implies at its very heart to have access to formal international negotiations and therefore to be supplied with resources, such as information or international assistance, denied to non-sovereign actors. Sovereignty therefore implies much more than just an intersubjective meaning that puts emphasis on the recognition of a certain legal status (see also Ruggie 1986). To give just one example: during its occupation by Iraq, the state of Kuwait was virtually dissolved but its government nevertheless had access to international resources, which were sufficient to resurrect the state. Internal delegitimization and even civil war may simultaneously lead to reduced domestic authority and a strengthening of the government's supply with goods provided by the international system. Being recognized as a sovereign therefore means having access to power resources that are denied to non-sovereign actors. What was obviously important for the government of Kuwait holds also true for the highly industrialized countries of the OECD: by being able to rely on means of international policy formulation and multilateral negotiations, governments have access to policy-arenas which are removed from public supervision and societal pressure groups. The macroeconomic response of the European Union to the perceived competitive challenge by the newly industrializing countries (NICs) in the mid-1980s, for example, would have been far more difficult to implement if it had to be conducted solely under conditions of domestic politics. Neither the unions nor consumer organizations were sympathetic to the prospect of a shift in bargaining power between capital on the one hand and labor and diffuse interest groups on the other, which the Internal Market Programme of 1985 entailed. The latter therefore would surely have opposed the turn to neoclassical economics far more than they actually did, if governments did not have the ability to disclaim responsibility and point to the imperatives of European integration. Sovereignty is therefore not only a legal category but an important power resource for all governments. Taking into account the increasing importance of decisions taken at the international level, ranging from the liberalization of capital flows and trade in goods and services to efforts in coping with ecological issues such as the greenhouse effect, the importance of sovereignty for understanding global governance therefore may be increasing rather than diminishing.

CITIES AND MICROREGIONS IN WORLD POLITICS

During the 1990s, sociology and urban studies produced a growing body of literature that explores possible linkages between global economic processes and local politics. Writers such as Manuel Castells (1993, 1994) and Saskia Sassen (1991, 1994) have highlighted the impact of a liberalized world economy on urban social structures and on the reconfiguration of economic spaces. In her frequently cited work on *The Global City* (Sassen 1991), Saskia Sassen argues that it is becoming less accurate to speak of global cities like New York, London, and Tokyo as parts of a national economy; these cities have an increasingly transnational orientation that is at least as strong as their integration within their respective domestic economies: "growth in the new industrial complex is based less on the expansion of final consumption by a growing middle class than on exports to the international markets and on intermediate consumption by organizations rather than individuals. The key, though not necessarily the largest, markets are not the consumer markets but the global markets for capital and services. These are the markets that shape society and economy" (Sassen 1991: 333). According to Sassen, global cities are characterized not only by rapid technological innovation but also by a new kind of intercommunal division of labor which constitutes a transterritorial marketplace separated from international structures. In global financial relations, it is Tokyo that serves as a center for the export of capital, London that centralises and distributes capital flows to and from the Euro-markets, and New York that is the main receiver of capital flows and the main locus of investment decision-making (Sassen 1991: 327). The importance of cities in global economic affairs can at least partially be explained by the uneven spread of new information and communication technologies. This process does not only lead, as is often argued, to improved opportunities for the population as a whole to participate in the emerging global information society (Wriston 1992), but also to a new centralization of 'informational power' (Strange 1988). There can be little doubt that a growing number of individuals have access to personal computers, fax machines, and the Internet. The most sophisticated technology, however, and the necessary know-how to use these techniques is centralized in the headquarters of multinational corporations, banks, and sometimes even universities. The major importance of telecommunications for modern business administration demands the concentration of these instruments at those points where the infrastructure is most advanced (Castells 1994). And these places are not suburban sites, but are the cities of the global metropoles.

Recent work on global governance has reacted to this body of literature and started to consider if and how far subnational territorial units should be integrated into its analysis. James Rosenau, for example, argues that cities and microregions are likely to be major control centres in the world politics of the twenty-first century. Due to their growing economic importance, he argues, they seem destined to emerge as either partners or adversaries of states. Ultimately, so Rosenau speculates, global cities may lose their status as mere objects of states' policies and could constitute an intercommunal polity, which builds on their crucial role for conducting cross-border economic and political affairs (Rosenau 1995: 27). Echoing Rosenau's statement is the observation by Petrella that "the new world order taking shape is not the one imagined by the obsolete statesmen of the cold war era. Rather than an order of nation-states weighing in on a new global balance of power, an archipelago of technologically highly developed city-regions — or mass-consumer *technopoles*—is evolving" (Petrella 1991: 59). Petrella describes an order that is deeply divided between a network of dynamic, affluent and hyper-developed city regions, encompassing one eighth of the world's population, and an impoverished, vast, disconnected, and disintegrated wasteland that comprises the rest of the world. Similarly, Manuel Castells sets high hopes on the future potential of cities in being able to bridge the gap between local communities and global politics: he argues that cities "could manage the articulation between the space of flows and the space of places, between functions and experience, between power and culture, thus recreating the city of the future by building on the new foundations of their past" (Castells 1994: 32). Perhaps the most visionary point of view has been formulated by William Drodziak who interprets recent dynamics in intercommunal networking as indicating a "resurrection of city-states." This, he argues, will not only reshape but even revolutionize the political landscape of Europe. Drozdiak identifies a new historical dynamism that will ultimately transform the political structure of Europe by creating a new kind of 'Hanseatic' League that consists of thriving city-states (Drodziak 1994).

The most serious shortcoming of these contributions is that they amount to little more than illustrations and anecdotes. Systematic empirical studies providing an overview of the forms of local foreign policy and the options available to subnational territorial units are still rare. As interesting as this literature may be for drawing scepticism on state-centered concepts of global governance, it does not help very much in understanding the foreign policies of cities and microregions. This deficit is propelled by the underlying assumption of most of this literature that cities and microregions need to be viewed as being "places and sites rather than actors" (Friedmann 1995: 22). And indeed, at first glance there seem to be good reasons for treating them as passive reflections of states' policies rather than as actors in their own right. Although global cities are economic giants, their political potential and their economic function as command-and-control centers of the world economy do not easily translate into political power. As Boulding already argued thirty years ago, "there are virtually no channels in society or in the world at large by which the city as such can exercise bargaining power" (Boulding 1968: 1120). Because of this gap between the economic potential and the transborder political activities of subnational territorial units, the causal path in most arguments that attempt to theorize the global-local connection runs from the top down. There have been few serious attempts to systematize the local-global connection with regard to the active responses of subnational territorial units to external challenges. We also find a body of studies dealing with the urban management of transnational problems, for example, air and water pollution, housing for the new poor, and so on.[10] However, these studies are not based on any wider understanding of changes in structures of global politics and so almost always restrict themselves to searching for local answers within a local urban policy context.

INTERNATIONAL PROCESSES AND LOCAL INTERESTS

The first analytical problem one faces in any attempt to devise a systematic approach to the analysis of subnational territorial units is the definition of the object of interest. Subnational territorial units are at least as heterogeneous as states. They range from globally oriented, economically powerful, and highly innovative megacities to small and rather traditional urban agglomerations without the financial or human resources that would enable them to think and act globally. Very much like states, subnational territorial units can be differentiated according to their size, the population they represent, their economic ressources, and so on. Unlike states, however, their legal status varies widely. Some of them, as the German *Länder* (federal states) for example, have a constitutional right to participate in foreign affairs. Others such as the Spanish *provincias* are strictly prohibited to engage in any international affairs.[11] All of these units, however, have one important element in common: they are assumed to act as political institutions. As opposed to nongovernmental organizations, furthermore, they do not represent special interest groups but are elected by a territorially defined group. The legitimacy of their political demands therefore is not dependent on some moral objective and the content of their demands, but is in itself a democratic expression of concerns that are legitimized as such. If we take these aspects together, we can define subnational territorial units as political institutions at a regional or local level with a rather high degree of democratic legitimacy and the political task to further the interests of their constituencies. But *who* are the constituencies and *what* are their interests? In order to approach these questions, the following argument proceeds in an inductive manner, identifying three important international processes and asking to what extent these affect local social groups. The three global processes are identified as: (1) the civilization of international relations, (2) the debordering of economic and social relations, and (3) the democratization of nation-states. Due to their effects on the balance between the regulatory competence of the nation-state and local political institutions, each of these processes forms a central tenet of the argument presented.

Civilization of International Relations

States and subnational territorial units have a long history of competitive rivalry that dates back to the early Middle Ages and the emergence of territorially constituted, rather than personally constituted, rule (see also Tilly 1990; Giddens 1985). With regard to this historical conflict, Taylor (1995a; 1995b) has argued for an understanding of the state as a container of power which subordinated cities to the supremacy of states: "Rather than mutuality between state and city, states seemed bent on destroying cities either physically or economically" (Taylor 1995a: 51). It has been pointed out by historians that the Italian city-states and the Hanse were, in fact, viable alternatives to the territorial state for the better part of two centuries, fully able to levy taxes and raise armies (Spruyt 1994c). The end of mutuality between cities and states in the Middle Ages was therefore primarily a process of coercive subordination of cities that was motivated by the financial demands of the military machineries of the emerging nation-states. The civilization of international relations since World War II has—at least in the OECD area—significantly reduced local actors' perceptions of threat by external enemies. In a world in which the need for domestic actors to cooperate against external enemies is rapidly declining, subnationalities and regions can assert their autonomy with less fear: "being, for example, an active advocate of Breton culture and interest," as Hirst and Thompson (1996: 177) argue, "will no longer have the effect of weakening France in its life or death conflicts with Germany." The civilization of international relations therefore implies nothing less than a decreasing importance of the state's capacity to make war, and to draw on the lives and property of its citizens in order to do so. The legitimacy of the monopolization of transborder interest representation by the nation-state, which in the eighteenth, nineteenth and early twentieth centuries was based on the permanent danger of war and the need to coordinate the political and economic resources of society, has been eroded. To be sure, the nation-state is still the primary guarantor of international security. Peaceful interaction between the nation-states of the OECD area, however, is today perceived as not constituting a valid argument for subordinating the interests of local actors. With its successful provision of international security, the nation-state has lost an important argument formerly used to discipline societal actors. Coercion, as Taylor (1995a: 59) argues, may still be required internally, but city-states were always able to deal with internal dissent. The external conditions for a new political prospering of city-states therefore are rather promising. The growing transnational political activities of subnational territorial units may thus be interpreted as a process of emancipation of subnational actors from the monopoly of the state in regulating transnational political processes. With the diminishing ability of the state to fulfill its redistribution and security functions, we may also expect the decline of the state's contribution to the formation of society and identity. As Rosenau has argued, the modern nation-state is immersed in a crisis of authority and legitimacy, according to which identity and authority are relocated 'downwards', in the direction of subnational groups, including ethnic and tribal groups and minorities, local governments, interest groups, and civic organizations (Rosenau 1992a: 18). There can be little doubt that in Eastern Europe and in some social segments of Western European societies the nation-state is politically as vital as ever, and is even increasingly seen as an institution that promises to provide national stability in an era of turmoil. However, this can be explained by pointing to the specifics of post-communist societies with their lack of democratic and pluralistic traditions and to the social problems associated with long-term structural unemployment in Western Europe. At least for the majority of people living in the OECD world, the 'imagined community' (Anderson 1991) of the nation is in retreat. The state might still be able to uphold its identity-building function for some time, but its society-building function is vanishing, and, as some observers argue, cities are increasingly filling the gap by replacing states in the construction of social identities: "Hence, alongside the erosion of national economy we can glimpse the erosion of nation-state. The incredible spatial congruence that was simultaneously a power, economic, and cultural container is clearly unravelling" (Taylor 1995a: 58; see also King 1995).

Economic and Social Debordering

While subnational territorial units have gained considerably in importance as locations of economic activity in the last decade, their sociopolitical record tends to reflect fragmentation and political paralysis. Due to the mobility of capital and to intercommunal competition for investment by multinational corporations it has become increasingly difficult for the local authorities of subnational territorial units to extract economic resources (Afheldt 1994). In fact, communal economic politics is only too often best characterized as a competition of laxity, which contributes to the paradox that the headquarters of nearly all the multinational corporations of the world are located in the global cities, but at the same time the latter are often close to financial bankruptcy. Moreover, the debordering of economic spaces leads to an analogous debordering of social spaces. Territorial categories no longer serve as discrete demarcations between the richer part of the global population and the marginalized remainder. Unevenly distributed capacities to participate in the global economy, the reduced social competence of welfare states and economically motivated migration have led to an increasing social polarization in the metropoles of the global economy. From Berlin to Paris, New York, Los Angeles, or Shanghai, local social cleavages deepen and give rise to concerns about the viability of the social preconditions civil societies depend on. In a significant number of American cities, not only the poor are concentrated in ghettos such as the South Bronx, the banlieues in Paris or East Los Angeles, but also the rich are increasingly retreating from a commonly shared public space and are 'coccooning' in private housing areas with privatized public services and privately organized security services (Soja 1989). Manuel Castells (1993) has described this process as a tendency toward a growing 'social schizophrenia' in which local communities reestablish the social cleavages of the nineteenth century. State-centered social and political control over the development of a territorially defined community, which was (at least in Western Europe) a defining feature of the welfare state, is being replaced by an aterritorial logic of capital and information flows in contradiction to the needs of territorial communities (Castells 1993: 343).

Under the conditions of a globally integrated economy and a territorially fragmented polity, we are therefore witnessing a social process of parallel global integration of local elites and marginalization of those people who are unable to participate in the global economy. Furthermore, in most advanced capitalist countries, eligibility criteria for redistributive programs are being tightened in hand with a reduction of money available. In Germany, this has led to a reduction in unemployment benefits and an increasing demand for social assistance (*Sozialhilfe*). Whereas the former are paid by state institutions (unemployment insurance), the latter is provided by local administrations. This implies nothing less than an institutional reorientation of financial support for the unemployed and marginalized from the central state to local institutions. To be sure, subnational territorial units never sought to take over state functions in providing for basic needs — the federal government imposed these costs by misusing them as a dumping ground for policies it wanted to get rid of. Thus, subnational territorial units in the world society are structured by a dialectic of integration and fragmentation, following which they are developing not only into centers of economic command and control, but also into sites of social poverty and inequality. Along with the civilization of international relations, this is gradually changing the meaning of security in urban spaces. It is no longer the external enemy who poses the main threat to the wealth and health of people living in subnational territorial units, but the internal social stratum of the marginalized and unemployed who are not able to earn an adequate income or find social acceptance in a legal manner. The rapid growth in private security services, which can be observed in countries as different as the United States, the United Kingdom, or Germany, may thus be interpreted as a response by private local actors to the inability of the nation-state to guarantee a relatively safe public space. Whereas nation-states have been able to banish the external danger of war, their internal monopoly of power no longer translates into effective domestic maintenance of the peace. Reductions in military expenditure at the level of the nation-state are at least partially offset by an increase in private spending on civil security at the local level. In this perspective it is not international anarchy and the classical international security dilemma that poses the main danger to the security of the inhabitants of urban spaces, but the local social fragmentation resulting from (inter)governmental policies.

Democratization

The third process to be noted is the democratization of OECD societies. Not least due to the role of the media, public political consciousness is today far greater than ever before. A growing number of individuals today are no longer willing to accept a high degree of governmental autonomy and are pressing for effective participation in the political process. As Hobbs (1994) argues, frustration at the state's diminishing ability to cope with issues such as security and environmental issues in addition to experiencing remoteness from the decision-making process of central governments, has prompted local leaders and their constituents to act on international issues. Although small groups' chances of participating in the decision-making processes of central government are restricted, they are more able to influence local political institutions. This orientation toward local non-governmental organizations and political institutions is no longer only an instrument for influencing local or domestic politics. It also has an influence on international relations. Due to the rise of global communications and the global spread of news, many people today feel affected by such diverse issues as pollution in the North Sea, the thinning of the ozone layer, or environmental catastrophes wherever they occur. The debordering of information flows and the global character of a variety of problems have led to a debordering in the perception of risks citizens face in the North. Consequently, local NGOs no longer restrict themselves to campaigning on local issues, but insist on having a voice in the formulation of international politics. Grassroots movements from a variety of social strata have begun to respond to global processes of political and economic restructuring by channelling their energy into 'municipal foreign policy', a transnational politics that transcends the formal realities of international affairs (Kirby and Marston 1995; Hobbs 1994).

In summary, we can understand the incentives of local actors to go abroad as political responses to either new opportunities for the articulation of local interests, the threatened social stability of local communities, and/or the reorientation of individuals away from the nation-state and toward local levels of governance.

SUBNATIONAL TERRITORIAL UNITS AND STATES: COOPERATION OR CONFLICT?

After having identified crucial motives of subnational territorial units to escape the political container of the nation-state, it might be interesting to see to what extent interests translate into reality. It is especially interesting in this regard to compare the rather successful story of regions in Europe to the failures that American cities have been facing in the late 1980s and early 1990s. The two stories point to some important potentials as well as limitations which subnational territorial units face when they challenge state sovereignty.

Promoting Interadministrative Partnership: A Look at Europe

During the entire history of European integration, one of its most pressing challenges has been the criticism expressed with regard to the European Union's (and formerly the EC's) inefficiencies and its lack of democratic legitimacy (see also Weiler et al. 1995). It has been argued that whereas the European bureaucracy has become ever more involved in a broad range of policy areas, much of its policy output has been ineffective and too rigid. In launching the Single Market Programme in 1985, the European Commission reacted to its critics. It stressed the importance to accompany further integration with the principle of subsidiarity, that is: "working from the bottom up, rebuilding from below, from small entities rooted naturally in a solidarity of interests and a convergence of feelings" (Delors 1994: 53). The principle of subsidiarity was in the beginning primarily intended as a device for delineating the competencies between Brussels and the member-states; subnational territorial units such as the European regions were not assumed to be covered by the principle (Kersbergen and Verbeek 1994). However, subsidiarity rapidly became an instrument used by subnational actors to challenge Brussels as well as their national centers by imposing on them the need to prove superior capabilities in managing public affairs. The by far most important instrument for regions and municipalities in this undertaking in the EU is the EC's structural fund policy. It was incorporated into the Community treaty framework with the Single European Act (Article 130(c)). Shortly thereafter in 1988, the Community undertook its first comprehensive reform of its structural funds by doubling fund expenditure in real terms over the period 1989–1993. This happened at a time when real spending on national regional policy was declining across much of Europe. In the aftermath of the Maastricht Treaty, the member-states even agreed on further expansion of the overall cohesion budget; by the end of the EU's next financial period (1994–1999), cohesion spending will reach ECU 141 billion in constant 1992 prices, or one third of the total EU budget (Anderson 1995: 146).

Alongside this impressive budget expansion, there have been fundamental innovations in the administration of the structural funds. For the first time, it is the administrations of the regions themselves that come to play a pivotal role in allocating resources and in developing and monitoring programs. To improve vertical coordination, the Community sought to develop lasting partnerships with regional and local authorities and has opened offices in several regions. It regularly sends official delegations to eligible regions and requires national governments to consult with local and regional authorities in the drafting of program applications (Anderson 1995: 145). The Commission also created the Consultative Council of

Local and Regional Authorities (CCLRA), which was to be consulted on general questions of regional development and on the regional implications of Community activities. These consultations include pan-European associations of regional and local governments, such as the Association des Régions d'Europe and the Union Nationale des Villes et Pouvoirs Locaux. The efforts of the Commission to decentralize administrative structures are met by many local governments with enthusiasm: "Virtually every regional government receiving significant structural funds is now directly represented in Brussels (and in many cases Strasbourg), where they shepherd their proposals through the Community political process, monitor EC regulations, and lobby the Commission and Parliament" (Marks 1992: 214). Due to the institutional reforms strengthening the role local administrations play in the structural fund policy of the EU, it is no longer the memberstates that monopolize the conduct of affairs between European institutions and European societies but increasingly regional and local governments. They have become important interlocutors (Marks 1992: 214).[12] Another important instrument in strengthening the role of subnational territorial units in European governance is the Council of European Municipalities and Regions (CEMR). It is the first European institution composed exclusively of delegates from subnational territorial units, and it is accepted by the member states of the European Union as an important part of the European policy-making process. It has to be consulted on all questions that could affect the affairs of regions and serves as a forum for the exchange of expertise and for planning intercommunal policy initiatives.

The impact on state sovereignty of these institutional developments, however, should not be overemphasized. Although the members of the CEMR control funds amounting to over $15 billion, it has no power to veto any policy proposals by the member states, having only an advisory status. The Maastricht Treaty does not regard subnational territorial units as legal subjects of the Treaty and therefore guarantees them no standing independent of the states of which they are a part. Furthermore, rights of participation do not always easily translate into effective participation. In Germany, for example, the individual states (*Länder*) have (according to Art. 23 of the German Basic Law) the right to give an opinion on all issues at stake in the European Union whenever their interests are concerned *before* the German government enters into negotiations. If their interests are of primary concern (for example, issues concerning education or foodstuffs control), the government is obliged not only to take their preferences into consideration but even to adopt their position.[13] This has led some observers to question to what extent the German government is able to pursue any coherent policy in Europe at all. In reality, however, the Länder often do not exercise this right due to the fact that coordination among them is too slow and that they do not command the necessary administrative resources to develop common positions in due time (see also Oschatz 1995).

To interpret the European Union as leading to the outflanking of the state would not only mean overemphasizing the importance of subnational territorial units but misunderstanding the character of the EU. The Union still is and probably will remain for the foreseeable future a legal community in which legal resources and factual influence correlate closely. There can be little doubt that a 'Europe of Regions' that is not backed by the necessary legal powers attributed to subnational territorial actors is not much more than a heuristic concept or at best a political vision. This does not mean, however, that sovereignty in the EU has not changed its meaning. If, as defined above, the access to international negotiations is an important element of sovereignty, then member-states today do in fact share sovereignty with non-nation-state actors, even if only to a limited degree. Their formal recognition as being competent actors with a legitimate concern and the right to be heard whenever their interests are being dealt with, implies a least an acceptance on part of the member states that a European polity may neither rest solely on intergovernmentalism nor on supranationalism nor on a combination of the two. For being accepted by the European peoples as a legitimate way of governance, it needs to be supplemented by some form of local democracy. Ultimately, therefore, the political message of the institutional regionalization of Europe is the nation-states' acknowledgment that European democracy needs to build on an integration of subnational territorial units into the interexecutive polity of the European Union.

Beyond the Limits: A Look at the United States

Whereas the European state system's reaction to the demands of local governments has been rather cooperative by way of integrating them into the EU's polity, the reaction of the federal government of the United States has been very different, ranging from benign neglect to open confrontation. Most large North American cities today have a growing number of personnel devoted to international issues, handling interactions with foreign cities as well as foreign national governments. In the last few years they also have begun to develop their own foreign trade and investment policies (for an overview, see also Stanley Foundation 1994b). One of the methods used here is the maintenance of offices abroad to advance economic contracts, attract investments, and promote tourism. As Joenniemi and Sweedler (1995: 6) point out: "Issues such as how cities compete in the global market, trade concessions for foreign companies to locate within a city, infrastructure to provide a 'world class' transport and telecommunications system, the training and education of people who are knowledgeable in international affairs and tourism, are all topics that city officials are now dealing with." For example, California set up a California World Trade Commission in 1985, which by 1993 had offices in Tokyo, Hong Kong, Mexico City, London, and Frankfurt. Furthermore, in 1993, the California Trade and Commerce Agency was created to deal with 'foreign' trade—with foreign nations and the other forty-nine American states (Goldsborough 1993: 90).

All this has been perceived by the American government as well as by American courts as being unproblematic in legal terms; and indeed, the American constitution provides scope for cross-border activities of local levels of governance. Nowhere does the Constitution even mention the terms 'foreign relations', 'foreign policy', or 'international affairs'. It only grants a few narrowly defined powers concerning foreign policy to each of the three branches of national government (Congress, the president, and federal courts). Behind this background it seems rather surprising that American courts have, in a couple of decisions in 1989 and 1990, asserted that the federal government has exclusive jurisdiction over all matters affecting international affairs and curbed the discretion of local cross-border activities. Shumann (1992: 159–61) lists three decisions that have delivered serious blows to state and local activism. In the first, *Board of Trustees v. City of Baltimore,* from September 1989, the highest court in Maryland upheld a Baltimore ordinance that prohibited city investment in firms doing business in South Africa only because it deemed the measure to be minimal and indirect. By implication, this meant that local activism was to be regarded as unconstitutional if it disrupted the foreign policy of the federal government. In the second decision, *United States v. City of Oakland*, in April 1990, the Justice Department won a case against Oakland's 'nuclear free-zone'. The federal judge argued that the Oakland law had gone too far by banning firms involved in the manufacture of nuclear weapons from doing any contracting and subcontracting work on nuclear warheads or delivery systems within city limits, and by requiring the city to stop investing in or entering into contract with these firms as well as limiting the transportation of nuclear materials on the city's streets. The federal judge concluded that the law was "so comprehensive, so complete, so all-encompassing that it cannot help but conflict with the rights and authority of the federal government" (cited in Shumann 1992: 160). The third decision, *Perpich v. Department of Defense*, in June 1990, concerned a case in which thirteen states tried to ban or limit their National Guard troops' training in Honduras. Congress responded to these efforts very quickly by attaching to the National Defense Authorization Act an amendment that withdrew gubernatorial discretion over the training of the militias. According to the amendment, governors were forbidden to block exercises for their National Guard units "because of any objection to the location, purpose, type, or schedule of such active duty" (cited ibid.). The Supreme Court, which had to give the decision, therefore, had no choice but to rule the efforts of the thirteen states as being illegal. The message of all of the three decisions was clearly the same: whenever local activism was threatening to become a serious disturbance of the federal government's foreign policy interests, the courts argued that this should be stopped.[14] In doing so, the judicial branch adopted an understanding, which holds that the federal government enjoys exclusive power—as opposed to superior power—in foreign affairs, and thereby narrowed the constitutional scope for cities and states.[15]

To be sure, there are strong arguments for opposing local activism in foreign affairs: as far as foreign policy is ultimately concerned with questions of war and peace, with deciding who is to live and who is to die, it should at least have a certain degree of coordination, expertise, and nonvolatility. It seems futile to have the U.S. foreign policy divided into hundreds of different foreign policies, conducted by whoever perceives himself to be competent. "Too many subnational initiatives abroad" as Duchacek (cited in Hobbs 1994: 78) pointed out, "may lead to chaotic fragmentation and so invite foreign meddling or cause a nation to speak with stridently conflicting voices on the international scene." Ultimately, so the argument, local measures at best dilute federal policy; at worst they render federal action ineffectual. As the example of the EU tells us, however, nation-states do not need to perceive cross-border local activism as a threat in general. The reason why the reaction of the American federal government has been so different from the member-states of the European Union was exactly because the challenge was so different in nature. Whereas European cities and regions were only claiming to be represented in affairs concerning distributional and economic issues, cities and states in the United States had been active in politically sensitive issues of high politics: activities against the arms race (through 'nuclear freeze' resolutions), against 'constructive engagement' with South Africa (through divestment ordinances), and against the carrot and stick-politics of the United States in Central America (through trying to limit the supply of troops).[16] "While trade and transborder cooperation for the most part pose no danger to the effective maintenance of federal foreign policy," State Department legal assistant Peter Spiro declared (cited in Hobbs 1994: 69), "foreign policy and defense-related measures represent 'local interference' and pose serious challenges and potential danger to the federal decision-making process in these areas." By reflecting a broad opposition against the central elements of the foreign policy of the Reagan and Bush administrations and by interfering with major concerns of American 'high politics', local governments had simply overstretched the tolerance of the federal government. And, not surprisingly, it was exactly those cases in which American courts were delivering their blows against state and local activism.

CONCLUSION

For the foreseeable future, the state will remain of significant importance because it is the only actor on the stage of world politics that can conduct effective international agreements and therefore promise to establish effective governance beyond the state. Behind this background, a transnational system with sovereignty in terms of formal access to international policy-formulation and decision-making assigned to nonterritorial actors is neither analytically plausible nor normatively acceptable. NGOs serve important ends in focusing public awareness on the importance of international politics for domestic policy outcomes. Their integration into the global polity, however, will for the foreseeable future neither question the sovereignty of the nation-state nor its central authority in formulating cross-border politics. State policies relying on sovereignty and clear-cut territorial delineation within distinct borders may no longer be the *only* mode of global interaction, but are obviously still highly relevant. The state remains a powerful focus of societal identification and political authority, despite its reduced autonomy and the increasing relevance of competing loyalties and identities that coexist with it at the subnational, transnational, and even supranational levels. Today's local communities and other subnational territorial units rarely command the resources and the necessary political room for maneuver which would enable them to coerce the nation-state into sharing sovereignty; they rely on some degree of benevolence, as the examples of the EU and the United States have shown. More often than not, local communities are under extreme financial pressure and possess only strictly limited political competencies in foreign policy. However, the ongoing political integration of Europe and the strengthening of the principle of subsidiarity may lead to swifter changes in the future. The urbanization of the world's population has greatly increased the political and economic relevance of subnational territorial units vis-à-vis nation-states. Neither the state's regulative competence nor its function as a facilitator promoting processes of identity formation and society building is as important as it used to be. Global cities and large urban conglomerations are no longer only sites and locations in the world economy without any independent influence on global processes and politics. They are also gaining importance as part of an emerging linkage between local politics and world affairs, moving beyond their traditional role as passive reflections of state policies. Empirical and theoretical studies in International Relations have until now paid only little attention to these processes. By and large, the discipline remains trapped in the tradition of analyzing conflicts between states as the main tool for describing and explaining global governance. The concept of world society therefore is at least an important heuristic device for challenging the claim of a state-centered global polity. Due to the skepticism with which it meets traditional ways of conceptualizing governance beyond the state, it furthermore invites empirical research that aims at identifying and describing structures of international governance attributable to nonstate actors. If it succeeds in doing so, it helps to provide evidence that international relations theory is vital as ever and lives up to the task of trying to understand an ever-changing world.

12

The Better Half of World Society

Ingo Take

International relations has a great deal of catching up to do, from the point of view of getting transnational politics incorporated into the analysis of international political processes, and thus rectifying what has up to now been the dominant state-centered perspective. Ensuring greater attention is paid to the reciprocal relations between political systems—or parts thereof—social groups, NGOs,[1] and international institutions is one of the aims of the World Society Research Group. The present chapter, which offers a systematic review of the mechanisms via which NGOs interact with national, transnational, and international players, and through which they thus also influence international relations, is intended as a contribution to achieving that aim.

The extent to which cross-border relations are now institutionalized and actors are dispersed can be demonstrated by reference to, amongst other things, the increase in transnational NGOs operating relatively independently of territorial frontiers in the most diverse fields of politics.[2] Given that transnational NGOs thus embody two crucial aspects of the change in international relations (from the point of view of the concept of world society), they may quite rightly be described as 'protagonists of world society'.

In what follows here, an account will first be given of why the usual analytical framework (geared mainly to influence as it is exerted on states) needs to be extended to include influence exerted on the social level. Secondly, the range of strategies available to NGOs as a means of exerting influence will be reviewed, and separate descriptions will then be given of the mechanisms of influence used by NGOs at the social level, national level, and international level.

LEVELS OF INFLUENCE

Most of the studies investigating the importance of NGOs concentrate chiefly on the national and international levels, neglecting in particular NGO activities geared to the social level. Most analysts (whether neorealist or neoinstitutionalist) continue to view the state as the central actor in the international system, despite the oft-noted diminution in its power to direct affairs. As a result, they conceive of political influence mainly in terms of influence on governmental decision-makers. From this perspective, transnational NGOs appear solely as actors who either seek to influence the policies of a state (influence at national level), or seek to create, within the international system, the kinds of conditions that help to increase or decrease international cooperation (influence at international level). Strategies of influence geared to the social level are either completely left out of account or are viewed as not of an essentially political character (Wapner 1996: 312). Such a view does not do justice to the true radius of impact of nongovernmental organizations. It is precisely when influence at the national or international level comes up against its limits that the NGOs redouble their activities at the social level.[3] They provide the public with additional information on particular issues and try to put across to it alternative perspectives and beliefs; they form networks with other NGOs, in order to pool their resources; they endorse products and, where appropriate, call for boycott measures; in addition, they point up potential solutions by supporting the development of environmentally friendly products; and lastly, they subsidize environmental and developmental projects in many different parts of the world.[4] NGOs are therefore not simply pressure groups; a number of them also have their own identities as actors, geared chiefly to the social level. Any analysis of the influence of NGOs on international politics must therefore address all three levels (the social, the national, and the international), if it wishes to comprehend the true radius of impact of NGOs (Take 1996: 9). Hence, in what follows, I shall attempt to show, by means of concrete examples, how NGOs organize their influence at the various levels.[5] Before that, however, I shall conduct a systematic review of the strategies they use to make their influence felt.

THE STRATEGIES WHICH NGOS USE TO EXERT INFLUENCE

If one wishes to examine the influence of NGOs on the social level or on political decision-makers, cognitive factors such as ideas, perceptions, preferences, and the learning process offer highly promising avenues to understanding. Interests can change without there having been any shift in positions of power. Such change can often only be understood in the light of learning processes[6] and new insights by political decision-makers. The NGO activities described in what follows here would seem to justify the assumption that NGOs can at least encourage this kind of change. Learning processes and new insights must therefore also be taken into consideration in the analysis. They make empirically acquired knowledge about the influence of NGOs both on the social level and on political decision-makers (national level) more explicable.

A further elucidatory framework is provided by the second-order problems analyzed by Zangl as part of his conjectures on the formation of international regimes (Zangl 1994).[7] With their help, it is possible to show how the NGOs, by controlling and, where appropriate, imposing sanctions on state actors, or by carrying out certain distributive functions, encourage the genesis or further development of international cooperation. These elements will therefore also be included in my analysis of NGO influence.

At the *social level*, the dominant strategy is that of the provision of information to, and education of, the population by the NGOs. Thus, the NGOs are often the first to inform the public of environmentally damaging practices or human rights violations. By awarding consumer seals of approval for environmentally friendly products, calling for the boycotting of particular products (that do not come up to these standards), and developing environmentally sustainable products, they not only guide the population toward more environmentally aware behavior, they also contribute to finding solutions to the problems. The latter also occurs, for example, when they themselves take over the running of nature-conservation projects or of beach cleanup operations, or help to identify hazardous substances by conducting self-financed expert scientific investigations. The second-order problems analyzed by Zangl bring other strategies within the compass of the analysis: NGOs help ensure that agreed measures are implemented, either by monitoring application at the individual level—for example, by private companies (problem of monitoring)—or, in the case of violations, by bringing public pressure to bear on those responsible (problem of sanctions). Another social strategy that should be mentioned is the formation of transnational networks by NGOs for the purposes of pooling their— albeit mostly very limited—resources. Transnational networks enable the NGOs to respond, at least in part, to the demands (mainly for additional information or for monitoring services) that are made on them from the national or international quarter (international organizations, international regimes, etc.). The implications of this, however, are two-edged (more will be said about this below).

At the *national level*, the NGOs seek to improve the political decision-makers' awareness of problems—through lobbying, through credible representation of public interests, and through the provision of additional information—and thus also to promote the genesis of international cooperation. (These types of influence also become more comprehensible within a cognitively based explanatory framework.) In addition, by organizing 'counter-conferences' alongside official national or international conferences, the NGOs try to ensure that public pressure is channelled promptly—that is, before all the decisions have been made and ratified—onto what they have identified as weak points. In parallel with this, they endeavor to improve states' political and administrative capacities by carrying out their own scientific studies and by supporting public projects. Translation of internationally agreed measures into national laws, and the implementation of these, is promoted by the NGOs in that they monitor enforcement and, where appropriate, engage in penalizing activities.

Influence at the *international level* brings into the foreground strategies such as mediation between the various national delegations, the provision of additional information, lobbying, and the drafting of alternative legal wordings and declarations. In addition, the NGOs seek strategic alliances with 'leader states',[8] as a means of increasing their range of options for exerting influence.

To sum up: it may be seen that the strategies used by NGOs vary from one level of influence to another, but that overlaps may be noted at certain points. Using examples from one area of policy in particular—namely, international protection of the North Sea—I shall, in what follows, show by what means transnational NGOs manage to exert influence on international relations.

NGO INFLUENCE ON THE SOCIAL LEVEL

A dominant NGO strategy at this level is the provision of information to, and education of, the population in regard to particular threats, risks, or violations of international agreements. Identifying new threats is generally something done by scientists or scientific communities (*epistemic communities*); but these new discoveries are highly unlikely to attain to public awareness through the medium of the epistemic communities alone. It is, rather, the NGOs, with the help of the mass media, who ensure that they come to the public's attention: only when a subject is publicly discussed can it be expected gradually to become part of public consciousness (Luhmann 1990b: 65). NGOs therefore organize all kinds of information events, particularly for the people affected. The increase in the numbers of oil-infested birds washed up in the German Bight during the winter of 1983 was something that environmental groups were amongst the first to identify and that they almost single-handedly made public. In the official progress report published by the secretariat of the Fourth International Conference on the Protection of the North Sea (NSC 4), this is cited as one of the incidents that prompted Germany to propose the calling of an international conference for the protection of the North Sea (Progress Report 1995: 24). And local environmental groups responded to the 'catastrophic summer' of 1988 (algal bloom, seal deaths) by organizing hundreds of information events, whereas the politicians confined themselves to superficial placatory statements, thus leaving people in a state of uncertainty.

The innovations that have occurred in the field of communications technology, of which NGOs are making ever greater use, has made it possible for the latter to influence the ideas, values, political convictions, and perceptual models of people all over the world. This happens, on the one hand, via the process of public information and education described above, and, on the other, through activities that are designed to have maximum impact on the public (often taking the form of spectacular actions that ensure media attention). Such actions are intended, by appealing to people's consciences, to promote the spread of information (for example, about damage to the environment) and the adoption of alternative perspectives (for example, on the causes of an environmental threat). Activists go as far as to risk their own lives in such actions, in order to show the public how serious they consider the threats to be. The organization that best embodies this strategy is Greenpeace, which uses the latest telecommunications technology to get its headline-grabbing activities through to the public. An example of a successful action of this kind was the Greenpeace campaign against the dumping of weak sulphuric acid in the North Sea. Greenpeace launched its first action on North Sea protection on 13 October 1980, in the Federal Republic of Germany. Using two life rafts, activists managed to prevent the dump ship *Kronos* from setting sail and discharging so-called 'weak' sulphuric acid into the North Sea. In 1981, Greenpeace used its ship *Sirius* for the first time to disrupt the shuttle traffic between Nordenham and the dumping area off Helgoland. In full view of the media, and thus also of the public, Greenpeace activists leaped down in front of the bow of the oncoming *Kronos*. Greenpeace was here linking in seamlessly to traditional 'popular hero' motifs, surrounding itself with a 'Robin Hood' aura. Thanks to these actions, it managed to make acid dumping into a symbol for the reckless pollution of the North Sea.

The aim of these kinds of campaigns is to expose environmentally dangerous practices using international mass communications (the public become eyewitnesses to environmentally damaging activities), and thus to demonstrate strength of action long before international politics is in a position even to decide on effective countermeasures. At the same time, the particular organization's point of view is communicated to the public, and the power of governments to define the problem is thus removed, or at least challenged.[9]

A quite different strategy of influence at the social level is environmental sponsorship. The basic idea underlying environmental sponsorship is rooted in the principle of reciprocity. The NGOs obtain support from the companies concerned, in the form of money, benefits in kind, and so on; the companies hope, in return, for positive effects on their internal working ambience and their external image. Where environmentally based marketing, supported by NGOs, rests on a solid basis of environmentally aware management and environmentally sustainable products and production processes, the companies concerned can advertise their environmentally sound production arrangements to the public and thus establish pointers (for example, in regard to what is technically possible in environmental terms, or concerning the fact that environmental sustainability does not necessarily involve higher costs) and at the same time indirectly induce rival companies to imitate them. Of course, there is a danger here that the NGOs will be abused or exploited by the companies for their own purposes; but in general NGOs are capable of defending themselves against this kind of abuse—as is shown by the example of Friends of the Earth Germany (FoEG). FoEG rejects the notion of a wholesale award of its logo, instead backing the idea of ecological consultancy for the companies. What form this can take in practice is illustrated by the contractually agreed cooperation between BUND and the Hertie chain of department stores. Under the influence of FoEG, Hertie has banned plastic carriers from its food departments, has removed all pesticides from its stocks, and has carried out a comprehensive check of packaging, with a view to its reduction. The cooperation between BUND and Hertie has altered the organizational structure of the company along environmentally sustainable lines. This benefits both the company (a brochure with the BUND logo is given out about each action, thus securing good publicity) and the environmental group, which thus acquires ecological competence in the economic sector.

A confrontational strategy that is used for influencing private companies consists in NGOs monitoring the implementation of legal regulations or, where appropriate, using the publicly highly effective device of calling for a boycott. This strategy is most effective in cases where avoiding the relevant company's products does not involve the consumer in too much effort or expense. An equally positive factor as far as a boycott's chances of success are concerned is if the company is being asked to make relatively minor structural adjustments—for example, discontinuing a line or avoiding the use of particular raw materials and other substances in the production process. Another example of the imposition of sanctions on environmentally hazardous practices by industry is the suit that a number of German environmental groups filed with the *Oberverwaltungsgericht* [Higher Administrative Court] in Hamburg in 1988 on behalf of seals. This suit was directed against the incineration of waste at sea and against the dumping of weak sulphuric acid. Although it had no legal basis whatever, the industrial companies against whom it was filed found themselves under considerable public pressure. As a result, the date that had originally been fixed for halting incineration at sea was brought forward.

For larger NGOs, providing proposals as to how problems may be solved is an additional strategy, which, alongside the traditional protest activities against environmentally dangerous practices, is acquiring increasing importance. WWF's contributions in the field of research into North Sea conditions, for example, have won official praise:

> WWF continues to take an active part in research, monitoring, protection and management of North Sea ecosystems, species and habitats [...]. WWF's projects range from education, site purchase, conservation management, proposals for legislation to total or partial funding of research and studies. Surveys include the status and trends of species and ecosystems in various parts of the North Sea. Studies have been made on mortality and diseases [...] as well as on other effects of contamination or exploitation [...]. Habitat and species conservations management often needs monitoring and this has been promoted and supported by WWF. (Andersen and Niilonen 1995: 184)

Amongst the proposals for solutions there are some that are intended to point out to social actors (with a view to imitation), new, more environmentally friendly ways of dealing with nature. One example is the Greenpeace-sponsored development of the CFC-free refrigerator[10] and the 3-liter car ('Smile'), one of the purposes of which was to show the public (and not so much the car industry in this case) that it was perfectly possible to create a product of this degree of environmental friendliness.[11]

Precisely because of the increasing institutionalization of cross-border relations, it is, moreover, a reasonable assumption that by creating transnational networks, NGOs are able to work in a way that is cost-effective, avoids duplication, and pools resources, thus improving their chances of exerting influence at the transnational and international level as well (Walk and Brunnengräber 1994: 623). In addition, where a large number of NGOs come together to form a single network, they can more easily attract the attention of the political decision-makers and win greater regard from them than can individual NGOs alone. But this kind of enmeshment does bring with it certain problems. The NGOs in the South, for example, are dependent on the resources of those in the North. Whether this dependence has a positive effect (material support, additional information) or a negative one (being patronized or exploited) remains an open question. The heterogeneity of the NGOs and the simultaneous pressure that exists to formulate joint goals within the framework of transnational networks can lead to the NGOs' getting together on a lowest-common-denominator basis, which can result in the loss of crucial NGO qualities. Incorporation into networks may also bring with it an additional workload and a trend toward bureaucracy.

NGO INFLUENCE ON THE NATIONAL LEVEL

The influence of NGOs has increased over recent years precisely because NGOs are different from states. In the first place, they concentrate primarily on a single issue (for example, North Sea protection) or a single area (for example, environmental protection), leaving other issues out of the picture, whereas states have to cope with a large number of different issues, with national security necessarily always enjoying top priority. Secondly, NGOs generally address principle-based questions of a kind that are either entirely ignored by governments or at least subordinated to immediate strategic foreign-policy interests. It is true that the state remains the principal actor when it comes to solving problems, because it is the only one able to translate the relevant measures into valid law. But its ability to solve problems is being considerably curtailed because of the increased demands on it in an ever greater number of fields and because of the growing number of actors involved. This is especially true in the case of global problems, which can only be resolved through international cooperation. The reasons for this lie, amongst other things, in the length of the decision-making chain between the international and the local level; the countless possibilities, which the states involved in the cooperation have for blocking the process; the inadequacy of measures for monitoring and penalizing the conduct of the states in regard to implementation; the lowest-common-denominator policy that is often necessitated (by the international framework); and the meager information that political decision-makers possess about actual conditions on the spot (Rucht 1996: 36).[12]

Since the United Nations first came into being, the NGOs in particular have gradually expanded their capacities for coping with global problems. Nowadays, they are in a better position to provide information,[13] to interpret that information in a scientifically sound manner, and, in addition, to work out viable schemes for solving problems. They thus help states to cope with two characteristic features of global problems. For one thing, such problems are characterized by great complexity, which makes it difficult for governments to come to any concrete position on where their own interests lie. They therefore need outside help with definition. Secondly, global problems are often characterized by a history of policy failure—that is, problem-solving strategies previously applied have so far had no success, or only minor success. The search is therefore on for new problem-solving ideas. Hence, new political strategies will have a greater chance of success if, amongst other things, they provide a broader understanding of complex problematic situations and if they hold out the prospect of better policy results. However, one should bear in mind that what is defined as policy failure and as complexity is determined by the perceptions and interpretations of the political decision-makers (who, in their turn, are influenced, amongst other things, by the perceptions and interpretations of the public).[14] In many cases, the quality of the information with which NGOs make their entry into the political process wins them recognition as actors on the international political stage, and puts them in a position to challenge governments' monopoly on definition. However, it does also happen that, by stressing the ethical character of a problem, or by painting a situation black, NGOs depart from the bounds of objectivity.[15] Such strategies can indeed help to extend the circle of people who feel touched by the issue, and thus give added impetus to public pressure; but they also harbor the danger that public and governmental recognition of the NGOs will be damaged if the information is shown to be unobjective.

The rapid growth of the environmental movement at the beginning of the 1980s led to mounting pressure on the political classes to increase their own activities in this area. The contribution, which environmental groups have made to reinforcing this movement is clear for all to see and surely needs no further proof here. What will, however, be demonstrated in the following pages, is the practical way in which the NGOs exert pressure on the political decision-makers. They employ various strategies to do this: (1) they present themselves, in contrast to the political classes, as championing the interests of a broad cross-section of the public;[16] (2) they give the affected people a voice (for example, in cases of human rights violations, discrimination, environmentally dangerous practices) and thus sharpen politicians' awareness of the problems; and (3) they often provide factual arguments, ideas, and counterproposals that find their way into politicians' decision-making.

All these cognitive strategies—this is my thesis—exert an influence on the perceptions of the political decision-makers and thus on their political actions. I am not thereby claiming that the NGOs determine the conduct of states; but they do, by their activities, extend the framework from within which governments select their options for action. In this way, NGOs acquire a not insignificant role in determining both political priorities and the way in which a particular issue is discussed.

The pressure exerted by committed citizens and NGOs—working upward from the national to the international level—helps increase the chances of international co-ordination, cooperation, and even acceleration of national efforts. Mayer-Tasch actually describes this "national grass-roots and lobby pressure" as the "true driving-force in international (environmental) politics" (Mayer-Tasch 1990: 174).[17] National governments react to this stimulus by passing it on to the international level. There, it both helps to put the notorious procrastinators of international cooperation (the so-called 'laggard states') under pressure and acquires an opportunity of being translated into international legislation of varying degrees of effectiveness. Thus, Britain's voluntary adherence to the process of cooperation to protect the North Sea becomes much more comprehensible if the explanation includes the pressure that transnational NGOs have exerted through their public accusations and protest actions—especially since, for one thing, Britain is least affected by the pollution of the North Sea and, for another, is subject to hardly any intrinsically domestic pressure to participate in international measures to protect the North Sea.

The nature and extent of what is mostly an industrially generated threat is thus made known in the face of those interest groups that advocate further industrial growth.[18] The environmental movements, so we note with Ulrich Beck, have often emerged from this 'exposure-centered conflict' as the victors—even in international terms (for example, the international campaign against the planned sinking of the oil rig *Brent Spar* initiated by Greenpeace in 1995[19]).

Once an issue has finally been fixed as an item on the political agenda, with (or without) the help of the NGOs, the discussion about the most effective strategy for countering the particular trend then begins. Here, the 'accountability-centered conflict' (Beck 1995: 15) comes to the fore. It involves the responsible parties being identified and made answerable for their actions. As the conflict about the sinking of the *Brent Spar* oil platform showed, NGOs are particularly successful in this kind of case if their actions incorporate vivid symbolic elements.[20] The Greenpeace campaign against Shell demonstrated clearly for the first time that, where far-reaching decisions are to be made, neither multinational concerns nor government ministers can simply ignore public opinion when mobilized.

The increasing integration of social actors into national and international political processes[21]—which also ensures a whole variety of personal contacts between government representatives, staff of international organizations, and NGO representatives[22]—opens up to the NGOs a range of options for exerting influence on the way their states conduct themselves in foreign affairs. It enables them, for example, to foster the translation of international agreements into national regulations, by monitoring this process and keeping the public informed about its progress. Thus, Greenpeace got some of its own scientists onto the London Dumping Convention's (LDC's)[23] panel of experts that was looking at the scientific aspects of the dumping of radioactive waste at sea. These scientists pointed to the many uncertainties that existed in regard to the effects that dumping has on the marine environment, and they highlighted the effects of previous dumping. The extension of the moratorium on the dumping of radioactive waste at sea can probably legitimately be regarded as a political consequence of these revelations, because dumping would have relieved many politicians of a considerable problem — in other words, would undoubtedly have been in their interest (Stairs and Taylor 1992: 123). Where regulations are violated by governments, or even where there is dilatoriness in implementing them, the NGOs turn to the public and thus put governments under pressure. For example, the proposal by the Oslo Commission that waste incineration at sea should be halted by the 1990s produced only dilatory attempts at implementation by the North Sea countries. In 1987–1988, Greenpeace responded by publishing a list naming the major suppliers to the incineration vessels Vesta and Vulcanus II (see also Greenpeace 1988). Greenpeace also sent rubber dinghies out against the incineration vessels — not, of course, without first having ensured the kind of media presence that would guarantee the problem was played out before the public. The date that had originally been set for the halting of these environmentally dangerous practices was promptly brought forward.

By exposing environmentally dangerous practices and identifying those responsible for them, environmental groups also enable politicians to act in a focused manner. Ecological issues are thus translated into political ones by the NGOs. This also increases pressure on the political decision-makers to act, because failure to respond to such a clear infringement of the rules brings with it the charge that the state is not willing to ensure the well-being of its people (because it allows damage to be done to the bases of its life).

The 'counter-meetings' that NGOs hold, generally in the run-up to international conferences, serve two purposes: first, they are intended to give the public a different perspective than that dictated by economic interests; second, they aim to make the people aware, in advance, of the weak points in the expected declaration. Public pressure is thus focused on these points, and the political decision-makers are pressurized into doing further rectificatory work on them.

Basing myself on Putnam's 'two-level' model,[24] I should like here to posit the additional thesis that strong (NGO-mediated) reservations on the part of the population in regard to a particular political practice sometimes provide national negotiators from leader states with a welcome aid in arguing for particular agreements. Germany and the Netherlands employed this strategy against Britain when a ban on the dumping of oil platforms was under discussion.

Since environmental problems do not stop at national borders, there has to be cooperation at the international level. The genesis and development of international cooperation on the protection of the environment is fostered by NGOs—this is my next thesis—because they involve themselves in monitoring the translation of internationally agreed measures into national laws or regulations (operationalization) and their application (implementation),[25] and because they improve states' political and administrative capacities at the national level. This bolstering effect on the part of NGOs can be demonstrated by reference to the second-order problems analyzed by Zangl, each of which influences the genesis of international cooperation in proportion to how pronounced it is. The less pronounced a problem, the better the chances of international cooperation coming about. In what follows, I should therefore like to describe these problems and the way in which NGOs help defuse them, thus fostering the genesis of international cooperation.

The risk that a state will contravene agreements concluded at the international level can only be effectively countered by guaranteeing reciprocal monitoring of state measures to implement such agreements (second-order problem). Only thus can states acquire the kind of information about other states' behavior which allows them then to respond in the appropriate way. However, acquisition of the relevant information entails certain costs. These so-called 'monitoring costs' include, for one thing, the resources expended to monitor the other actors; they also include the loss of sovereignty—much lamented by nation-states—that is a concomitant of being monitored by others.[26] These monitoring costs thus constitute a problem the solution of which is a precondition for effective decentralized cooperation.

Those NGOs interested in the development of international cooperation can help defuse this problem by acting as monitors within their own states, keeping an eye both on the translation and on the implementation of internationally agreed norms and measures. If a government fails to adhere to international regulations, the social actors inform the other states of this infringement. Mutual monitoring exercised in this way[27] results in fewer costs to the states involved, and the second-order problem of monitoring thus decreases in importance.

In order to be able to fulfill this monitoring function effectively, Greenpeace, for example, has its own laboratory ship (the *Beluga*), for measuring the pollution burden of rivers, and also a mobile air-measurement station. In almost all the North Sea countries, nature-conservation groups monitor the beaches and collect evidence of environmental damage.[28] Thus, after NSC 2, as a result of intervention by environmental groups, Germany was obliged to enforce legally a third stage of purification for sewage-treatment plants in 1989 (instead of, as originally planned, in 1992). Another example of how national implementation of international resolutions have been monitored is the WWF's pollutant release and transfer register. The register was established by the Hamburg-based Ökopol-Institut, at the behest of the WWF; by means of a statistical survey of municipal and industrial dischargers along the German North Sea coast, it assesses the conduct of the Federal Republic of Germany, a participant in the regime, in regard to implementation. In exercising their monitoring functions, the NGOs also base themselves on official reports on activity and implementation. If states fall behind the goals agreed at the international level, the NGOs move into action. Thus, Greenpeace used data compiled by the Oslo Commission to condemn the British government publicly for its practice in regard to dumping. Similar examples have been provided by environmental groups in Denmark, Sweden, Germany, and the Netherlands (Haas 1993b: 175). But the NGOs also supplement their evaluations of official reports with their own research. The WWF, for example, in parallel with the official report on implementation, investigated how matters stood in member-countries with regard to the aim of halving register entries for thirty-six hazardous substances by the year 1995, as agreed at NSC 3.[29] The results show that all the North Sea countries exhibit considerable shortcomings in regard to implementing the resolutions on reduction.

If particular actors behave like 'free riders'—in other words, if they fail to observe the jointly concluded agreements—it has to be possible to inflict some sanction. This means there must be the option of excluding the actor concerned from the cooperation and from the benefits associated with it. But even the imposition of sanctions on 'free riders' sometimes entails considerable costs (second-order problem). Hence, every participant in international cooperation is keen to leave the imposition of sanctions on a defaulting state to the other participants.

The sanction problem too becomes less acute where social actors exert influence. A government's nonobservance of internationally agreed measures is made known to the public by social actors (for example, through protest action at a conference venue—before the eye of the television cameras—through demonstrations, or even through fully fledged campaigns against a particular policy). The result for the government concerned can range from a general loss of popularity up to and including deprival of the votes of whole sections of the electorate. (Thus, at the height of the environmental movement in the early 1980s, 'green' parties emerged all over Europe and wooed voters away from the established parties.) Some of the costs of sanctions are thus borne at the social level. The participants in the cooperation are thus spared having to create reliable sanctions mechanisms in certain problem areas (in the case of environmental regimes, this is quite often the case).

A further strategy of the NGOs is to increase states' problem-solving capacities by providing additional information, doing their own research, drawing up proposals, and carrying out feasibility studies. The official recognition, which a number of NGOs have enjoyed as providers of information to government decision-makers, has meant not only an increase in the legitimacy of the NGOs; it also points to the fact that information provided by them is being incorporated into the political decision-making process. But the enhancement of nation-states' capacities is not confined to the input of additional information. The execution of national regulations by industrial concerns is an obvious weak point in the field of national environmental policy. Local authorities mostly do not have sufficient capacities to monitor to what extent industrial companies are actually observing the laws or regulations. This monitoring function is taken over by the NGOs, in that they identify polluters, publicize their names, and, where appropriate, conduct actions or campaigns against them.

CONTRIBUTION AT THE INTERNATIONAL LEVEL

At the international level, NGOs contribute to the genesis of international cooperation by mediating between the positions of the various national actors involved, fueling the process of international cooperation with additional information, engaging in lobby work, submitting alternative proposals, and forming alliances with the so-called leader states.

Within the framework of decentralized cooperation, several cooperative interactive outcomes are generally negotiated simultaneously. The participants have varying preferences in regard to the different outcomes. Participants generally concur about the goal of their cooperation, but there is by no means always agreement about the measures to be used to achieve it. In a situation involving this kind of difficulty, one talks of there being a distribution problem (second-order problem): as long as joint measures cannot be agreed, the emergence of a Pareto optimal solution[30] remains in doubt.

The NGOs can help to defuse this problem by acting as mediators between the various governmental actors, by highlighting the points they have in common, and by pointing up alternative solutions.[31] Thus, in the field of international environmental policy, dilemma games[32] often assume the character of coordination games,[33] the structure of which makes the genesis of international cooperation more likely than would be the case with dilemma games.[34] Once they become more integrated into processes of international cooperation, it is easier for the NGOs to exert this kind of influence.

By providing additional information to the institutions involved in international cooperation, the NGOs make the job of formulating effective binding measures easier for them. NGOs also foster international cooperation by participating in scientific projects set up by states for this purpose. As a result, the international expert groups formed to look at the individual areas of international cooperation have, over recent years, not only become more open to participation by NGO representatives; they are increasingly frequently calling on the latter's expertise and skills. In this way, NGOs are acquiring greater influence on international negotiations.[35] The points at which NGOs have influenced the final drafting of a declaration, and the extent of that influence, can be demonstrated in the domain of North Sea protection by reference to the minutes of the informal meetings (which NGO representatives attend). Thus, in August 1984—in other words, one month before the close of the official preparatory meeting, and a good two months before NSC 1—a hearing took place at which various NGOs had an opportunity to present their proposals, "which then found their way into the subsequent conference preparations" (Ehlers 1985: 103). In the course of the cooperation on North Sea protection, NGOs managed, amongst other things, to secure acceptance for a ban on particular hazardous substances and a moratorium on the import of radioactive waste. Furthermore, thanks to their intervention, accommodation was reached on the issues of pollution caused by shipping, the reduction of waste, the use of fertilizers, and pollution from offshore installations.

The conferences organized by the NGO side, and the alternative draft declarations worked out by it, are not confined to criticism of the process of international cooperation; they also provide a range of alternatives to the official draft declarations. The more closely the alternative proposals are geared to the official draft treaties, the greater their chance of being realized.[36] This kind of policy of 'small steps' may well be regarded by many (including some members of NGOs, as well as certain sections of the population) as unequal to the problems involved, but it has been successfully pursued at the international level, and concrete proof of this may be found in minutes of meetings, proposals, draft declaration, and concluding documents.

Cooperation with so-called leader states is another strategy used by the NGOs to influence the international negotiating process. If the NGOs succeed in recruiting allies who have decision-making power, their chances of exerting influence increase considerably. NGOs are therefore always on the lookout for potential allies, at the same time taking care not to subordinate themselves to these allies' interests. One task identified by the NGOs is that of highlighting everything that can be achieved by individual states acting alone, both on concrete issues and from the point of view of political impact. Hence, states that are ready to engage in these kinds of solo efforts must be supported. The task is then to work with these allies to point up practicable solutions that might persuade other states to follow suit. At the 16th meeting of the Oslo and Paris Commissions, the environmental groups pressed in particular for a ban on the use of chlorinated paraffins. In pushing their demands, the environmental groups could be sure of the support of Sweden, which had already achieved a 90 per cent reduction in the use of such types of paraffin since 1986. By pointing out to the other treaty members a practicable method of reducing their use, the environmental groups and Sweden helped advance the development of international safeguards. One year later, this coalition secured the adoption of a resolution providing for chlorinated paraffins to be discontinued by 1999. The Dutch delegation had the support of the NGOs in seeking to get North Sea oil and gas extraction included in the declaration—and was also successful (OSPAR Convention 1992: ch. VI, §52).

CONCLUSION

The influence of the NGOs documented here is geared to the realities of international politics. What can be achieved within this framework is by no means insignificant, and it contributes to a more appropriate treatment of global problems. It would be wrong to describe international agreements as ineffective because they are not always implemented conscientiously by nation-states. If one considers the novel character of many global problems, and their complex nature, one cannot set expectations about the effectiveness of international agreements too high. It is simply the fact that the conflict-fraught business of working out international norms and rules, and the repeated failure to implement them at the national level, are such that the treatment of global problems only does partial justice to the issues involved. The time lags involved in implementation also have an obstructive effect. By improving basic knowledge and thus helping to reduce reaction times, the NGOs help to counteract these defects in international cooperation.

The increasing number of international conferences on global problems[37] has also led to an increase in the number of NGOs active at the international level.[38] This trend is both the cause and the effect of the increased regard in which NGOs are held by political decision-makers in governments, international bodies, and commissions (Rucht 1996: 35). This is reflected, firstly, in the increasing official acceptance of NGOs as participants, *rapporteurs*, or indeed members of delegations at international conferences.[39] Secondly, an increasing number of NGOs are being financially supported by national or international bodies.[40] This increased integration brings with it an increase in NGOs' opportunity to influence political decisions. The transnational NGOs, amongst others, are thus helping to ensure that social internationalization is being brought at least partially into congruence with political internationalization.

The integration of transnational NGOs into international decision-making processes also increases the legitimacy of agreements concluded at the international level. This is indicated by the high level of public regard, which NGOs have now acquired. The boundaries in the new areas of conflict often run in different directions than they do in the conflict-areas in which, for example, our existing party-system was formed. For this reason, the individuals affected can hardly entrust the articulation of their interests to what are partly traditional institutions. They are therefore increasingly placing their trust in the new transnational actors.[41] A refusal by states to include NGOs in international political processes could, against this background, end up causing damage to the states themselves.

Hence, in conclusion, one should note that political decision-making processes at the international level are characterized by a tendency to destroy options (because they depend on solutions capable of securing a consensus) rather than create alternatives. And it is the latter that should be the true task of politics. But as long as the political decision-makers in states and international organizations do not show themselves capable of solving long-term global problems, transnational NGOs will enjoy increasing support from the public. It is they who, to an ever greater extent, are pointing up alternatives and thus demonstrating a capacity for action of a kind which, in the eyes of the public, is lacking in other actors. They are thus throwing down a challenge to national and international institutions to tackle these problems in a more effective way. The integration of NGOs therefore offers international politics a chance to win back some of its lost problem-solving capacity.

Notes

NOTES TO CHAPTER 1

The present version of this chapter was written by Mathias Albert, Lothar Brock, Hilmar Schmidt, Ingo Take, Christoph Weller, and Klaus Dieter Wolf. The World Society Research Group is a working group of scholars at the Darmstadt University of Technology and the Johann Wolfgang Goethe University Frankfurt.

1. The Weberian terms *Vergesellschaftung* and *Vergemeinschaftung* are translated here in such a way as to make it clear that in our understanding, they refer to processes rather than to static or already existent entities or relationships; if they are simply translated as 'society' and 'community', this nuance is lost.

2. Our undertaking links up with the present debate on globalization (see Beisheim and Walter 1997), though globalization as such is not at the center of our work. Much of the debate hinges around the question whether there is anything new in globalization. Our understanding is that there are structural changes in the world economy that have to be taken into account in any analysis of world affairs. Whether these are subsumed under the term 'globalization' or not does not concern us here.

3. This would mean, for example, that an interaction-based perspective, which we have taken as our starting point, would be supplemented by a system-theoretical perspective. In this regard, Luhmann's radically different contribution to the world society debate may yet prove to be helpful (Luhmann 1997; see also Albert 1997).

4. The idea of a world community was inherent in the Enlightenment, whose project was a universal one. This project continues to affect our conceptions of world politics today in the obligation adopted by the United Nations to, in the words of the Preamble to the Charter, "save succeeding generations from the scourge of war," and also in the policy of protecting human rights, which has so far been pursued within the U.N. framework.

NOTES TO CHAPTER 2

1. We employ the term 'world of states' in order to denote that the characterization as a 'system' in the way it is commonly employed in IR does not adequately describe the societal (and maybe even communal) dimension of relations between states (see also the

final section of this chapter below); the term 'system of states' is then employed only to point to the systemic dimensions of relations between states where traditionally used in reference to the development of sovereign states.

2. Wherever 'territoriality' came into play (notably in the 'English School'), it rather meant a framework condition pointing toward the unchangeability of the international system or 'international society' as a system of states than a possible breaking point out of which substantial change could emerge.

3. Sack (1986); Duchacek (1986); Duchacek et al. (1988); Agnew (1994); Cappellin and Batey (1994); Demko and Wood (1994); Taylor (1994, 1995a); closely connected is the literature on world cities and industrial locations; see also Soja (1989); Castells and Hall (1994); Scott (1988); Amin and Thrift (1992); Henry (1992); also the literature on new regionalism and localism: for example, Hettne and Inotai (1994).

4. Jones (1959); Kristof (1959); Hansen (1994); Martinez (1986); Herzog (1992).

5. Relevant in respect to the theory of international relations are, among others: Kratochwil (1986); Ruggie (1993); also: Held (1991a); Connolly (1991); Walker (1993).

6. This development may also be conceived as part of a comprehensive change of world order in the transition from modernity to postmodernity; see Ruggie (1993).

7. See Bauböck (1994); Kratochwil (1994); Beiner (1995); see also Rosenau (1992b); Agnew (1993); Faist (1999).

8. See Jones (1959); Kristof (1959); Kratochwil (1986); Duchacek (1986); Herzog (1992).

9. See part 2 of Kratochwil (1986); Jones (1959: 243–44); Ruggie (1993: 190).

10. Duchacek (1986); Nijkamp (1994); Martinez (1994); Engel and Rogers (1994); see also Helliwell (1998).

11. Duchacek (1984); Sassen (1991); Scott (1988); Amin and Thrift (1992); Hettne and Inotai (1994); Delamaide (1994); Ohmae (1993); Lash and Urry (1994).

12. The *Länder* compare to U.S. states, whereas the *Regierungsbezirke* are subunits of the individual states which form an additional administrative layer between state and county (*Landkreis*).

13. See for example: Kaplan (1993); Meehan (1993); Bauböck (1994); Close (1995); Beiner (1995); Roberts (1995).

NOTES TO CHAPTER 3

I would like to thank Gerard Holden for the translation, and am grateful for the valuable comments on earlier versions of this chapter to the colloquium of the Political Science Institute at the Darmstadt University of Technology, the World Society Research Group, and in particular to Heidrun Abromeit, Lothar Brock, Tillmann Elliesen, Gunther Hellmann, Andrea Liese, Gerald Mörsberger, Rainer Schmalz-Bruns, Hilmar Schmidt, Thomas Schmidt, Christina Schrade, Ingo Take, Cornelia Ulbert, Jürgen Wilzewski, Klaus Dieter Wolf, and Michael Zürn.

1. Weber (1968: vol. I, part one, ch. I, § 9); see also Esser (1988).

2. See the abundant literature on globalization; an excellent overview of this literature can be found in Beisheim and Walter (1997).

3. The fact that individual advantage is central to the assumptions of this social-psychological theory does not necessarily place it in the vicinity of rational choice approaches, as this psychological gain is not accessible to any intentional calculation.

4. Social identity theory is set out in more detail in the fourth section of this chapter.

5. Weber himself can be cited to make more plausible the association of collective identities with his concept of community formation: "All kinds of other visible differences can, in a given case, give rise to repulsion and contempt [...]. Seen from their positive aspect, however, these differences may give rise to consciousness of kind, which may become as easily the bearer of group relationships" (Weber 1968: vol. I, 387). See also Estel (1994: 15).

6. Weber emphasizes this dimension of community-formation in his discussion of 'race': "Of course, race creates a 'group' [*Gemeinschaft*] only when it is subjectively perceived as a common trait [...]. The resulting social action is usually merely negative: those who are obviously different are avoided and despised or, conversely, viewed with superstitious awe" (Weber 1968: vol. I, 387).

7. See the respective arguments laid down in chapter 1; see also Weller (1997).

8. "While the possibility of personal identity seems plausible, collective identity appears problematic," comments Assmann (1993: 240). "The terms 'collective', 'local', 'national', and 'ethnic' identity are often used in such a way that it remains entirely unclear who the subject of these concepts is, that is, who is identical to what. It is not unreasonable to suspect that what is going on here is the same kind of terminological short-circuit as occurs with concepts like *'Volkspersönlichkeit'* [the 'personality of a people'; the eds.]. It is at least advisable to begin with a rather more precise definition of the terminology involved" (Bausinger 1978: 205; see also Bausinger 1986: 143).

9. See Assmann (1993) for a discussion of essentialist notions of collective identity.

10. For similar remarks see also Katzenstein (1996b: 22), and Neumann (1996: 140). "We need to situate the debates about identity within all those historically specific developments and practices which have disturbed the relatively 'settled' character of many populations and cultures" (Hall 1996: 4). See also Bausinger (1978: 204).

11. For discussions of this question, see Lapid (1996), Kratochwil (1996), Zalewski and Enloe (1995), Katzenstein (1996b), and Jepperson et al. (1996).

12. I have singled out Zalewski and Enloe's treatment of the question because it appears in a "collection of essays about the major theoretical questions today" (Booth and Smith 1995b: xi), because its title (*Questions about Identity in International Relations*) indicates that it is relevant to my subject, and because the editors of this collection describe the individual contributions as essays "on the state of thinking about their particular topic" (Booth and Smith 1995b: xi).

13. In an exemplary review of Wæver et al.'s book, McSweeney (1996) has sharply criticized the concept of 'societal security' put forward by these authors, and argued that a contradictory concept of identity lies at the root of the problem. I shall not, however, repeat here the details of McSweeney's critique.

14. Wæver's presentation of the concept shows occasional signs of a constructivist approach, but this is not compatible with the definition of societal security as "the security of a social agent which has an independent reality and which is more than and different from the sum of its parts" (Wæver 1993: 26); on this point see McSweeney (1996: 84).

15. The main reason for Katzenstein's choice of his research question is the fact that traditional utilitarian theories based on the rational choice approach are clearly inadequate to the task of offering an adequate representation or a satisfactory explanation of events, and above all of changes, in international relations in the 1990s (Katzenstein 1996b: 22; Jepperson et al. 1996: 40). In Katzenstein's view, the central problem is the assumption made within traditional theoretical approaches that the interests of states are laid down from the start.

16. The title of the volume, *The Culture of National Security: Norms and Identity in World Politics*, is also to be understood in this way: "The empirical essays in this volume focus on the ways in which norms, institutions, and other cultural features of domestic and international environments affect state security interests and policies" (Jepperson et al. 1996: 37).

17. These authors do discuss this aspect of their use of the concept, but there is no theoretical discussion, and the problem is 'solved' by means of an analogy: "The term [identity] comes from social psychology, where it refers to the images of individuality and distinctiveness ('selfhood') held and projected by an actor and formed (and modified over time) through relations with significant 'others'. Thus the term (by convention) references mutually constructed and evolving images of self and other. Appropriation of this idiom for the study of international relations may seem forced, since states obviously do not have immediately apparent equivalents to 'selves'. *But nations do construct and project collective identities, and states operate as actors.* A large literature on national identity and state sovereignty attests to this important aspect of international politics. We employ the language of 'identity' to mark these variations. For the purpose of this project, more specifically, we employ 'identity' as a label for the varying construction of nationhood and statehood" (Jepperson et al. 1996: 59, my emphasis).

18. Once again, McSweeney's critique of Wæver et al. is relevant; in particular McSweeney (1996: 87–90).

19. Wendt (1992: 396–98); the quotation is from Berger (1966: 111).

20. "I treat states as agents having identities" (Wendt 1994: 392). When Wendt uses the terms 'collective identity', 'corporate identity', and 'social identity' (Wendt 1994), they always refer to interstate relations. In 1994, Wendt treated the claim that "states are the principal units of analysis for international political theory" as one of the three 'core claims' (Wendt 1994: 385) of his IR constructivism. He made only minor changes to this thesis in a revised version of his 1994 article published in 1996—"states are the principal actors in the system" (Wendt 1996: 48). However, his very clear response to Mearsheimer abandons this argument and reduces the fundamental assumptions of his IR constructivism to two (see Wendt 1995).

21. "Structuration theory makes it impossible to classify collective entities as actors. A collective unit such as a state can only exist if and when it is reproduced via the institutionalized practices of bureaucrats, politicians, and societal agents who make their own demands. The assumption that the state is an actor reifies the state when what is needed is a problematization of the mechanisms which reproduce it" (Jaeger 1996: 320). Although Jaeger voices this criticism from a perspective that is explicitly indebted to structuration theory (Jaeger 1996: 315), it is just as relevant in a social-constructivist context (see Berger and Luckmann 1967: 55).

22. Risse-Kappen uses the term differently in his book *Cooperation Among Democracies* (1995b), where populations as totalities are the bearers of collective identity: "One would expect a collective identity to emerge when democracies interact in an institutionalized setting such as an alliance. While Americans do not cease to remain Americans, and Europeans remain Europeans (or British, German, and French), they nevertheless identify with each other and care about each other's fate. Liberal theory assumes that the *content* of this collective identity refers to shared values such as human rights, the rule of law, and democratic governance" (Risse-Kappen 1995b: 204, emphasis in original).

23. If one searches for a systematic discussion of 'collective identity' in Risse-Kappen's liberal-constructivist approach, one gets the impression that he could in fact manage with-

out the term and could base his analysis on nothing more than values, norms, and a 'sense of community' (Risse-Kappen 1996: 371; 1995b: 39); even so, Risse-Kappen repeatedly stresses collective identity when he makes general statements (for example, Risse-Kappen 1995b: 4, 26, 195; 1995c: 506; 1996: 358–59, 385).

24. Surprisingly enough, Neumann (1996) also fails to appreciate the potential of Social Identity Theory. Neumann's valuable review of the literature on concepts of identity in International Relations does deal with this school of thought in its treatment of the question of 'Self and Other in International Relations', and in connection with the observation that "the working boundary between an 'us' and a 'them' is the home turf of social psychology" (Neumann 1996: 144; an earlier article, Neumann 1992, is also relevant here). But he fails to see that Social Identity Theory would be eminently suited to developing further the research strategy he sketches: "The focus for studies of identity formation should therefore be the socially placed one of how these boundaries come into existence and are maintained. Students of international relations have studied physical and economic borders for a long time. The concern with these types of boundaries needs to be complemented by a focus on how *social* boundaries between human collectives are maintained. [...] Any social field will harbour more than one type of politically relevant collective identity. Particular care must be taken not to prejudice analyses by singling out only one type of human collective, say, nations, and neglecting others. [...] Collective identities emerge as *multifaceted*, and must be studied as such" (Neumann 1996: 167, emphases in original). My argument is that the concept of collective identity in world society, which I am in the process of developing here, can go a considerable way toward answering the questions posed by Neumann.

25. Estel (1994) provides a comprehensive overview that also goes beyond the question of national identity; see also Brand (1993).

26. Larsen et al. (1993) use an equally multidimensional concept of national identity in their study of American national identity.

27. Anderson's concept of an 'imagined community' fits in very well with Weber's 'community formation', according to which concept it is also quite possible that those involved do not know each other and need not be participants in any active process of negotiation of a communal identity (Weber 1968: vol. I, 365), and which only requires that something be subjectively experienced as a common feature (Weber 1968: vol. I, 387). On this point see also Estel (1994: 37), and Fuchs et al. (1993: 350).

28. "Recent research on nationalism emphasizes, quite correctly, that 'the nation' was a kind of blueprint, an artefact resting on the desire to find something held in common, something shared" (Jeismann 1993: 14). Weber himself comments on this (Weber 1968: vol. I, 397–8), and see also Estel (1994).

29. Fuchs et al. (1993: 391) regard the process of West European unification and the waves of migration affecting some West European countries as factors that could have led to a 'weakening or eclipsing of national-state identities' in this region. "Divisions between nation-states play virtually no role in the construction of collective identities in the countries of Europe" (Fuchs et al. 1993: 395). This finding is based on representative surveys of public opinion conducted in the (then) twelve EU countries in Fall 1988.

30. Fuchs et al. (1993: 396) argue, on the basis of their opinion poll data, that "at least the initial signs of European identity-formation" can be observed. About the formation of a European collective identity see also Weller (1997).

31. My examination of national identity has stressed the institutional benefits that make it logical for individuals to attach themselves emotionally to specific communities. The de-

cisive role here is played by the positive evaluation, that is the attachment of a higher value to the ingroup than to the outgroup (see Weller 1995). However, this perspective does not provide us with any way of identifying the requirements and conditions of changes in collective identities and their significance for political action. For this reason, it is necessary to employ social-psychological theories in order to advance the debate further.

32. There are similarities between this feeling of belonging and the concept of the 'we-group'; on this point see Elwert (1989) and Leggewie (1994: 53). Social categorization carried out in this way is directly related to the practice of according a lower value to 'other' groups for the purpose of deriving a positive social identity from the superiority of one's own group, in order to derive benefit for the individual's own feeling of self-worth (see above, also Weller 1992; Tajfel and Turner 1986; Oakes et al. 1994). However, this aspect of social categorization plays only a minor role in the context under discussion here.

33. This conceptualization of 'collective identities' should be distinguished from an understanding of the term as meaning something essential (*wesenhaft*), which individuals can partake of in order to create their I-identity; this understanding is usually associated with a normative idea (see, for instance, Habermas 1976).

34. The effects of collective identity-formation can vary greatly. Perceiving oneself primarily as a member of a group can be quite appropriate in one situation, problematic in a different situation, and even dangerous in a third. A player in a women's football team will perceive herself primarily as a team member during the game, because the competitive situation makes it perfectly clear how her perceptions should be categorized, and even seems to determine them in a normative sense ('one for all and all for one'). However, in the context of a post-match social event it would seem to be quite possible that the difference between the two teams will hardly matter anymore, as social contact with players from the other team and an individual self-perception comes to dominate. It could also be the case that meeting male functionaries at this gathering brings out a quite different categorization of the situation, and the two women's teams form a collective identity, because the difference between the two teams seems smaller than that between them and the male functionaries. The metacontrast principle states that categorization occurs at the point where the greatest difference is perceived, and collective identities are formed according to this categorization.

35. See Axtmann (1995: 93, 97). Alonso (1995: 587) comments: "Among the forces challenging citizenship as a primary identity are three which I shall call supranational, subnational and transnational."

36. Over twenty years ago, Habermas posed the question of "whether the reality of the world society that is coming into being is compatible with an identity formed with reference to territories" (Habermas 1976: 110). However, Habermas uses a much less precise concept of identity than the one I have developed here with the help of Self-Categorization Theory.

37. Gephart (1993: 463–64) speaks of the "tragic paradox at the heart of universalistic community-building. [...] It seems that the formation of emotional communities is only possible if others are excluded."

38. Senghaas' (1995) analysis is a convincing one: there is no sign of any geocultural conflict formations coming into being, but a 'geo-material' conflict constellation seems quite possible. Cultural factors would then be added to this, which would lead to dominant collective identities similar to those of the Cold War, with an accompanying preparedness to use violence and a danger of escalation.

39. Huntington's thesis of the 'Clash of Civilizations' has of course itself contributed to the tendency to use this primitive model as a way of interpreting international politics. In this sense, the thesis itself can be understood as an attempt to form a new 'Western' collective identity by offering or proposing a particular categorization for the perception of international politics (on this point see Hummel and Wehrhöfer 1996). The best way of telling whether this categorization offer actually succeeds in bringing into being a new collective identity that determines action will be to observe the extent to which it comes to dominate the presentation in the mass media of international politics as a whole.

NOTES TO CHAPTER 5

This chapter first appeared as "International Theory and International Society: The Viability of the Middle Way" in the Review of International Studies (1995) 21, 183–196. For the World Society Colloquium in Frankfurt, 6–7 October 1995—a shortened version of which is reprinted here—I took the opportunity to correct some errors, add some references, remove some examples of parochial axe-grinding, and extend the argument at one or two points. A still earlier version was presented to the Ford Foundation funded International Society Seminar at the L.S.E. in February 1994. I am grateful to James Mayall, Molly Cochran, John Charvet, Mervyn Frost, Hayo Krombach, and other participants in the seminar for their comments, two anonymous referees for the Review of International Studies.

1. Apart from sources listed below, the ideas expressed here have been influenced by the work of a number of authors; see Mayall (1990); Jackson (1995); James (1993); Griffiths (1992).

2. The classic reference here, of course, is Waltz (1979); see also the papers collected in Keohane (1986) and, for a recent extension of the root idea, Buzan, Jones, and Little (1993). M. E. Brown et al. (1995) is the best recent source for neorealism.

3. This last point is entailed by Waltz's view that, once established, balances of power can be managed—in much the same way that competition can be managed amongst oligopolists, that is, without this implying any underlying desire to cooperate.

4. Modern cosmopolitans such as Henry Shue, Charles R. Beitz, and Thomas Pogge seem to have rather given up on 'institutional' cosmopolitanism, concentrating instead on 'moral' cosmopolitanism—see, for example, the papers by Pogge and Beitz in Brown, *Political Restructuring*. Whether this is wise is debatable, since any moral commitment to cosmopolitan values must surely eventually be given institutional form if it is to affect actual state, or individual, conduct. On the other hand, the unwillingness of modern cosmopolitans to go down the world government route is also understandable. Perhaps the answer here is to re-examine what is meant by a 'state'; Martin Shaw goes down this route, arguing that 'global state institutions already exist'—see Shaw (1994).

5. This does not preclude reference by theorists of international society to nonstate actors, such as individuals, any more than the state centricity of traditional international law prevents that discourse from recognising that in certain circumstances entities other than states can possess international legal personality.

6. See, most obviously, Burton (1972), and, rather more elaborately argued (1968). Actually, cobwebs usually have centres (and spiders) so the metaphor is not particularly apt.

7. Burton's 'turn' to human needs comes with *Deviance Terrorism and War* (London: Pinter, 1979). Burtonian thought which was once quite significant, at the cutting edge of non-conventional IR theory in Britain and in parts of the United States, is now somewhat in the doldrums; however, all, save the youngest generation of British IR scholars associate the term World Society with Burtonian thought, which may present some minor difficulties—specific to the UK—for the German World Society Project.

8. For 'regimes' see Krasner (1982); key neoliberal works would include Axelrod and Keohane (1985), and Keohane (1989b). The recent collection Baldwin (1993) is a good way of following the story, while Evans and Wilson (1992) and Buzan (1993) are to the point.

9. This discussion relies heavily on Grieco (1993).

10. For example, this point is exemplified by Bull's comment that "A purely fortuitous balance of power we may imagine to be simply a moment of deadlock in a struggle to the death between two contending powers ..." (Bull 1977: 105), emphasis added.

11. 'Second best' is a rather ugly formulation, but not without precedent; as I am reminded by a referee, one of Manning's subheadings is 'The Second Best of Six Possible Worlds'—although in his view the 'best' that we should work toward is "a greater degree of order through more effectively functioning inter-governmental arrangements", that is, a better international society rather than a world community. This means he is not a 'second bester' in the sense that the term is used here (Manning 1975: 9).

12. Although these two conceptions are attributed here to different individuals, it has to be acknowledged that they are, in the last resort, theoretical constructs; it need not be a matter for concern that the thought of any actual thinker of substance contains elements of both positions.

13. Edmund Burke, especially in the *Letters on a Regicide Peace*, is probably the best source here.

14. This is, of course, procedural justice—impartial rules, impartially applied—rather than social or distributive justice.

15. In terms of Martin Wight's threefold classification, Kantian thought is clearly not compatible with the idea of an international society; see M. Wight International Theory ed. G. Wight and B. Porter (London: Allen and Unwin,1991). But Wight's use of Kant is problematic; see Hurrell (1990) for an argument that Kant was more of a statist than the tradition allows—which is compatible with the view argued here.

16. Emphasis in original.

17. In Brown (1992a) it is argued that Kant put considerable emphasis on the practical objections to a world republic—laws losing force at a distance and so on. The change of tack here is partly the result of discussion with Laberge (1994) whose paper 'Kant and the Constitution of International Society' argues the thesis presented in the main body of the present chapter.

18. Wight's personal convictions are discussed in Hedley Bull's biographical writings on Wight, in particular (1976).

19. Compare A. J. P. Taylor commenting on the norms of nineteenth-century diplomacy "Many diplomats were ambitious, some vain or stupid, but they had something like a common aim—to preserve the peace of Europe without endangering the security of their own country" (1954: xxiii). The fact that Wight's reference comes at the end of *Power Politics*, usually thought of as the work of Wight least oriented toward notions of international society, and that Taylor is usually thought of as a radical critic of the

old order, is of some significance. That both authors refer to Europe is also interesting and will be returned to below.

20. The papers collected in Bull and Watson (1984a) address exactly this issue, and it is clear that no assumption of the universal applicability of European customs can be made.

21. See Rawls (1993) for the original formulation. In a recent Amnesty International Lecture, "The Law of Peoples" in S. Shute and S. Hurley (eds.) *On Human Rights* (1993), Rawls extends the 'political not metaphysical' formula to relations between allegedly just societies with different internal characteristics. J. Charvet in *The Idea of an International Ethical Order* (Seminar in International Political Theory, L.S.E., November 1992) also examines this position.

22. Brown (1988) for an illustration of this habit. Just as seventeenth-century English writers on toleration usually had a clause somewhere in the text excluding Roman Catholics from the benefits of this virtue, so Islamic thinkers could be forgiven for imagining that current Western writers on tolerance have similar reservations directed at them.

23. Clearly what follows can do no more than skate over the surface of this topic. For more sustained analysis (often against the position outlined here) see, for example, Donnely (1989, 1993), Renteln (1990), Shue (1980), Vincent (1986) and, of particular interest, the essays in Shute and Hurley (1993).

24. Soviet-controlled countries also abstained, but their abstention could, charitably, be described as based on a different interpretation of the inheritance of the European Enlightenment, rather than on opposition to it.

25. This seems to be the implication of the discussion following p. 239.

26. Thus, while the government of the Islamic Republic of Iran always maintained the fiction that it was not actually holding American diplomats as hostages in 1979–1981—the hostage-takers were said to be 'students'—it has not taken the same line with respect to the death threats made against Salman Rushdie, much less 'domestic' acts such as the persecution of the Baha'i religious movement.

27. Martin Shaw's (1994) thinking on 'weak global state institutions' looks in the same direction.

28. It might be thought that the 'zone of peace' is rather less peaceful and somewhat smaller than Singer and Wildavsky anticipated in (presumably) 1991–1992 when writing their book. However, they have quite a robust idea of peace; in their terms even an extreme anomic event such as the explosion of a nuclear device in a city in the 'zone of peace' by external enemies from the zone of conflict would be less threatening to the peoples of the zone of peace than the threat of extermination with which they have had to live for two generations. A rational choice theorist would set this up as a trade-off between the remote possibility of total disaster as against a larger possibility (probability even) of a less-than-total catastrophe.

NOTES TO CHAPTER 6

I am grateful for comments on earlier drafts from Asbjørn Sonne Nørgaard, Robert Jackson, Stephen Krasner, and Michael Zürn as well as from seminar participants at the University of British Columbia and JW Goethe University in Frankfurt. Research for this chapter was supported by the Danish Social Science Research Council. An earlier version of this chapter was published in *The Journal of Political Philosophy* (Sørensen 1998).

1. "So long as anarchy endures, states remain like units." "To call states 'like units' is to say that each state is like all other states in being an autonomous political unit. It is another way of saying that states are sovereign" (Waltz 1979: 93, 95). Hendrik Spruyt has recently traced the development of sovereign statehood as the key form of political organization (see Spruyt 1994b). I shall not dispute the fact that all states share the attribute of formal sovereignty (that is, constitutional independence, the content of which will be defined in a moment); but I reject that such formal sovereignty denotes autonomous 'like units' as argued by neorealists.

2. "We abstract from every attribute of states except their capabilities" (Waltz 1979: 99).

3. Although one can claim that no such thing as a standard group of states of the modern post-Westphalia type can be found empirically, my argument about the unlike 'premodern' and 'postmodern' units still holds as I will try to show below. For a good overview of the 'Westphalian system', see, for example, Zacher (1992).

4. A comprehensive scope also characterizes Gourevitch (1978), although he did not seek the identification of different main types of units.

5. Hall and Ikenberry (1989: 66). Hall and Ikenberry mention the case of Italy and argue that "the fundamental policy of the United States was to establish a historic class compromise which ruled out the extreme right and the extreme left," loc.cit. In broader historical terms such interventions in the domestic affairs of states are the rule, not the exception; "after every major war since 1815, the victorious powers consciously reorganized the societies of the losing states. They did this, not to reduce their military capabilities, but to make them into certain kinds of states" (Cronin 1994: 17–18).

6. See Leujrdik 1986. Krasner (1995: 245–46) emphasized the severe problems such interventions pose for neorealism because they violate that theory's ontological given: the autonomy of sovereign states.

7. These remarks on decolonization are indebted to the penetrating analysis by Jackson (1990); quote from p. 85. See also Barkin and Cronin (1994); Cronin (1994).

8. Hirst and Thompson (1992: 361); see also Holm and Sørensen (1995b); Thrift (1994: 365–81).

9. A view developed in Holm and Sørensen (1995b). The position taken here differs from the World Systems approach developed by Immanuel Wallerstein and others. World Systems analysts conceive of an integrated world economy existing and expanding since the fifteenth century. The present view perceives of such an integrated world economy emerging only in recent decades.

10. Since World War II, economic globalization has taken place in a context increasingly characterized by three distinct groups of states: the planned economies of the East led by the Soviet Union; the industrialized countries of the West led by the United States and organized in what was to become the OECD; and the developing countries of the South, many of which only gained independence during the decades after the war. It is the OECD countries that have been most involved in and consequently most affected by economic globalization. Data to that effect can be found in UNCTC 1992; UNCTAD (1990); Siebert (ed.) (1991); Nicolaides (1990: 283–95).

11. An important determinant of whether specific countries will lose or gain from processes of globalization is their capacity for constructive domestic response to the challenges that globalization posit. There was an intense debate in the seventies and early eighties about the effects of transnational corporations' activities in developing countries.

Were they 'engines of growth' or 'spearheads of imperialism'? It turned out that a great deal of that debate could be resolved when focus was moved from the transnationals themselves to the interplay between transnationals on the one hand and the economic and political capacities of the host countries on the other. See Sørensen (1983). For a recent treatment of the interplay, applied to the United States as a host country, see Crystal (1994).

12. Current economic reality in the advanced industrialized countries is thus a mixture of 'truly globalized' and 'interdependent national' economies. It is not surprising, therefore, that different analyses can come up with results which stress either the 'national' or the 'globalized' aspect. For an example of the former, see Hirst and Thompson (1992). Other recent analyses stressing the aspect of globalization include Stopford and Strange (1991); Ohmae (1993: 78–87); Reich (1991); Mackenzie and Lee (1991).

13. Cerny (1994: 21–26). The remarks in this and the following paragraph in the main text draw on Cerny's analysis. See also Cerny (1995).

14. A point much emphasized in Anthony Giddens' work. See for example, Giddens (1985); see also Krasner (1993a: 301–22).

15. A point also made by Keohane in Keohane (1995: 175–77).

16. Many authors have noted this trend; see for example, Zürn (1995: 137–165); Held (1991b); Zacher (1992).

17. Max Weber defined the ideal type as follows: "An ideal type if formed by the one-sided accentuation of one or more points of view and by the synthesis of a great many diffuse, discrete, more or less present and occasionally absent concrete individual phenomena, which are arranged according to one-sided emphasized viewpoints into a unified analytical construct. In its conceptual purity, the mental construct (*Gedankenbild*) cannot be found empirically anywhere in reality." Weber emphasized that the ideal type is "no 'hypothesis' but it offers guidance to the construction of hypotheses. It is not a description of reality but it aims to give unambiguous means of expression to such a description" (Weber 1949: 90). Ideal types have frequently been used in the discipline of IR (international relations); Waltz's reflections on units and structure are based on the economic ideal types of the market and the firm. The concept of 'complex interdependence' set forth by Keohane and Nye is an ideal type.

18. Some of what follows draws on Sørensen (1994).

19. "National politics is the realm of authority, of administration, and of law" (Waltz 1979: 113).

20. Jackson prefers the term that is in the title of his book, *Quasi-states*. Spruyt has recently argued that "the state system has increasingly become isomorph, in that sovereign, territorial rule is ubiquitous [...]" (Spruyt 1994a: 34). See also Spruyt (1994b: 527–57). The differentiation of state units undertaken here does not dispute such isomorphism, which pertains only to the level of formal, juridical sovereignty.

21. Ayittey (1985); see also the works mentioned in note 31.

22. One penetrating analysis is Keohane (1989b).

23. See for example, Hettne and Inotai (1994); Cox (1992: 132–60). This does not necessarily mean that a world of coherent regions is in the making because the regionalism label covers many different types of relationships; see also Kahler (1995: 19–27).

24. Formally, states retain the freedom of choice: they can opt out of cooperation. Thus political (and economic) autonomy remains an option, but outside of a few special cases such an option would have disastrously negative consequences for the standard of living. See also Keohane (1995: 253).

25. See for example, Keohane and Hoffmann (eds.) (1991); Garrett (1992: 533-60); Schmitter (1992).

26. For a parallel line of reasoning, see Nørgaard (1994: 245-87).

27. "By making use of multiple routes, many entrances and more phases, national actors from the public and private sector are more difficult to co-ordinate by national governments. They have their own sources of information, networks and influence positions, independent from the national coordinating office" (Van Schendelen 1993: 278). See also Nørgaard (1994).

28. Cerny (1994: 48). See also Strange (1994b). For the alternative view that EU cooperation increases the centrality of the state, see Moravcsik (1994).

29. Constitutional independence of other states means that sovereignty is a "legal, absolute, and unitary condition." Legal in that the sovereign state is not subordinate in law to any other state; absolute in that sovereignty is either present or absent; and unitary in that the state is supreme authority within its jurisdiction. Quote is from James (1986: 39); see also Jackson (1990: 32-40).

30. Before decolonization and the emergence of the development assistance regime, the idea that every colonial area could eventually achieve a level of development comparable to the modern, economically advanced countries was considered absurd. Today, development of poor countries is sooner considered a right that includes the obligation of the advanced countries to redistribute wealth in favor of the poor. This new outlook is a result of the nonreciprocity sovereignty game played by premodern states. Jackson (1990) gives a fascinating and detailed account of how this transformation took place. At the same time, it must be stressed that the flow of resources is not only one way; specific groups in rich countries have exploited premodern states. The current situation in premodern states is thus the result of the interplay in earlier periods of domestic and international causes and processes. The 'development problem' is about why this interaction has led to social and economic development in some countries and underdevelopment and misery in others.

31. Helman and Ratner (1992-93: 3-21); see also Deibel (1993: 13-33); Lyons and Mastanduno (1993: 517-32); Etzioni (1992-93: 21-35).

32. A similar view is set forth in Ayoob (1995).

33. Three domestic conflicts alone have each cost the lives of 500,000 to one million people; they were in Sudan, Ethiopia, and Mozambique. Estimates are from Copson (1994: 29). Copson's analysis stresses how the "causes of every war [in Africa] were, at their root, internal" (Copson 1994: 103).

34. See for example, Marks (1992: 191-224); Leibfried and Pierson (1992: 333-66).

35. Karl Deutsch defined a security community as follows: "A security community is a group of people which has become 'integrated'. By integration we mean the attainment, within a territory, of a 'sense of community' and of institutions and practices strong enough and widespread enough to assure [...] dependable expectations of 'peaceful change' among its population. By sense of community we mean a belief [...] that common social problems must and can be resolved by processes of 'peaceful change'" (Deutsch and Burrell 1957: 5).

36. Kant (1970). For recent applications, see for example, Russett (1993); Singer and Wildawsky (1993). Commercial liberalism goes back to at least Richard Cobden (1903), see also the treatment in Waltz (1959: 104). For current arguments, see for example, Rosecrance (1986); Keohane and Nye (1989).

37. One way of conceptualizing the difference may be in the terms suggested recently by Arie Kacowicz. He distinguishes between (a) a pluralistic security community ("with stable expectations of peaceful change, in which the member states share common norms, values, and political institutions, sustain an identifiable common identity, and are deeply interdependent"); (b) a zone of stable peace ("[no expectations of violence], in which peace is maintained on a reciprocal and consensual basis. In the case the probability of war is so small that it does not really enter into the calculations of any of the people involved"); (c) a zone of negative peace ("[mere absence of war], in which peace is maintained only on a precarious basis by threats, deterrence, or a lack of will or capabilities to engage in violent conflict at a certain time.") The EU is a pluralistic security community; relations between EU, the United States, and Japan have elements of both (a) and (b), and the relationship between Greece and Turkey has elements of (b) and (c) (Kacowicz 1995: 3–4).

38. "So long as the major states are the major actors, the structure of international politics is defined in terms of them" (Waltz 1979: 94).

39. See the argument in Krasner (1993b).

NOTES TO CHAPTER 7

1. This chapter takes stock of an approach to the study of governance beyond the state that was first presented to a workshop on 'The Transformation of Governance in the European Union' at the ECPR Joint Sessions of Workshops in Oslo in March 1996. The ins and outs of this theoretical approach have subsequently been explored in different various directions. In addition to provisional results that have already been published and that have mainly dealt with the further elaboration of the conceptual framework of the basic argument (see for example, Wolf 1999), this article provides some empirical illustrations of the patterns of interaction that characterize the practice of the new raison d'état.

2. A number of authors have drawn attention to the phenomenon that "states increasingly exercise sovereignty in multilateral, international institutions which are distanced from societal control" (Thompson 1995: 230). Wendt notes: "As state actors pool their de facto authority over transnational space, they remove it from direct democratic control. Territorial electorates may still retain the formal right to 'unelect' their leaders, but the ability to translate this right into tangible policy change [...] is constrained by the commitments that states have made to each other." More or less explicit interventions in this debate can also be found in the work of Moravcsik (1993a: 507), Müller (1993: 76), Hoffmann (1987), or Ikenberry et al. (1988: 240).

3. I refer to 'the state' with different meanings in particular theoretical contexts. This should not be misunderstood as terminological inconsistency. As previously stated, the concept around which my own argument is built differs from the realist unitary actor model as well as from a liberal view that distinguishes between state and society but allows the state no specific interests other than those it pursues on behalf of society. For further discussion of this point see Wolf (1999).

4. Nordlinger makes a similar comment: "[A] state's involvement in an international network of states is a basis for potential autonomy of action and against groups and economic arrangements within its jurisdiction" (Nordlinger 1981: 23).

5. In his paper prepared for the International Studies Association Convention in Washington, D.C., in Feburary 1999, James Raymond Vreeland (1999) offers an impressive account of cases in which the IMF has been used as a scapegoat by national governments whose interests were not so much in the loans themselves but rather in the IMF conditions.

6. The famous first seven words of the Charter read "We the peoples of the United Nations." The only other instance in which reference is made to civilian participation is Article 71, which provides for the possibility of consultative arrangements with nongovernmental organizations in the Economic and Social Council of the UN.

NOTES TO CHAPTER 8

An earlier version of this chapter was presented at the Twentieth Annual Conference of the British International Studies Association, Southampton, 18–20 December 1995. Panel: "World Society—Continental Perspectives."

1. Ernst-Otto Czempiel picks out the growth in importance of societies and societal actors as the greatest single change in the international system during recent decades (Czempiel 1993). For Czempiel, the relationship between political systems and their societies is the "real cause of structural change in world politics" (Czempiel 1991: 105). Czempiel characterizes as follows the way in which the societal interest works: "It is directed outwards and demands a juster distribution of goods. Above all, though, it is directed inwards, and here it demands the right to participate in decisions taken by the political systems and that societal interests should be taken into consideration in foreign policy" (Czempiel 1993: 105).

2. Krippendorff (1963); Zürn (1993); to name but a few.

3. Prittwitz (1990); Jänicke and Mönch (1988); Jänicke and Weidner (1995); Breitmeier (1996).

4. Crepaz (1994); Therborn (1987).

5. On this point see *Die Zeit,* 6 September 1996: 13.

NOTES TO CHAPTER 9

An earlier version of this chapter was presented at the 1995 faculty seminar of the Zentrum für Europäische Rechtspolitik, University of Bremen, as well as at the 1995 Summer Institute on 'The Political Economy of European Integration,' funded by the German American Academic Council. A German version of this chapter has been published in *Politische Vierteljahresschrift* 37:1, 27–55. I wish to thank the participants of these seminars and particularly Thomas Gehring, Edgar Grande, Markus Jachtenfuchs, Frank Schimmelfennig, Dieter Wolf as well as the reviewers of the *Politische Vierteljahresschrift* (PVS) for helpful comments. Vicki May and Tina Menge translated the original German manuscript.

1. For a survey of the newly provoked discussion, see Kreile (1992) and Sbragia (1992). For more recent contributions see also Jachtenfuchs and Kohler-Koch (1996a).

2. Furthermore, Rosenau (1990), Camilleri and Falk (1992) and Zacher (1992) have prophesied the end of the state system even beyond Europe.

3. See Héritier et al. (1994) for a shrewd analysis of this issue on the basis of the European ecological policy that started out from the opposite hypothesis.

4. For arguments to this effect see also Thompson and Krasner (1989), who note the continuously increasing significance of the nation state in the whole of the western world. For a very shrewd analysis of this debate see Sørensen (1996).

5. Prominent representatives of this point of view are Giddens (1985) and Tilly (1990).

6. Leading representatives of this point of view are North (1981) and Spruyt (1994c).

7. For an informative survey see Alemann and Heinze (1979), particularly the articles by Lehmbruch and Schmitter.

8. For a general survey of these international regimes and organizations see Rittberger and Zangl (1994).

9. Deutsch and Burrell (1957) conceptualize boundaries of social transactions as the places where a critical reduction in the frequency of certain types of transaction take place.

10. These terms are discussed by the World Society Research Group (chapter 1), Holm and Sørensen (1995a) and Zürn (1996). For a comprehensive set of data see now Beisheim et al. (1999).

11. See the identical findings by Rittberger and Zürn (1990) as well as Young and Osherenko (1993).

12. See Zürn (1998) for an analysis of 'governance beyond the nation-state' based on this concept.

13. Exemplary for the area of welfare policy are the articles by Leibfried and Pierson (1995).

14. See Kohler-Koch (1994: 4), who states unequivocally that "European organization of interest groups grows in response and not in advance of integrative steps."

15. Reasons for the asymmetrical interest representation on the European level are given by Traxler and Schmitter (1995).

16. These features are convincingly demonstrated by Grande (1994). He calls it the paradox of weakness.

17. Using this formulation I exclude the question of which constitutional provisions should be protected against majority decisions. See the contributions in Preuß (1994).

18. A multi-level governance system is distinguished by two features from ordinary international governance in the form of international regimes. First, different sectoral regulations are so closely interwoven that they constitute a new political space or territory, albeit with loosely defined borders. In contrast, international governance defined as the sum of international regimes lacks a territorial focus. Second, international regimes are usually conceptualized as passive institutions formed by nation-states, which themselves are independent of the regimes. The concept of multilevel governance assumes that political institutions at different levels merge with each other into one political system and can no longer be thought of as distinct political systems. For an overview on regime analysis see Rittberger (1993), Levy, Young, and Zürn (1995), and more recently Hasenclever, Mayer, and Rittberger (1997). Gehring (1994) applies regime theory to the European Community.

19. A fourth question that is relevant for democratic theory but which is not discussed there is: Under which *social conditions* are given democratic institutions able to function and endure? See for example, Dahl (1989) and Held (1987) as two of the most important of the more recent contributions in the field of democratic theory. An impressive survey about theories of democracy is provided by Schmidt (1995).

20. For an authoritative representation of the points of view concerning this question see Dahl (1989).

21. This argument has been made by, for example, Weiler (1989), Kielmansegg (1994), Sbragia (1992), and Scharpf (1993a).

22. See Tomuschat's (1993, 496) criticism of the judgment on Maastricht by the Federal Constitutional Court.

23. See also Lepsius (1990a: 53), who defines modernization politics as the scheduled restructuring of "human coexistence by means of institutional reform and institution-building."

24. See also the analysis by Evans (1993), which reveals how the central decision-makers are able to exploit their positions as 'hinges' in two-level games.

25. For a survey on the Maastricht referenda see Luthardt (1993).

26. Frey (1994) discusses this with regard to Switzerland.

27. The meaning 'constitution' in this respect is broader than the legal term, which is bound to traditional statehood. By 'constitutional matters' here is meant all aspects of European *polity* structuring.

28. See Riker (1955) for a very instructive analysis of the development of the American Senate.

NOTES TO CHAPTER 10

The authors are members of the World Society Research Group. We would like to thank the other members of the Group as well as Rainer Schmalz-Bruns, Thomas Schmidt, and Michael Zürn for valuable suggestions regarding revisions to the text.

1. We here define NGOs exclusively as nongovernmental, non-profit-making organizations that pursue goals that are in the public interest. The term is used solely in this sense in the present chapter. We thus follow the traditional understanding of NGOs, which excludes industrial and trade organizations and other organizations guided by private interests. The definitions given by the U.N. and the Union of International Associations are drawn up either in such general terms that no meaningful use of them is possible or in such strict terms that a whole series of organizations that fulfill the above-mentioned criteria would be excluded from consideration.

2. See Union of International Associations, *Yearbook of International Organizations 1992–1993*.

3. On this, see the analysis of international politics in regard to the protection of the ozone layer, where American environmental groups have sought to exert a direct influence on European ozone policy (Benedick 1991).

4. For critical comment on this, see Smith (1992) and Litfin (1993).

5. We use the concept of globalization as defined in the University of Bremen's DFG project on this theme. Globalization in this sense may be understood to mean any "increase in the intensity and range of cross-border links for exchange or interaction, be it in the form of economic transactions, cultural and informal exchange-processes, or the cross-border exchange of environmental pollutants" (DFG-Projekt, Universität Bremen).

6. See Bundesministerium für Umwelt, Naturschutz und Reaktorsicherheit (ed.).

7. Thus, in November 1996, representatives of all the national Greenpeace offices jointly agreed the political areas in which work in 1997 was to be concentrated. The main theme for 1997 was climate protection.

8. When asked what institutions would have to be particularly active in future if environmental protection measures were to be implemented quickly and effectively, 67 percent of those questioned named environmental groups, *Allensbacher Jahrbuch der Demoskopie* (1993: 930).

9. Thus, a statement at the international NGO conference in Paris (1992) stipulated that all citizens have the right to take part in decision-making processes that affect their lives and environment (*Die Zeit*, 6 September 1996: 13).

10. It is precisely thanks to this transparency that there can be (and is) any discussion about Greenpeace's internal structure.

11. As the NGOs have gradually increased their ability to operate effectively in media terms, a reciprocal relationship has grown up between the mass media and the NGOs. This relationship is undoubtedly not always problem-free but cannot be examined in detail here.

12. This statement implies that the NGOs provide, on the one hand, information about political decision-making processes which, for one reason or another, is withheld by state actors, and, on the other, additional, alternative points of view on particular problems. This is not to imply that information provided by NGOs is in principle more neutral or better than that from the governmental side.

13. But the implementation of these ideas can very well fail because of excessively hierarchical decision-making structures such as are often to be found in the large transnational NGOs.

14. Mayer-Tasch describes this "national grass-roots and lobby pressure" as the "real driving-force behind international environmental policy". "National governments", he continues, "pass it on to the international level, where, on the one hand, it can put pressure on the notorious thwarters of environmental progress and, on the other, be translated into international environmental legislation of very varying degrees of effectiveness" (Mayer-Tasch 1990: 174).

15. A number of delegates from various countries made comments to this effect at the Fourth International Conference for the Protection of the North Sea.

16. This integration occurs as part of problem-solving. There is no discussion here of the types of reaction to be expected from states on strategic grounds—that is, in order to safeguard autonomy of action (Wolf 1999).

17. One factor that militates against a 'classic' corporatist integration of the NGOs is their lack of a hegemonial status in the problem area; another is the limited executive power which NGO leaderships have vis-à-vis their members. However, there is a rudimentary hierarchization of internal structures in large NGOs too, and also some centralization of NGOs as a result of the formation of organized networks.

18. We cite by way of example: Haufler (1993); Leathermann, Pagnucco and Smith (1993); Martens (1993); Stairs and Taylor (1992); and Zürn (1992b).

NOTES TO CHAPTER 11

I wish to thank the World Society Research Group and especially Lothar Brock and Klaus Dieter Wolf for detailed comments on earlier drafts. Remaining errors are my own.

1. For the purpose of this chapter, governance may be defined "as referring to activities backed by shared goals that may or may not derive from legal and formally pre-

scribed responsibilities and that do not necessarily rely on police powers to overcome defiance and attain compliance [...]. It embraces governmental institutions, but it also subsumes informal, non-governmental mechanisms whereby those persons and organizations within ist purview move ahead, satisfy their needs, and fulfill their wants" (Rosenau 1992a: 4).

2. Similarly, but more recent, Held (1991b) has posed this question.

3. See also Strayer and Munro and Anderson who depict the political structure of the Middle Ages as a "patchwork of overlapping and incomplete rights of government" which were inextricably superimposed and tangled, and in which "different juridical instances were geographically interwoven and stratified, and plural allegiances, asymmetrical suzerainties and anomalous enclaves abounded" (cited in Ruggie 1993: 148–49).

4. The same holds true for the fact that even individual multinational corporations sometimes exert significant influence on goverments, especially in third world countries (Vernon 1971).

5. More elaborated on these issues see also Franck (1990) and Chayes and Chayes (1995).

6. I am indebted to Lothar Brock for sensitizing me on this issue.

7. For pertinent discussions on the meaning and analytical value of the concept see also Ruggie (1986), Ashley (1986), Krasner (1989), Beitz (1991), and more recently Thompson (1995).

8. As Kratochwil has put it: "we observe the virtually universal recognition of territorial sovereignty as the organizing principle of international politics" (Kratochwil 1986: 27).

9. Thompson (1995: 219) similarly defines sovereignty as "the recognition by internal and external actors that the state has the exclusive authority to intervene coercively in activities within its territory." For an investigation of the changing norms of sovereignty, see also Barkin and Cronin (1994). For a very different conception of sovereignty as 'popular sovereignty', see also Held (1995, ch. 2).

10. For pertinent literature, see also Fuchs et al. (1994), Kasarda and Parnell (1993), Goetz (1993), Fainstein et al. (1994), Judge et al. (1995).

11. For a very informative overview on the different constitutional settings of European regions see also Hasselbach (1996, ch. 2).

12. See also Marks (1996) for an account of the different ways in which local and regional governments participate in European structural policy.

13. Gesetz über die Zusammenarbeit von Bund und Ländern in Angelegenheiten der Europäischen Union vom 12. März 1993, § 5 und 6.

14. See also also the case *Zschernig v. Miller* in which the Supreme Court in 1941 struck down an Oregon statute "because of its great potential for disruption or embarrasment" of the federal government's foreign policy (Shumann 1986: 166–67).

15. For a more extended discussion of the legal aspects, see also Hobbs (1994: 80–84).

16. See also the following impressive summary of local activism: "As of 1991, more than 900 localities passed resolutions supporting a 'freeze' in the arms race; 197 demanded a halt to nuclear testing; 120 refused to cooperate with the Federal Emergency Management Agency's nuclear-war exercises; 126, plus 27 states divested more than $20 billion from firms doing business in South Africa; 86 formed linkages with Nicaragua and, along with grassroots activists, provided more to the Nicaraguan people than all the military aid Congress voted for the *contras*; 80, along with the U.S.

Conference of Mayors, demanded cuts in the Pentagon's budget; 73 formed sister-city relations with Soviet cities (roughly 50 more are pending); 29 provided sanctuary for Guatemalan and Salvadoran refugees; 20 passed stratospheric protection ordinances phasing out ozone-depleting chemicals; and at least 10 established funded offices of international affairs—in essence municipal state departments" (Shumann 1992: 158–59). For a more detailed analysis of the cross-border activities of American cities and states, see also Hobbs (1994: 20–36) and Kirby and Marston (1995).

NOTES TO CHAPTER 12

1. I here define NGOs exclusively as nongovernmental, non-profit-making organizations whose activities are geared to public interests. I thus follow the traditional understanding of NGOs, which excludes industrial and trade organizations and other organizations guided by private interests (see also note 1 to chapter 10).

2. According to figures in the *Yearbook of International Organizations*, 176 NGOs were registered in 1909 and 4,696 in 1992 (Union of International Associations 1992/3: 1535).

3. This is not to say that the national level is then less important as a partner in dialogue. Rather, the shift in attention toward the social level may be seen as an additional strategy, the importance of which appears to depend on how good the prospects are of influencing the national or international level.

4. The NGOs spend $5 billion per year on such projects (Haas 1996: 42).

5. In Take (1996), I did this in detail for the field of North Sea protection policy. Within the present framework, however, I have to restrict my use of empirical findings considerably.

6. The term 'learning' is here used in Nye's sense: "Learning often involves a shift from overly simple generalizations to complex, integrated understandings grounded in realistic attention to detail" (Nye 1987: 378).

7. The second-order cooperation problems are the problems of monitoring, sanctioning, and distribution, the severity of which influences the chances of a genesis (and, as I shall show, the development) of international cooperation. The first-order problem is often illustrated in research on political cooperation by means of the prisoner's dilemma. In this, cooperation by all puts each actor and all actors together in a better position than the mutual damage through self-interested action. And yet, for each actor in the prisoner's dilemma there is an incentive to rely on self-interest. If one attempts to get out of this dilemma, one is confronted, amongst other things, with the above-mentioned second-order problems.

8. The term 'leader state' is used to describe states that actively promote the process of international cooperation and, at the national level, implement laws that provide models for the international level.

9. Politicians, civil servants, the representatives of social interests, and experts all operate in the same political context—that is, they are all tied to the same public discourses and have to take part in these if they want to push through their ideas and interests and gain acceptance. If they succeed in steering the public discourse in their chosen direction—that is, make a particular political issue or solution into an integral, or indeed dominant, part of

the internal political debate relating to acceptance—they acquire a certain power of definition in regard to future political behavior. The importance of this factor is highlighted in particular by Eder (1996: 206).

10. The production and consumption of CFCs had to be phased out until the 31.12.96 according to the 'Montreal Protocol on Substances that Deplete the Ozone Layer'. Until then, CFCs were used in (the production-processes of) refrigerators, for example.

11. It should, by way of qualification, be said that at present only a few NGOs have the resources to develop this kind of solution.

12. These shortcomings in intergovernmental problem-solving at the same time constitute the general preconditions for successful action by transnational social actors.

13. Not only that based on scientific findings, but also that based on the testimony of people affected by the particular situation—a fact that gives it a special persuasive force that is often lacking in purely scientific findings.

14. On this, see, for example, Hall (1993).

15. See, for example, Peterson (1992) regarding the whaling regime.

16. The importance of the NGOs as representatives of public interests was also highlighted by UN Secretary-General Boutros-Boutros Ghali when he described them as a basic form of representation, which in some sense guaranteed the political legitimacy of the United Nations.

17. This thesis is founded on the widely accepted realization "that national governments as a rule are motivated by nothing so much as the desire to retain power" (Mayer-Tasch 1990: 174). But since retention of power generally depends more on national than on international acceptance of the particular policy being pursued, the national level represents a very promising starting point for NGO influence.

18. These include not only industrial and trading concerns, but also governments and, ultimately, consumers.

19. Although Shell UK obtained the necessary permit for deepwater disposal from UK authorities, which have handled every aspect of the approval process in accordance with established national and international politics and standards, they were both forced to change their policy due to international pressure.

20. Shell's decision about the sinking of the *Brent Spar* oil-platform provided all the preconditions needed for a successful campaign. It involved visual impact, symbolic contents, and a powerful adversary. The action therefore went off like a stage performance. Greenpeace did all the preparatory media work to ensure that its message reached the whole world and that pressure was thus put on the political decision-makers.

21. For example, not one government at NSC 4 omitted to meet the NGOs and acquaint themselves with their views, proposals, and criticisms.

22. These contacts are characterized both by constructive cooperation and by pressure exerted on the political decision-makers either directly or indirectly (via the public), with the NGO representatives often being acknowledged as authentic champions of public interests.

23. The LDC is one of the international cooperation agreements that make up the international regime ensuring North Sea protection.

24. Governments can exploit the internal political configuration in such a way that the outcome of international negotiations is affected (restricted win-set); or they can speed up the achievement of internal political goals through deliberate measures at the international level (Putnam 1988: 434).

25. In order to be effective, international law needs to be linked back into national law—that is, it needs to be translated into national laws, and these legal regulations then need to be implemented systematically at the social level (for example, in relation to arms exporters, industrial polluters, and so on). At the level both of translation and of implementation, NGOs function as monitoring bodies, with the ability, where appropriate, to resort to sanctions (public condemnation, demonstrations, calls for boycotts, and so on).

26. These latter, however, are not real costs. Rather, they depend on the perception of the national actors.

27. This monitoring can also be done by social actors from other states or by social actors operating transnationally.

28. In Germany this job is done by Jordsand, in the Netherlands by the Landelijke Vereniging tot Behoud van de Waddenzee (LVBW).

29. The report is entitled *What Reductions? North Sea Ministers Maths Homework and a Lot of Hot Air*.

30. In this kind of outcome, no participant can opt out without damaging another. It therefore represents the optimum outcome for all participants together.

31. But mediation activities are geared not only to ministers and parliamentarians but also to representatives of international organizations, members of national delegations, and the representatives of other groups.

32. Dilemma games highlight problems of cooperation in international relations: in this context, collectively rational and individually rational outcomes of interaction come partly asunder, with the result that cooperation is needed in order to be able to achieve outcomes that are both collectively and individually desirable (Zürn 1992a: 153–61).

33. Coordination games are characterized by the fact that, once agreement is reached, there is no longer any incentive for any party to deviate from the agreement (Zangl 1994: 291–93).

34. That the actions of transnational NGOs described here should facilitate not only the creation of forms of international cooperation but also their further development is readily explicable. Because there is cost-free monitoring of nation-states' conduct in regard to implementation, it is easier for the political decision-makers to adopt additional measures. The sanctions options listed above can also be used to put pressure on governments to improve outdated standards and to speed up the introduction of new measures. And the defusing of the distribution problem makes it easier for governments to agree on new measures.

35. The involvement of the NGOs in the legislative process also means that the laws ultimately passed by a government have greater legitimacy in the eyes of the public (the same is true for the agreements concluded at the international level).

36. This was confirmed to me by various representatives of national delegations at NSC 4.

37. Between 1972 and 1989 a total of 20 UN conferences took place. In the much shorter period between 1990 and 1996, however, the number had already reached 26.

38. The reason for this lies, firstly, in the fact that an increasing number of people feel they are affected by global problems, and, secondly, that the NGOs feel duty-bound to monitor international agreements and to press for the further development of cooperation.

39. According to figures cited by Princen and Finger, 150 official delegations at the Rio conference had NGO representatives in their ranks (Princen and Finger 1994: 4). NGOs

have been involved in the London Dumping Conference since 1980, and they enjoy consultative status in various other international commissions. However, there are still a number of international bodies and organizations (for example, the FAO) that continue to make heavy weather of granting NGOs any kind of rights.

40. In Germany, a number of jobs in environmental NGOs are, for example, financed out of local sewage taxes. The Dutch NGOs receive even more generous state support, which renders inter-NGO competition for resources virtually superfluous.

41. Asked what groups or institutions would have to be particularly active in future to ensure that environmental protection measures were implemented quickly and effectively, 67 percent of people mentioned environmental groups; only 37 percent were ready to entrust this task to the parties, and only 24 precent to the trade unions (Allensbacher Jahrbuch der Demoskopie 1984–92, 1993: 930). Another survey shows that 77 percent of Germans believe that Greenpeace is the most active champion of the environment and trust it most of all. Only 29 percent show the same trust in the German ministry of the environment (ibid.: 937). This public regard for the NGOs is also reflected in mass-media reporting (Rucht 1996: 36).

References

Adler, Emmanuel, and Peter M. Haas. 1992. Epistemic Communities, World Order and the Creation of a Reflective Research Program. *International Organization* 46:1, 367–90.
Afheldt, Horst. 1994. *Wohlstand für niemand? Die Marktwirtschaft entläßt ihre Kinder.* München: Kindermann.
Agnew, John. 1993. Representing Space. Space, Scale and Culture in Social Science. In *Place, Culture, Representations*, ed. Duncan, et al., 251–71, London: Routledge.
———. 1994. The Territorial Trap: The Geographical Assumptions of International Relations Theory. *Review of International Political Economy* 1:1, 53–80.
Albert, Mathias. 1996. *Fallen der (Welt-)Ordnung. Internationale Beziehungen und ihre Theorien zwischen Moderne und Postmoderne.* Opladen: Leske und Budrich.
———. 1997. Toward Generative Differentiation? The International Political System in World Society. Paper presented at the Identities, Borders, Orders workshop, 19–21 January at Las Cruces.
———. 1999. Observing World Politics: Luhmann's Systems Theory of Society and International Relations. *Millennium* 28: 2 (in print).
Albert, Mathias, and Lothar Brock. Forthcoming. What Keeps Westphalia Together? Integration and Fragmentation in the Modern System of States. In *Identities, Borders, Orders: New Directions in IR Theory*, ed. Albert, et al. Minneapolis, Minn.: University of Minnesota Press.
Albert, Mathias, and Yosef Lapid. 1997. On Dialectics and IR Theory: Some Remarks on the Hazards of a Proposed Marriage. *Millennium* 26:3, 403–15.
Alemann, Ulrich von, and Rolf G. Heinze, eds. 1979. *Verbände und Staat. Vom Pluralismus zum Korporatismus.* Opladen: Westdeutscher Verlag.
Allen, Christopher. 1989. Corporatism and Regional Economic Policy in the Federal Republic of Germany. The 'Meso' Politics of Industrial Adjustment. *Publius. The Journal of Federalism* 19:4, 147–64.
Allensbacher Jahrbuch der Demoskopie 1984–92, Band 9, 1993. München: Saur.
Alonso, William. 1995. Citizenship, Nationality and Other Identities. *Journal of International Affairs* 48:2, 585–99.
Altvater, Elmar. 1994. Operationsfeld Weltmarkt oder: Vom souveränen Nationalstaat zum nationalen Wettbewerbstaat. *Prokla* 24:4, 517–47.
Amin, Ash, and Nigel Thrift. 1992. Neo-Marshallian Nodes in Global Networks. *International Journal of Urban and Regional Research* 16:4, 571–87.

Amin, Samir. 1991. *Delinking. Towards a Polycentric World.* London: ZED Books.
Andersen, Jesper, and Tonny Niilonen. 1995. *Fourth North Sea Conference Secretariat, Danish EPA: Progress Report.* 4th International Conference, Esbjerg, 8–9 June 1995. Copenhagen.
Anderson, Benedict. 1991. *Imagined Communities: Reflections on the Origin and Spread of Nationalism.* Revised Ed. London: Verso.
Anderson, Jeffrey. 1992. *The Territorial Imperative. Pluralism, Corporatism and Economic Crisis.* Cambridge: Cambridge University Press.
———. 1995. Structural Funds and the Social Dimension of EU Policy: Springboard or Stumbling Block? In *European Social Policy. Between Fragmentation and Integration*, ed. Leibfried, et al., 123–58. Washington, D.C.: The Brookings Institution.
Apel, Karl-Otto. 1988. *Diskurs und Verantwortung. Das Problem des Übergangs zur postkonventionellen Moral.* Frankfurt/M.: Suhrkamp.
Apter, David E., and Carl G. Rosberg, eds. 1994. *Political Development and the New Realism in Sub-Saharan Africa.* Charlottesville: University Press of Virginia.
Archibugi, Daniele, and David Held, eds. 1995. *Cosmopolitan Democracy. An Agenda for a New World Order.* Cambridge: Polity Press.
Ashley, Richard K. 1986. The Poverty of Neoralism. In *Neorealism and Its Critics*, ed. Robert O. Keohane, 255–300. New York: Columbia University Press.
———. 1989. Living on Border Lines. Man, Poststructuralism and War. In *International/Intertextual Relations. Postmodern Readings of World Politics*, ed. Der Derian, et al., 259–322. Lexington, Mass.: Lexington Books.
Assmann, Aleida. 1993. Zum Problem der Identität aus kulturwissenschaftlicher Sicht. *Leviathan* 21:2, 238–53.
Avineri, Schlomo, and Avner de-Shalit, eds. 1992. *Communitarianism and Individualism.* Oxford: Oxford University Press.
Axelrod, R., and Robert O. Keohane. 1985. Achieving Co-operation under Anarchy. *World Politics* 38:1, 226–54.
Axtmann, Roland. 1995. Kulturelle Globalisierung, kollektive Identität und demokratischer Nationalstaat. *Leviathan* 23:1, 87–101.
Ayittey, George B. N. 1992. *Africa Betrayed.* New York: St. Martin's Press.
Ayoob, Mohammed. 1995. *The Third World Security Predicament.* Boulder, Colo.: Lynne Rienner.
Bach, Maurizio. 1993. Vom Zweckverband zum technokratischen Regime: Politische Legitimation und institutionelle Verselbständigung in der Europäischen Gemeinschaft. In *Nationalismus – Nationalitäten – Supranationalität*, ed. Winkler, et al., 288–308. Stuttgart: Klett Cotta.
Bachrach, Peter, and Morton S. Baratz. 1970. *Power and Poverty. Theory and Practice.* Oxford: Oxford University Press.
Baldwin, David A., ed. 1993. *Neoliberalism and Neorealism: the Contemporary Debate.* New York: Columbia University Press.
Banks, Michael, ed. 1984. *Conflict in World Society. A New Perspective on International Relations.* Hertfordshire: Harvester Wheatsheaf.
Barkin, J. Samuel, and Bruce Cronin. 1994. The State and the Nation: Changing Norms and the Rules of Sovereignty in International Relations. *International Organization* 48:1, 107–30.
Barnett, Michael N. 1997. Bringing in the New World Order. Liberalism, Legitimacy, and the United Nations. *World Politics* 49:4, 526–51.

Bartelson, Jens. 1995. *A Genealogy of Sovereignty*. Cambridge: Cambridge University Press.
Bauböck, Rainer. 1994. *Transnational Citizenship. Membership and Rights in International Migration*. Aldershot: Edward Elgar.
Bauer, Eva. 1993. Zur Entstehung soziologischer Theorie. Anfänge soziologischen Denkens. In *Soziologische Theorie. Abriß der Ansätze ihrer Hauptvertreter*, 2d ed., ed. Julius Morel, 1–31. München: Oldenbourg.
Bausinger, Hermann. 1978. Identität. In *Grundzüge der Volkskunde*, ed. Bausinger, et al., 204–11. Darmstadt: Wissenschaftliche Buchgesellschaft.
———. 1986. Kulturelle Identität — Schlagwort oder Wirklichkeit. In *Ausländer—Inländer. Arbeitsmigration und kulturelle Identität*, ed. Hermann Bausinger, 141–59. Tübingen: Vereinigung für Volkskunde.
Bean, Frank D., Roland Chanove, Robert G. Cushing, Rodolfo De la Garza, Rodolfo, Gary P. Freeman, Charles W. Haynes, and David Spener. 1994. *Illegal Mexican Migration and the United States/Mexico Border: The Effects of Operation Hold the Line on El Paso/Juárez*. Austin, Tex.: Population Research Center, University of Texas at Austin.
Beck, Ulrich. 1986. *Risikogesellschaft*. Frankfurt/M.: Suhrkamp. [*Risk Society*. London: Sage, 1992].
———. 1991. Der Konflikt der zwei Modernen. In *Die Modernisierung moderner Gesellschaften. Verhandlungen des 25. Deutschen Soziologentages in Frankfurt am Main 1990*, ed. Wolfgang Zapf, 40–53. Frankfurt/M.: Campus.
———. 1995. Der grüne Spaltpilz. Warum Kohl Greenpeace unterstützt. *Süddeutsche Zeitung*, 8/9 July 1995, 15.
———. 1996. Unser Schicksal ist die Nötigung, das Politische neu zu erfinden. *Das Parlament*, 30–31, 12 July 1996, 12.
———. 1997. *Was ist Globalisierung? Irrtümer des Globalismus – Antworten auf Globalisierung*. Frankfurt/M.: Suhrkamp.
Beiner, Ronald. 1995. Why Citizenship Constitutes a Theoretical Problem in the Last Decade of the Twentieth Century. *Theorizing Citizenship*, ed. Roland Beiner, 1–28. Albany, N.Y.: SUNY Press.
Beisheim, Marianne, Sabine Dreher, Gregor Walter, Bernhard Zangl, and Michael Zürn. 1999. *Im Zeitalter der Globalisierung? Thesen und Daten zur gesellschaftlichen und politischen Denationalisierung*. Baden-Baden: Nomos.
Beisheim, Marianne, and Gregor Walter. 1997. Globalisierung: Kinderkrankheiten eines Konzepts. *Zeitschrift für Internationale Beziehungen* 4:1, 153–80.
Beitz, Charles R. 1991. Sovereignty and Morality in International Affairs. In *Political Theory Today*, ed. David Held, 236–54. Cambridge: Polity Press.
———. 1994. Cosmopolitan Liberalism and the States System. In *Political Restructuring in Europe: Ethical Perspectives*, ed. Chris Brown, 123–36. London: Routledge.
Benedick, Richard E. 1991. *Ozone Diplomacy. New Directions in Safeguarding the Planet*. Cambridge, Mass.: Harvard University Press.
Berding, Helmut, ed. 1994. *Nationales Bewußtsein und kollektive Identität. Studien zur Entwicklung des kollektiven Bewußtseins in der Neuzeit 2*. Frankfurt/M.: Suhrkamp.
Berfield, Susan. 1993. Global Changes and Domestic Transformations. Southern California's Emerging Role. In *Global Changes and Domestic Transformations: Southern California's Emerging Role* (Vantage Conference, San Diego, April 29–March 1, 1993), ed. The Stanley Foundation, 15–26. Muscatine, Iowa: Stanley Foundation.
Berger, Peter. 1966. Identity as a Problem in the Sociology of Knowledge. *European Journal of Sociology* 7:1, 32–40.

Berger, Peter L., and Thomas Luckmann. 1967. *The Social Construction of Reality*. London: Penguin.

Biersteker, Thomas J. 1992. The 'Triumph' of Neoclassical Economics in the Developing World: Policy Convergence and Bases of Governance in the International Economic Order. In *Governance Without Government*, ed. Rosenau, et al., 102–31. Cambridge: Cambridge University Press.

Bode, Thilo. 1995. Igittigitt, Qualitätskontrolle. Ein Ökoverband muß wie ein Konzern geführt werden, Spiegel Spezial No. 11. *Die Macht der Mutigen*, 122–24.

Böhret, Claus, and Göttrik Wewer, eds. 1993. *Regieren im 21. Jahrhundert zwischen Globalisierung und Regionalisierung*. Opladen: Leske und Budrich.

Booth, Ken. 1995. Global Ethics. Human Wrongs and International Relations. *International Affairs* 71:1, 103–26.

Booth, Ken, and Steve Smith, eds. 1995a. *International Political Theory Today*. Cambridge: Polity Press.

———. 1995b. Preface. In *International Political Theory Today*, ed. Booth, et al., xi–xii. Cambridge: Cambridge University Press.

Boulding, Kenneth E. 1968. The City as an Element in the International System. *Daedalus* 97:4, 1111–23.

Brand, Karl-Werner. 1993. Zur Neustrukturierung kollektiver Identitäten. Nationalistische Bewegungen in West- und Osteuropa. In *Lebensverhältnisse und soziale Konflikte im neuen Europa*, ed. Bernhard Schäfers, 549–57. Frankfurt/M.: Campus.

Breitmeier, Helmut. 1996. *Wie entstehen globale Umweltregime? Der Konfliktaustrag zum Schutz der Ozonschicht und des globalen Klimas*. Opladen: Leske und Budrich.

Breitmeier, Helmut, and Klaus Dieter Wolf. 1993. Analysing Regime Consequences: Conceptual Outlines and Environmental Explorations. In *Regime Theory and International Relations*, ed. Volker Rittberger, 339–60. Oxford: Oxford University Press.

Breuilly, John. 1994. *Nationalism and the State*. 2d ed. Chicago, Ill.: University of Chicago Press.

Brock, Lothar. 1993. Im Umbruch der Weltpolitik. *Leviathan* 21:2, 163–73.

———. 1994. Brüche im Umbruch der Weltpolitik. In *Frieden und Konflikt in den internationalen Beziehungen*, ed. Krell, et al., 19–37. Frankfurt/M.: Campus.

Brown, Chris. 1988. Ethics of Co-existence: The International Theory of Terry Nardin. *Review of International Studies* 14:3, 213–22.

———. 1992a. *International Relations Theory: New Normative Approaches*. Hemel Hempstead: Harvester Wheatsheaf.

———. 1992b. 'Really-Existing Liberalism' and International Order. *Millennium* 21:3, 313–28.

———. 1993. Sorry Comfort: The Case against International Theory. In *International Relations and Pan-Europe: Theoretical Approaches and Empirical Findings*, ed. Frank Pfetsch, 85–100. Hamburg: Lit.

———, ed. 1994. *Political Restructuring in Europe: Ethical Perspectives*. London: Routledge.

———. 1995. International Political Theory and the Idea of World Community. In *Political Theory Today*, ed. Booth, et al., 90–109. Cambridge: Cambridge University Press.

———. 1996. Cultural Pluralism, Universal Principles and International Relations Theory. In *National Rights and International Obligations*, ed. Jones, et al., 166–82. Oxford: Westview.

Brown, Michael E., Sean M. Lynne-Jones, and Steven E, eds. 1995. *The Perils of Anarchy: An International Society Reader*. Cambridge, Mass.: The MIT Press.

Brown, Rupert. 1988. *Group Processes. Dynamics within and between Groups*. Oxford: Basil Blackwell.

———. 1990. Beziehungen zwischen Gruppen. In *Sozialpsychologie. Eine Einführung, Berlin*, ed. Stroebe, et al., 400–29. Berlin: Springer.

Brown, Seyom. 1988. *New Forces, Old Forces, and the Future of World Politics*. Glenview, Ill.: Scott Foresman.

Brunkhorst, Hauke. 1996. Demokratie als Solidarität unter Fremden. Universalismus, Kommunitarismus, Liberalismus. *Aus Politik und Zeitgeschichte*, B 36/96, 21–28.

Bull, Hedley. 1969. The Case for a Classical Approach. In *Contending Approaches to International Politics*, ed. Knorr, et al., 20–38. Princeton, N.J.: Princeton University Press.

———. 1976. Martin Wight and the Theory of International Relations. *British Journal of International Studies* 2:2, 101–16.

———. 1977. *The Anarchical Society. A Study of Order in World Politics*. London: Macmillan.

Bull, Hedley, and Adam Watson, eds. 1984a: *The Expansion of International Society*. Oxford: Oxford University Press.

———. 1984b. Introduction. In *The Expansion of International Society*, ed. Bull, et al., 1–9. Oxford: Oxford University Press.

———. 1984c. Conclusion. In *The Expansion of International Society*, ed. Bull, et al., 430–37. Oxford: Oxford University Press.

Bundesministerium für Umwelt, Naturschutz und Reaktorsicherheit. *Konferenz der Vereinten Nationen für Umwelt und Entwicklung im Juni 1992 in Rio de Janeiro—Dokumente—Agenda 21*. Bonn: Köllen.

Burke, Peter. 1992. We, the People: Popular Culture and Popular Identity in Modern Europe. In *Modernity and Identity*, ed. Lash, et al., 293–308. Oxford: Blackwell.

Burley, Anne-Marie, and Walter Mattli. 1993. Europe before the court: a political theory of legal integration. *International Organization* 47:1, 41–76.

Burton, John W. 1968. *System, States, Diplomacy, Rules*. Cambridge: Cambridge University Press.

———. 1972. *World Society*. Cambridge: Cambridge University Press.

———. 1979. *Deviance Terrorism and War*. London: Pinter.

Business Council for a Sustainable Future, ed. 1994. *Business Council Case-Studies of Clean Energy Technology Deployment*. Washington, D.C.: Business Council for a Sustainable Future.

Buzan, Barry. 1993. From International System to International Society: Structural Realism and Regime Theory meet the English School. *International Organization* 47:3, 327–52.

———. 1994. The interdependence of security and economic issues in the 'new world order'. In *Political Economy and the Changing Global Order*, ed. Stubbs, et al., 92–112. New York: St. Martin's Press.

Buzan, Barry, Charles Jones, and Richard Little. 1993. *The Logic of Anarchy*. New York: Columbia University Press.

Camilleri, Joseph A., and Jim Falk. 1992. *The End of Sovereignty? The Politics of a Shrinking and Fragmenting World*. Aldershot: Elgar.

Cappellin, Roberto, and P. W. J. Batey, eds. 1994. *Regional Networks, Border Regimes and European Integration*. London: Pion.
Castells, Manuel. 1993. *The Informational City. Information Technology, Economic Restructuring and the Urban-Regional Process*. 4th ed. Oxford: Blackwell.
———. 1994. European Cities, the Informational Society, and the Global Economy. *New Left Review*, 204, 18–32.
Castells, Manuel, and Peter Hall. 1994. *Technopoles of the World. The Making of 21st Century Industrial Complexes*. London: Routledge.
Cerny, Philip G. 1993. Plurilateralism: Structural Differentiation and Functional Conflict in the Post-Cold War World Order. *Millennium* 22:1, 28, 31.
———. 1994. Patterns of Financial Globalization: Financial Market Structures and the Problem of Governance. Paper presented at the annual International Studies Association meeting, 28 March–1 April in Washington, D.C.
———. 1995. International Finance and the Erosion of State Policy Autonomy. Paper for the annual meeting of International Studies Association, 21–25 February in Chicago.
Charvet, John. 1992. In: The Idea of an International Ethical Order. Seminar in International Political Theory, L.S.E., November 1992.
Chayes, Abram, and Antonia Handler Chayes. 1995. *The New Sovereignty. Compliance with International Regulatory Agreements*. Cambridge, Mass.: Harvard University Press.
Childers, Erskine, and Brian Urquart. 1994. *Renewing the United Nations System*. Uppsala: Dag Hammarskjöld Foundation.
Claasen, Claus Dieter. 1994. Europäische Integration und demokratische Legitimation. *Archiv des Öffentlichen Rechts* 119:2, 239–60.
Clark, Ann Marie, Elisabeth J. Friedman, and Kathryn Hochstetler. 1998. The Sovereign Limits of Global Civil Society: A Comparison of NGO Participation in UN World Conferences on the Environment, Human Rights, and Women. *World Politics* 51:1, 1–35.
Close, Paul. 1995. *Citizenship, Europe and Change*. London: Macmillan.
Cobden, Richar. 1903. *Political Writings*. 2 vols. London: Fischer-Unwin.
Cohen, Bernhard C. 1995. *Democracies and Foreign Policy. Public Participation in the United States and the Netherlands*. Madison, Wis.: University of Wisconsin Press.
Colás, Alejandro. 1996. The Promises of International Civil Society, Paper presented at the 37th Annual Convention of the International Studies Association, April 16–20 in San Diego.
Connolly, William E. 1991. Democracy and Territoriality. *Millennium* 20:3, 436–84.
Connor, Walker. 1994. Man is a Rational Animal. In *Ethnonationalism. The Quest for Understanding*, ed. Walker Connor, 195–209. Princeton, N.J.: Princeton University Press.
Cooper, Richard. 1968. *The Economics of Interdependence*. New York: McGraw-Hill.
Copson, Raymond W. 1994. *Africa's Wars and Prospects for Peace*. Armonk, N.Y.: M.E. Sharpe.
Cox, Robert W. 1981. Social Forces, States and World Orders. Beyond International Relations Theory. *Millennium* 10:2, 126–55.
———. 1987. *Production, Power and World Order. Social Forces in the Making of History*. New York: Columbia University Press.
———. 1992. Towards a Post-Hegemonic Conceptualization of World Order. In *Governance Without Government*, ed. Rosenau, et al., 132–60. Cambridge: Cambridge University Press.

——. 1994. Global Restructuring. Making Sense of the Changing International Political Economy. In *Political Economy and the Changing Global Order*, ed. Stubbs, et al., 45–59. Toronto: St. Martin's Press.

Crepaz, Markus M.L. 1994. From Semisovereignty to Sovereignty. The Decline of Corporatism and Rise of Parliament in Austria. *Comparative Politics* 27:1, 45–65.

Cronin, Bruce. 1994. Distinguishing Between a Domestic and an International Issue: The Changing Nature of Sovereignty and Obligation in International Relations. Paper for the American Political Science Association annual meeting, September 1–4 in New York.

Crystal, Jonathan. 1994. The Politics of Globalization: Explaining the Reactions to Incoming Foreign Direct Investment in the United States. Paper for American Political Science Association annual meeting, September 1–4 in New York.

Czada, Roland. 1994. Konjunkturen des Korporatismus: Zur Geschichte eines Paradigmenwechsels in der Verbändeforschung. In *Staat und Verbände, Politische Vierteljahresschrift*, Special Issue 25, ed. Wolfgang Streeck, 37–64. Opladen: Westdeutscher Verlag.

Czempiel, Ernst-Otto. 1981. *Internationale Politik. Ein Konfliktmodell*. Paderborn: Schöningh.

——. 1991. *Weltpolitik im Umbruch*. München: Beck.

——. 1993. Die neue Souveränität—ein Anachronismus? Regieren zwischen nationaler Souveränität, europäischer Integration und weltweiten Verflechtungen. In *Regieren in der Bundesrepublik 5, Souveränität, Integration, Interdependenz: Staatliches Handeln in der Außen- und Europapolitik*, ed. Hartwich et al., 145–58. Opladen: Leske und Budrich.

——. 1994. Vergesellschaftete Außenpolitik. *Merkur* 48:1, 1–14.

Dahl, Robert A. 1989. *Democracy and its Critics*. New Haven, Conn.: Yale University Press.

——. 1994. A Democratic Dilemma: System Effectiveness versus Citizen Participation. *Political Science Quarterly* 109:1, 23–34.

Dahrendorf, Ralf. 1994. Die Zukunft des Nationalstaats. *Merkur* 48:9/10, 751–61.

De la Garza, Rodolfo, Angelo Falcon, and Chris F. Garcia. 1996. Will the Real Americans Please Stand Up: Anglo and Mexican American Support of Core American Political Values. *American Journal of Political Science* 40:2, 335–51.

De la Garza, Rodolfo, and Jesús Velasco, eds. 1997. *Bridging the Border. Transforming Mexico-U.S. Relations*. Lanham, Md.: Rowman and Littlefield.

Deibel, Terry L. 1993. Internal Affairs and International Relations in the Post-Cold War World. *The Washington Quarterly* 16:3, 13–33.

Delamaide, Darrell. 1994. *The New Superregions of Europe*. New York: Penguin.

Deleuze, Gilles, and Félix Guattari. 1987. *A Thousand Plateaus: Capitalism and Schizophrenia*. Minneapolis, Minn.: University of Minnesota Press.

Delors, Jaques. 1994. A Necessary Union. In *The European Union. Readings on the Theory and Practice of European Integration*, ed. Nelsen, et al., 51–64. Boulder: Lynne Rienner.

Demko, George J., and William B. Wood. 1994. *Reordering the World: Geopolitical Perspectives on the 21st Century*. Boulder, Colo.: Westview.

Deutsch, Karl W. 1953. *Nationalism and Social Communication*. 2d ed. Cambridge, Mass.: MIT Press.

———. 1968. *Die Analyse internationaler Beziehungen. Konzeptionen und Probleme der Friedensforschung*. Frankfurt/M.: Europäische Verlagsanstalt. [*The Analysis of International Relations*. Englewood Cliffs: Prentice Hall, 1978].

———. 1973. *Politische Kybernetik. Modelle und Perspektiven*. 3d ed. Freiburg: Rombach.

Deutsch, Karl W., and Sidney A. Burrell. 1957. *Political Community and the North Atlantic Area*. Princeton: Princeton University Press.

DFG-Projekt. 'Gesellschaftliche Bestimmungsfaktoren von politischer Integration und politischer Fragmentierung in der OECD-Welt'. Universität Bremen, unpublished manuscript.

Diehl, Michael. 1990. The Minimal Group Paradigm: Theoretical Explanations and Empirical Findings. *European Review of Social Psychology*, 1, 263–92.

Donnely, Jack. 1989. *Universal Human Rights in Theory and Practice*. Ithaca, N.Y.: Cornell University Press.

———. 1993. *International Human Rights*. Boulder, Colo.: Westview.

Drodziak, William. 1994. Revying up Europe's 'Four Motors'. *Washington Post*, 27 March 94, C3.

Dubiel, Helmut. 1994. *Ungewißheit und Politik*. Frankfurt/M.: Suhrkamp.

Duchacek, Ivo D. 1984. The International Dimension of Subnational Self-Government. *Publius* 14:4, 5–31.

———. 1986. *The Territorial Dimension of Politics Within, Among and Across Nations*. Boulder, Colo.: Westview.

———. 1988. Multicommunal and Bicommunal Polities and Their International Relations. In *Perforated Sovereignties and International Relations. Trans-Sovereign Contacts of Subnational Governments*, ed. Duchacek, et al., 3–28. New York: Greenwood Press.

Duchacek, Ivo D., Daniel Latouche, and Garth Stevenson, eds. 1988. *Perforated Sovereignties, and International Relations. Trans-Sovereign Contacts of Subnational Governments*. New York: Greenwood Press.

Dunning, John H. 1994. *Multinational Enterprises and the Global Economy*. Wokingham: Addison-Wesley.

Easton, David. 1965. *A Systems Analysis of Political Life*. New York: Wiley.

Eder, Klaus. 1996. The Institutionalisation of Environmentalism: Ecological Discourse and the Second Transformation of the Public. In *Risk, Environment and Modernity. Towards a New Ecology*, ed. Lash, et al., 203–23. London: Sage.

Ehlers, Peter. 1985. Die erste Internationale Nordseeschutz-Konferenz. *Natur und Recht* 3, 126–30.

Elazar, Daniel J. 1988. Introduction. In *Perforated Sovereignties and International Relations. Trans-Sovereign Contacts of Subnational Governments*, ed. Duchacek, et al., iii–xix. New York: Greenwood Press.

Elias, Norbert. 1970. *Was ist Soziologie?* Weinheim: Juventa. [*What is Sociology?* New York: Columbia University Press, 1978].

———. 1976. *Über den Prozeß der Zivilisation*. 2 vols. Frankfurt/M.: Suhrkamp. [*The Civilizing Process*. Oxford: Blackwell, 1994].

———. 1987. Wandlungen der Wir-Ich-Balance. In *Die Gesellschaft der Individuen*, by Norbert Elias, 207–315. Frankfurt/M.: Suhrkamp. [*The Society of Individuals*. Oxford: Blackwell, 1991.]

Elwert, Georg. 1989. Nationalismus und Ethnizität. Über die Bildung von Wir-Gruppen. *Kölner Zeitschrift für Soziologie und Sozialpsychologie* 41:3, 440–64.
Engel, Charles, and John H. Rogers. 1994. How Wide is the Border?, Cambridge, Mass./Washington, D.C.: National Bureau of Economic Research (Working Paper No. 4829).
Esser, Hartmut. 1988. Ethnische Differenzierung und moderne Gesellschaft. *Zeitschrift für Soziologie* 17:4, 235–48.
Estel, Bernd. 1994. Grundaspekte der Nation. In *Das Prinzip Nation in modernen Gesellschaften. Länderdiagnosen und theoretische Perspektiven*, ed. Estel, et al., 13–81. Opladen: Westdeutscher Verlag.
Etzioni, Amitai. 1962. A Paradigm for the Study of Political Unification. *World Politics* 15:1, 44–74.
———. 1992-93: The Evils of Self-Determination. *Foreign Policy*, 89 (Winter): 21–35.
Evans, Peter B. 1993. Building an Integrative Approach to International and Domestic Politics. Reflections and Projections. In *Double-Edged Diplomacy: International Bargaining and Domestic Politics*, ed. Evans, et al., 397–430. Berkeley: University of California Press.
Evans, Peter B., Harold K. Jacobson, and Robert D. Putnam, eds. 1993. *Double-Edged Diplomacy: International Bargaining and Domestic Politics*. Berkeley: University of California Press.
Evans, Tony, and Peter Wilson. 1992. Regime Theory and the English School of International Relations: A Comparison. *Millennium* 21:3, 329–51.
Evers, Tilmann. 1994. Supranationale Staatlichkeit am Beispiel der Europäischen Union: Civitas Civitatum oder Monstrum? *Leviathan* 22:1, 115–34.
Fainstein, Susan S., Ian Gordon, and Michael Harloe. 1994. *Divided Cities: New York and London in the Contemporary World*. Oxford: Blackwell.
Faist, Thomas. 1999. *Overcoming Immobility and Building Bridges: International Migration and Transnational Social Spaces*. Oxford: Oxford University Press (forthcoming).
Falk, Richard. 1992. *Explorations at the Edge of Time*. Philadelphia, Penn.: University of Pennsylvania Press.
Fisher, William E. 1969. An Analysis of the Deutsch Sociocausal Paradigm of Political Integration. *International Organization* 23:2, 254–90.
Forsyth, Murray. 1994. Federalism and Confederalism. In *Political Restructuring in Europe: Ethical Perspectives*, ed. Chris Brown, 50–65. London: Routledge.
Foucault, Michel. 1992. *Wahnsinn und Gesellschaft. Eine Geschichte des Wahnsinns im Zeitalter der Vernunft*. 5th ed. Frankfurt/M: Suhrkamp.
Fowler, Robert. 1991. *The Dance With Community. The Contemporary Debate in American Political Thought*. Lawrence, Kan.: University Press of Kansas.
Franck, Thomas M. 1990. *The Power of Legitimacy Among Nations*. Oxford: Oxford University Press.
Frey, Bruno S. 1994. Direct Democracy: Politco-Economic Lessons from Swiss Experience. *American Economic Review* 84:2, 338–42.
Frey, Hans-Peter, and Karl Haußer. 1987. Entwicklungslinien sozialwissenschaftlicher Identitätsforschung. In *Identität. Entwicklungen psychologischer und soziologischer Forschung*, ed. Frey, et al., 3–26. Stuttgart: Enke.
Friedman, John. 1986. The World City Hypothesis. *Development and Change* 17:1, 69–83.
———. 1995. Where We Stand: a Decade of World City Research. In *World Cities in a World System*, ed. Knox, et al., 21–47. Cambridge: Cambridge University Press.

Frost, Mervyn. 1986. *Towards a Normative Theory of International Relations*. Cambridge: Cambridge University Press.

Fuchs, Dieter, Jürgen Gerhards, and Edeltraud Roller. 1993. Ethnozentrismus und kollektive Identitätskonstruktionen im westeuropäischen Vergleich. In *Lebensverhältnisse und soziale Konflikte im neuen Europa*, ed. Bernhard Schäfers, 390–98. Frankfurt/M.: Campus.

Fuchs, Roland J., Ellen Brennan, Joseph Chamie, Fu-Chen Lo, and Juha L. Uitto. 1994. *Mega-City Growth and the Future*, Tokyo: United Nations University Press.

Ganster, Paul, and Eugenio O. Valenciano, eds. 1993. *The Mexican-U.S. Border Region and the Free Trade Agreement*. San Diego, Calif.: Institute for Regional Studies of the Californias, San Diego State University.

Gantzel, Klaus-Jürgen, ed. 1975. *Herrschaft und Befreiung in der Weltgesellschaft*. Frankfurt/M.: Campus Verlag.

Garreau, Joel. 1981. *The Nine Nations of North America*. Boston, Mass.: Avon.

Garrett, Geoffrey. 1992. The European Internal Market: The Political Economy of Regional Integration. *International Organization* 46:2, 533–60.

Gaubatz, Kurt Taylor. 1994. The Hobbesian Problem and the Micofoundations of International Relations Theory. Paper for the 1994 Annual Meeting of the American Political Science Association, Sept. 1–4, New York.

Gehring, Thomas. 1994. Der Beitrag von Institutionen zur Förderung der internationalen Zusammenarbeit. Lehren aus der institutionellen Struktur der Europäischen Gemeinschaft. *Zeitschrift für Internationale Beziehungen* 1:2, 211–42.

———. 1995. Regieren im internationalen System. Verhandlungen, Normen und Internationale Regime. *Politische Vierteljahresschrift* 36:2, 197–219.

Gellner, Ernest. 1991. *Nationalismus und Moderne*. Berlin: Rotbuch Verlag. [*Nations and Nationalism*. Oxford: Blackwell, 1983].

Gephart, Werner. 1993. Partikulare Identitäten und die Grenzen der Gemeinschaftsbildung in Europa. In *Lebensverhältnisse und soziale Konflikte im neuen Europa*, ed. Bernhard Schäfers, 459–65. Frankfurt/M.: Campus.

Giddens, Anthony. 1985. *The Nation State and Violence*. Cambridge: Polity Press.

Gilpin, Robert. 1989. The Theory of Hegemonic War. In *The Origin and Prevention of Major Wars*, ed. Rotberg, et al., 15–37. Cambridge: Cambridge University Press.

Glass, James M. 1995. *Shattered Selves. Multiple Personality in a Postmodern World*. Ithaca, N.Y.: Cornell University Press.

Glick Schiller, Nina, Linda Basch, and Christina Szanton-Blanc, eds. 1992. *Towards a Transnational Perspective on Migration*. New York: Academy of Sciences.

Goetz, Edward G. 1993. The New Localism From a Cross-National Perspective. In *The New Localism: Comparative Urban Politics in a Global Era*, ed. Goetz, et al., 199–221. London: Sage.

Göhler, Gerhard. 1995. Einleitung. In *Macht der Öffentlichkeit—Öffentlichkeit der Macht*, ed. Gerhard Göhler, 7–21. Baden-Baden: Nomos.

Goldgeir, James, and Michael McFaul. 1992. A Tale of Two Worlds: Core and Periphery in the Post-Cold War Era. *International Organization* 46:1, 467–92.

Goldsborough, James O. 1993. California's Foreign Policy. *Foreign Affairs* 72:2, 88–96.

Gourevitch, Peter. 1978. The Second Image Reversed: The International Sources of Domestic Politics. *International Organization* 32:4, 881–911.

Grabher, Gernot. 1994. *Lob der Verschwendung*. Berlin: Edition sigma.

Grande, Edgar. 1994. *Vom Nationalstaat zur europäischen Politikverflechtung. Expansion und Transformation moderner Staatlichkeit – untersucht am Beispiel der Forschungs- und Technologiepolitik*. Konstanz. (Habilitation thesis).

———. 1996. Das Paradox der Schwäche. Forschungspolitik und die Einflußlogik europäischer Politikverflechtung. In *Europäische Integration*, ed. Jachtenfuchs, et al., 373–99. Opladen: Leske und Budrich.

Greenpeace. 1988. *Greenpeace Report* 4. Amsterdam: Greenpeace.

Greven, Michael T. 1993. Ist die Demokratie modern? Zur Rationalitätskrise der politischen Gesellschaft. *Politische Vierteljahresschrift* 34:3, 399–413.

Grieco, Joseph M. 1993. Anarchy and the Limits of co-operation. In *Neoliberalism and Neorealism: the Contemporary Debate*, ed. David A. Baldwin, 116–40. New York: Columbia University Press.

Griffiths, Martin. 1992. *Realism, Idealism and International Politics: A Reinterpretation*. London: Routledge.

Guéhenne, Jean M. 1994. *Das Ende der Demokratie*. München: Artemis und Winkler.

Haas, Peter M. 1993a. Epistemic Communities and the Dynamics of International Environmental Cooperation. In *Regime Theory and International Relations*, ed. Volker Rittberger, 168–201. Oxford: Oxford University Press.

———. 1993b. Protecting the Baltic and the North Seas. In *Institutions for the Earth*, ed. Haas, et al., 133–81. Cambridge, Mass.: MIT Press.

———. 1996. The Future of International Environmental Governance, Paper presented at the 37th Annual Convention of the International Studies Association, April 16–20 in San Diego.

Habermas, Jürgen. 1976. Können komplexe Gesellschaften eine vernünftige Identität ausbilden? In *Zur Rekonstruktion des Historischen Materialismus*, by Jürgen Habermas, 92–126. Frankfurt/M.: Suhrkamp.

———. 1981. *Theorie des kommunikativen Handelns*. 2 vols. Frankfurt/M.: Suhrkamp. [*The Theory of Communicative Action*. Boston: Beacon Press, 1984].

———. 1983. Moralbewußtsein und kommunikatives Handeln, Frankfurt/M.: Suhrkamp.

———. 1995. Kants Idee des Ewigen Friedens—aus dem historischen Abstand von 200 Jahren. *Kritische Justiz* 28:3, 293–319.

———. 1996. *Die Einbeziehung des Anderen. Studien zur politischen Theorie*. Frankfurt/M.: Suhrkamp.

Hall, John A., and John G. Ikenberry. 1989. *The State*. Milton Keynes: Open University Press.

Hall, Peter A. 1993. Policy Paradigms, Social Learning, and the State. The Case of Economic Policymaking in Britain. *Comparative Politics* 25:3, 275–96.

Hall, Stuart. 1996. Introduction: Who Needs 'Identity'? In *Questions of Cultural Identity*, ed. Hall, et al., 1–17. London: Sage.

Hänsch, Klaus. 1986. Europäische Integration und parlamentarische Demokratie. *Europa Archiv* 41:7, 191–200.

Hansen, Niles. 1994. Barrier Effects in the U.S.-Mexico Border Area. In *New Borders and Old Barriers in Spatial Development*, ed. Peter Nijkamp, 87–104. Newcastle upon Tyne: Avebury.

Hardin, Garrett. 1968. The Tragedy of the Commons. *Science*, 162, 1243–48.

Harris, Ian. 1993. Order and Justice in 'The Anarchical Society'. *International Affairs* 69:4, 725–41.

Harvey, David. 1982. *The Limits to Capital*. Oxford: Blackwell.
——. 1989. *The Condition of Postmodernity*. Oxford: Blackwell.
Hasenclever, Andreas, Peter Mayer, and Volker Rittberger. 1997. *Theories of International Regimes*. Cambridge: Cambridge University Press.
Hasselbach, Kai. 1996. *Der Ausschuß der Regionen in der Europäischen Union*. Köln: Carl Heymanns Verlag.
Haufler, Virginia. 1993. Crossing the Boundary between Public and Private: International Regimes and Non-State Actors. In *Regime Theory and International Relations*, ed. Volker Rittberger, 94–111. Oxford: Oxford University Press.
Haushofer, Karl. 1927. *Grenzen in ihrer geographischen und politischen Bedeutung*. Berlin: K. Vowinckel.
Hegel, Georg Wilhelm Friedrich. 1975. *The Philosophy of Right*. Chicago: Encyclopaedia Britannica/University of Chicago.
Hein, Wolfgang. 1994. Globale Vergesellschaftung und politische Selbstorganisation auf internationaler Ebene. In *Weltbild – Weltordnung. Perspektiven für eine zerbrechliche und endliche Erde*, ed. Wolfgang Hofkirchner, 107–24. Münster: Agenda Verlag.
Held, David. 1987. *Models of Democracy*. Stanford, Calif.: Stanford University Press.
——. 1991a. Democracy and Globalization. *Alternatives* 16:2, 201–08.
——. 1991b. Democracy, the Nation-State and the Global System. In *Political Theory Today*, ed. David Held, 197–235. Cambridge: Polity Press.
——. 1995. *Democracy and the Global Order. From Modern State to Cosmopolitan Governance*. Cambridge: Polity Press.
Helleiner, Eric. 1994. *States and the Reemergence of Global Finance. From Bretton Woods to the 1990s*. Ithaca, N.Y.: Cornell University Press.
Helliwell, John F. 1998. *How Much Do National Borders Matter?* Washington, D.C.: The Brookings Institution.
Helman, Gerald B., and Steven B. Ratner. 1992–93: Saving Failed States. *Foreign Policy*, 89 (Winter), 3–21.
Henrich, Dieter. 1979. 'Identität'—Begriff, Probleme, Grenzen. In *Identität*, ed. Marquard, et al., 133–86. München: Fink.
Henry, Nick. 1992. The New Industrial Spaces. Locational Logic of a New Production Era? *International Journal of Urban and Regional Research* 16:3, 376–96.
Héritier, Adrienne, ed. 1993a. *Policy-Analyse. Kritik und Neuorientierung, Politische Vierteljahresschrift*, Special Issue 24. Opladen: Westdeutscher Verlag.
——. 1993b. Policy Analyse. Elemente der Kritik und Neuorientierung. In *Policy-Analyse. Kritik und Neuorientierung, Politische Vierteljahresschrift*, Special Issue 24, ed. Adrienne Héritier, 10–36. Opladen: Westdeutscher Verlag.
Héritier, Adrienne, Susanne Mingers, Christoph Knill, and Martina Becka 1994. *Staatlichkeit in Europa. Ein regulativer Wettbewerb: Deutschland, Großbritannien, Frankreich in der Europäischen Union*. Opladen: Leske und Budrich.
Herrera, Eduardo Barrera. 1992. The Phantom of the Operators. Global Networks and Flexible Production. Paper presented at the 18th Conference of the International Association of Mass Communication Research, Guaruja, Brasil.
Herz, John. 1957. Rise and Demise of the Territorial State. *World Politics* 9:4, 473–79.
——. 1968. The Territorial State Revisited. *Polity*, 1, 11–34.
——. 1976. *The Nation-State and the Crisis of World Politics*. New York: David McKay.

Herzog, Lawrence A. 1991. Cross-national Urban Structure in the Era of Global Cities: The US-Mexico Transfrontier Metropolis. *Urban Studies* 28:4, 519–33.

——. 1992. Changing Boundaries in the Americas. An Overview. In *Changing Boundaries in the Americas*, ed. Lawrence Herzog, 3–24. San Diego, Calif.: UCSD/Center for U.S.-Mexican Studies.

Hesse, Joachim Jens, and Arthur Benz. 1990. *Die Modernisierung der Staatsorganisation*. Baden-Baden: Nomos.

Hettne, Bjorn, and Andras Inotai. 1994. *The New Regionalism: Implications for Development and Peace*. Helsinki: WIDER.

Hirst, Paul, and Grahame Thompson. 1992. The Problem of 'Globalization': International Economic Relations, National Economic Management and the Formation of Trading Blocs. *Economy and Society* 21:4, 357–96.

——. 1996. *Globalization in Question—The International Economy and the Possibilities of Governance*. Cambridge: Polity Press.

Hobbs, Heidi H. 1994. *City Hall Goes Abroad: The Foreign Policy of Local Politics*. London: Sage.

Hoffmann, Stanley. 1983. Reflections on the Nation-State in Western Europe Today. *Journal of Common Market Studies* 21:1, 21–37.

——, ed. 1987. *Janus and Minerva: Essays in the Theory and Practice of International Politics*, Boulder, Colo.: Westview.

Holm, Hans-Henrik, and Georg Sørensen eds. 1995a. *Whose World Order? Uneven Globalization and the End of the Cold War.* Boulder, Colo.: Westview.

——. 1995b. Introduction: What Has Changed? In *Whose World Order? Uneven Globalization and the End of the Cold War*, ed. Holm, et al., 1–19. Boulder, Colo.: Westview.

Hrbek, Rudolf, and Sabine Weyand. 1994. *betrifft: Das Europa der Regionen*. München: Beck.

Hudson, Valerie M., Susan Sims, and John C. Thomas. 1993. The Domestic Political Context of Foreign Policy-Making: Explicating a Theoretical Construct. In *The Limits of State Autonomy. Societal Groups and Foreign Policy Formulation*, ed. Skidmore, et al., 49–101. Boulder, Colo.: Westview.

Hughes, Barry B. 1993. Delivering the goods: the EC and complex governance. In *The 1992 Project and the Future of Integration in Europe*, ed. Smith, et al., 46–64. New York: M. E. Sharpe.

Hukkinen, Janne. 1995. Corporatism as an Impediment to Ecological Sustenance: the Case of Finnish Waste Management. *Ecological Economics* 15:1, 59–75.

Hummel, Hartwig, and Birgit Wehrhöfer. 1996. Geopolitische Identitäten. Kritik der Ethnisierung einer sich regionalisierenden Welt als paradigmatische Erweiterung der Friedensforschung. *WeltTrends*, 12, 7–34.

Huntington, Samuel. 1993. The Clash of Civilizations? *Foreign Affairs* 72:3, 22–49.

——. 1996. *The Clash of Civilizations and the Remaking of World Order*. New York: Simon and Schuster.

Hurrell, Andrew. 1990. Kant and the Kantian Paradigm in International Relations. *Review of International Studies* 16:3, 183–205.

Hurrell, Andrew, and Benedict Kingsbury, eds. 1992. *The International Politics of the Environment*. Oxford: Oxford University Press.

Ikenberry, John G., David A. Lake, and Michael Mastanduno. 1988. Introduction: Approaches to Explaining American Foreign Policy. *International Organization* 42:1, 1–14.
Jachtenfuchs, Markus. 1995. Ideen und internationale Beziehungen. *Zeitschrift für Internationale Beziehungen* 2:2, 417–42.
Jachtenfuchs, Markus, and Beate Kohler-Koch, eds. 1996a. *Europäische Integration*. Opladen: Leske und Budrich.
——. 1996b. Regieren im dynamischen Mehrebenen-System. In *Europäische Integration*, ed. Jachtenfuchs, et al., 15–44. Opladen: Leske und Budrich.
Jackson, Robert H. 1990. *Quasi-states: sovereignty, international relations and the Third World*. Cambridge: Cambridge University Press.
——. 1994. Continuity and change in the states system. In *States in a Changing World. A Contemporary Analysis*, ed. Jackson, et al., 345–67. Oxford: Oxford University Press.
——. 1995. The Political Theory of International Society. In *International Political Theory Today*, ed. Booth, et al., 110–28. Cambridge: Cambridge University Press.
Jackson, Robert H., and Carl G. Rosberg. 1982. *Personal Rule in Black Africa. Prince, Autocrat, Prophet, Tyrant*. Berkeley: University of California Press.
Jaeger, Hans-Martin. 1996. Konstruktionsfehler des Konstruktivismus in den Internationalen Beziehungen. *Zeitschrift für Internationale Beziehungen* 3:2, 313–40.
James, Alan. 1986. *Sovereign Statehood*. London: Allen and Unwin.
——. 1993. System or Society. *Review of International Studies* 19:3, 269–88.
Jänicke, Martin. 1987. *Staatsversagen. Die Ohnmacht der Politik in der Industriegesellschaft*. München: Piper.
——. 1993a. Ökologische und politische Modernisierung in entwickelten Industrienationen. In *Umweltpolitik als Modernisierungsprozeß*, ed. Volker Prittwitz, 15–30. Opladen: Leske und Budrich.
——. 1993b. Vom Staatsversagen zur politischen Modernisierung? Ein System aus Verlegenheit sucht seine Form. In *Regieren im 21. Jahrhundert zwischen Globalisierung und Regionalisierung*, ed. Böhret, et al., 63–77. Opladen: Leske und Budrich.
Jänicke, Martin, and Helmut Mönch. 1988. Ökologischer und wirtschaftlicher Wandel im Industrieländervegleich. In *Staatstätigkeit. International und historisch vergleichende Analyse*, ed. Manfred G. Schmidt, 389–405. Opladen: Leske und Budrich.
Jänicke, Martin, and Helmut Weidner, eds. 1995. *Successful Environmental Policy. A Critical Evaluation of 24 Cases*. Berlin: Edition Sigma.
Jeismann, Michael. 1993. Alter und neuer Nationalismus. In *Grenzfälle. Über neuen und alten Nationalismus*, ed. Jeismann, et al., 9–26. Leipzig: Reclam.
Jepperson, Ronald L., Alexander Wendt, and Peter J. Katzenstein. 1996. Norms, Identity, and Culture in National Security. In *The Culture of National Security. Norms and Identity in World Politics*, ed. Peter J. Katzenstein, 33–75. New York: Columbia University Press.
Joas, Hans. 1993. Gemeinschaft und Demokratie in den USA. Die vergessene Vorgeschichte der Kommunitarismus-Diskussion. In *Gemeinschaft und Gerechtigkeit*, ed. Brumlik, et al., 49–62. Frankfurt/M.: Fischer.
Joenniemi, Pertti, and Alan Sweedler. 1995. The Role of Cities in International Relations. New Features in the Baltic Sea Region. Kiel: PFK (PFK-Texte No. 36).
Joerges, Christian. 1991. Markt ohne Staat? Die Wirtschaftsverfassung der Gemeinschaft und die regulative Politik. In *Staatswerdung Europas? Optionen für eine Europäische Union*, ed. Rudolf Wildenmann, 225–68. Baden-Baden: Nomos.

———. 1995. Das Recht im Prozeß der europäischen Integration. Ein Plädoyer für die Beachtung des Rechts durch die Politikwissenschaft. EUI Working Paper No. 95/1, Florenz.

Joerges, Christian, and Jürgen Neyer. 1997. Transforming Strategic Interaction into Deliberative Problem-Solving: European Comitology in the Foodstuffs Sector. *Journal of European Public Policy* 3:3, 609–25.

Johnston, R.J. 1994. One World, Millions of Places: The End of History and the Ascendency of Geography. *Political Geography* 13:2, 111–21.

Jones, Stephen B. 1959. Boundary Concepts in the Setting of Place and Time. *Annals of the Association of American Geographers* 49:3, 241–55.

Judge, David, Gerry Stroker, and Harold Wolman, eds. 1995. *Theories of Urban Politics*. London: Sage.

Kacowicz, Arie M. 1995. Pluralistic Security Communities in the Third World? The Intriguing Cases of South America and West Africa. Paper for the annual meeting of the International Studies Association, Chicago, February 21–25.

Kahler, Miles. 1995. A World of Blocs. Facts and Factoids. *World Policy Journal* 12:1, 19–27.

Kant, Immanuel. 1902–1955. *Kants gesammelte Schriften*. Edition prepared by the Königlich-Preußischen Akademie der Wissenschaften. 23 vols. Berlin and Leipzig: de Gruyter.

———. 1970. Perpetual Peace: A Philosophical Sketch. In *Kant's Political Writings*, ed. Hans J. Reiss, 93–130. Cambridge: Cambridge University Press.

Kaplan, William, ed. 1993. *Belonging. The Meaning and Future of Canadian Citizenship*. Montreal: University of Toronto Press.

Kapstein, Ethan B. 1991. We are Us: The Myth of the Multi-National. *The National Interest* 7:4, 55–62.

———. 1993. Territoriality and Who is 'US'? *International Organization* 47:3, 501–03.

Kasarda, John D., and Allan M. Parnell, eds. 1993. *Third World Cities: Problems, Policies, and Prospects*. London: Sage.

Katzenstein, Peter J. 1976. International Relations and Domestic Structures: Foreign Economic Policies of Advanced Industrial States. *International Organization* 30: 1, 1–49.

———. 1984. *Corporatism and Change*. Ithaca, N.Y.: Cornell University Press.

———. 1985. *Small States in World Markets. Industrial Policy in Europe*. Ithaca, N.Y.: Cornell University Press.

———, ed. 1996a. *The Culture of National Security. Norms and Identity in World Politics*. New York: Columbia University Press.

———. 1996b. Introduction: Alternative Perspectives on National Security. In *The Culture of National Security. Norms and Identity in World Politics*, ed. Peter J. Katzenstein, 1–32. New York: Columbia University Press.

Kenworthy, Lane. 1990. Are Industrial Policy and Corporatism Compatible? *Journal of Public Policy* 10:3, 233–65.

Keohane, Robert O., ed. 1986. *Neorealism and Its Critics*. New York: Columbia University Press.

———. 1989a. *International Institutions and State Power*. Boulder, Colo.: Westview.

———. 1989b. The Demand for International Regimes. In *International Institutions and State Power*, ed. Robert O. Keohane, 101–32. Boulder, Colo.: Westview.

———. 1995. Hobbes's Dilemma and Institutional Change in World Politics: Sovereignty in International Society. In *Whose World Order? Uneven Globalization and the End of the Cold War*, ed. Holm, et al., 165–87. Boulder, Colo.: Westview.

Keohane, Robert O., and Stanley Hoffmann, eds. 1991. *The New European Community: Decisionmaking and Institutional Change.* Boulder, Colo.: Westview.

Keohane, Robert O., and Joseph S. Nye Jr. 1989. *Power and Interdependence: World Politics in Transition.* 2d ed. Boston: Little Brown.

Kersbergen, Kees van, and Bertjan Verbeek. 1994. The Politics of Subsidiarity in the EU. *Journal of Common Market Studies* 32:2, 215–36.

Kielmansegg, Peter Graf. 1994. Läßt sich die Europäische Gemeinschaft demokratisch verfassen? *Europäische Rundschau* 22:2, 23–33.

Kincaid, John. 1984. The American Governors in International Affairs. *Publius* 14:4, 95–106.

King, Anthony. 1995. Re-presenting World Cities: Cultural Theory/Social Practice. In *World Cities in a World-System*, ed. Knox, et al., 215–31. Cambridge: Cambridge University Press.

Kirby, Andrew, and Sallie Marston, with Kenneth Seasholes. 1995. World Cities and Global Communities: The Municipal Foreign Policy Movement and New Roles for Cities. In *World Cities in a World-System*, ed. Knox, et al., 267–79. Cambridge: Cambridge University Press.

Kitschelt, Herbert. 1996. Demokratietheorie und Veränderungen politischer Beteiligungsformen. Zum institutionellen Design postindustrieller Gesellschaften. *Forschungsjournal Neue Soziale Bewegungen* 9:2, 17–29.

Kline, John M. 1984. The International Economic Interests of U.S. States. *Publius* 14:4, 81–93.

Knox, Paul L., and Peter J. Taylor, eds. 1995. *World Cities in a World-System.* Cambridge: Cambridge University Press.

Kohler-Koch, Beate. 1993. Die Welt regieren ohne Weltregierung. In *Regieren im 21. Jahrhundert zwischen Globalisierung und Regionalisierung*, ed. Böhret, et al., 109–41. Opladen: Leske und Budrich.

———. 1994. The Evolution of Organized Interests in the EC. Driving Forces, Co-Evolution or New Type of Governance, Paper prepared for XVIth IPSA Congress, August 1994 in Berlin.

Kondylis, Panajotis. 1992. *Planetarische Politik nach dem Kalten Krieg.* Berlin: Akademie Verlag.

König, Helmut. 1993. Dieter Senghaas und die Zivilisationstheorie. *Leviathan* 21:4, 453–60.

Kößler, Reinhart, and Henning Melber. 1993. *Chancen einer internationalen Zivilgesellschaft*, Frankfurt/M.: Suhrkamp.

Krasner, Stephen D., ed. 1982. *International Regimes. International Organization* 36:2, special issue.

———. 1989. Sovereignty: An Institutional Perspective. In *The Elusive State: International and Comparative Perspectives*, ed. James A. Caporaso, 69–96. London: Sage.

———. 1993a. Economic Interdependence and Independent Statehood. In *States in a Changing World. A Contemporary Analysis*, ed. Jackson, et al., 301–22. Oxford: Clarendon Press.

———. 1993b. Westphalia and All That. In *Ideas and Foreign Policy. Beliefs, Institutions and Political Change*, ed. Goldstein, et al., 235–65. Ithaca, N.Y.: Cornell University Press.

———. 1994a. International Political Economy: Abiding Discord. *Review of International Political Economy* 1:1, 13–19.

———. 1994b. Contested Sovereignty: The Myth of Westphalia. Paper for the American Political Science Associaion annual meeting, September 1–4, New York.

———. 1995. Sovereignty and Intervention. In *Beyond Westphalia? State Sovereignty and International Intervention*, ed. Lyons, et al., 228–50. Baltimore, Md.: Johns Hopkins University Press.

Kratochwil, Friedrich. 1986. Of Systems, Boundaries, and Territoriality. *World Politics* 39:1, 27–52.

———. 1994. Citizenship: On the Border of Order. *Alternatives* 19:4, 485–506.

———. 1996. Is the Ship of Culture at Sea or Returning. In *The Return of Culture and Identity in IR Theory*, ed. Lapid, et al., 201–22. Boulder, Colo.: Lynne Rienner.

Kreile, Michael, ed. 1992. *Die Integration Europas* (PVS-Sonderheft 23). Opladen: Westdeutscher Verlag.

Krippendorff, Ekkehart. 1963. Ist Außenpolitik 'Außenpolitik'? *Politische Vierteljahresschrift* 4:3, 243–66.

Kristof, Ladis K.D. 1959. The Nature of Frontiers and Boundaries. *Annals of the Association of American Geographers* 49:3, 269–82.

Küng, Hans. 1990. *Projekt Weltethos*. München: Piper.

Laberge, Pierre. 1994. Kant and the Constitution of International Society. Unpublished paper presented to Ethikon Conference on the Constitution of International Society, January 1994, California.

Langewiesche, Dieter. 1995. Nation, Nationalismus, Nationalstaat: Forschungsstand und Forschungsperspektiven. *Neue Politische Literatur* 40:2, 190–236.

Lapid, Yosef. 1996. Culture's Ship: Return and Departures in International Relations Theory. In *The Return of Culture and Identity in IR Theory*, ed. Lapid, et al., 3–20. Boulder, Colo.: Lynne Rienner.

Lapid, Yosef, and Friedrich Kratochwil, eds. 1996. *The Return of Culture and Identity in IR Theory*. Boulder, Colo.: Lynne Rienner.

Larsen, Knud S., Carolyn Killifer; Gyorgy Csepeli, Krum Krumov, Ludmilla Andrejeva, Nadia Kashlakeva, Zlatka Russinova, and Laszlo Pordany. 1993. National Identity: Group-specific or Common Stereotypes. In *Conflict and Social Psychology*, ed. Knud S. Larsen, 213–24. London: Sage.

Lash, Scott, and John Urry. 1994. *Economies of Signs and Space*. London: Sage.

Leatherman, Janie, Ron Pagnucco, and Jackie Smith. 1993. International Institutions and Transnational Social Movement Organizations: Challenging the State in a Three-level Game of Global Transformation. Unpublished manuscript. Kroc Institute for International Peace Studies, University of Notre Dame. Unpublished manuscript.

Lefebvre, Henri. 1991. *The Production of Space*. Oxford: Blackwell.

Leggewie, Claus. 1994. Ethnizität, Nationalismus und multikulturelle Gesellschaft. In *Nationales Bewußtsein und kollektive Identität. Studien zur Entwicklung des kollektiven Bewußtseins in der Neuzeit 2*, ed. Helmut Berding, 46–65. Frankfurt/M.: Suhrkamp.

Lehmbruch, Gerhard. 1982. Introduction: Neo-Corporatism in Comparative Perspective. In *Patterns of corporatist policy-making*, ed. Lehmbruch, et al., 1–28. London: Sage.

Leibfried, Stephan, and Paul Pierson. 1992. Prospects for Social Europe. *Politics and Society* 20:3, 333–66.

———, eds. 1995. *European Social Policy. Between Fragmentation and Integration.* Washington, D.C.: The Brookings Institution.

Lenk, Kurt. 1993. Probleme der Demokratie. In *Politische Theorien von der Antike bis zur Gegenwart*, ed. Hans-Joachim Lieber, 933–86. Bonn: Bundeszentrale für politische Bildung.

Lepsius, M. Rainer. 1990a. Modernisierungspolitik als Institutionenbildung: Kriterien institutioneller Differenzierung. In *Interessen, Ideen und Institutionen*, ed. Rainer M. Lepsius, 53–62. Opladen: Westdeutscher Verlag.

———. 1990b. Nation und Nationalismus in Deutschland. In *Interessen, Ideen und Institutionen*, ed. Rainer M. Lepsius, 232–46. Opladen: Westdeutscher Verlag.

Leujrdik, J. Henk. 1986. *Intervention in International Politics.* Leeuwarden, Netherlands: Eisma B.V.

Levy, Marc A., Oran Young, and Michael Zürn. 1995. The Study of International Regimes. *European Journal of International Relations* 1:3, 267–330.

Lewin, Leif. 1994. The Rise and Decline of Corporatism: The Case of Sweden. *European Journal of Political Research* 26:1–2, 59–79.

Lipschutz, Ronnie. 1992. Reconstructing World Politics. The Emergence of Global Civil Society. *Millennium* 21:3, 389–420.

———. 1994. Who are We? Why are We Here? Political Identity, Ecological Politics, and Global Change, Paper presented at the International Studies Association Annual Meeting, 28 March–1 April, Washington, D.C.

List, Martin. 1992. Weltgesellschaft, Staatengemeinschaft und umfassende Sicherheit im Rahmen ökologischer Verträglichkeit. *polis*, no. 21, Hagen: Fernuniversität.

Litfin, Karen. 1993. Ecoregimes: Playing Tug of War with the Nation-State. In *The State and Social Power in Global Environmental Politics*, ed. Lipschutz, et al., 94–117. New York: Columbia University Press.

Locher, Birgit. 1996. Feminismus ist mehr als 'political correctness'. Anmerkungen und Ergänzungen zu Gert Krells Literaturbericht. *Zeitschrift für Internationale Beziehungen* 3:2, 381–97.

Luhmann, Niklas. 1990a. Identität—was oder wie? In *Soziologische Aufklärung 5: Konstruktivistische Perspektiven*, by Niklas Luhmann, 14–30. Opladen: Westdeutscher Verlag.

———. 1990b. *Ökologische Kommunikation. Kann die moderne Gesellschaft sich auf ökologische Gefährdungen einstellen?* Opladen: Westdeutscher Verlag.

———. 1997. *Die Gesellschaft der Gesellschaft.* 2 vols. Frankfurt/M.: Suhrkamp.

Luthardt, Wolfgang. 1993. European Integration and Referendums: Analytical Considerations and Empirical Evidence. In *The State of the EC: The Maastricht Debates and Beyond*, ed. Cafruny, et al., 53–71. Boulder, Colo.: Lynne Rienner.

Lyons, Gene M., and Michael Mastanduno. 1993. International Intervention, State Sovereignty and the Future of International Society. *International Social Science Journal*, 138 (November), 517–32.

Mackenzie, Richard B., and Dwight R. Lee. 1991. *Quicksilver Capital: How Rapid Movement of Wealth Has Changed the World.* New York: Free Press.

Majone, Giandomenico. 1993. Deregulation or Re-regulation, Policymaking in the European Community Since the Single Act, EUI-Working Paper SPS 93/9, Florenz.
——. 1996. *Regulating Europe*. London: Routledge.
Maluschke, Günther. 1975. Hegel und das Problem der Staatsräson. In *Staatsräson. Studien zur Geschichte eines politischen Begriffs*, ed. Roman Schnur, 569–90. Berlin: Duncker und Humblot.
Mann, Michael, ed. 1990. *The Rise and Decline of the Nation State*. Oxford: Blackwell.
Manning, C. A. W. 1975. The Nature of International Society, Reissued. London: Macmillan.
Marks, Gary. 1992. Structural Policy in the European Community. In *Euro-Politics: Institutions and Policymaking in the New European Community*, ed. Alberta M. Sbargia, 191–224. Washington, D.C.: The Brookings Institution.
——. 1993. Structural policy and multilevel governance in the EC. In *The State of the EC: The Maastricht Debates and Beyond*, ed. Cafruny, et al., 391–410. Boulder, Colo.: Lynne Rienner.
——. 1996. Politikmuster und Einflußlogik in der Strukturpolitik. In *Europäische Integration*, ed. Jachtenfuchs, et al., 313–44. Opladen: Leske und Budrich.
Martens, Jens. 1993. Dabeisein ist noch nicht alles. Die NGOs in den Vereinten Nationen: Akteure, Kritiker, Nutznießer. *Vereinte Nationen* 41:5, 168–71.
——. 1995. Die Bedeutung der NGOs wächst. Nicht mehr länger nur auf der Zuschauertribüne. *Das Parlament* 42/95, 13.10.95, 13.
Martinez, Oscar, ed. 1986. *Across Boundaries: Transborder Interaction in Comparative Perspective*. El Paso, Tex.: Texas Western Press.
——. 1994. *Border People. Life and Society in the U.S.-Mexico Borderlands*. Tucson, Ariz.: University of Arizona Press.
Mayall, James. 1990. *Nationalism and International Society*. Cambridge: Cambridge University Press.
Mayer-Tasch, Peter C. 1990. Umweltinitiativen und internationale Umweltpolitik. *Zeitschrift für Politik* 37:2, 172–79.
Mayntz, Renate. 1993. Policy-Netzwerke und die Logik von Verhandlungssystemen. In *Policy-Analyse. Kritik und Neuorientierung, Politische Vierteljahresschrift*, Special Issue 24, ed. Adrienne Héritier, 39–56. Opladen: Westdeutscher Verlag.
Mayntz, Renate, and Fritz W. Scharpf, eds. 1995. *Gesellschaftliche Selbstregelung und politische Steuerung*. Frankfurt/M.: Campus.
McGrew, Anthony G., and Paul G. Lewis, eds. 1992. *Global Politics. Globalization and the Nation-State*. Cambridge: Polity Press.
McSweeney, Bill. 1996. Identity and Security: Buzan and the Copenhagen School. *Review of International Studies* 22:1, 81–93.
Mead, George Herbert. 1967. *Mind, Self, and Society: From the Standpoint of a Social Behaviorist, Fifteenth Impression*. Chicago, Ill.: The University of Chicago Press.
Meehan, Elizabeth. 1993. *Citizenship and the European Community*. London: Sage.
Mercer, Jonathan. 1995. Anarchy and Identity. *International Organization* 49:2, 229–52.
Miller, Toby. 1993. *The Well-Tempered Self. Citizenship, Culture, and the Postmodern Subject*. Baltimore, Md.: Johns Hopkins University Press.
Milner, Helen. 1983: *Resisting Protectionism: Global Industries and the Politics of International Trade*. Princeton: Princeton University Press.
——. 1991. The Assumption of Anarchy in International Relations Theory: A Critique. *Review of International Studies* 17:1, 67–85.

Milward, Alan S., George Brennan, and Frederico Romero. 1992. *The European Rescue of the Nation State*. Berkeley: University of California Press.

Möller, Franz, and Martin Limpert. 1993. Informations- und Mitwirkungsrechte des Bundetags in Angelegenheiten der Europäischen Union. *Zeitschrift für Parlamentsfragen* 24:1, 21–32.

Moravcsik, Andrew. 1993a. Preferences and Power in the European Community: A Liberal Intergovernmentalist Approach. *Journal of Common Market Studies* 31:4, 473–524.

———. 1993b. Introduction. Integrating International and Domestic Theories of International Bargaining. In *Double-Edged Diplomacy: International Bargaining and Domestic Politics*, ed. Evans, et al., 3–42. Berkeley: University of California Press.

———. 1994. Why the European Community Strengthens the State: Domestic Politics and International Cooperation. Paper for the annual meeting of American Political Science Association, 1–4 September, New York.

Morphet, Sally. 1996. NGOs and the Environment. In *The consience of the world. The influence of non-governmental organisation in the UN System*, ed. Peter Willetts, 116–46. Washington, D.C.: The Brookings Institution.

Müller, Harald. 1993. Verrechtlichung, Innen- und Außenpolitik in: *Internationale Verrechtlichung*, ed. Klaus Dieter Wolf, 56–81. Pfaffenweiler: Centaurus Verlag.

———. 1994. Internationale Beziehungen als kommunikatives Handeln. *Zeitschrift für Internationale Beziehungen* 1:1, 15–44.

Müller, Harald, and Thomas Risse-Kappen. 1990. Internationale Umwelt, gesellschaftliches Umfeld und außenpolitischer Prozeß in liberaldemokratischen Industrienationen. In *Theorien der Internationalen Beziehungen, Politische Vierteljahresschrift*, Special Issue 21, ed. Volker Rittberger, 357–400. Opladen: Westdeutscher Verlag.

Nardin, Terry. 1983. *Law, Morality, and the Relations of Nations*. Princeton, N.J.: Princeton University Press.

Narr, Wolf-Dieter, and Alexander Schubert. 1994. *Weltökonomie. Die Misere der Politik*. Frankfurt/M.: Suhrkamp.

Navari, Cornelia, ed. 1991. *The Condition of States. A Study in International Political Theory*. Philadelphia, Penn.: Open University Press.

Neumann, Iver B. 1992. Identity and Security. *Journal of Peace Research* 29:2, 221–26.

———. 1996. Self and Other in International Relations. *European Journal of International Relations* 2:2, 139–74.

Newman, David, ed. 1999. *Boundaries, Territory and Postmodernity*. London: Frank Cass.

Neyer, Jürgen. 1995. Globaler Markt und territorialer Staat. Konturen eines wachsenden Antagonismus. *Zeitschrift für Internationale Beziehungen* 2:2, 287–315.

Neyer, Jürgen, and Dieter Wolf. 1996. Zusammenfügen, was zusammengehört. *Zeitschrift für Internationale Beziehungen* 3:2, 399–423.

Nicolaides, Phedon. 1990. Services in Growing Economies and Global Markets. *The Pacific Review* 59:4, 283–95.

Nijkamp, Peter, ed. 1994. *New Borders and Old Barriers in Spatial Development*. Newcastle upon Tyne: Avebury.

Nordlinger, Eric A. 1981. *On the Autonomy of the Democratic State*. Cambridge, Mass.: Harvard University Press.

Nørgaard, Asbjørn Sonne. 1994. Institutions and Post-Modernity in IR. The 'New' EC. *Cooperation and Conflict* 29:3, 245–87.

North, Douglass C. 1981. *Structure and Change in Economic History*. New York: Norton.
Nuscheler, Franz. 1995. Universalität und Unteilbarkeit der Menschenrechte? Zur Kakophonie des Wiener Wunschkonzerts. *Österreichische Zeitschrift für Politikwissenschaft* 24:2, 199–210.
Nye, Joseph S. 1987. Nuclear Learning and U.S.-Soviet Security Regimes. *International Organization* 41:3, 371–402.
O'Brien, Richard. 1992. *Global Financial Integration. The End of Geography*. London: Pinter.
Oakes, Penelope J., S. Alexander Haslam, and John C. Turner. 1994. *Stereotyping and Social Reality*. Cambridge, Mass.: Blackwell.
Oakeshott, Michael. 1975. *On Human Conduct*. Oxford: Oxford University Press.
Offe, Claus. 1975. *Bildungsreform. Eine Fallstudie über Reformpolitik*. Frankfurt/M.: Suhrkamp.
———. 1984. Politische Legitimation durch Mehrheitsentscheidung. In *An den Grenzen der Mehrheitsdemokratie*, ed. Guggenberger, et al., 150–83. Opladen: Westdeutscher Verlag.
Ohmae, Kenichi. 1993. The Rise of the Region State. *Foreign Affairs* 72:2, 78–87.
Oschatz, Georg-Bernd. 1995. Die Bundesregierung an der Kette der Länder?—Zur europapolitischen Mitwirkung des Bundesrates. *Die öffentliche Verwaltung* 48:10, 437.
OSPAR Convention 1992: 1992 Ministerial Meetings of the Oslo and Paris Commissions.
Owen, John M. 1994. How Liberalism Produces Democratic Peace. *International Security* 19:2, 87–126.
Pappi, Franz Urban. 1993. Policy-Netze: Erscheinungsform moderner Politiksteuerung oder methodischer Ansatz? In *Policy-Analyse. Kritik und Neuorientierung, Politische Vierteljahresschrift*, Special Issue 24, ed. Adrienne Héritier, 84–94. Opladen: Westdeutscher Verlag.
Pedersen, Thomas. 1992. *Maastricht-traktaten i frderalistisk belysning* (The Maastricht Treaty From a Federalist Perspective). Aarhus: Department of Political Science, University of Aarhus.
Perham, Margery. [1946] 1967. *Colonial Sequence*. Reprint. London: Methuen. (Quoted from Jackson 1990.)
Peterson, M. J. 1992. Whalers, Cetologists, Environmentalists, and the International Management of Whaling. *International Organization* 46:1, 147–86.
Petrella, Riccardo. 1991. World City-States of the Future. *New Perspectives Quarterly* 8:4, 59–64.
Plessner, Helmuth. 1981. Grenzen der Gemeinschaft. Eine Kritik des sozialen Radikalismus. In *Gesammelte Schriften, Vol. V: Macht und menschliche Natur*. Frankfurt/M.: Suhrkamp, 7–134.
Pogge, Thomas W. 1994. Cosmopolitanism and Sovereignty. In *Political Restructuring in Europe: Ethical Perspectives*, ed. Chris Brown, 89–122. London: Routledge.
Potter, David. 1996. Non-Governmental Organisations and Environmental Policies. In *Environmental Policy in an International Context. Prospects for Environmental Change*, ed. Blowers, et al., 25–49. London: Arnold.
Preuß, Ulrich K., ed. 1994. *Zum Begriff der Verfassung. Die Ordnung des Politischen*. Frankfurt/M.: Fischer.
Princen, Thomas E., and M. Finger, eds. 1994. *Environmental NGO's in World Politics. Linking the local and the global*. London: Routledge.

Prittwitz, Volker v. 1990. *Das Katastrophenparadox. Elemente einer Theorie der Umweltpolitik.* Opladen: Leske und Budrich.

———, ed. 1993a. *Umweltpolitik als Modernisierungsprozeß.* Opladen: Leske und Budrich.

———. 1993b: Reflexive Modernisierung und öffentliches Handeln. In *Umweltpolitik als Modernisierungsprozeß*, ed. Volker Prittwitz, 31–51. Opladen: Leske und Budrich.

Purnell, Robert. 1973. *The Society of States. An Introduction to International Politics.* London: Wiedenfeld and Nicolson.

Putnam, Robert D. 1988. Diplomacy and Domestic Policy: the Logic of Two-level Games. *International Organization* 42:3, 429–60.

Quaritsch, Helmut. 1975. Staatsraison in Bodins 'Republique'. In *Staatsräson. Studien zur Geschichte eines politischen Begriffs*, ed. Roman Schnur, 43–63. Berlin: Duncker und Humblot.

Ratzel, Friedrich 1896. Die Gesetze des räumlichen Wachstums von Staaten. *Petermanns Geographische Mitteilungen*, 42, 97–103.

———. 1903. *Politische Geographie.* 2d ed., München: Oldenbourg.

Rawls, John. 1993. *On Human Rights.* New York: Basic Books.

Reich, Robert B. 1983. *The Next American Frontier.* New York: Times Books.

———. 1990. Who is US? *Harvard Business Review* 68:1, 53–64.

———. 1991. *The Work of Nations: Preparing Ourselves for 21st Century Capitalism.* New York: Alfred A. Knopf.

Renteln, Alison D. 1990. *International Human Rights.* London: Sage.

Richter, Emanuel. 1990. Weltgesellschaft und Weltgemeinschaft. Begriffsverwirrung und Klärungsversuche. *Politische Vierteljahresschrift* 31:2, 275–79.

———. 1991. Erkenntniskritik versus kritische Ontologie. Gemeinschaft und Gesellschaft bei Kant und Tönnies. In *Hundert Jahre 'Gemeinschaft und Gesellschaft'. Ferdinand Tönnies in der internationalen Diskussion*, ed. Clausen, et al., 189–213. Opladen: Leske und Budrich.

———. 1992. *Der Zerfall der Welteinheit. Vernunft und Globalisierung in der Moderne.* Frankfurt/New York: Campus.

———. 1997. Demokratie und Globalisierung. Das Modell einer Bürgergesellschaft im Weltsystem. In *Politische Beteiligung und Bürgerengagement in Deutschland. Möglichkeiten und Grenzen*, ed. Klein, et al., 173–202. Bonn: Bundeszentrale für politische Bildung.

Rieger, Elmar. 1995. Politik supranationaler Integration. Die Europäische Gemeinschaft in institutionentheoretischer Perspektive. In *Politische Institutionen im Wandel. Kölner Zeitschrift für Soziologie und Sozialpsychologie*, Special Issue 35, ed. Birgitta Nedelmann, 349–67. Opladen: Westdeutscher Verlag.

Riker, William. 1955. The senate and American federalism. *American Political Science Review* 49:2, 452–69.

Risse-Kappen, Thomas. 1991. Public Opinion, Domestic Structure, and Foreign Policy in Liberal Democracies. *World Politics* 43:4, 479–512.

———. 1994. Demokratischer Frieden? Unfriedliche Demokratien? Überlegungen zu einem theoretischen Puzzle. In *Frieden und Konflikt in den internationalen Beziehungen*, ed. Krell, et al., 159–89. Frankfurt/M.: Campus.

———. 1995a. Reden ist nicht billig. Zur Debatte um Kommunikation und Rationalität. *Zeitschrift für Internationale Beziehungen* 2:1, 171–84.

———. 1995b. *Cooperation Among Democracies. The European Influence on U.S. Foreign Policy*. Princeton, N.J.: Princeton University Press.
———. 1995c. Democratic Peace—Warlike Democracies? A Social Constructivist Interpretation of the Liberal Argument. *European Journal of International Relations* 1:4, 491–517.
———. 1996. Collective Identity in a Democratic Community: The Case of NATO. In . In *The Culture of National Security. Norms and Identity in World Politics*, ed. Peter J. Katzenstein, 357–99. New York: Columbia University Press.
Rittberger, Volker with the assistance of Peter Mayer, ed. 1993. *Regime Theory and International Relations*. Oxford: Oxford University Press.
Rittberger, Volker, and Bernhard Zangl. 1994. *Internationale Organisationen. Politik und Geschichte*. Opladen: Leske und Budrich.
Rittberger, Volker, and Michael Zürn. 1990. Towards Regulated Anarchy in East-West-Relations. Causes and Consequences of East-West Regimes. In *International Regimes in East-West Politics*, ed. Volker Rittberger, 9–63. London: Pinter.
Roberts, Bryan. 1995. The Social Content of Citizenship in Latin America. *International Journal of Urban and Regional Research* 20:7, 38–65.
Ronge, Volker. 1979. *Bankenpolitik im Spätkapitalismus, Starnberger Studien 2*. Frankfurt/M.: Suhrkamp.
Rosecrance, Richard. 1986. *The Rise of the Trading State*. New York: Basic Books.
Rosenau, James N. 1990. *Turbulence in World Politics*. Brighton: Harvester Wheatsheaf.
———. 1992a. Governance, Order, and Change in World Politics. In *Governance without Government*, ed. Rosenau, et al., 30–57. Cambridge: Cambridge University Press.
———. 1992b. Citizenship in a Changing Global Order. In *Governance without Government*, ed. Rosenau, et al., 272–94. Cambridge: Cambridge University Press.
———. 1995. Governance in the Twenty-first Century. *Global Governance* 1:1, 13–34.
Rosenau, James N., and Ernst-Otto Czempiel, eds. 1992. *Governance without Government*. Cambridge: Cambridge University Press.
Rucht, Dieter. 1996. Multinationale Bewegungsorganisationen: Bedeutung, Bedingungen, Perspektiven. *Forschungsjournal Neue Soziale Bewegungen* 9:2, 30–41.
Ruggie, John G. 1983. International regimes, transactions, and change: embedded liberalism in the postwar economic order. In *International Regimes*, ed. Stephen D. Krasner, 195–231. Ithaca, N.Y.: Cornell University Press.
———. 1986. Continuity and Transformation in the World Polity. In *Neorealism and Its Critics*, ed. Robert O. Keohane, 131–57. New York: Columbia University Press.
———. 1993. Territoriality and Beyond. Problematizing Modernity in International Relations. *International Organization* 47:1, 139–74.
———. 1994. Trade, protectionism and the future of welfare capitalism. *Journal of International Affairs* 48:1, 1–12.
Russett, Bruce. 1993. *Grasping the Democratic Peace. Principles for a Post-Cold War World*. Princeton, N.J.: Princeton University Press.
Sack, Robert. 1980. *Conceptions of Space in Social Thought. A Geographic Perspective*. Minneapolis: University of Minnesota Press.
———. 1986. *Human Territoriality. Its Theory and History*. Cambridge: Cambridge University Press.
Sandbrook, Richard. 1985. *The Politics of Africa's Economic Stagnation*. Cambridge: Cambridge University Press.

Sandholtz, Wayne, and John Zysman. 1989. 1992 – recasting the European bargain. *World Politics* 42:1, 95–128.
Sassen, Saskia. 1991. *The Global City.* Princeton, N.J.: Princeton University Press.
———. 1994. *Cities in the World Economy.* Thousand Oaks: Pine Forge Press.
Sbragia, Alberta M. 1992. Thinking about the European future: the uses of comparison. In *Europolitics. Institutions and Policymaking in the 'New' European Community,* ed. Alberta M. Sbragia, 257–91. Washington, D.C.: The Brookings Institution.
Scharpf, Fritz W. 1985. Die Politikverflechtungs-Falle: Europäische Integration und deutscher Föderalismus im Vergleich. *Politische Vierteljahresschrift* 26:4, 323–56.
———. 1991. Die Handlungsfähigkeit des Staates am Ende des zwanzigsten Jahrhunderts. *Politische Vierteljahresschrift* 32:4, 621–34.
———. 1993a. Autonomieschonend und gemeinschaftsverträglich: Zur Logik der europäischen Mehrbenenpolitik. MPIFG Discussion Paper 93/9, Köln.
———. 1993b. Legitimationsprobleme der Globalisierung. Regieren in Verhandlungssystemen. In *Regieren im 21. Jahrhundert zwischen Globalisierung und Regionalisierung,* ed. Böhret, et al., 165–85. Opladen: Leske und Budrich.
———. 1994. Community and Autonomy. Multilevel Policy-Making in the European Union. RSC Working Papers (94:1). Florence: European University Institute.
Schelling, Thomas C. 1960. *The Strategy of Conflict.* Cambridge, Mass.: Harvard University Press.
Schmalz-Bruns, Rainer. 1996. Demokratietheoretische Aspekte einer ökologischen Modernisierung der Politik. In *Konfliktregelung in der offenen Bürgergesellschaft,* ed. Feindt, et al., 37–64. Dettelbach: Röll.
Schmidt, Hilmar. 1995. Nation-States and their Capacity to Adapt to World Society, Paper presented at the 20th Annual Conference of the British International Studies Association, 18–20 December, Southampton.
———. 1996. Konfliktlinien der internationalen Klimapolitik. Das Klimaspiel und die USA als Spielverderber? In *Klimapolitik. Naturwissenschaftliche Grundlagen, internationale Regimebildung und Konflikte sowie nationale Problemerkennung und Politikimplementation,* ed. Hans-Günter Brauch, 129–40. Berlin: Springer.
Schmidt, Manfred G. 1993. Theorien in der international vergleichenden Staatstätigkeitsforschung. *Policy-Analyse. Kritik und Neuorientierung, Politische Vierteljahresschrift,* Special Issue 24, ed. Adrienne Héritier, 371–93. Opladen: Westdeutscher Verlag.
———. 1995. *Demokratietheorien.* Opladen: Leske und Budrich.
Schmidt, Samuel, and David Lorey, eds. 1994. Policy Recommendations for Managing the El Paso-Ciudad Juarez Metropolitian Area (PROFMEX Urban Studies Series). El Paso, Tex.: El Paso Community Foundation und Center For Inter American and Border Studies, University of Texas at El Paso.
Schmitter, Philippe C. 1981. Neokorporatismus: Überlegungen zur bisherigen Theorie und weiteren Praxis. *Neokorporatismus,* ed. Ulrich v. Alemann. 62–79. Frankfurt: Campus.
———. 1992. *Interests, Powers and Functions: Emergent Properties in the European Polity.* Working paper. Stanford University.
Schmuck, Otto, and Wolfgang Wessels, eds. 1989. *Das Europäische Parlament im dynamischen Integrationsprozeß: Auf der Suche nach einem zeitgemäßen Leitbild.* Bonn: Europa Union Verlag.
Schnur, Roman, ed. 1975. *Staatsräson. Studien zur Geschichte eines politischen Begriffs.* Berlin: Duncker und Humblot.

Scott, Allen J. 1988. *New Industrial Spaces. Flexible Production Organisation and Regional Development in North America and Western Europe*. London: Pion.
Scott, James. 1989. Transborder Cooperation, Regional Initiatives, and Sovereignty Conflicts in Western Europe: The Case of the Upper Rhine Valley. *Publius* 19:1, 139–56.
———. 1996. Dutch-German Euroregions. A Model for Transboundary Cooperation? In *The Future of Borders and Border Regions in Europe and Northamerica*, ed. Scott, et al., 11–24. Berlin: Institut für Regionalentwicklung und Strukturplanung.
Senghaas, Dieter. 1994. *Wohin driftet die Welt? Über die Zukunft der friedlichen Koexistenz*. Frankfurt/M.: Suhrkamp.
———. 1995. Die Wirklichkeiten der Kulturkämpfe. *Leviathan* 23:2, 197–212.
Sharpe, Laurence J. 1993. The European Meso. An Appraisal. In *The Rise of Meso Government in Europe*, ed. Laurence C. Shapre, 1–39. London: Sage.
Shaw, Martin. 1994. *Global Society and International Relations. Sociological Concepts and Political Perspectives*. Cambridge: Polity Press.
Shue, Henry. 1980. *Basic Rights*. Princeton, N.J.: Princeton University Press.
Shumann, Michael H. 1986. Local Foreign Policies. *Foreign Policy* 65:4, 154–74.
———. 1992. Courts v. Local Foreign Policies. *Foreign Policy* 86:3, 158–77.
Shute, Stephen, and Susan Hurley, eds. 1993. *On Human Rights: The Oxford Amnesty Lectures* 1993. New York: Basic Books.
Siebert, Horst, ed. 1991. *Capital Flows in the World Economy*. Tübingen: J. C. B. Mohr.
Siegelberg, Jens. 1994. *Kapitalismus und Krieg. Eine Theorie des Krieges in der Weltgesellschaft*. Münster: Lit Verlag.
Simonis, Georg. 1972. Außenpolitischer Handlungsspielraum und politische Autonomie. In *Gesellschaftlicher Wandel und politische Innovation. Politische Vierteljahresschrift*, Special Issue 4, Opladen: Westdeutscher Verlag, 282–314.
Singer, Max, and Aaron Wildavsky. 1993. *The Real World Order: Zones of Peace/Zones of Turmoil*. Chatham, N.J.: Chatham House.
Skidmore, David, and Valerie M. Hudson, eds. 1993. *The Limits of State Autonomy. Societal Groups and Foreign Policy Formulation*. Boulder: Westview.
Skocpol, Theda. 1979. *States and Social Revolutions: A Comparative Analysis of France, Russia, and China*. Cambridge: Cambridge University Press.
Skriver, Ansgar. 1993. Die westlichen Menschenrechtsorganisationen können vom Süden lernen—Zu den Perspektiven nach der Wiener Menschenrechtskonferenz. *Gewerkschaftliche Monatshefte* 44:9, 521–31.
Smith, Anthony D. 1991. *National Identity*. London: Penguin.
———. 1992. National Identity and the Idea of European Unity. *International Affairs* 68:1, 55–76.
Smith, John, R. Pagnucco, and W. Romeril. 1994. Transnational Social Movement Organisations in the Global Political Arena. *Voluntas* 5:2, 123–54.
Smith, Martin J. 1993. *Pressure, Power and Policy. State Autonomy and Policy Networks in Britain and the United States*. Hertfordshire: Harvester Wheatsheaf.
Smith, Michael. 1992. Modernization, Globalization and the Nation-State. In *Global Politics. Globalization and the Nation-State*, ed. McGrew, et al., 253–68. Cambridge: Polity Press.
Soja, Edward. 1989. *Postmodern Geographies. The Reassertion of Space in Critical Social Theory*. London: Verso.

Sørensen, Georg. 1983. *Transnational Corporations in Peripheral Societies*. Aalborg: Aalborg University Press.

———, ed. 1993. *Political Conditionality*. London: Frank Cass.

———. 1994. *International Relations After the Cold War*. Working paper. Aarhus: Department of Political Science, University of Aarhus.

———. 1996. Individual security and national security. The state remains the principal problem. *Security Dialogue* 27:4, 371–86.

———. 1998. States are Not 'Like Units': Types of State and Forms of Anarchy in the Present International System. *The Journal of Political Philosophy* 6:1, 79–98.

Spruyt, Hendrik. 1994a. The Evolution of Sovereignty and Institutional Isomorphism. Paper presented at the American Political Science Association Conference, 1–4 September, New York.

———. 1994b. Institutional selection in international relations: state anarchy as order. *International Organization* 48:4, 527–57.

———. 1994c. *The Sovereign State and Its Competitors*. Princeton, N.J.: Princeton University Press.

Stahl, Karin. 1995. Nichtregierungsorganisationen und internationale Organisationen: Partizipationsmöglichkeiten und Demokratisierungspotentiale am Beispiel der UN-Konferenz 'Umwelt und Entwicklung'. In *Nichtregierungsorganisationen und Entwicklung: Auf dem Wege zu mehr Realismus*, ed. Hanisch, et al., 237–53. Hamburg: Deutsches Übersee-Institut.

Stairs, Kevin, and Peter Taylor. 1992. Non-Governmental Organizations and the Legal Protection of the Oceans: A Case Study. In *The International Politics of the Environment*, ed. Hurrell, et al., 110–41. Oxford: Oxford University Press.

Stanley Foundation, ed. 1994a. *Shaping American Global Policy: The Growing Role of the Pacific Northwest*. Report of a New American Global Dialogue Conference, 7–8 September 1994, Snoqualmie, Washington. Muscatine, Iowa: Stanley Foundation.

———. 1994b. *The Changing Face of American Foreign Policy: The Role of the State and Local Actors*. A Report of a New American Global Dialogue Conference, 27–29 October 1994, Warrenton, Virginia. Muscatine, Iowa: Stanley Foundation.

Stewart, Jenny. 1992. Corporatism, Pluralism and Political Learning: A Systems Approach. *Journal of Public Policy* 12:3, 243–55.

Stichweh, Rudolf. 1994. Nation und Weltgesellschaft. In *Das Prinzip Nation in modernen Gesellschaften*, ed. Estel, et al., 83–96. Opladen: Westdeutscher Verlag.

Stopford, John, and Susan Strange, with John S. Henley. 1991. *Rival States, Rival Firms: Competition for World Market Shares*. Cambridge: Cambridge University Press.

Strange, Susan. 1988. *States and Markets*. London: Pinter.

———. 1994a. Rethinking Structural Change in the International Political Economy: States, Firms, and Diplomacy. In *Political Economy and the Changing Global Order*, ed. Stubbs, et al., 103–15. London: Macmillan.

———. 1994b. Wake up, Krasner! The World has Changed. *Review of International Political Economy* 1:2, 209–19.

Strayer, J.R. 1970. *On the Medieval Origins of the Modern State*. Princeton, N.J.: Princeton University Press.

Streeck, Wolfgang, ed. 1994a. *Staat und Verbände, Politische Vierteljahresschrift*, Special Issue 25. Opladen: Westdeutscher Verlag.

———. 1994b. Einleitung des Herausgebers. Staat und Verbände: Neue Fragen. Neue Antworten? In *Staat und Verbände, Politische Vierteljahresschrift,* Special Issue 25, ed. Wolfgang Streeck, 7–34. Opladen: Westdeutscher Verlag.

Tajfel, Henri, and John C. Turner. 1986. The Social Identity Theory of Intergroup Behavior. In *Psychology of Intergroup Relations.* 2d ed., ed. Worchel, et al., 7–24. Chicago, Ill.: Nelson-Hall.

Take, Ingo. 1996. *Der Einfluß von Umweltverbänden auf internationale Regime* (Master Thesis). Bremen: University of Bremen.

Taylor, A. J. P. 1954. *The Struggle for Mastery in Europe,* London: Oxford University Press.

Taylor, Charles. 1992. Atomism. *Communitarianism and Individualism,* ed. Avineri, et al., 29–50. Oxford: Oxford University Press.

———. 1994. Was ist die Quelle kollektiver Identität? In *Projekt Europa. Postnationale Identität: Grundlage für eine europäische Demokratie?* ed. Dewandre, et al., 42–46. Berlin: Schelzky & Jeep.

Taylor, Peter J. 1994. The State as a Container: Territoriality in the Modern World System. *Progress in Human Geography* 18:6, 151–62.

———. 1995a. World Cities and Territorial States: The Rise and Fall of their Mutuality. In *World Cities in a World System,* ed. Knox, et al., 48–62. Cambridge: Cambridge University Press.

———. 1995b: Beyond Containers. Internationality, Interstateness, Interterritoriality. *Progress in Human Geography* 19:1, 1–15.

Therborn, Gustaf. 1987. Does Corporatism Really Matter? The Economic Crisis and Issues of Political Theory. *Journal of Public Policy* 7:3, 259–84.

———. 1992. Lessons from 'Corporatist' Theorizations. In *Social Corporatism: A Superior Economic System?* ed. Pekkarinen, et al., 24–43. Oxford: Clarendon Press.

Thompson, Janice E. 1995. State Sovereignty in International Relations: Bridging the Gap between Theory and Empirical Research. *International Studies Quarterly* 39:2, 213–33.

Thompson, Janice E., and Stephen D. Krasner. 1989. Global transactions and the consolidation of sovereignty. In *Global Changes and Theoretical Challenges. Approaches to World Politics for the 1990s,* ed. Czempiel, et al., 195–219. Lexington, Mass.: Lexington Books.

Thorup, Cathryn L. 1991. The Politics of Free Trade and the Dynamics of Cross-Border Coalitions in U.S.-Mexican Relations. *Columbia Journal of World Business* 26:2, 12–26.

Thrift, Nigel. 1994. Globalisation, Regulation, Urbanisation: The Case of the Netherlands. *Urban Studies* 31:3, 365–81.

Tibi, Bassam. 1995. *Der religiöse Fundamentalismus im Übergang zum 21. Jahrhundert.* Mannheim: BI-Taschenbuchverlag.

Tilly, Charles. 1990. *Coercion, Capital, and European States, AD 990–1990.* Oxford: Basil Blackwell.

Tomuschat, Christian. 1993. Die Europäische Union unter der Aufsicht des Bundesverfassungsgerichts. *Europäische Grundrechte-Zeitschrift* 20:20–21, 489–96.

Tönnies, Ferdinand. 1972. *Gemeinschaft und Gesellschaft. Grundbegriffe der reinen Soziologie.* 3r ed. Darmstadt: Wissenschaftliche Buchgesellschaft. [Community and Association. London: Routledge and Paul, 1955.]

Tönnies, Sibylle. 1995. *Der westliche Universalismus. Eine Verteidigung klassischer Positionen*. Opladen: Westdeutscher Verlag.

Traxler, Franz, and Philippe C. Schmitter. 1995. The emerging Euro-polity and organized interests. *European Journal of International Relations* 1:2, 191–218.

Tsoukalis, Loukas. 1993. *The New European Economy. The Politics and Economics of Integration*. Oxford: Oxford University Press.

Tyson, Laura. 1991. They are not Us: Why American Ownership Still Matters. *The American Prospect* 2:4, 37–49.

UNCTAD. 1990. *Trade and Development Report 1990*. New York: United Nations.

UNCTC. 1992. *World Investment Report: Transnational Corporations as Engines of Growth*. New York: United Nations.

Union of International Associations. 1993. *Yearbook of International Organizations,* vol 3. 10th ed. München: Saur.

Van Schendelen, Marinus C. P. M. 1993. Conclusion: From National State Power to Spontaneous Lobbying. In *National Public and Private EC Lobbying*, ed. Van Schendelen, et al., 275–91. Dartmouth: Dartmouth Publishing Company.

Vernon, Raymond. 1971. *Sovereignty at Bay: the Multinational Spread of US Enterprises*. New York: Basic Books.

Vila, Pablo. 1994. The Construction of Social Identities in the Border. Some Case Studies in Ciudad Juarez/El Paso. In *Sociological Explorations Focus on the Southwest*, ed. Daudistel, et al., 51–64. Minneapolis, Minn.: University of Minnesota Press.

Vincent, R.J. 1984. Edmund Burke and the Theory of International Relations. *Review of International Studies* 10:3, 205–18.

———. 1986. *Human Rights and International Relations*. Cambridge: Cambridge University Press.

Viotti, Paul R., and Mark V. Kauppi. 1993. *International Relations Theory. Realism, Pluralism, Globalism*. 2d ed. New York: Macmillan.

Vreeland, James R. 1999. The IMF: Lender of Last Resort or Scapegoat?, Paper Prepared for the International Studies Association Conference, 16–21 February, Washington, D.C.

Waarden, Frans van. 1992. The Historical Institutionalization of Typical National Patterns in Policy Networks between State and Industry. A Comparison of the USA and the Netherlands. *European Journal of Political Research* 21:1–2, 131–62.

Wæver, Ole. 1993. Societal Security: The Concept. In *Identity, Migration and the New Security Agenda in Europe*, ed. Wæver, et al., 17–40. London: Pinter.

Wæver, Ole, Barry Buzan, Morten Kelstrup, and Pierre Lemaitre. 1993. *Identity, Migration and the New Security Agenda in Europe*. London: Pinter.

Walk, Heike, and Achim Brunnengräber. 1994. Motivationen, Schwierigkeiten und Chancen der Nicht-Regierungsorganisationen bei der Bildung von Netzwerken. *PROKLA* 24: 97, 623–42.

Walker, R. B. J. 1993. *Inside/Outside: International Relations as Political Theory*. Cambridge: Cambridge University Press.

Wallerstein, Immanuel. 1974, 1980, 1989. *The Modern World System*. New York: Academic Press.

———. 1991. *Geopolitics and Geoculture. Essays on the Changing World System*. Cambridge: Cambridge University Press.

Waltz, Kenneth N. 1959. *Man, the State, and War*. New York: Columbia University Press.

———. 1979. *Theory of International Politics*. Reading, Mass.: Addison Wesley.
Walzer, Michael. 1974. Civility and Civic Virtue in Contemporary America. *Social Research* 41:4, 593–611.
———. 1990. The Communitarian Critique of Liberalism. *Political Theory* 18:1, 6–23.
———. 1995. The Concept of Civil Society. In *Toward a Global Civil Society*, ed. Michael Walzer, 7–27. Oxford: Berghahn.
Wapner, Paul. 1996. *Environmental Activism and World Civic Politics*. New York: State University of New York Press.
Weber, Max. 1947. *The Theory of Social and Economic Organization*. Translated by A. M. Menderson and Talcott Parsons. Edited with an Introduction by Talcott Parsons. New York: Free Press.
———. 1949. *The Methodology of the Social Sciences*, translated and edited by Edward A. Shils and Henry A. Finch. New York: Free Press.
———. 1968. *Economy and Society: An Outline of Interpretive Sociology*, edited by Guenther Roth and Claus Wittich. 2 vols. New York: Bedminster Press.
Wehner, Burkhard. 1992. *Nationalstaat—Solidarstaat—Effizienzstaat*. Darmstadt: Wissenschaftliche Buchgesellschaft.
Weidner, Helmut. 1995. Reduction in SO_2 and NO_2 Emissions from Stationary Sources in Japan. In *Successful Environmental Policy. A Critical Evaluation of 24 Cases*, ed. Jänicke, et al., 146–72. Berlin: Edition Sigma.
Weiler, Joseph H. 1987. *The European Community in Change: Exit, Voice and Loyalty*. Saarbrücken: Universität des Saarlandes.
———. 1989. Europäisches Parlament, europäische Integration, Demokratie und Legitimität. In *Das Europäische Parlament im dynamischen Integrationsprozeß: Auf der Suche nach einem zeitgemäßen Leitbild*, ed. Schmuck, et al., 73–94. Bonn: Europa Union Verlag.
Weiler, Joseph H., Ulrich Haltern, and Franz C. Mayer. 1995. European Democracy and its Critique. *West European Politics* 18:3, 4–39.
Weißmann, Karlheinz. 1993. Die Wiederkehr eines Totgesagten: Der Nationalstaat am Ende des 20. Jahrhunderts. *Aus Politik und Zeitgeschichte*, B 14/93, 3–10.
Weller, Christoph. 1992. Feindbilder und ihr Zerfall. Eine Analyse des Einstellungswandels gegenüber der Sowjetunion (Tübinger Arbeitspapiere zur Internationalen Politik und Friedensforschung Nr. 18), Tübingen.
———. 1993. Das scheinbare Verschwinden der Feindbilder. *Das Baugerüst* 45:3, 210–14.
———. 1995. Feindbilder und Krieg. *Berliner Debatte—Initial* 6/95, 69–78.
———. 1997. Collective Identities in International Relations: The Case of a European Collective Identity, Paper presented at the Workshop on 'Theoretical, Methodological and Empirical Questions in the Study of National Identities' at the European University Institute, 21–22 November 1997, Florence.
———. 1998. *Bedingungen und Möglichkeiten außenpolitischen Einstellungswandels: Erklärungen des Feindbild-Zerfalls gegenüber der Sowjetunion am Ende des Ost-West-Konflikts*. PhD. diss. Darmstadt University of Technology. Darmstadt.
Welsh, Jennifer M. 1995. *Edmund Burke and International Relations*. London: Macmillan.
Wendt, Alexander. 1987. The Agent-Structure Problem in International Relations Theory. *International Organization* 41:3, 335–70.
———. 1992. Anarchy is What States Make of It: The Social Construction of Power Politics. *International Organization* 46:2, 391–425.

———. 1994. Collective Identity Formation and the International State. *American Political Science Review* 88:2, 384–96.
———. 1995. Constructing International Politics. *International Security* 20:1, 71–81.
———. 1996. Identity and Structural Change in International Politics. In *The Return of Culture and Identity in IR Theory*, ed. Lapid, et al., 47–64. Boulder, Colo.: Lynne Rienner.
Westle, Bettina. 1994. Nationale Identität der Deutschen nach der Vereinigung: Zur Asymmetrie deutschen Nationalstolzes. In *Wahlen und politische Einstellungen im vereinten Deutschland*, ed. Rattinger, et al., 453–98. Frankfurt/M.: Lang.
Wewer, Göttrik. 1993. Die Zukunft des Regierens in einer turbulenten Welt. In *Regieren im 21. Jahrhundert zwischen Globalisierung und Regionalisierung*, ed. Böhret, et al., 9–27. Opladen: Leske und Budrich.
Wight, Martin. 1978. *Power Politics*. Leicester: Leicester University Press.
Willetts, Peter. 1982. The Impact of Promotional Pressure Groups on Global Politics. In *Pressure Groups in the International System*, ed. Peter Willetts, 179–200. New York: Pinter.
———, ed. 1996a. *'The conscience of the world'. The influence of non-governmental organisation in the UN System*. Washington, D.C.: The Brookings Institution.
———. 1996b: Introduction. In *The conscience of the world'. The influence of non-governmental organisation in the UN System*, ed. Peter Willetts, 1–14. Washington, D.C.: The Brookings Institution.
———. 1996c: The Consultative Status for NGOs at the United Nations. In *The conscience of the world'. The influence of non-governmental organisation in the UN System*, ed. Peter Willetts, 31–62. Washington, D.C.: The Brookings Institution.
Williams, Shirley. 1991. Sovereignty and accountability in the European Community. In *The New European Community. Decisionmaking and Institutional Change*, ed. Keohane, et al., 155–76. Boulder, Colo.: Westview.
Wilson, James Q., and John J. Dilulio. 1995. *American Government: Institutions and Policies*. 6th ed. Lexington, Mass.: Heath & Co.
Wolf, Klaus Dieter. 1991. *Internationale Regime zur Verteilung globaler Ressourcen. Eine vergleichende Analyse der Grundlagen ihrer Entstehung am Beispiel der Regelung des Zugangs zur wirtschaftlichen Nutzung des Meeeresbodens, des geostationären Orbits, der Antarktis und zu Wissenschaft und Technologie*. Baden-Baden: Nomos.
———. 1995. Capitalism Meets the Democratic Peace. *Mershon International Studies Review* 39:2, 239–45.
———. 1999. Defending State Autonomy. International Governance in the European Union. In *The Transformation of Governance in the European Union*, ed. Beate Kohler-Koch, 230–47. London: Routledge.
Wriston, Walter. 1992. *The Twilight of Sovereignty*. New York: Macmillan.
Young, Oran R., and Gail Osherenko. 1993. International regime formation: findings, research priorities, and applications. In *Polar Politics. Creating International Environmental Regimes*, ed. Young, et al., 223–61. Ithaca, N.Y.: Cornell University Press.
Zacher, Mark W. 1992. The Decaying Pillars of the Westphalian Temple: Implications for International Order and Governance. In *Governance without Government*, ed. Rosenau, et al., 58–101. Cambridge: Cambridge University Press.
Zalewski, Marysia, and Cynthia Enloe. 1995. Questions about Identity in International Relations. In *International Political Theory Today*, ed. Booth, et al., 279–305. Cambridge: Cambridge University Press.

Zander, Jürgen. 1982. Introduction to: *Ferdinand Tönnies, Die Tatsache des Wollens.* Aus dem Nachlaß herausgegeben und eingeleitet von Jürgen Zander. Kiel: Schleswig-Holsteinische Landesbibliothek, 11–37.

Zangl, Bernhard. 1994. Politik auf zwei Ebenen. Hypothesen zur Bildung internationaler Regime. *Zeitschrift für Internationale Beziehungen* 1:2, 279–312.

Zimmerling, Ruth. 1991. *Externe Einflüsse auf die Integration von Staaten. Zur politikwissenschaftlichen Theorie regionaler Zusammenschlüsse.* Freiburg: Alber.

Zürn, Michael. 1992a. *Interessen und Institutionen in der internationalen Politik. Grundlegung und Anwendung des situationsstrukturellen Ansatzes.* Opladen: Leske und Budrich.

———. 1992b: Weltordnung ohne Weltstaat. Plädoyer für mehr Demokratie in der internationalen Politik. *Der Überblick* 28:3, 58–61.

———. 1992c: Jenseits der Staatlichkeit. Über die Folgen der ungleichzeitigen Denationalisierung. *Leviathan* 20:4, 490–513.

———. 1993. Bringing the Second Image (back) In: About the Domestic Sources of Regime Formation. In *Regime Theory and International Relations*, ed. Volker Rittberger, 282–314. Oxford: Oxford University Press.

———. 1995. The Challenge of Globalization and Individualization: A View from Europe. In *Whose World Order? Uneven Globalization and the End of the Cold War*, ed. Holm, et al., 137–65. Boulder, Colo.: Westview.

———. 1996. Global dangers and international co-operation: are we on the way to a world risk society? *Law and State* 53/54, 69–89.

———. 1998. *Regieren jenseits des Nationalstaates. Globalisierung und Denationalisierung als Chance.* Frankfurt/M.: Suhrkamp.

Zürn, Michael, and Ingo Take. 1996. Weltrisikogesellschaft und öffentliche Wahrnehmung globaler Gefährdungen. *Aus Politik und Zeitgeschichte*, B 24–25/96, 3–12.

Index

accountability, democracy and, 159
accountability-centered conflict, 173
actors, differentiation of, 8–11
Afghanistan, 104
American-Mexican border, 35
Amnesty International, 180
anarchy, 114
Anti-Fast-Track campaign, 42
arms race, 196
ASEAN. *See* Association of South East Asian Nations
Asian Pacific Economic Cooperation, 26
Association des Régions d'Europe, 193
Association of European Border Regions, 34
Association of South East Asian Nations (ASEAN), 14
autonomy, 182–85

BECC. *See* Border Environment Cooperation Commission
Board of Trustees v. City of Baltimore, 195
Border Environment Cooperation Commission (BECC), 35
borders, 5, 33–36
Brent Spar oil rig, 172, 182
Burtonians, 93–94

Cable News Network (CNN), 32
California Trade and Commerce Agency, 194
California World Trade Commission, 194
Canadian-American border, 35
capital control centers, 28
Cascadia Transportation/Trade Task Force, 35
CCLRA. *See* Consultative Council of Local and Regional Authorities
CEMR. *See* Council of European Municipalities and Regions
Central America, 35
China, 22, 184
Christian world, 41
citizens and states, relationships between, 20
citizenship, granting, 31
civil security, 190
CNN. *See* Cable News Network
cobweb model, 2–3
Cold War, 64, 67
collective identities, 45–46
colonialism, 104
commercial liberalism, 115
Committee of Regions, 34
Common Market, 154
communitarians, modern, 15
community, 92; categories, 74–76; history of concept, 71–74; in political theory, 71; introduction, 69–71; liberals *versus* communitarians, 77–78; orientation to, 76–77; problems in application of concept, 79–85
community formation, 1, 11–12, 41
competition, global relationships, 24

congruence, democratic communities, 158
Consultative Council of Local and Regional Authorities (CCLRA), 192–93
consumers, citizens as, 27
controls, territorially defined, 22
copyright violations, 107
corporatism, 141–43
Council of European Municipalities and Regions (CEMR), 193
counterfeiting, 107
cross-border local activism, 196
cross-border refugees, 180
cultural pessimism, 15
cultural relativism, 85
Czechoslovakia, 104

debordering, 5; definition of, 20; demarcation, 33–40; economic dimensions, 24–27; meaning, 21–24; multiple statehood, 27–30; transnational communities and coalitions, 30–33; world society, 40
decision networks, transparent, 167
decolonization, 104
de-democratization, 119
de-hierarchization, 124
democracy, 81–82
democratic corporatism, 138
democratization, 32, 191
destructive violence, 59
divestment ordinances, 196
Dominican Republic, 104

East-West conflict, 21, 65
ecology. *See* environmental issues
economic decision-making processes, centralization of, 26
economic globalization, 30
economic regions, 23
economy, 113
ECOSOC, 170
EEC. *See* European Economic Community
embedded liberalism, 164
emotions, humanity's capacity to control, 15–16
English School approach: desirability of international society, 94–97; international theory, 91–92; society and community, 92–94; viability of international society, 97–101
enterprise *versus* civil association, 95
environmental issues, 35, 203; Greenpeace, 176, 180, 203, 205–8; international cooperation, 10; preservation, 32; protection, 12; security, 136
epistemic communities, 87
equality, 32
Eritrea, 39
Ethiopia, 39
ethnic divisions, 110
EU. *See* European Union
Euregio, 29–30
Euro-markets, 185
Europe, medieval, 22
European Court of Justice, 154
European Economic Community (EEC), 152
European identity, 60
European integration, 193
European Monetary Union, 127, 129
European Parliament, 30, 149–50, 161–62
European Union (EU), 9, 14, 103, 115; autonomous power, 111–12; debordering, 24, 30, 33–34, 39; intergovernmental cooperation, 119; policy formation, 181; raison d'état, 124–28
European *versus* Republican, 101
Europe-wide referenda, 165–68
evasions of sovereignty, 28

Federal Aviation Administration (FAA), 182
Federal Republic of Germany, 60
feminist research, identity and, 51–52
flexible manufacturing, 107
FoEG. *See* Friends of the Earth Germany
Food and Drug Administration (FDA), 182
Fordism, 106
free-trade areas, 24
Friends of the Earth Germany (FoEG), 203

GATT, 152
Gemeinschaft, 6–7
Gemeinschaftshandeln, 12
German *Länder,* 34, 187, 193
Gesellschaft, 6–7
global cities, 9, 185–87
global communities, 89
global economy, 106
global governance, 137, 170–73, 186
global network, 7
global society formation, process of, 11
global sourcing, 5, 25
global strategic alliance building, 5
globalism, 51, 69, 135
globalization, 25, 40, 48, 107
grassroots movements, 191
greenhouse effect, 169
Greenpeace, 176, 180, 203, 205–8
Grotian tradition, regime analysis, 94

hegemony, 3
Holy Roman Empire, 22, 37
human rights, 12, 14, 32, 99, 131
humanitarian organizations, 180
Hungary, 104

identity: bearers of, 50, 55; collective, 49, 64–68; definition of, 49; democratic communities, 158; formation, 47; international relations, 51–57; maintaining a positive social, 50; national, 57–59; reflexive concepts of, 50; self-categorization theory, 63–64; social identity theory, 61–63; as social-scientific concept, 59–61
IGO. *See* Intergovernmental Organization
imperialism, 4
inclusion and exclusion, degrees of, 86
industrialization, Mexico, 35
ingroup *versus* outgroup, 59
INS. *See* U.S. Immigration and Naturalization Service
institutional cosmopolitanism, 101
integration, 37
interaction, levels and spheres of, 8–11
interest rates, 107
intergovernmental cooperation, 119, 121

Intergovernmental Organization (IGO), 111–12
International Boundary and Water Commission, 36
International Center for Sustainable Cities, 35
international community, 1–2
International Monetary Fund, 4, 129
international order, 16, 92
international political economy, 179
international politics, collective identities in, 64–66
International Relations (IR), 2, 13
international society, 2, 7, 11
international system, 2, 11
International Telegraphic Union, 37
INTERREG program, 34–35
interstate borders, 20
interstate economic relations, 24
IR. *See* International Relations
Iraq, 184
Islamic world, 41

juridical statehood, 110

Kosovo, 39
Kuwait, 184

LACE. *See* Linkage Assistance and Cooperation for the European Border Regions
Laos, 104
League of Nations, 105
liberal interdependence, 106
liberalizations, global policy of, 26
Linkage Assistance and Cooperation for the European Border Regions (LACE), 34
local activism, 195
local interests, 187
London Dumping Convention, 208

Maastricht Treaty, 127, 150–56, 192–93
media, collaboration with, 172
mediators, 174
meta-contrast principle, 67
meta-strategies, 122

Mexamerica, 36, 39
microregions, 186
Middle Ages, 188
migration, 31, 39
military, 110
modernization risks, 136
moral cosmopolitanism, 101
MTV, 32
multilevel governance: democratic process, 156–60; Europe-wide referenda, 165–68; Maastricht Treaty, 150–56; overview, 149–50; strengths and weaknesses, 160–64
multinational corporations, 180, 185
multiple identities, 33
multiple statehood, 27–30

NADBank. *See* North American Development Bank
NAFTA. *See* North American Free Trade Agreement
National Defense Authorization Act, 195
nationality, definition of, 58
nationhood, 113
nation-states, 120, 134–36, 189
NATO, 36, 65
neocorporatists, 143
neoliberal institutionalism, 93
neorealist international relations theory, 103
Nestlé campaign, 42
network analysis methods, 140
network design, 41
newly industrialized country (NIC), 184
NGO *See* nongovernmental organization
NIC. *See* newly industrialized country
nongovernmental organization (NGO), 9–10, 28, 138, 146, 167, 199–214; global governance, democratizing, 170–73; international politics, 174; international problem solving, 173–74; international-level integration, 175; national-level integration, 174–75; nonprofit, 182; overview, 169; problems, 176–78; world society, 170
nonstate actors, 10–11, 23–24
North American Development Bank (NADBank), 35

North American Free Trade Agreement, 26–27, 35–39, 42
nuclear freeze resolutions, 196
nuclear weapons, 174
nuclear-free zones, 195

OECD. *See* Organization for Economic Cooperation and Development
Olympic Games, 63
Operation Blockade, 38
Operation Gatekeeper, 38
Operation Hold the Line, 38
Organization for Economic Cooperation and Development (OECD), 4, 26, 68, 116, 183–84

Pacific Corridor Enterprise Council, 35
Pacific Northwest Economic Region, 35
particularism, 85
Party of Institutionalized Revolution (PRI), 39
peace, domestic maintenance of, 190
peace, zones of, 102
Peace of Westphalia, 22
Perpich v. Department of Defense, 195
pluralism, 51, 141
policy formation, transgovernmental, 181
policy networks as phenomenon, 140–41
political autonomy, 122
political community, 57
political geography, 19–20, 21, 28
political innovation, 33–36
political liberalism, 120
political modernization, 138, 143–45
political regions, 23
politics, internationalization of, 1
politics, territorial references, 20
polity, 113
PRI. *See* Party of Institutionalized Revolution
private security services, 190
problems, nongovernmental organizations, 176–78
procedural legitimacy, lack of, 183
property rights, 107
protectionism, 24
Pugwash Club, 174

raison d'état: challenges to autonomy of states, 123–24; domestic dimensions of, 122–23; as feature of international governance, 128–31; intergovernmental self-commitments in the European Union, 124–28; introduction, 119–22
realism, 51, 104
Red Cross, 180
redistributive programs, 190
regimes, 8, 37
region-states, rise of, 179
relative locations, primacy of, 25
republican liberalism, 115
reversibility, prerequisite of democracy, 159
Rheinschiffahrtskommission, 37
risk societies, 15
Roman Empire, 22

Schengen Agreement, 39
Second Industrial Revolution, 106
self-categorization theory, 63–64
self-government, obstacles, 105
Single European Act, 115, 128, 149–50
Single Market Treaty, 115
social assistance, 190
social categorization, 62
social cleavage, 190
social fragmentation, 45–46, 191
social identity theory, 46, 56
social networks, 140
social reality, 54
social schizophrenia, 190
society and community, relationship between, 11–15, 47–49
society-formation process, 45
soft states of inclusion, 88
sovereignty, 113, 182–85
Soviet disarmament, 65
space, definition of, 23
state actors, 23–24
state autonomy, erosion of, 179
state identity, 56
states, problem-solving processes: corporatism, 141–43; nation-state and world society, 134–36; network analysis method, 140; pluralism, 141; policy networks as phenomenon, 140–41; political modernization, 143–45; society and, 138–40; world society capacity, 136–38
structural realism, 120
subnational territorial units, 187–91, 191–92

Taiwan, 184
tax havens, 107
technopoles, 186
telecommunications, importance of, 185
territorial representation, democratization of, 166–67
territoriality: changing role of, 5; definition of, 23; space and, 19, 21
territory and state, relation between, 19
Third Conference on the Law of the Sea, 21
Third Industrial Revolution, 106, 111
trade wars, 24
transborder phenomena, 20
transborder society formation, 1
transnational capital flows, 107
transnational coalitions, 23–24
transnational communities, 5, 31, 33–36
transnational relations, 13
transnationalized regions, 25
trans-statehood, 5
turmoil, zones of, 102

unemployment benefits, 190
Union Nationale des Villes et Pouvoirs Locaux, 193
unitary subjectivity, 33
United Nations, 114–15; Charter, 59, 130; Conference on Environment and Development, 177; decolonizaton, 105
United States v. City of Oakland, 195
Universal Declaration (1948), 99
Universal Postal Union, 37
universalism, 14, 83
unlike units: anarchy, different forms of, 113–16; functional and structural differentiation, 108–13; power and interdependence, 104–8
Upper Rhine region, 38

U.S. Border Patrol, 43
U.S. hegemony, 28
U.S. Immigration and Naturalization Service (INS), 38, 43
USSR, 65

Vergemeinschaftung, 1–2, 6–7, 11–14, 45
Vergesellschaftung, 1–2, 6–8, 13–15, 41
Vienna Human Rights Conference (1993), 14
Vietnam, 104
violence, 16
voting rights, 175

Warsaw Pact, 65
welfare provisions, 107
welfare state, 190
World Bank, 4
world cities, 24
world goods, globally standardized, 32
world news, 32
world republic, 96
world society, 2, 11; collective identities in, 66–68; contributions, international-level, 211–13; driving force behind, 135; evolution of, 21; levels of influence, 199–200; national-level influence, 205–11; NGO strategies, 200–202; social-level influence, 202–5
world systems, 24, 92
World Trade Organization, 4
World Wildlife Federation (WWF), 204
worldwide sense of life, 32
WWF. *See* World Wildlife Federation

zones of peace/zones of conflict, 102, 116

About the Contributors

Mathias Albert is assistant professor at Darmstadt University of Technology. His research interests include IR theory and sociology, international security, and transnational law. His works include *Fallen der (Welt-)Ordnung* [Pitfalls of (World) Order] (1996) and *Identities, Borders, Orders: New Directions in IR Theory* (forthcoming 2000: ed. with D. Jacobson and Y. Lapid); he is currently working on a book on *The Politics of World Society: Identity, Law and Security*.

Lothar Brock holds a Chair in International Relations at Johann Wolfgang Goethe-University in Frankfurt/M. and is a Research Director at Peace Research Institute Frankfurt. He has worked extensively on development issues and North-South relations, issues of peace and conflict, as well as IR theory.

Chris Brown is the author of *International Relations Theory: New Normative Approaches* (1992) and *Understanding International Relations* (1997) and currently holds a Chair in International Relations at the London School of Economics. He is immediate past Chair, and current honorary president of the British International Studies Association.

Jürgen Neyer is a research fellow in the Center for European Law and Politics and Lecturer at the University of Bremen. His research interests include European integration, international law, and political theory.

Emmanuel Richter is 'Privatdozent' at the University of Kassel. He was recently visiting professor of German and European Studies at the University of California, Irvine. His publications include *Der Zerfall der Welteinheit. Vernunft und Globalisierung in der Moderne* [The Decline of Cosmopolitanism. Enlightenment Reason and Globalization in Modernity] (1992); *Die Expansion der Herrschaft. Eine demokratietheoretische Studie* [The Extension of Rule. A Study in Democratic Theory] (1994); *Das republikanische Europa. Aspekte einer nachholenden Zivilisierung* [Republican Europe. The Delayed Development of a Civil Society] (forthcoming 1999).

Hilmar Schmidt is currently a research associate at the Institute of Political Science at Darmstadt University of Technology. He mainly works on issues of international cooperation, concepts of globalization, and international environmental politics, as well as foreign policy analysis.

Georg Sørensen is a professor of political science at the University of Aarhus. Among his publications are *Whose World Order* (1995; ed. with Hans-Henrik Holm) and *Introduction to International Relations* (1999; with Robert Jackson).

Ingo Take is currently a research associate at the Institute of Political Science at Darmstadt University of Technology. His main areas of research are nongovernmental organisations, international cooperation, concepts of globalization, and international environmental politics.

Christoph Weller is the managing editor of the German *Journal of International Relations* (*Zeitschrift fuer Internationale Beziehungen*) and a research fellow at the Institute for Intercultural and International Studies, Bremen University, and received his doctorate from the Darmstadt University of Technology.

Klaus Dieter Wolf holds the Chair in International Relations at the Institute of Political Science at Darmstadt University of Technology. He received his doctorate from the University of Tuebingen. He is co-director of the World Society Research Group and founding editor of the German *Journal of International Relations* (*Zeitschrift fuer International Beziehungen*). He is currently preparing a book titled *Die Neue Staatsräson* [The New Raison d'Etat].

Michael Zürn is currently professor of International and Transnational Relations, co-director of the Institute for Intercultural and International Studies (InIIS), University of Bremen, and co-director of the Center for European Law and Policy, Hansestadt Bremen. He is also executive editor of the the German *Journal of International Relations* (*Zeitschrift für Internationale Beziehungen*). His most recent publications include *Regieren jenseits des Nationalstaates* [Governing Beyond the Nation-State] (1998) and articles in *International Studies Quarterly* and *World Politics*.